1994

How did the ideals of liberty, equality and fraternity evolve out of the corporate structure of the Old Regime in France? This study investigates the evolution of a new ideal of the polity in 1789 and the reaction of French society to it.

Concentrating especially on the restructuring of the administration and judiciary, the author argues that the new political stucture created by the Constitution of 1791 was the most equitable and participatory national political system in the world. In particular, by the standards of the eighteenth century, the polity enacted by the National Assembly was more inclusive than exclusive, and the Constitution of 1791 was much more of an object of consensus than has been acknowledged. Challenging criticisms of the Assembly and the constitution, it is argued that the achievements of the National Assembly deserve greater recognition than they have traditionally received.

# The remaking of France

# The remaking of France

*The National Assembly and the Constitution of 1791*

Michael P. Fitzsimmons

*Auburn University at Montgomery*

CAMBRIDGE
UNIVERSITY PRESS

Published by the Press Syndicate of the University of Cambridge
The Pitt Building, Trumpington Street, Cambridge, CB2 1RP
40 West 20th Street, New York, NY 10011–4211, USA
10 Stamford Road, Oakleigh, Melbourne 3166, Australia

© Cambridge University Press 1994

First published 1994

Printed in Great Britain at the University Press, Cambridge

*A catalogue record for this book is available from the British Library*

*Library of Congress cataloguing in publication data*

Fitzsimmons, Michael P., 1949–
  The remaking of France: the National Assembly and the Constitution of
1791 / Michael P. Fitzsimmons.
    p.    cm.
  Includes bibliographical references and index.
  ISBN 0 521 45407 7
    1. France. Assemblée nationale constituante (1789–1791) – Influence.
2. France – Politics and government – 1789–1799 – Citizen participation.
3. France. Constitution (1791)  4. Nationalism – France – History –
18th century.  5. Political participation – France – History – 18th century.
I. Title.
DC165.F57  1994
944.02′1 – dc20  93–35732  CIP

ISBN 0 521 45407 7 hardback

UP

*To the memory of*
James E. Fitzsimmons (1921–1987)
Kathryn J. Fitzsimmons (1923–1989)
Kevin S. Fitzsimmons (1951–1991)

The passage of the Red sea – was it more miraculous than that from the old regime to the new?

Speech of the priest Charles Hervier during a celebration of Louis's acceptance of the Constitution, September 25, 1791

# Contents

# Preface

In the spring of 1789 French society gathered for the first time in 175 years to elect men to a national body called to address a political and financial crisis. It was a crisis universally acknowledged to be national in scope. The mode of government established in France since the Estates-General last met in 1614 – royal absolutism mediated through privileged corporatism – had failed. Those electing deputies to the Estates-General saw the two chief tasks of the men whom they were choosing as remedying the fiscal situation and, more importantly, providing France with a constitution. There were certainly sharp differences over the constitution, beginning with the fundamental question of whether or not there already was one, but at the same time a common expectation prevailed that the objectives of the deputies would not require more than three or four months to complete. It was also believed that, apart from greater uniformity being brought about by the elimination of disparities in the administration of France, the basic configuration of the kingdom would remain essentially unchanged.

Before the end of 1789, however, sovereignty had been transferred from the monarch to the nation. The three estates of the kingdom no longer existed, provinces had been abolished, the *parlements* suspended and the National Assembly had irrevocably committed itself to a comprehensive restructuring of the polity that would extend the life of the original Estates-General to nearly two and one half years. By the time it disbanded on September 30, 1791, the National Assembly had transformed the kingdom so completely that many deputies simply referred to much of what had preceded them as 'the old regime.' Indeed, the men who left the National Assembly in Paris that September 30 entered a society radically different – politically, socially, economically and religiously – from that which had existed when most among them had entered the Estates-General in Versailles on May 4, 1789. The transformation was primarily of their own making. It was all the more extraordinary, however, in that it could not possibly have been foreseen by any of them when they arrived at Versailles as deputies.

During the past several years historians of the French Revolution have increasingly turned away from consideration of its social origins to focus instead on political and cultural elements. The present work is associated with this newer approach, for it argues that the beginnings of the Revolution are to be found in the attempt to reform the French state during the period after the Assembly of Notables in 1787. The primary goal of this effort was to shape a more rationally ordered state through fiscal changes and uniformity of administration. Ultimately, the Estates-General became perceived as the vehicle for accomplishing this task, but the traditional voting procedure of that body would have permitted the clergy and the nobility to block reform. As a result, a major dimension of the effort to reform the state involved amending the historical format for the Estates-General. In every other respect, however, social distinctions were to be respected and upheld.

This study is an examination of the manner in which the limited aspirations for the Estates-General of 1789 became transformed into the much broader movement that has come to be known as the French Revolution. The critical turning point in this process was the night of August 4, 1789, when the National Assembly formulated a new ideal of the polity. The essence of this ideal was a conception of the nation itself as a source of equity, which led to the replacement of privileged corporatism by laws common to all. This transformation led the National Assembly into virtually every facet of French life, but the hopes of the Assembly for the realization of its new ideal of the polity had two key foci – civil administration and justice – and it is on these two spheres that this work will concentrate.

This book is divided into two parts, with its structure reflecting one of its primary arguments – that the National Assembly, although occasionally lagging behind public opinion in some parts of France, conceived a new ideal of the polity on the night of August 4 and reshaped the polity in accordance with that new ideal. Most of France, although surprised by the scope of change, nevertheless accepted it and ultimately, through its electoral choices, adopted it. The structure of this book – examining first the actions of the National Assembly, then the reaction to those actions throughout France – stems from a conviction that two distinct dynamics were at work.

Part one treats the formulation and elaboration of a new political ethos in the National Assembly from 1789 to 1791, when deputies often found themselves in an unsettled situation as rapid shifts in opinions and outlooks occurred. Furthermore, in Paris especially, beginning in the autumn of 1789, there were alternative – and, in a few instances, competing – outlets for political expression, including popular protest, political clubs and the press. Popular protest, however, does not seem to have affected the Assembly after October, 1789 – the only incident that might be cited, the violence at the Champ de Mars in July, 1791, was ignited by a decision already taken, and it ultimately galvanized support for the Assembly. Moreover, although clubs and the press somewhat diminished the ability of the National Assembly to shape public opinion after September, 1789, the Assembly nevertheless remained the locus of political power. Indeed, these institutions, especially the clubs, with many deputies among their membership, sought primarily to discuss or to influence the work of the National Assembly, not to compete with it.

Part two deals with the reaction of French society to the changes enacted by the Assembly. As one newspaper, *Affiches, annonces et avis divers du département de l'Yonne*, noted in June, 1791, in areas beyond Paris the focal point of political life was, and had been, the constitutional debates and legislation of the National Assembly. The rapid sequence of events at Versailles and Paris often required major adjustments by inhabitants of towns and regions across France. Such adjustments were sometimes difficult, involving the acceptance of a new and rapidly formed identity as well as a myriad of new institutions designed to achieve it. Literally overnight one was no longer Breton or Burgundian or Languedocian, but French, and the initial sense of displacement was compounded by the subsequent destruction of such centuries-old institutions as provinces, provincial estates and *parlements*. The shock was all the more intense for its total unexpectedness. Participants in elections to the Estates-General had believed that they were sending deputies to Versailles to resolve the financial situation and to produce a constitution in accordance with the *cahiers* and mandates given to those deputies. They had no idea that these elections would produce the outcome that they did. Ultimately, however, the stature of the National Assembly became so great, and the moral authority of its new ideals so unassailable, that virtually all locales in France relinquished their mandates and yielded to the imperatives of the Assembly. This growing consensus, in turn, augmented the confidence and power of the Assembly, and it is this mutual reinforcement that is the subject of this study.

This work is not a general history of the Revolution between 1789 and 1791, but a study of the development of a new ideal of the polity by the National Assembly and the acceptance and realization of that ideal by French society. There were innumerable other events concurrent with this process – municipal revolutions, the Great Fear, peasant *jacqueries*, provisioning crises and other such upheavals. These events will be mentioned, but they have found their historians. In comparison with the drawing up of the constitution and the realization of the new administrative and judicial structure, however, they were brief and impermanent. This is not to deny their influence or importance, but by September, 1791, as Frenchmen celebrated the new constitution with processions, the firing of cannons, *Te Deums*, bonfires and general illuminations, the crises and difficulties that had accompanied its completion were all but forgotten.

For the most part, the National Assembly has been treated unfavorably by scholars. During its final weeks opinion in Paris turned against it, and historians have generally tended to adopt that viewpoint in judging the Assembly. This study, however, deliberately moves beyond Paris, beyond the opinions of Gorsas, Loustalot or Marat, for example, whose polemical reporting could often color events, to examine attitudes toward the National Assembly more broadly. It seeks a better understanding of events by considering them from within the National Assembly through the letters and journals of deputies and through the reaction from provinces and departments as recorded in the minutes, records or accounts of assemblies, elections, festivals or ceremonies in cities, towns and villages. This is in no way to dismiss the press, for it is a valuable source in gauging reaction to many of these occurrences. But by capturing events directly rather than through the filter of the press or other outside sources, it is possible to reconstruct more accurately the milieu in which the National Assembly operated and to appreciate the ways in which it both shaped and responded to events and changing beliefs of a society in flux.

The National Assembly self-consciously viewed its program as national in scope, and so I have sought to make my examination of the response to its actions correspondingly nationwide. To have pursued a case study based on one or several departments would have run counter to the intent and outlook of the Assembly and would not have presented adequately the full range of responses to its program. Consequently, although I obviously could not achieve comprehensive coverage, I have sought to focus on as many areas or regions of the kingdom as possible.

One of the pleasures of appearing in print is the opportunity it affords to offer a permanent record of thanks, and I am indebted to a number of individuals and institutions. I would like to thank the Auburn University at Montgomery Research Council for its support of this project at both its beginning and end with Research Grants-in-Aid. It also benefitted from a Short-Term Fellowship in Residence from the Newberry Library, for which I am equally grateful. Most especially, I would like to express my gratitude to the National Endowment for the Humanities for a fellowship that enabled me to spend the 1988–89 academic year in France.

My research was greatly facilitated by the kind assistance of countless archivists and librarians in both the United States and France. In France the staff of the *Archives nationales*, various departmental and municipal archives, and municipal libraries were attentive and responsive to what must have seemed at times to be a bewildering array of requests. In the United States the members of the staff of the Newberry Library, especially the Special Collections Department, were unfailingly courteous and helpful, and the time spent there saved me several weeks of research in France. Likewise, the Interlibrary Loan unit of the Auburn University at Montgomery Library efficiently processed numerous requests. I would also like to thank Millie Weaver for her help in preparing the manuscript. Finally, I am grateful to Alan Stahl of the American Numismatic Society for his help with the cover photograph and to William Davies and Katherine V. Boyle for their efforts in seeing this volume through the publication process.

The historical profession is supposed to be a collegial enterprise and my experience has happily confirmed this ideal. Alan Forrest, Patrice Higonnet and Donald Kelley supported my pursuit of this project. Michael Sydenham, Kenneth Margerison and Alan Forrest read early drafts of this work and offered useful and incisive criticisms. Melvin Edelstein generously shared his work and thoughts with me. My colleagues, both past and present, in the Department of History at Auburn University at Montgomery have provided a supportive working environment, especially Elizabeth Dunn, John Fair and Kandice Hauf. For their encouragement along the way I am also grateful to Rory Browne, William Doyle, Claudine Ferrell, Jan Goldstein, Susan Suleiman, Liana Vardi and Isser Woloch. Rochelle Ziskin provided astute suggestions, consistently wise counsel and assisted in other ways too numerous to mention; I was fortunate to have such a wonderful teammate.

As always, there are some acknowledgments that go deeper. As I began this project my father was diagnosed with terminal cancer. Other completely unanticipated losses followed, but because I was insulated somewhat by distance the burden of these later deaths fell more heavily on my sister, Kelly. I want to express my love and admiration for her and for the way in which she handled many difficult matters. Her assumption of various obligations enabled me to complete this study earlier than would otherwise have been the case.

Finally, despite her own losses and sorrow, Theresa Fitzsimmons remained steadfastly supportive throughout this difficult period. As is the case with my sister, there is nothing that I can say that would adequately express my gratitude.

# Abbreviations

AD        Archives départementales
ADG     Archives de Guerre (Vincennes)
AM       Archives municipales
AN       Archives nationales
*AP*       *Archives parlementaires de 1787 à 1860 : recueil complet des débats législatifs et politiques des chambres françaises, first series (1787–1799)*, ed. J. Mavidal and E. Laurent, 82 vols. (Paris, 1867–1913)
BHVP   Bibliothèque historique de la ville de Paris
BM       Bibliothèque municipale
BN       Bibliothèque nationale

*Part One*

# 1    The crisis of the Old Regime

A kingdom in which the provinces are unknown to one another ... where
privileges upset all equilibrium, where it is not possible to have either
steadfast rule or consensus, is obviously a very imperfect kingdom

Calonne to Louis XVI, August 20, 1786

In presenting a memorandum to the monarch that candidly delineated
several deficiencies in the structure and administration of the kingdom,
the Controller-General of Finances, Charles-Alexandre de Calonne,
sought to make Louis XVI comprehend that modifications in the
traditional method of governance were imperative. Under the Old
Regime, French society was organized corporatively. In order to bypass
the Estates-General, the traditional institution for popular consent, the
Crown, in exchange for recognition of the imposition of its authority, had
bolstered the corporate framework of French society. As a result, a
demarcation remained between the state and society – the Crown was
less an integral part of society than a separately constituted entity.[1] The
metaphors and vocabulary of theorists sought to emphasize a holistic
image of the polity and to portray it as an organic whole, but the reality
was quite different.[2]

1 See, for example, Elizabeth Fox-Genovese, *The Origins of Physiocracy: Economic
Revolution and Social Order in Eighteenth-Century France* (Ithaca, 1976), p. 108; Michael
Sonenscher, *The Hatters of Eighteenth-Century France* (Berkeley, 1987), pp. 6–8; Gail
Bossenga, *The Politics of Privilege: Old Regime and Revolution in Lille* (Cambridge, 1991),
p. 7. On the evolution and structure of French society under the Old Regime, see François
Jean Olivier-Martin, *L'Organisation corporative de la France de l'ancien régime* (Paris,
1939); Emile Coornaert, *Les Corporations en France avant 1789* (Paris, 1941); Roland
Mousnier, *The Institutions of France Under the Absolute Monarchy 1598–1789*, 2 vols.
(Chicago, 1979–1984); William H. Sewell, Jr., *Work and Revolution in France: The
Language of Labor from the Old Regime to 1848* (Cambridge, 1980), pp. 16–61; Hubert
Méthivier, *L'Ancien régime en France XVIᵉ, XVIIᵉ, XVIIIᵉ siècles* (Paris, 1981); David
Parker, *The Making of French Absolutism* (London, 1983); Pierre Goubert and Daniel
Roche, *Les Français et l'ancien régime*, 2 vols. (Paris, 1984); William Beik, *Absolutism and
Society in Seventeenth-Century France: State Power and Provincial Aristocracy in Languedoc*
(Cambridge, 1985), which offers some nuances.
2 William H. Sewell, Jr., "Etat, corps and ordre: some notes on the social vocabulary of
the French Old Regime," *Sozialgeschichte Heute: Festschrift für Hans Rosenberg zum 70.
Geburtstag*, ed. Hans Ulrich Wehler (Göttingen, 1974), pp. 48–68.

3

Inextricably connected with this corporate structure – indeed, its very underpinning – was privilege. Privilege was the primary instrument of government and therefore the chief medium of political exchange between the state and society. At the beginning of each reign, for example, one method used by the new monarch to announce his accession to the throne was to issue an edict that confirmed the privileges of different provinces. Through this edict, the monarch tacitly acknowledged the rights of his subjects, who in turn implicitly recognized the legitimacy of his claim. This became a starting point of the reign that, in substance if not in form, was perhaps as important as the coronation ceremony. It is an indication of how vital an element privilege was that one scholar has, in fact, argued that privileged corporatism in France was "the functional equivalent" of constitutionalism in England.[3]

In contemporary usage, then, privilege was not a pejorative term, but simply a descriptive, juridic one. The *Encyclopedia*, for example – significantly, under a sub-heading of "government" – defined privilege entirely without irony or ridicule as useful or honorific distinctions enjoyed by some members of society that were not enjoyed by others.[4] Whether under the appellation of *privilèges, statuts particuliers, lois privées* or other designations, they were a principal device of the Crown for dealing with the different constituent elements of society. Consequently, privilege was a concept largely devoid of emotional content, for it permeated society, with virtually every corporate entity possessing privileges of some kind.[5] The pervasiveness of privilege in no way lessened its value; on the contrary, since every privilege, no matter how insignificant, served to differentiate one corporate body from another and

3 On privilege as a medium of exchange, see, for example, AD Côte d'Or C 2975, C 2976, C 2977; AD Ille-et-Vilaine C 3130, C 3131; AD Haute-Garonne C 42, letters-patent of king, confirming privileges of province of Languedoc, October 28, 1774; on privileged corporatism as the equivalent of constitutionalism, see David Bien, "The *Secrétaires du Roi*: absolutism, corps and privilege under the Ancien Régime," *Vom Ancien Régime zur Französischen Revolution*, ed. Ernst Hinrichs, Eberhard Schmitt and Rudolph Vierhaus (Göttingen, 1978), pp. 153–168, especially p. 159. For more on the centrality of privilege to the Old Regime polity, see David Bien, "Offices, corps, and a system of state credit: the uses of privilege under the Ancien Régime," *The Political Culture of the Old Regime*, ed. Keith M. Baker (Oxford, 1987), pp. 89–114; for a consideration of the coronation ceremony, see Richard A. Jackson, *Vive le Roi! A History of the French Coronation from Charles V to Charles X* (Chapel Hill, 1984).

4 *Encyclopédie, ou Dictionnaire raisonné des sciences, des arts et des métiers, par une société des gens de lettres*, Denis Diderot and Jean Lerond d'Alembert, eds., 17 vols. (Paris, 1751–1765), XIII: 389. To give but one example of its use in government, see AD Rhône 9 C 58, entry of February 21, 1789.

5 In the *Encyclopedia*, for example, following the general entries on privilege, there were nineteen cross references to related discussions of specific privileges. See *Encyclopédie*, XIII: 391. See also C. B. A. Behrens, *The Ancien Regime* (London, 1967), especially pp. 46–62.

to enhance the standing of its possessor, each one was zealously defended against encroachment, even by the Crown. The Brittany Affair in particular illustrates the role of privilege under the Old Regime and buttresses the notion of it as a surrogate for constitutionalism, for it developed into a major constitutional crisis.

This obsession with maintaining and defending privilege – by guilds, professional bodies, provinces, municipalities and other entities – fostered a narrow, circumscribed outlook that splintered French society and in which broader societal concerns had little place. This state of affairs was entirely satisfactory to the Crown, for it allowed the Crown to act as arbiter and to claim that it alone could act for the greater interests of the kingdom. Indeed, Gail Bossenga has argued that privilege was a critically important vehicle in the growth of the power of the Crown under the Old Regime.[6] There was a pitfall in this course, however; if the use of privilege facilitated imposition of the will of the Crown on society, it also hindered the ability of the Crown to reform the kingdom, even in a limited and salutary fashion.[7]

For the most part, as long as its authority was not challenged in the fundamental fashion that it had been from the late sixteenth to the mid-seventeenth century, the Crown was generally prepared to compromise or even to yield when its claims collided with entrenched privilege. Conversely, as long as it respected their immunities and privileges, most corporate bodies were not inclined to confront the Crown. It was through this compromise that privileged corporatism became the superintending principle of Old Regime society.[8]

The developing financial crisis that led Calonne to draft his memorandum imperiled this compromise, for it made clear that one of the most important sectors of privilege, its fiscal component, had become a

---

6 Gail Bossenga, "City and state: an urban perspective on the origins of the French Revolution," *The Political Culture of the Old Regime*, ed. Baker, pp. 115–140. See also Bossenga, *The Politics of Privilege*, p. 8.

7 Perhaps the best example of this near the end of the Old Regime is the experience of Turgot. See Douglas Dakin, *Turgot and the Ancien Regime in France* (London, 1939), especially pp. 245–246; Edgar Faure, *12 mai 1776. La Disgrace de Turgot* (Paris, 1961) and Keith M. Baker, *Condorcet: From Natural Philosophy to Social Mathematics* (Chicago, 1975), pp. 55–72, 202–214.

8 Two incidents from the reign of Louis XV reveal the nature of this compromise. During the tenure of the Controller-General Machault d'Arnouville, Louis XV yielded on the *vingtième* after it provoked protest among major privileged groups. On the other hand, Louis's vigor and tenacity in the episode of the Maupeou *parlements*, despite the opposition it raised, arose from the fact that the *parlements* had challenged the sovereignty of the Crown. It was a struggle that ended only with Louis's death. On Machault, see Marcel Marion, *Machault d'Arnouville. Etude sur l'histoire du contrôle général des finances de 1749 à 1754* (Paris, 1891); on Maupeou, Robert Villiers, *L'Organisation du Parlement de Paris et des conseils supérieurs d'après la réforme de Maupeou* (Paris, 1937).

luxury that the state literally could no longer afford. The deterioration of the Crown's financial position – its debt had tripled in the previous fifteen years and more than half of its revenues were slated for debt service – led Calonne to urge Louis to embark upon a major reform of the kingdom, and especially to attack fiscal privilege.[9]

A leading scholar of French finances, J. F. Bosher, who characterized Calonne as "a determined conservative in the vital matters of financial administration," has argued that by confining his program only to the *taille* and other such impositions Calonne did not fully attack the problem, and Bosher's brilliant study demonstrates that this is undeniably true.[10] At the same time, however, it was precisely Calonne's conservatism that made his proposals – however limited their utility – so significant, for if a "determined conservative" such as Calonne could raise the matter of privilege as a problem in the polity, it is not at all surprising that the theme subsequently resonated with a larger public. Indeed, although one can only speculate, as Bosher later did, about Louis's hesitation in convening the Assembly of Notables, it is plausible that at least one element may have been an awareness by Louis or Vergennes, his principal adviser, of the explosive and potentially destabilizing effect an attack on privilege might have.[11]

Whatever his intentions were, Calonne's memorandum contained several proposals for reform, but its most significant element was a "territorial subvention" or proportional land tax to be paid in kind by all landowners, with no exceptions. Fully aware that the *parlements* and provincial estates would oppose his program, he sought to outmaneuver them by presenting his program to an "assembly of notables," a device that had last been utilized by Richelieu in 1626, also in a financial crisis. Confident of their approval, he hoped in this way to preempt the opposition of the *Parlement* of Paris, which would have to register the proposals before they could be put into effect. Louis delayed giving his approval for their convocation until late December and, as a result, the Assembly did not convene until February 22, 1787.

The Assembly was preeminently a gathering of representatives of major privileged corporations in France, but Calonne was confident that he could convince them of the need for reform. From the outset the Crown made it clear that privilege was the critical issue in the resolution

9 On the financial crisis, see especially J. F. Bosher, *French Finances 1770–1795: From Business to Bureaucracy* (Cambridge, 1970) and, more cautiously due to their excessive pro-Necker orientation, Robert D. Harris, *Necker, Reform Statesman of the Ancien Regime* (Berkeley, 1979) and *Necker and the Revolution of 1789* (Lanham, Md., 1986).
10 Bosher, *French Finances*, pp. 179–180.
11 See J. F. Bosher, *The French Revolution* (New York, 1988), pp. 98–100.

of the financial crisis before them. Louis concluded his brief opening speech to the Notables by expressing the hope that they would not oppose private interests to the greater public good. Calonne was even more explicit. He presented an analysis of the fiscal situation and told the Notables that it was no longer possible simply to rely on the expedients of the past. He asserted that there were only two courses of action available, and that one of them – admission of state bankruptcy – was unthinkable. The only remaining solution was the destruction of what Calonne called "abuses," by which he clearly meant the pecuniary privileges enjoyed by most of the Notables. He then outlined his program, emphasizing at the conclusion of his presentation that the ultimate aim of the proposed measures was "the well-being of the nation."[12]

Angered by the seemingly pliant role to which they had been consigned, and dismayed by Calonne's attack on privilege, the Notables resisted his program from the beginning. Their opposition was both resolute and ingenious, and successfully avoided the pitfalls in which Calonne had sought to trap them. In order not to alienate public opinion, the Notables endorsed the principle of fiscal equality and even voluntarily renounced their proposed exemption from the *capitation*. For most of the Notables, however, these actions, as Albert Goodwin has argued, were merely ploys to deceive public opinion, for they then proceeded to oppose the land tax vigorously, citing constitutional and administrative grounds. Furthermore, they took advantage of the inaccessibility of the accounts on which Calonne had based his calculation to express doubt about the need for the tax.[13]

In the following weeks relations between Calonne and the Notables deteriorated as they took no action on his program. Although their public pronouncements endorsed fiscal equality, their meetings in committee revealed that many had a private agenda in which the preservation of privilege was the primordial concern. The Estates of Brittany, for example, had sent their deputies to the Assembly without any instructions or mandate, an action that they sought to conceal by not mentioning it in the register of the meeting. After their deputation arrived at Versailles, the Estates continued to remind them that they had no mandate to negotiate the matters under discussion. On March 20, then, in the first committee, the Breton Notables stated that the privileges of

12 *Procès-verbal de l'Assemblée de Notables, tenue à Versailles, en l'année 1787* (Paris, 1788), pp. 42, 45–66, especially p. 59.
13 See Albert Goodwin, "Calonne, the assembly of French notables of 1787 and the origins of the *Révolte Nobiliaire*," *English Historical Review*, 61 (1946), 202–234, 329–377, especially 344–345.

the province could not be discussed or negotiated and asserted that any modification of the system of taxation was solely the prerogative of the province itself. Similarly, a representative of Burgundy vigorously defended the privileges of that province in the committee of which he was a member, pointedly noting that Louis XVI himself had confirmed these privileges at the time of his accession to the throne.[14]

Utterly exasperated at the disparity between their private adhesion to fiscal privilege and their public renunciation of it, Calonne commissioned a pamphlet against them, claiming that the reestablishment of financial equilibrium was in the interest of all and that the burden of the Crown's proposed measures would not fall on the people. After presenting an outline of the reforms that the Crown had recommended, he went on to note the equivocal attitude of the Notables toward it and speculated on some of the possible reasons for their stance. He acknowledged that the tax burden would be heavier, but asserted that it would fall only on those who did not currently pay enough. Stating that privileges would be sacrificed, he asked if the Notables preferred to overburden the non-privileged, the people. He then seemed to defend the Notables by reminding his readers that they had, in fact, already agreed to the sacrifice of their fiscal privileges and to the recommendation that the land tax should be extended to all land without exception. He stated that it would therefore be wrong to believe that reasonable doubts on the part of the Notables represented a malevolent opposition, for such sentiments would be injurious to the nation.[15] The unmistakable implication of this passage, however, was to indicate to the Notables that further opposition on their part could give rise to the notion of malevolence.

Calonne then took the extraordinary step of having the pamphlet disseminated without charge, not only in Paris but also in provincial towns. Many were distributed through the clergy, who were urged to read it to their flocks from the pulpit. Its publication, and particularly the method of diffusion utilized by Calonne, which obviously intensified the pressure on the Notables, poisoned relations between them, and on

14 On Brittany, AD Ille-et-Vilaine C 1799, letter of Bertrand to Calonne and Breteuil, January 10, 1787; AD Ille-et-Vilaine C 3899, letter of commission of Estates of Brittany to Bishop of Dol, February 2, 1787, letters of commissioners of Estates to deputies at Assembly of Notables, March 28, 1787 and April 3, 1787; AD Côte d'Or C 3476, *Cahier des délibérations du premier bureau présidé par M. Frère du roi, Assemblée des Notables, 1787*, I. On Burgundy, AD Côte d'Or C 3476, *Observations en forme d'avis sur les differens mémoires présentés à l'Assemblée des Notables en 1787, Bureau de S. A. S. Mgr. le Prince de Condé, M. l'abbé de la Fare. Observations conservatoires des droits et privilèges de la Province de Bourgogne* (undated, but between March 7 and 23, 1787).
15 Charles-Alexandre Calonne, "Avertissement," *De l'État de la France, présent et à venir*, 5th ed. (London, 1790), pp. 436–440.

April 8, soon after its appearance, Louis dismissed Calonne from office because of the lingering stalemate.[16]

Although he dismissed Calonne, Louis still wished to implement the program that Calonne had devised. At the same time, he realized that the objections of the Notables could not simply be ignored or impugned and that the proposals would have to be modified. Therefore, on April 23, in a personal address to the Notables to urge the passage of the land tax, Louis made several significant concessions. He met, in fact, nearly all of the objections that the Notables had raised; among other actions, he agreed to limit the duration of the tax and to make it proportional to the amount of the deficits, as they had asked.[17] He also agreed to grant them access to the financial accounts prepared by Calonne. Furthermore, shortly afterward, during the interval when the accounts were being transmitted to the Notables, Louis appointed a leading member of the opposition within the Notables, Loménie de Brienne, archbishop of Toulouse, minister without portfolio, and Brienne quickly took control of finances for the Crown.

Soon after the appointment of Brienne, the Notables began to examine the accounts. The figures were difficult to understand, and although they could not agree on the size of the deficit, the Notables generally agreed that it was a considerable amount. Their chief response, however, was simply to urge the king to pursue greater economies than those previously announced and to suggest various administrative measures to prevent future deficits.

Brienne, in contrast, sought to focus their attention on the current deficit. In a conference on May 9 with several key members of the Notables, he stressed the need for dealing with the deficit immediately, so that state credit could be restored in both the international and domestic markets. Recognizing that the Notables had not been able to agree on the amount of the deficit, Brienne suggested taking an average of the different estimates to calculate an amount. He announced a further cut in state expenditures of approximately forty million *livres*, although he warned the Notables that no additional reductions could be expected. Finally, to treat the remainder of the deficit, Brienne proposed a land tax, to be a fixed amount and paid in money, as the Notables had earlier suggested, and two indirect taxes. The proposals were essentially similar

16 Goodwin, "Calonne, the assembly of French notables of 1787 and the origins of the *Révolte Nobiliaire,*" 358; see also *Correspondance secrète inédite sur Louis XVI, Marie Antoinette, la cour et la ville de 1777 à 1792*, ed. Mathurin François Adolphe de Lescure, 2 vols. (Paris, 1866), II: 125.
17 On the recognition from within the Notables that he had met nearly all of their objections and that the interests of the nation were at stake, see AN M 788, dossier 2[17], document 89.

to those put forward by Calonne, except that they incorporated recommendations brought forward by the Notables, especially the provision making the land tax repartitional rather than proportional.[18]

In the days following the meeting, however, the Notables, who were dismayed to see Brienne adopt much of Calonne's program, did not consider the projects that he had proposed.[19] Instead, they examined deficiencies in financial administration and formulated various measures that the Crown, in effect, agreed to consider. Only afterward, slowly and reluctantly, did the Assembly agree to consider Brienne's program. They opposed one of the indirect taxes and were divided on the other. Most important, on May 19 the Notables indicated that they could not approve the land tax.

The various committees into which the Assembly had been subdivided for deliberations advanced different reasons for their opposition. Some justified their position by stating that the complexity of the financial accounts kept them from determining the size of the deficit, which in turn meant that they could not estimate the amount of revenue that the tax should produce, how long it should be in effect or even whether it was needed at all. Others declared that the Assembly should not anticipate the decision of the *parlements*. Lastly, all but one of the committees rejected the tax on the principle that since the Assembly was not a representative body, it was not truly empowered to consent to it.[20] In the face of such intransigence, Brienne realized that he had little choice but to dissolve the Assembly, which he did on May 25.

In recent years, scholars have sought to reexamine the goals of the Assembly of Notables or to offer new explanations for the conduct of its members. Bosher, for example, discounts defense of privilege as a primary factor, just as Vivian Gruder had done before him.[21] Their arguments have merit and cannot be dismissed but, as the correspondence from Brittany and Burgundy shows, one must also continue to

18  Goodwin, "Calonne, the assembly of French notables of 1787 and the origins of the *Révolte Nobiliaire*," 368–369; AN M 788, dossier 2[17], document 113.
19  See *Correspondance secrète*, ed. de Lescure, II: 142–143.
20  Goodwin, "Calonne, the assembly of French notables of 1787 and the origins of the *Révolte Nobiliaire*," 373.
21  Bosher, *The French Revolution*, pp. 101–106; Vivian R. Gruder, "No taxation without representation: the assembly of notables of 1787 and political ideology in France," *Legislative Studies Quarterly*, 7 (1982), 263–279; "Paths to political consciousness: the assembly of notables of 1787 and the 'Pre-Revolution' in France," *French Historical Studies*, 11 (1984), 323–355; "A mutation in elite political culture: the French notables and the defense of property and participation, 1787," *The Journal of Modern History*, 56 (1984), 598–634; "The society of orders at its demise: the vision of the elite at the end of the Ancien Régime," *French History*, 1 (1987), 210–237. A critique of some of Gruder's arguments can be found in Michael P. Fitzsimmons, "Privilege and the polity in France, 1786–1791," *The American Historical Review*, 92 (1987), 269–295, especially 274–275.

take defense of privilege strongly into account.[22] Indeed, in the final analysis, there were several undercurrents at the Assembly of Notables, but this was less evident to contemporary observers than it has been to historians.

Rather, what was much more apparent to contemporaries was that after more than three months the Assembly had disbanded without resolving in any way the financial crisis that had been the reason for its convocation.[23] Since they had, in fact, negotiated with the Crown on the land tax and other issues during those three months, the protestation of the Notables that they could not assent to the land tax rang hollow. Rather, their sudden abdication, particularly after the Crown had met most of their demands and adopted virtually all of their recommendations, led to the perception that they were unwilling to yield their fiscal privileges in the interest of the solvency of the state. To most contemporaries, it appeared that privilege had triumphed over the well-being of the nation.

Up until the publication of Calonne's pamphlet, which one scholar has characterized as the most ambitious attempt to cultivate the French public since Necker's *Compte rendu*, the proceedings of the Assembly had not been made public.[24] Calonne's action, however, made its deliberations much more general, and the revelations made at the Assembly of Notables shocked virtually all Frenchmen who had an interest in public affairs.[25] In an age when economics was for the most part only imperfectly understood, the deficit and its consequences were not fully comprehended, but there was a pervasive sense that it was inimical to France.[26] Even more important, however, the perception that privilege had triumphed over the financial equilibrium and general well-being of

---

22 See AD Ille-et-Vilaine C 1799, letter of Bertrand to Calonne and Breteuil, January 10, 1789; AD Côte d'Or C 3476, *Cahier des délibérations du premier bureau présidé par M. frère du Roi, Assemblée des Notables*, I; AD Côte d'Or C 3476, *Observations en forme d'avis sur les différens mémoires présentées à l'Assemblée des Notables en 1787. Bureau de S. A. S. Mgr. le Prince de Condé, M. l'abbé de la Fare. Observations conservatoires des droits et privilèges de la Province de Bourgogne* (undated, but between March 7 and 23, 1787). For more on the defense of privilege at the Assembly of Notables, see Bailey Stone, *The Parlement of Paris, 1774–1789* (Chapel Hill, 1981), p. 161.

23 See *Correspondance secrète*, ed. de Lescure, II: 145.

24 See William Doyle, *Origins of the French Revolution*, 2nd edn. (Oxford, 1988), p. 102.

25 See BM Nantes Collection Dugast-Matifeux, tome 12, fol. 8; *Correspondance secrète*, ed. de Lescure, II: 145; Jean-Paul Rabaut de Saint-Etienne, *Précis de l'histoire de la Révolution française* (Paris, 1827), p. 131.

26 See Rabaut de Saint-Etienne, *Précis de l'histoire de la Révolution française*, p. 131. Many pamphlets opened with an elementary explanation of what a deficit was. See, for example, *Considérations interéssantes sur les affaires présentes* (Paris, 1788), p. 3, or *Le véritable patriotisme* (N.p., 1788), pp. 1–2. For a retrospective indication of the unease that contemporaries felt about the financial crisis, see AN C 117, dossier 325, document 12; AN C 117, dossier 329, document 25.

the nation led many to begin to reconsider the nature of the French state. Was it primarily an aggregate of privileged individuals and corporations, or was it a grander entity defined by common bonds and ideas?[27]

Thus, while Calonne's pamphlet did not produce the immediate effect that he had desired, the theme that he had adduced – that there was perhaps a fundamental opposition between the fiscal advantages enjoyed by the clergy and the nobility and the general well-being of the state – legitimized the questioning of privilege. A prominent characteristic of the period between the dissolution of the Assembly of Notables and the opening of the Estates-General was the extent to which the traditional notion of the state underwent a fundamental reexamination. Initially, this reconsideration was amorphous and heterogeneous, but a prevalent theme was concern about the role of privilege in the body politic. Although it would not fully crystallize until 1788, the substance of this revaluation became a movement away from acceptance of privilege as a valid instrument of government to rejection of it as injurious to the common weal.[28]

In Paris, however, the course of events that followed the dismissal of the Assembly of Notables had a more familiar outline. The desperate efforts of the Crown to register edicts to alleviate the fiscal crisis resulted in the exiling of the *Parlement* of Paris to Troyes and led to the traditional charge of despotism. The *Parlement* deliberately sought to make the cause of the nation its own, as the Assembly of Notables had not, by stridently advocating the convocation of the Estates-General. Although it was primarily a delaying tactic, and a prospect that the *Parlement* saw ultimately as being to its own advantage, this stance, combined with the support that the *Parlement* gained in its perceived struggle with despotism, obscured the fact that its opposition to the Crown's program was virtually as self-interested as that of the Notables had been. As a result of this misapprehension, from this time until late 1788 the *Parlement* came increasingly to be identified with the nation and began to emerge as its chief representative.[29]

27 Rabaut de Saint-Etienne, *Précis de l'histoire de la révolution française*, p. 134. Fox-Genovese, *The Origins of Physiocracy*, pp. 114–117, has argued that this question was implicit in the earlier work of Quesnay. While undeniably true, the difference in 1787 was that the reality of the deep fiscal problems revealed during the Assembly of Notables, as well as the failure of the Notables to resolve them, went beyond the more theoretical concerns of Quesnay and became the catalyst for a much sharper focus on the question.
28 See Fitzsimmons, "Privilege and the polity in France," 276–277; Ran Halevi, "La révolution constituante: les ambiguités politiques," *The Political Culture of the French Revolution*, ed. Colin Lucas, (Oxford, 1988), pp. 69–70.
29 See Jean Egret, *La Pré-Révolution française* (Paris, 1962), pp. 147–203, especially pp. 168–181. See also Bailey Stone, *The French Parlements and the Crisis of the Old Regime* (Chapel Hill, 1986), pp. 83–84. See, too, AD Côte d'Or E 642, no. 56.

The defense of noble fiscal privileges by several provincial *parlements* in 1787 served, however, to focus greater attention on privileges, especially fiscal privilege.[30] Indeed, the provincial *parlements* were much more resolutely opposed to the Crown's program for addressing the financial crisis and continued to resist an extension on the existing land tax (*vingtième*) even after the *Parlement* of Paris had accepted it from its exile at Troyes. Furthermore, the continued opposition of provincial *parlements* to even minimal fiscal equity meant that privilege loomed as a much larger issue in the provinces than it did in Paris.

In 1788, in fact, the course of events enabled provincial concerns to dominate political developments. In May, 1788, the Keeper of the Seals, Chrétien-François de Lamoignon reorganized the judiciary. Among other measures, the reorganization created a supreme plenary court that deprived the *Parlement* of Paris of its political role and significantly redefined the scope of its judicial functions.[31] Lamoignon also ordered that all of the *parlements* be suspended and that their members be placed on indefinite vacation, but only the *Parlement* of Paris obeyed the stricture against further meetings.[32]

The subservience of the *Parlement* of Paris allowed the political focus to shift from Paris to the provinces and enabled provincial concerns to emerge with greater strength.[33] In the provinces, Rennes and Grenoble became two preeminent centers of opposition[34] and the political mobilization that began in 1788 in defense of the *parlements* in these two locales had an afterlife that ultimately formed a frame of reference on which contemporaries drew until the opening of the Estates-General.

In Brittany the nobility, the dominant political group in the province, took the lead in opposition, seeking above all to preserve its traditional privileges. They attempted to enlist the support of the clergy and the Third Estate in their cause, but met with only limited success, especially

30 Egret, *La Pré-Révolution française*, p. 205.
31 In yet another indication of a growing ideal of the nation, Egret argues that the Lamoignon measures were the expression of "a visible desire for national unification." Jean Egret, "Les origines de la Révolution en Bretagne (1788–1789)," *Revue Historique*, 113 (1955), 192.
32 Egret, *La Pré-Révolution française*, p. 257. For more on the Lamoignon edicts, see Marcel Marion, *Le Garde des sceaux Lamoignon et la réforme judiciaire de 1788* (Paris, 1905) and John F. Ramsey, "The judicial reform of 1788 and the French Revolution," *Studies in Modern European History in Honor of Franklin Charles Palm*, ed. Fredrick J. Cox, Richard M. Brace, Bernard C. Weber and John F. Ramsey, (New York, 1956), pp. 217–238.
33 See, for example, AD Côte d'Or E 642, no. 35, no. 36, no. 47. For a broader consideration of this theme, see Robert Chagny, ed., *Aux Origines provinciales de la Révolution* (Grenoble, 1990).
34 On Rennes and Grenoble as early focal points, see AD Côte d'Or E 642, no. 32, no. 33; Marquis de Bombelles, *Journal*, ed. Jean Grassion and François Durif, 2 vols. (Geneva, 1978–1982), II: 205.

with respect to the Third Estate. Only with great difficulty were the nobility able to form a deputation of members of all three orders to present a memorandum to the king. The restoration of the *Parlement* of Rennes represented a triumph for the aristocratic resistance, but in the process of mobilization against the Lamoignon edicts the Third Estate had also begun to articulate its own political grievances, setting the stage for a vigorous effort to reform the Breton constitution in order to lessen the dominance enjoyed by the nobility in the Estates.[35]

The situation in Dauphiné contrasted sharply with that of Brittany, for in Dauphiné a broadly based coalition of all three orders joined together in a sense of common purpose and were fused by concern for the well-being of the nation. On June 7, 1788, in the "day of the tiles," citizens of Grenoble protested the dismissal of their *parlement*. A week later prominent members of all three orders in Grenoble gathered and, in addition to demanding the recall of the *parlement* and the convocation of the Estates-General, asserted the right of citizens to assemble and deliberate on matters of importance to the nation. They therefore invited the three orders of the different cities and towns of the province to send deputies to Grenoble to form a new assembly.[36]

The general assembly of members of all orders of municipalities that met on July 21 at the château of Vizille, outside Grenoble, in defiance of the intendant, had several innovative features that captured the attention of much of the rest of France. The Third Estate was numerically predominant, the orders met in common, and issues were decided through votes by head rather than by order. The assembly at Vizille adopted resolutions requesting not only the recall of the *parlements* and the convocation of the Estates-General, but also calling for the re-establishment of the estates of Dauphiné, with double representation for the Third Estate and vote by head. Most important, the assembly transcended purely provincial concerns and invoked the ideal of the nation, going so far as to renounce the privileges of the province in the interest of the nation, claiming that national unity was necessary for France to move forward.

The following month of August brought the contending issues of despotism and privilege into much clearer focus as the Crown announced a date for the convening of the Estates-General and, just over a week later, suspended payment on the debt. Although the latter act caused

---

35 See Egret, "Les origines de la Révolution en Bretagne," 193–197. See also AD Ille-et-Vilaine C 3899, undated list of demands of Third Estate of Brittany.
36 *Délibération de la ville de Grenoble, du samedi quatorze juin mil sept cent quatre-vingt-huit, à l'Hôtel de Ville de Grenoble, sur les dix heurs du matin* (N.p., n.d.).

tension in Paris,[37] the two events served to make the unrest in the realm less amorphous by clarifying what had heretofore been competing issues in the public consciousness. With a fixed date for the convening of the Estates-General and bankruptcy, despotism was clearly no longer the critical issue, for a bankrupt monarch could hardly be a despotic one.

Instead, privilege became the chief concern as the suspension of payment generally banished whatever doubts there might have been about the existence or magnitude of the fiscal crisis. Given the parlous financial condition of the state, the fiscal privileges of the clergy and the nobility were the principal issue to be resolved.[38] The contrast between the manifest financial needs of the state and fiscal privileges set up a clear antithesis between them – privilege and the nation became mutually exclusive categories.[39]

The position of the Crown during most of this period, however, was ambiguous, even passive. On the one hand, with the perception that it had struggled unsuccessfully against privilege at the Assembly of Notables, the Crown could be viewed as a victim of privilege.[40] On the other hand, as the source and guarantor of privilege and the traditional ally of what was commonly called the "privileged orders," the Crown could also be seen as deeply implicated in it.[41] Amidst the conviction that France was being crippled by privilege, the ambiguity of its position led to an overshadowing of the Crown – as the notion of "regenerating" France grew, the word "nation" gained usage over that of "kingdom," which was associated with privilege.[42]

---

37 See, for example, *Correspondance secrète du comte de Mercy-Argenteau avec l'Empereur Joseph II et le Prince de Kaunitz*, ed. Alfred d'Arneth and Jules Flammermont, 2 vols. (Paris, 1889–1891), II: 189; AD Côte d'Or E 642, no. 51.

38 On August, 1788, as a watershed in clarifying issues for the chief theorist of the era, the abbé Sieyès, see AN 284 AP 3, dossier 2, part 2. It was at this time that Sieyès began to compose his *Essay on Privileges*, although it did not appear until several months later. See also Bombelles, *Journal*, II: 207.

39 See, for example, AN AB[XIX] 3494 (13), letter of February 2, 1789; AN H[1] 207, dossier 1, document 22; AN B[a] 57, liasse 141, dossier 1, document 20.

40 [Joseph-Antoine-Joachim Cérutti] *A la mémoire auguste de feu monseigneur le Dauphin, Père du Roi* (N.p., n.d.), pp. vii–ix, xi.

41 *Mémoire des princes présentés au Roi* (N.p., n.d.).

42 On the conviction that France was being crippled by privilege, see *Le dernier mot du tiers-état à la noblesse de France* (N.p., n.d.), p. 1; *Qu'est-ce que la Noblesse, et que sont ses privilèges?* (Amsterdam, 1789), pp. 1–2; *Considérations sur l'injustice des prétensions du clergé et de la noblesse* (N.p., 1789), pp. 20–21. For the rise of the word "nation" over "kingdom," Cornwell B. Rogers, *The Spirit of Revolution in 1789: A Study of Public Opinion as Revealed in Political Songs and other Popular Literature at the Beginning of the French Revolution* (Princeton, 1949), p. 39 n. For a good discussion of the idea of regeneration, see Mona Ozouf, "Regeneration," *A Critical Dictionary of the French Revolution*, ed. François Furet and Mona Ozouf, (Cambridge, Mass., 1989), pp. 781–791. For more on the rise of the idea of the nation, see François Furet, *Interpreting the French Revolution* (Cambridge,

With the convocation of the Estates-General no longer in doubt, its composition and procedure now assumed an elemental importance.[43] Since the task of regeneration was so comprehensive, and since the fiscal privileges of the clergy and the nobility were the significant issue to be deliberated, the traditional method of voting by order was not acceptable. Indeed, the dichotomy between privilege and the nation ultimately crystallized around this issue, which soon superseded the narrower issue of fiscal privilege.

The Crown, however, never departed from the equivocal position it assumed at the time it announced the date for the convening of the Estates-General – simply renewing its solicitation of ideas about how the Estates-General should be constituted, a stance that gave the debate a strong sense of intensity and import. One scholar has argued, in fact, that the Crown's inconclusive stance was a calculated measure designed to encourage division in society. No longer able to postpone the convocation of the Estates-General, the Crown desired controversy over its composition and procedure in order to weaken it as an institution and to render its proceedings unobjectionable.[44] Indeed, more recently Bailey Stone has argued along similar lines, asserting that the decision of the *Parlement* of Paris on September 25, 1788, stating that the Estates-General should follow the precedents of 1614 was less a reactionary effort to assure control over the Estates-General than it was an attempt to impart some orderliness to the debate by defining what it believed were established principles.[45]

Whether desired by the Crown or not, the controversy continued unabated, particularly after the decision of September 25 by the *Parlement* of Paris and, more especially, that of a reconvened Assembly of Notables in November and December, 1788,[46] that the Estates-General should meet as it had in 1614. These opinions, particularly that of the Assembly of Notables – for the *Parlement*, in a vain attempt to regain its popularity, sought to amend its pronouncement in December – imparted additional vigor to the debate on privilege by expanding it to include political as well as fiscal privilege, and served also to sharpen the

1981), pp. 33, 42–43. The passivity of the Crown had been noted earlier by the Austrian ambassador. See *Correspondance secrète*, ed. d'Arneth and Flammermont, II: 137–138.
43  See BN Mss. Nouv. acq. fr. 17275, fol. 92; ADG A⁴ 56, p. 10. See also Antoine Rivarol, *Mémoires* (Paris, 1824), p. 7; Bombelles, *Journal*, II: 781–791.
44  Mitchell B. Garrett, *The Estates-General of 1789: The Problems of Composition and Organization* (New York, 1935), pp. 25–40. On the debate and the passivity of the Crown, see Guy-Marie Sallier, *Annales françaises 1774–1789* (Paris, 1813), pp. 234–241.
45  Stone, *The Parlement* of Paris, p. 167.
46  On the attention that the second Assembly of Notables commanded, see AM Arles AA 23, fol. 43.

antithesis between privilege and the nation more clearly than ever. As one pamphleteer observed, the king had twice convened the Notables to consult them on the interests of the throne and the nation. In 1787, he said, they had defended their privileges against the throne, and in 1788 they had defended their privileges against the nation.[47]

The changing contours of opinion – the shift from acceptance of privilege as a legitimate instrument of governance to repudiation of it as detrimental to the common good – are especially evident in the writings of the Abbé Emmanuel-Joseph Sieyès, whom several scholars have tended to view as the personification of the Revolution.[48] In this respect, then, it is worth examining two pamphlets written before he composed *Qu'est-ce que le Tiers Etat?* that particularly reflect the metamorphosis that occurred during this period on the issues of privilege and the nation.

In 1788, after the announcement by the Crown that the Estates-General would meet in May, 1789, Sieyès wrote his first pamphlet, *Vues sur les moyens d'exécution dont les représentans de la France pourront disposer en 1789*. In it, Sieyès asserted that the Estates-General was the organ of the entire nation rather than of particular constituent elements within society and argued that no province could ignore or veto its decisions.[49] The pamphlet is noteworthy mainly as a reflection of the new idea of the nation that began to form during the months before the opening of the Estates-General.

His next and more influential pamphlet, *Essai sur les privilèges*, was prompted by the decision of the *Parlement* of Paris and the reconvened Assembly of Notables that the Estates-General should follow the forms of 1614.[50] For the sake of argument, Sieyès conceded the legitimate (*pure*) origins of privilege in the polity, but argued that its current effect was either to exempt specific individuals from the law or to grant them the

---

47 [Cérutti], *A la mémoire auguste de feu de Monseigneur le Dauphin*, p. xi; see also AN B^a 57, liasse 141, dossier 1, document 20; Bertrand Barère, *Mémoires*, 4 vols. (Paris, 1842), I: 417–421; *Correspondance secrète*, ed. de Lescure II: 304; Bossenga, *The Politics of Privilege*, p. 96.

48 See, for example, Sewell, *Work and Revolution in France*, pp. 78–84; Patrice Higonnet, *Class, Ideology and the Rights of Nobles during the French Revolution* (Oxford, 1981), pp. 255–256; Jean-Denis Bredin, *Sieyès: la clé de la Révolution française* (Paris, 1988), and, less strongly, Colin Lucas, "Nobles, bourgeois and the origins of the French Revolution," *Past and Present*, 60 (August, 1973), 124, and Furet, *Interpreting the French Revolution*, p. 2. The fullest exposition, however, is Murray Forsyth, *Reason and Revolution: The Political Thought of the Abbé Sieyès* (New York, 1987), especially p. 37.

49 *Vues sur les moyens d'exécution dont les représentans de la France pourront disposer en 1789* (N.p., n.d.). See also Forsyth, *Reason and Revolution*, pp. 73–76; Paul Bastid, *Sieyès et sa pensée*, revised edn. (Paris, 1970), pp. 72–75.

50 The ideas expressed in the *Essai sur les privilèges* began to crystallize in August, 1788, but the pamphlet itself appeared in November, 1788. See AN 284 AP 3, dossier 2, part 2.

right to do something not intrinsically illegal. The essential character of privilege was to be outside of the law.

Since the goal of positive law (*la loi*) was to protect liberty and property in order to prevent injury to others in society, to exempt an individual from it was to bestow on him the right to injure others. Similarly, if he had the exclusive right to do something not intrinsically illegal, he in effect deprived others of a portion of their liberty, for anything that was not illegal was part of the civil domain and therefore belonged to all. Sieyès therefore concluded that by their very nature privileges were "unjust, odious and inconsistent with the ultimate aim of all political association."[51] After an extended discussion of the pernicious effect of privilege on society, Sieyès closed by calling for a vigorous attack on it.

Much like the subsequent *Qu'est-ce que le Tiers Etat?*, Sieyès's *Essai sur les privilèges* was a cogent articulation of a vague idea. The vehemence of Sieyès's denunciation, as well as, for example, his intolerance even of honorific privilege, were far more advanced positions than those generally current. But at the same time it is illustrative of the deeper concern about privilege that manifested itself following the ruling by the *Parlement* of Paris and the second Assembly of Notables and was one of the clearer expositions of the issue confronting France between 1787 and 1789, the deep-seated place of privilege in the polity. Along with his subsequent and better known work, it struck a responsive chord.[52]

The larger dimensions that the debate on privilege assumed during the autumn of 1788 so alarmed the princes of the blood that in December, 1788, they issued a declaration offering to give up the fiscal privileges of the clergy and the nobility in return for a cessation of the attacks on them.[53] It had no official standing, for they were not empowered in any way to represent the nobility as a whole, nor could they be said to represent the clergy. Furthermore, the tone of their statement was so imperious and petulant that it served primarily to intensify rather than to still the controversy; many writings appeared in response to it.[54] Some of

51 Edme Champion, ed., *Qu'est-ce que le tiers Etat? Par Emmanuel Sieyès, précédé de l'Essai sur les privilèges* (Paris, 1888). See also Forsyth, *Reason and Revolution*, pp. 90–96 and Bastid, *Sieyès et sa pensée*, pp. 55–56.

52 Etienne Dumont, *Souvenirs sur Mirabeau et sur les deux premières assemblées législatives*, new edition, ed. J. Bénétruy, (Paris, 1951), pp. 44–64. Another major statement on privilege was [Jean-Paul Rabaut de Saint-Etienne], *Considérations sur les intérêts du tiers-état, adressés au peuple des provinces, par un propriétaire foncier* (N.p., 1788).

53 *Mémoire des Princes présenté au Roi.*

54 See [F. M. Kerverseau and G. Clavelin], *Histoire de la révolution de 1789, et de l'établissment d'une constitution de France … par deux amis de la liberté*, 20 vols. (Paris, 1790–1803), I: 89. See also BN Mss. Fonds Français 6687, fols. 185, 188, 200. Responses included *A monseigneur comte d'Artois* (N.p., n.d.), *Réflexions sur le mémoire des princes, par un avocat de Province* (N.p., n.d.); *Examen du mémoire des princes, présenté au Roi* (N.p.,

the nobility in the provinces followed the lead of the princes and renounced their fiscal privileges. But just as the princes had weakened the effect of their action with the tone in which it was done, so, too, whatever goodwill might have been generated by the action of the provincial nobility was often greatly vitiated by the insistence on vote by order at the Estates-General that usually accompanied such renunciations.[55]

Since the September ruling of the *Parlement* of Paris and its subsequent affirmation by the reassembled Notables, the problem of privilege had been redefined; it had expanded beyond the narrow concept of fiscal privilege to focus more broadly on political privilege, especially vote by order. To many contemporaries, it appeared that the clergy and the nobility, in seeking to retain their traditional advantage in the Estates-General, were intent on checking the task of national regeneration. Having implicitly acknowledged the detrimental effect of privilege by offering to yield on the issue of taxation, they simultaneously sought to adhere to it by invoking the procedures of 1614.[56] To those interested in public affairs, however, the task of rehabilitating the nation was too fundamental and too comprehensive to be left chiefly to the clergy and the nobility – arguably, the elements in French society most responsible for the predicament that now confronted it. For the interests of the nation to counterbalance the predominance of privilege, it was crucial that the Third Estate's delegation be doubled to equal the number of deputies of the other two orders combined and that the vote be by head rather than order.[57]

In late December, 1788, the Crown decided the former by authorizing the Third Estate to have a deputation equal in number to the first two orders combined. The concomitant question of the method of voting was not addressed, however, not even in the following month when the Crown promulgated electoral arrangements for the Estates-General and, as a result, the dispute continued unabated.

The electoral provisions for the Estates-General lend credence to the belief that the Crown sought to encourage division in society over the

n.d.); *Modestes observations sur le Mémoire des Princes; faites au nom de 23 millions de citoyens françois* (N.p., 1788); *Ultimatum d'un citoyen du tiers-état, au mémoire des Princes, présenté au Roi. Seconde édition* (N.p., 1789).

55 See, for example, AN B$^a$ 24, liasse 40, dossier 6, document 7; AN B$^a$ 27, liasse 45, dossier 6, document 1; AN K 679, no. 26, no. 27; AD Yonne L 169.

56 See AN H$^1$ 149, dossier 1, documents 2, 11, 12, 17, 20, 23, 24.

57 See AN B$^a$ 57, liasse 141, dossier 1, document 20; AN H$^1$ 207, dossier 1, document 22; AN B$^a$ 11, liasse 5, dossier 12, document 6; BM Grenoble Ms. R 7082, convocation of town of Ambert, December 15, 1788. See also Bossenga, *The Politics of Privilege*, p. 96.

Estates-General, for they emphasized its atomized nature.[58] If this was the Crown's intention, however, it was largely neutralized by the process of drafting the *cahiers*, which gave rise in all three orders to an inchoate but ultimately unifying concept of the nation.[59] In ways both large and small, in fact, the *cahiers* illustrate the reaction against privilege as a superintending principle of society and the desire to see the nation given greater precision and definition. Two prominent goals of many of the *cahiers* were equality of taxation and uniformity within France, particularly legal and administrative uniformity – the antithesis of the congeries of customs and privileges then in place.[60] The elevation of the ideal of the nation manifested itself in lesser ways as well; several *cahiers*, for example, suggested that ennoblement be a product not of wealth or nobility, but of service to the nation.[61]

If doubling the Third and vote by head were the issues that defined the debate on privilege versus the nation, the symbolic sites of the dispute were the provinces of Brittany and Dauphiné.[62] Brittany became the symbol of the divisive effect that adherence to privilege could have, whereas Dauphiné represented union in the transcending of privilege and gave hope to much of the rest of France.

In Brittany the agitation that had been raised against perceived despotism earlier in 1788 generated an afterlife that evolved in an

---

58 For the regulations, see Armand Brette, *Recueil de documents rélatifs à la convocation des Etats-Généraux de 1789*, 4 vols. (Paris, 1894–1915). I: 66–87. R. B. Rose also discerned such motives in the electoral arrangements for Paris. See R. B. Rose, *The Making of the Sans-Culottes: Democratic Ideas and Institutions in Paris, 1789–1792* (Manchester, 1983), p. 24.

59 The word "nation" recurs consistently in the *cahiers*. Beatrice F. Hyslop, *French Nationalism in 1789 According to the General Cahiers*, revised edn. (New York, 1968), p. 31. The notion had been expressed in pamphlets, of course, but the drafting of the *cahiers* provided a more systematic method and institutional framework that enabled the concept to engage more of the populace and to establish itself. At the same time, it must be recognized that the concept of the nation was amorphous, and could be used in reference to such provinces as Brittany or Provence as easily as it could refer to France as a whole. See Norman Hampson, "The idea of the nation in revolutionary France," *Reshaping France : Town, Country and Region during the French Revolution*, ed. Alan Forrest and Peter Jones, (Manchester, 1991), pp. 13–25.

60 George V. Taylor, "Revolutionary and nonrevolutionary content in the *cahiers* of 1789: an interim report", *French Historical Studies*, 7 (Fall 1972) 495; Hyslop, *French Nationalism in 1789*, pp. 52–61.

61 AD Charente-Maritime 4 J 1574 (28); AN B$^a$ 25$^1$, liasse 42, dossier 2, document 2; AN AB$^{XIX}$ 3258, *cahier* of combined orders of nobility and Third Estate of Péronne, Montdidier and Roye, p. 32; AN AB$^{XIX}$ 3259, *cahier* of Third Estate of town of Châlons-sur-Marne, pp. 21–22, *cahier* of *senéchaussée* of Vannes, p. 6; George V. Taylor, "Noncapitalist wealth and the origins of the French Revolution," *The American Historical Review*, 72 (1967), 492.

62 See, for example, ADG A$^4$ 56, pp. 5–9; BN Mss. Nouv. acq. fr. 17275, fols. 5, 13, 17, 29v$^o$, 37v$^o$, 39v$^o$, 43–48v$^o$, 55, 57–58, 59–60, 73–76, 81–88, 114; AD Côte d'Or E 642, no. 42, no. 47. See also Bombelles, *Journal*, II: 205, 207.

altogether new direction. Against the backdrop of the financial crisis – now made manifest by the suspension of payment on the debt – provincial fiscal privileges were no longer merely a local grievance; they became national in scope, for they were inimical to the entire nation. Within Brittany, the province in which, in the judgment of the intendant, the burden of taxation was "assessed with the most injustice,"[63] the focus of resentment against privilege became the Estates of Brittany, which had historically overseen the assessment and collection of taxes.[64] In an effort to gain a more equitable distribution of taxation, the Third Estate in various towns began to agitate against the existing level of representation in the Estates, and those seeking change were ultimately able to draw on the moral force of the emerging idea of the nation.

The effort began in late 1788, as the biannual opening of the Estates of Brittany approached. Led principally by Nantes and Rennes, the Third Estate began to seek authorization to send extra deputies to the Estates along with their regular contingent. Many towns also wrote to the Crown to ask that they be allowed to choose their representatives to both the Estates of Brittany and the Estates-General. Furthermore, the Third Estate decided that if its demands were not met, its deputies would withdraw from the Estates, thereby rupturing them. To show the Crown that its actions were not directed against it or the nation in its time of financial distress, the Third Estate subsequently amended its position to agree to treat the awarding of the *don gratuit* before presenting its demands. At the same time, however, it persisted in its determination not to deliberate on any other matter unless its demands for equal taxation, greater representation in both the Estates of Brittany and the intermediary commission – the body that functioned between meetings of the Estates – and the right to name its deputies to the Estates-General were met.[65]

With a sense of resolve on both sides, uneasiness mounted as the opening of the Estates approached. Indeed, representatives of the Third Estate, including extra deputies sent by many locales, arrived in Rennes eight days before the opening of the Estates to coordinate their goals and

---

63 AD Ille-et-Vilaine C 1799, letter of Bertrand to Fourqueux, April 21, 1787.
64 See AN H¹ 564, extract from registers of deliberations of town of Quimper, November 13, 1788; AN H¹ 409, dossier 4, document 186, for an overview of the problem with the Estates. On the Estates, see Armand Rebillon, *Les Etats de Bretagne de 1661 à 1789* (Rennes, 1932).
65 AN H¹ 409, dossier 4, document 131; AN H¹ 419, letter of Bertrand to Necker, December 3, 1788; AN H¹ 563, extract from registers of town of Rennes, November 3, 1788, letter of mayor and *procureur-syndic* of Vitré, November 5, 1788 and attached deliberation of November 4, 1788, as well as the similar declarations of Pontivy, Ancenis and other towns. See also AN M 890, dossier 14; AN H¹ 419, document 212.

strategy. For its part, the nobility, equally determined to resist the demands of the Third Estate, arrived in unprecedented numbers in an attempt to overawe the Third Estate – between 1,200 and 1,300 came, leading the Third Estate from all over the province to send help and support to protect their deputies.[66]

Although an incident at a theater between law students and a nobleman on the evening of December 28 raised tensions, the Estates opened calmly on December 29 and the next day unanimously voted a *don gratuit* of one million *livres* annually for the years 1789 and 1790. On December 31, however, when the clergy pursued a routine request to renew the powers of the intermediary commissioners, the Third Estate opposed it, although the votes of the clergy and the nobility carried the motion. The two orders named their intermediary commissioners, but the Third Estate refused to do so until its demands had been presented. The clergy and nobility, however, refused to hear them and the meeting then adjourned. Because the rules required the participation of all three orders, the continuing refusal of the Third Estate to name its commissioners plunged the Estates into a stalemate that continued for several days. On January 7 the Crown suspended the Estates until February 3, during which time the deputies of the Third Estate were to return to their communities to obtain new powers authorizing them to deliberate and participate on all issues.[67]

The conflicting ideals of privilege and the nation that informed events can be seen in the actions of the opposing sides during the stalemate. On January 4, 1789, a group of young men in Rennes, consisting primarily of law students, sought to form a confederation with their peers in Nantes to protect the deputies of the Third Estate attending the Estates. They denounced the efforts of the nobles and their followers to interfere in the deliberations and activities of the Third Estate, and, claiming service to the fatherland (*la patrie*) as a chief goal, the group swore on "the altar of the fatherland" to defend it against its oppressors.[68]

Whereas the young men of the Third Estate of Rennes took the nation as their primary focus of concern, the nobility, in contrast, demonstrated

---

66 AN H¹ 419, letter of Bertrand to Necker, December 3, 1788; AN H¹ 563, extract from registers of town of Rennes, November 3, 1788, letter of mayor and *procureur-syndic* of Vitré, November 5, 1788 and attached deliberation of November 4, 1788; AN M 890, dossier 14.
67 AN H¹ 419, letter of Dufaure-Rochefort to Necker, December 30, 1788; *Procès-verbal* of Estates of Brittany, December 31, 1788, January 3, 1789, January 7, 1789; letters of comte de Thiard to Necker, December 30, 1788, January 4, 1789; AN C 12², decree of Council of State, January 3, 1789.
68 AD Ille-et-Vilaine 1 F 1842, letter of Moreau and others to club of Nantes, January 4, 1789.

the priority that it continued to give to privilege. On January 8, 1789, the day after the suspension of the Estates had been announced, the nobles reassembled in the meeting hall and, following the denunciation of an article in the decree suspending the Estates that seemed to portend an increased level of taxation of the province, took an oath to defend the Breton constitution, vowing never to participate in any administration contrary to the form of the Estates. Furthermore, the nobles and clergy continued to meet for several days after the ostensible suspension of the Estates.[69]

Despite efforts by the king's military representative, the comte de Thiard, to avert violence, the conflict culminated on January 26, 1789, in a riot between liveried servants and young patriots that resulted in fatalities after the former group had demanded the maintenance of the Breton constitution as well as a lowering of the price of bread. The nobility then took the extraordinary step of locking themselves in the meeting hall, where they remained for several days and nights, requesting help from the comte de Thiard, who worked to defuse tensions, thereby allowing the clergy and nobility to leave Rennes on February 1. The incident, however, heightened the antagonism between the two groups and graphically highlighted the contrast between privilege and the nation.[70]

The conflict between these contrasting ideals climaxed in the following weeks as the Third Estate, buoyed by the electoral regulations for the Estates-General, issued in late January, met during the spring to draft *cahiers* and to elect deputies in assemblies of *sénéchaussées*, as in the rest of France. The Crown had mandated that the clergy and nobility meet separately at Saint-Brieuc to elect their deputies. When the assembly opened on April 16, however, it ignored the instructions of the Crown for selecting deputies and instead sent a deputation to the comte de Thiard proposing that he send a courier to the court asking that the king order the municipalities and the deputies of the Third Estate to join the other two orders to form themselves into the Estates. Notified by the comte that this was not possible, the members of the two orders became quite angry. Although they now offered to renounce their fiscal privileges, it was, as the comte noted, a meaningless gesture, too late to have any significance. After a tumultuous and chaotic meeting, both orders,

69 AN H$^1$ 419, *Procès-verbal* of Estates of Brittany, January 8, 1789 and *passim*. See also AN K 684$^2$, no. 181; AN H$^1$ 419, document 124.
70 See, for example, AD Maine-et-Loire 1 J 51, protest and decree of law students of Angers, February 3, 1789. On the recognition of the depth of bitterness that preceded this incident, see AN AB$^{XIX}$ 3494 (13), letter of January 26, 1789. On the riot of January 26–27, see *Précis exact et historique des faits arrivés à Rennes, le 26 et 27 janvier 1789, et autres jours suivants* (N.p., n.d.).

largely at the behest of the nobility, refused to select representatives for the Estates-General. The comte de Thiard saw two motives in their action, the most important of which was the desire to oppose themselves to the Estates-General and whatever decisions might be made there as well as to any constitution that would be applicable to the entire kingdom. Secondly, the comte maintained that the clergy and nobles believed that by their abstention, the Estates-General, finding itself incomplete, would ask Brittany to send deputies through the Estates of Brittany, thereby necessitating the reassembling of the three orders at Saint-Brieuc in order to hold new elections.[71]

At a time when the rest of France sought to address the problems of the nation and to elect deputies to deal with them, the clergy and nobility of Brittany chose to stand apart and to assert instead the particular rights and privileges of their province.[72] By their actions they made Brittany – and especially the Breton constitution – a metaphor for privilege and the pernicious role it had in the polity.[73]

If Brittany was the chief symbol of privilege, it was Dauphiné that represented the emerging ideal of the nation. Like the movement in Brittany, developments in Dauphiné grew out of the resistance to the Lamoignon edicts during the spring and summer of 1788, but where ensuing events in Brittany had led to a divergence between the orders, in Dauphiné they were almost always an object of consensus, offering hope to much of the rest of France, a fact of which the Dauphinois were aware.

In the meeting at Vizille in June, 1788, the three estates had requested not only the recall of the parlements and the convocation of the Estates-General, but also the reestablishment of the Estates of Dauphiné. To this end, the three orders held a preliminary meeting in Romans in September, 1788, to propose an organizational structure for the Estates to the Crown. The meeting opened on September 10, and on September 15, in a gesture that indicated the spirit of goodwill under which they hoped to operate, the assembly abolished the *corvée*.[74] Yet, shortly afterward, in what would also be a characteristic of events in Dauphiné, there was uneasiness between the orders, for the clergy and nobility were

---

71 AN H¹ 419, letters of the comte de Thiard to Necker, April 18, and April 21, 1789; Egret, "Les origines de la Révolution en Bretagne (1788–1789)," 211–212, 214. See also AN H¹ 419, declaration of nobility assembled in town of Saint-Brieuc, April 16, 1789, declaration and protest of order of the church assembled in Saint-Brieuc, April 20, 1789. For an earlier statement of grievance, see H¹ 419, decree of clergy and nobility to Louis, March 4, 1789.
72 See BN Mss. Fonds Français 20706, fols. 170–188; BM Nantes Collection Dugast-Matifeux, t. 12, fols. 24–26.
73 See, for example, Jacques-Guillaume Thouret, *Vérités philosophiques et patriotiques sur les affaires présentes, 1788* (N.p., n.d.). See also *Correspondance secrète*, ed. de Lescure, II: 311.    74 AN Bᵃ 74², liasse 174, dossier 5, document 21², p. 14.

concerned about the "decisive influence" wielded by the Third Estate.[75] Nevertheless, aware that much of the nation was watching them, the three orders succeeded in working together and drafting a structure for the Estates, which they forwarded to the Crown when the Assembly adjourned on September 28.[76]

The Crown promulgated the structure of the reconstituted Estates on October 22, 1788, and the Estates, consisting of 144 members – twenty-four for the clergy, forty-eight for the nobility and seventy-two for the Third Estate – formally opened on November 2, 1788, with all voting done by head. In his opening speech, the archbishop of Vienne, the president of the assembly, noted that the model of Dauphiné could serve as an example not only for other provinces, but for the nation itself at the Estates-General. The president of the nobility, the comte de Morges, speaking in a more restrained fashion, also referred to public opinion, but alluded as well to the need for a balance between the orders in the estates.[77] His statement reflected the tension that underlay the Estates of Dauphiné – an awareness that they were a focal point for public opinion led the clergy and the nobility to subordinate as much as possible their uneasiness with the new procedures.

Since the Estates had just been reconstituted, there was no old business or continuing agenda, so the Dauphinois were able to concentrate as much on the form of representation at the Estates-General as on any other single issue. As a result, the Estates charged a commission to examine the issue of the number of deputies that Dauphiné ought to have at the Estates-General. The commission gave its report on December 9, and it set forth the principles that the province had adopted. Delivered by the archbishop of Embrun, the report observed that it was time that the "sacred title" of citizen be earned through the observation of the duties that this title imposed, and that all Frenchmen ought to unite as if they were members of the same family. Recommending the election of thirty deputies for the province, it went on to propose, for the Estates-General as a whole, that the orders and provinces deliberate in common, that voting be by head and that the Third Estate have as large a number of representatives as the First and Second Estates combined. The commission argued that love of the nation should direct all deliberations, and it offered to yield all of the privileges of Dauphiné in the interest of salutary reform.[78]

75 AN B$^a$ 74$^2$, liasse 174, dossier 5, documents 22, 26.
76 AN B$^a$ 74$^1$, liasse 174, dossier 4, document 36.
77 AN C 13, *Procès-verbal* of general assembly of three orders of province of Dauphiné, held in town of Romans, November 2, 1788, p. 8.
78 See *Procès-verbal des Etats de Dauphiné assemblés à Romans dans le mois de décembre 1788* (Grenoble, 1788), pp. 68–72.

*152,369*

In the aftermath of the decision of the *Parlement* of Paris that the Estates-General should observe the forms of 1614, the endorsement of that decision by the reconvened Assembly of Notables and the turmoil in Brittany that would culminate in December, 1788, and January, 1789, the deliberations in Dauphiné offered hope to much of the rest of France and elicited enormous admiration. Acknowledging a copy of the *procès-verbaux* of the proceedings at Romans that they had received in December, 1788, for example, the Third Estate of Alais wrote to express their admiration and to tell them that they had become an example for the entire kingdom. The Third Estate of Alais stated that they intended to use the *procès-verbaux* as their own guide in subsequent deliberations.[79]

The province was so consumed with the Estates-General that after the Crown approved double representation for the Third Estate, the Estates of Dauphiné proceeded to elect the deputies for the province without waiting for electoral procedures to be promulgated.[80] Indeed, on January 2, 1789, the Dauphinois officially proclaimed that their deputies to the Estates-General could not participate in the meeting unless the Third Estate had an equal number of deputies to those of the other two orders combined, unless the orders deliberated together and unless voting was conducted by head. The ratification of this mandate set off an emotional response in the assembly, and its author, Jean-Joseph Mounier, was immediately proclaimed as a deputy to the Estates-General. Furthermore, as other deputies were elected, they advanced to the center of the assembly to swear loyalty to this instruction.[81] The province explicitly prohibited its deputies from voting on any issue until these conditions had been met, and reserved the right to recall its deputies if they violated these guidelines.[82]

Although the working relationship between the orders in Dauphiné was generally harmonious, there were serious conflicts that occasionally arose. Indeed, only days after the promulgation of the mandate for deputies at the Estates-General, the nobility and clergy, fearful of the preponderance of the Third Estate, withdrew from the meeting, and similar withdrawals had occurred as early as September. But, in an indication of how aware the Dauphinois were of their place in public opinion in France, these ruptures were disguised or omitted in the official

---

79  AM Grenoble AA 41.
80  See, for example, AN AB^XIX 3494 (13), letter of January 23, 1789; AN B^a 74, liasse 174, dossier 3, document 9; Sallier, *Annales françaises*, p. 308.
81  AN B^a 75^2, liasse 175, dossier 8, document 1.
82  See *Pouvoirs des Députés de la Province de Dauphiné aux Etats-Généraux. Extrait du Procès-verbal des Etats de la Province de Dauphiné, assemblés à Romans* (N.p., n.d.), especially pp. 5–6, and, *Mandats donnés à Messieurs les députés du Dauphiné, pour leurs pouvoirs aux Etats-Généraux prochains* (N.p., n.d.).

*procès-verbaux* of the meetings, almost certainly in order to project a more favorable image.[83]

At all times, the province exhorted the rest of France to seize the occasion for the good of the nation. To all suggestions of using the Estates-General to advance specific, particular interests, the Dauphinois consistently responded that this would be counterproductive, and that the only objective should simply be the national interest.[84]

It would be incorrect, however, simply to see public posturing in the actions of the Dauphinois. They were proud of their efforts and believed that they represented a new mode of thinking, transcending traditional concern with privilege and prerogative.[85] The example of Dauphiné was widely admired and became a powerful symbol of aspirations that royal policy makers and the public alike could not fail to notice.[86] In the final analysis, Dauphiné became the tangible incarnation of the inchoate ideal of the nation, beside which Brittany, the symbol of privilege, was an object of invidious comparison.[87]

Although Brittany and Dauphiné were the two key foci, virtually all of France was engulfed by political ferment as the convening of the Estates-General produced a vague but powerful expectation of change.[88] Nevertheless, it would be incorrect to assume that in the dichotomy between privilege and the nation that developed in the agitation

83 See BM Grenoble Ms. R 7109, fol. 34; AN B^a 74^1, liasse 174, dossier 3, document 9; AN B^a 74^2, liasse 174, dossier 5, document 22; AN B^a 75^1, liasse 175, dossier 2, document 31; AN AB^XIX 3494 (13), letter of January 29, 1789. Their effort was not altogether successful, however, for rumors circulated of divisions between the orders at Romans. See BN Mss. Fonds français 6687, fols. 204–205.

84 See, for example, *Lettre écrite par plusiers citoyens du clergé, de la Noblesse et des communes de Dauphiné à Messieurs les Syndics-Généraux des Etats de Béarn* (N.p., n.d.); *Réponse des négociants de la ville de Grenoble, à MM. les juges-consuls de Montauban, Clermont-Ferrand, Châlons, Orléans, Tours, Besançon, Dunkerque & Saint-Quentin & à la Chambre de Commerce de Picardie, de Saint-Malo & de l'Isle en Flandre* (N.p., n.d.).

85 AN B^a 74^1, liasse 174, dossier 4, document 36.

86 AD Calvados C 6348, *mémoire* presented to king by mayor and aldermen of Avranches; AN AB^XIX 3494 (13), letter of January 29, 1789; *Mémoire autographe de M. de Barentin* (Paris, 1844), pp. 132–135; *Modestes observations sur le Mémoire des Princes; faites au nom de 23 millions de Citoyens François. 22 décembre 1788*, p. 9.

87 See, for example, AN AB^XIX 3494 (13), letter of February 19, 1789; *Pétition des citoyens domiciliés à Paris; Conservation des trois ordres et déstruction de leur rivalité; ou lettre du vicomte de Toustain, à M. l'abbé Brizard, de la Sociéte Patriotique-Bretonne* (N.p., 1789), p. 5.

88 There were disputes over representation of the Third Estate in Burgundy and Provence, for example, while events in the *pays de Vivarais* replicated those of neighboring Dauphiné. See AN H^1 203, dossier 3, document 1448; AN H^1 1240, dossier 1, document 22; AN AB^XIX 3492, dossier 7; AN AB^XIX 3494 (13), letter of January 26, 1789; Jean Egret, "La prérévolution en Provence 1787–1789," *Annales historiques de la Révolution française*, 26 (1954), 97–126; Monique Cubells, *Les Horizons de la liberté: Naissance de la révolution en Provence (1787–1789)* (Aix-en-Provence, 1987); AN K 679, no. 32, no. 33, no. 34; Sallier, *Annales françaises*, p. 220.

preceding the opening of the Estates-General there was widespread sentiment favoring the total extirpation of privilege within society. On the contrary, in most locales both the Third Estate and the nobility sought to retain privileges that were not pecuniary in nature. The Third Estate of Douai, for example, while seeking the suppression of all pecuniary privileges and exemptions, asked at the same time that the "usages, franchises, immunities and privileges" of Flanders be preserved, except those that the province itself might ask to have revoked. Similarly, the nobility of Cambrai and Cambrésis agreed to yield their pecuniary privileges and to submit to equal taxation, but sought to maintain and preserve the "constitutions and privileges" of the province.[89] Indeed, even Dauphiné, the very embodiment of the overcoming of privilege and of the newly emerging ideal of the nation, explicitly reserved the right to maintain possession of its privileges in the event that it was not possible to reach an agreement on reform at the Estates-General.[90] Ultimately, the goal of most participants was simply to readjust privilege, particularly fiscal and political privilege, so that it would no longer be able to compete with or take priority over the interests of the nation.[91] The major concern of the *cahiers*, equality of taxation, was the primary representation of this goal of readjusting privilege.[92]

The abolition of privilege and orders was not implicit in the nascent concept of the nation, which is why the liberal nobility – centered in the Patriot or National Party – could work toward the same goals as the Third Estate.[93] The objective for most was not the outright abolition of orders, but the doubling of the Third Estate's representation and voting by head. The belief among the Third Estate in particular was that vote by order would not truly express the national will because each order would merely vote its own self-interest and the concerns of the nation would be ignored.[94]

89 On Douai, see AM Douai AA 330, *cahier* of Third Estate of Douai; on Cambrai and Cambrésis, AN AB[XIX] 3258, *cahier* of nobility of Cambrai and Cambrésis. See also AN B[a] 57, liasse 136, dossier 6, document 3.
90 *Procès-verbal des Etats de Dauphiné, assemblés à Romans dans le mois de décembre 1788*, p. 121.
91 See, for example *Voeu de plusiers citoyens de trois ordres, et invitation à leur concitoyens d'y adhérer*, pp. 7–8; *Pétition des curés* (N.p., n.d.); *Le dernier mot du tiers-état à la noblesse de France* (N.p., n.d.). See also the statement of the clergy of Puy-en-Velay, in Hyslop, *French Nationalism in 1789*, p. 84.
92 All studies of the cahiers agree that equality of taxation was their primary concern. See Hyslop, *French Nationalism in 1789*, p. 84; Taylor, "Revolutionary and nonrevolutionary content in the *Cahiers* of 1789," 495; Furet, *Interpreting the French Revolution*, p. 42.
93 On the Patriot Party, see Daniel L. Wick, *A Conspiracy of Well-Intentioned Men: The Society of Thirty and the French Revolution* (New York, 1987).
94 Again, see especially AN H[1] 207, dossier 1, documents 21–22.

For the most part, then, the Third Estate was not seeking a dominant role, which is why Sieyès's *Qu'est-ce que le Tiers Etat?* is, in fact, atypical. Instead, most advocates of the Third Estate were simply seeking a role coequal to that of the other two orders in the management of the state. As one pamphleteer noted, "I have nowhere seen that the Third Estate has asked for superiority in voting, although it indeed has the right to do so; it has had the modesty to be intent on equality."[95] Most elements in the Third Estate were willing to recognize the continued existence of orders, albeit not as a basis for voting, and were also completely willing to accord the clergy and the nobility a general eminence and social standing.[96] Indeed, all over France the Third Estate made clear how modest and limited its goals were and how favorably disposed it was to the maintenance of social distinctions. The Third Estate of Dijon, for example, stated in January, 1789:

We will always respect distinctions founded on social order, and necessary to the glory and security of the state. The ministers of the altars will always have our respect; the heads of armies will always have our gratitude and our consideration; the Clergy and the Nobility will not cease to be distinct and separate orders. Honorific privileges, more worthy of them than pecuniary privileges, will forever class them in a rank properly superior to that of the Third Estate.[97]

In Picardy, a municipal assembly in Abbeville indicated that no attempt to infringe on social distinctions would be made, asserting that it was important to conserve them "to prevent the harm that would necessarily result from the confusion of ranks and conditions."[98] Municipal gatherings in Agen, Alençon, Bayonne, Sommière, Le Havre and other towns likewise affirmed the respect and social distinctions owed to the

95 *Modestes observations sur le Mémoire des Princes*, p. 25. See also, BM Grenoble Ms. R 7082, convocation ... of town of Ambert; *Cahier des délibérations proposés par les trois ordres réunis de la ville de Bayonne, assemblés le 21 mars 1789, pour procéder à l'élection de leurs députés aux Etats-Généraux; précédé d'un discours de M. le maire de la ville de Bayonne, à l'ouverture de l'Assemblée* (N.p., n.d.), p. 4.
96 AD Calvados C 6348, *Mémoire* presented to king by mayor and aldermen of town of Avranches; AD Seine-Maritime C 2185, fol. 116, Report of Rules Board on Estates-General; Rabaut de Saint-Etienne, *Considérations sur les intérêts du tiers-état*, pp. 64, 66–67; Thouret, *Vérités philosophiques et patriotiques sur les affaires présentes, 1788*, pp. 21–22, and *Avis des bons Normands à leurs frères tous les bons Français de toutes les provinces et de tous les ordres, sur l'envoi des lettres de convocation aux Etats-Généraux* (N.p., 1789), p. 12; [Joseph-Antoine-Joachim Cérutti], *Mémoire pour le peuple françois* (N.p., 1788), pp. 25–26.
97 AD Côte d'Or C 2987[6], *Requête au Roi, et délibération du Tiers-Etat de la ville de Dijon, du 18 janvier 1789*. For another example from that region, see the speech given by two barristers to a gathering in the town of Nuits late in 1788 in Egret, *La Pré-Révolution française*, p. 352.          98 AN B[a] 9, liasse 1, dossier 4, document 16.

clergy and nobility.[99] Even in the highly polarized atmosphere of Brittany, similar sentiments were evident:

Allow us to quote here the discourse of M. de Brienne, Archbishop of Toulouse, head of the Royal Council of Finances, at the conclusion of the first Assembly of Notables ... The minister believed ... it his duty to reassure the privileged about the preservation of their other privileges; he asserted that in a monarchy there were distinctions that it is important to preserve; he claimed that absolute equality is proper only in purely republican states, but he maintained that *an equal tax assessment does not imply the abasement of ranks and conditions* ...

*The unity of the Nation* in the different Orders that comprise it, the absolute abjuration *of all distinctions* when it is a question of contributing to public expenses, *civil liberty* extended to *every province*, the sacrifice *of all pecuniary exemptions, an equal tax assessment* that does not imply the *abasement of ranks and conditions*; such are, in reality, the real foundations for a beneficial regeneration, and for the public good.[100]

This attitude on the part of the Third Estate persisted throughout the period leading to the opening of the Estates-General. In Saintonge, the *cahier* of the Third Estate specified that the nobility, having made so honorable an abdication of its pecuniary privileges, should be maintained in all of its ancient prerogatives, and in Champagne the Third Estate voiced similar sentiments.[101] Similarly, the Third Estate of the *sénéchaussée* of Lyon explicitly requested that its deputies "maintain toward the deputies chosen by the two orders the deference and respect owed to their persons."[102] With the example of Dauphiné as a model, the Estates-General was to be the instrument for resolving the problems of the kingdom and the vehicle for the realization of a new role for the Third Estate in the management of the state, most concretely by the joint drafting of a new constitution for the nation.

In addition, again perhaps reflecting the Dauphinois injunction that the Estates-General be used solely to advance the national interest rather than to further any particular interest, there was a strong hope that the

99  On Agen, *Délibération de la ville et communauté d'Agen, dans l'intérêt de la ville et toute la Province d'Agenois, du 25 décembre 1788* (Agen, n.d.); on Alençon, see AN B$^a$ 11, liasse 5, dossier 12, document 6; AM Le Havre AA 49, address of thanks presented to king by municipal officers of town of Alençon, in general assembly; on Bayonne, *Cahier des délibérations proposés par les trois ordres réunis de la ville de Bayonne*, pp. 4–5; on Sommière, see AN K 679, no. 36; on Le Havre, AM Le Havre AA 44, address of thanks presented to king by municipal officers of town of Le Havre in general assembly. See also AM Le Havre AA 50, address of thanks presented to king by municipal officers of town of Honfleur.
100  AD Ille-et-Vilaine C 3900, *Mémoire des avocats du Parlement de Bretagne, sur les moyens d'entretenir l'union entre les différens Ordres de l'Etat* (emphases in original); for similar sentiments elsewhere in Brittany, see AN B$^a$ 25$^1$, liasse 42, dossier 2, document 2. See also AD Ille-et-Vilaine C 3899, undated list of demands of Third Estate of Brittany.
101  AD Charente-Maritime 4 J 1574 (28), *cahier* of third estate of *sénéchaussée* of Saintonge seated at Saint-Jean d'Angély; AN B$^a$ 31, liasse 55, dossier 6, document 5.
102  AN AB$^{XIX}$ 3259, *cahier* of Third Estate of *sénéchaussée* of Lyon, p. 17.

Estates-General would mark an end to a legacy of dissension and discord in France. The period preceding the convocation of the Estates-General had clearly shown France to be a nation divided against itself, revealing cleavages between state and society, between orders, between provinces as well as other fissures.[103] A yearning rather than a program, there was a frame of mind that viewed the Estates-General as an opportunity to transcend divisions and to join together in a sense of common purpose. The Third Estate of Lyon observed that no diversity of interests could exist between the first two orders and the third and expressed the hope that the deputies of the three orders joined together would present to the nation a model of harmony.[104] Likewise, in its *cahier* the Third Estate of the *bailliage* of Château-Thierry told its deputies:

It [the Third Estate] desires, it demands that they bring to this august assembly the good sense that will overcome obstacles that initially seem insurmountable; that they carefully avoid extreme opinions, impetuous parties, overly prompt assents, or overly opinionated opposition on questions immaterial to its rights and interests...

The Third Estate desires and demands that its deputies remember that they are not dispatched toward enemies whom they ought to face audaciously and proudly, but toward citizens with whom they are going to deal with the peace and happiness of the nation; that in the conflict of opinions necessary to the search for truth, that in the zeal [that is] inseparable from love of the public good, wisdom and moderation always should be the companions of boldness and steadfastness.[105]

Such heightened expectations for resolving the difficulties facing the nation through the Estates-General were not entirely fatuous, for it was clear not only that the nobility and, to a lesser extent, the clergy were prepared to renounce their fiscal privileges, but also, as many participants realized, that the goals of the nobility and the Third Estate were remarkably similar.[106] Unfortunately, however, the nobility in particular were not prepared to yield the privileged political position afforded them by the traditional structure of the Estates-General – indeed, many deputies of the nobility were strictly forbidden to vote by head, with some even specifically instructed to withdraw if the Estates-General

103 Sallier, *Annales françaises ... 1774–1789*, p. 192.
104 AN AB[XIX] 3259, *cahier* of Third Estate of *sénéchaussée* of Lyon, p. 17. See also BN Mss. Fonds Français 20706, fols. 67–68.
105 AN AB[XIX] 3259, *cahier* of Third Estate of *bailliage* of Château-Thierry, pp. 12–13. See also AN B[a] 25[1], liasse 42, dossier 2, document 2, fols. 8, 15; Thouret, *Avis des bons Normands*, p. 24; *Qu'est-ce-que la Nation? et Qu'est-ce-que la France?* (N.p., 1789), pp. 68–70, 72; *Conservation des trois ordres et déstruction de leur rivalité*.
106 AN AB[XIX] 3258, *cahier* of order of the nobility of province of Berry, pp. 3–4; AN AB[XIX] 3259, *cahier* of Third Estate of *sénéchaussée* of Nîmes, pp. 51–52. See also AN H[1] 149, dossier 1, documents 7, 8, 11; AN H[1] 148, dossier 2, documents 40, 41, 45, 53, 60.

adopted any method other than vote by order.[107] At the same time, most members of the Third Estate, as a practical matter, believed vote by head to be necessary for the nation's problems to be addressed successfully.[108] As the opening of the Estates-General approached, then, the attempt of major elements of the nobility to cling to the now discredited standard of privilege as an instrument of government caused the problem of privilege to assume an even greater magnitude and importance.[109]

107  See AN AB[XIX] 3258, *cahier* of nobility of Quercy, p. 3; *cahier* of order of nobility of *bailliage* of Alençon, pp. 10–11; *cahier* of order of nobility of *sénéchaussée* of Condom, p. 6; *cahier* and powers of nobility of *sénéchaussée* of Lannes, p. 3; AN B[a] 57, liasse 136, dossier 6, document 3. See also AD Calvados C 6345, undated protest of nobility of Normandy; AN H[1] 149, dossier 1, documents 2, 11, 12, 17, 20, 23, 24; AN K 679, no. 26, no. 27. In his study, Guy Chaussinand-Nogaret found 41 percent of the *cahiers* of the nobility favored vote by order, while only 8 percent favored voting by head. There was, to be sure, ambiguity in the remaining *cahiers*, and it is this ambiguity that he emphasizes, but these unambiguous positions more closely reflect the terms of the debate. Furthermore, even some of the ambiguous or seemingly more flexible *cahiers*, most of which initially specified vote by order, were unpromising. The nobility of the *bailliage* of Nemours specified vote by order, but stipulated that if that was rejected the vote by head was still to be taken in separate chambers. Similarly, the nobility of the *bailliage* of Troyes authorized voting by head only if two-thirds of the order of the nobility agreed to it. Indeed, the vote by order was the strongest single stance among the nobility. Guy Chaussinand-Nogaret, *The French Nobility in the Eighteenth Century: From Feudalism to Enlightenment* (Cambridge, 1985), pp. 134–137; on Nemours, see AN B[a] 57, liasse 139, dossier 3, document 5 or AN AB[XIX] 3258, *cahier* of powers and instructions of deputy of order of the nobility of *bailliage* of Nemours, p. 5; on Troyes, AN AB[XIX] 3258, *cahier* of order of the nobility of *bailliage* of Troyes, pp. 5–6. It should be noted, however, that others were clearly more flexible and afforded some room for maneuver. See AN AB[XIX] 3258, *cahier* of order of the nobility of *bailliages* of Mantes and Meulan, p. 6, *cahier* of order of the nobility of *bailliage* of Labour, p. 3, *cahier* of combined orders of the nobility and Third Estate of Péronne, Montdidier and Roye, p. 45.
108  BN Mss. Fonds Français 20703, fol. 44; André Morellet, *Mémoirs inédites de l'Abbé Morellet sur le dix-huitième siècle et sur la Révolution*, 2nd. edn., 2 vols. (Paris, 1822), I: 345.
109  Bombelles, *Journal*, II: 308; Jacques-Pierre Brissot de Warville, *Mémoires* (1754–1793), 2 vols. (Paris, 1911), II: 192, AD Calvados C 6345, conditions necessary for the legality of the Estates-General.

# 2    The formation of the new ideal of the polity

Despite these follies, it seems to me that the plurality will be for...
moderation, but I do not doubt that before the end of the month the
Third will resolve to declare that it is the nation, that it alone is the
nation.

Diary of the deputy Adrien Duquesnoy, May 15, 1789

On May 4, 1789, amidst high hopes and expectations among the deputies
and in the nation at large, the Estates-General opened at Versailles.[1] The
opening ceremony, with an emphasis on the distinction of orders that
denigrated the Third Estate, annoyed several Third Estate deputies. The
more substantive aspect of the problem of the distinction of orders
appeared soon afterward, however, and the impasse that developed in the
opening days of the Estates-General quickly established privilege –
specifically privilege as embodied in the procedures of 1614 – as the
primary obstacle to be overcome before the task of national regeneration
could be realized.[2]

Having agreed to consider yielding their pecuniary privileges, the
nobility believed that nothing more should be asked of them and
attempted to maintain deliberation by orders.[3] The day after the opening
ceremonies, the clergy and the nobility withdrew to their respective
chambers, while the Third Estate reassembled in the common meeting
room to await the other two orders. In the chamber of the nobility,
despite a plea by one of the liberal nobles that the present circumstances

1 For more on the opening phases of the Estates-General, see *Recueil de documents relatifs
aux séances des Etats-Généraux*, ed. Georges Lefebvre and Anne Terroine (Paris, 1953).
For an excellent account of the daily routine of deputies, see Edna Hindie Lemay, *La Vie
quotidienne des députés aux Etats-Généraux 1789* (Paris, 1987).
2 AN 284 AP 4, dossier 1, Consultation for commissioners of the Third charged to verify
powers. For an additional insight into awareness of how pejorative the concept of privilege
had become, see the letter of Louis XVI to Bailly in Félix-Sébastien Feuillet de Conches,
ed., *Louis XVI, Marie Antoinette et Madame Elizabeth : Lettres et documents inédits*, 6 vols.
(Paris, 1864–1873), III: 175.
3 Jacques-Antoine Creuzé-Latouche, *Journal des Etats-Généraux et du début de l'Assemblée
Nationale 18 mai – 29 juillet 1789*, ed. Jean Marchand (Paris, 1946), pp. 12–14; Adrien
Duquesnoy, *Journal d'Adrien Duquesnoy*, ed. Robert de Crevecoeur, 2 vols. (Paris, 1894),
I: 33–34.

called for union and concord among the orders, and despite a statement by the deputies from Dauphiné that they could deliberate only in common with the other two orders, the nobility decided by a large majority to constitute itself as an order and to verify the credentials of its members separately.[4] Indeed, the nobility was so adamant in preserving the distinction of orders that it initially refused to approve the credentials of some deputies because they had been chosen by electoral assemblies consisting of members of the Third Estate meeting in common with the nobility.[5]

At the same time, the clergy met in its chamber and began to verify the credentials of its members, but it stopped short of formally constituting itself as an order. On May 7 the Third Estate sent a deputation to the clergy to propose the verification of credentials in common. The clergy replied by acknowledging its regard for the Third Estate and stating its wish to establish harmony among the three orders, and therefore suggested naming commissioners from each order to reach some kind of agreement on the proposal advanced by the Third Estate.[6]

The deputies of the Third Estate believed unanimously in vote by head, and as a result were able to forge a consensus that provided an early cohesion. This cohesion was further reinforced by the conviction within the Third Estate that it represented the nation. Indeed, the fusion of these issues and the strength with which they were held can be seen distinctly in the comments of the deputy François Ménard de la Groye. In a private letter to his wife, this deputy, a modest man of moderate views, stated that the issue to be decided was whether the clergy or the nobility would submit to the nation or whether the nation would submit to them.[7] It is clear that the Third Estate was willing to recognize the existence of orders as long as they were not the basis for voting,[8] for the

4 AN KK 641, entry of May 6, 1789; BM La Rochelle Ms. 21, entry of May 6, 1789. For more on the position of those nobles who wished to retain vote by order, see Harriet Varrell Sullivan, "Defenders of privilege: a study of the political ideas which lay behind the defense of privilege at the French Constituent Assembly of 1789," Ph.D. dissertation, Radcliffe College (1956), especially p. 44.
5 BN Mss. Nouv. acq. fr. 4121, fols. 13–15; Procès-verbal des séances de la chambre de l'ordre de la noblesse aux Etats-Généraux, tenues à Versailles en 1789 (Versailles, 1789), pp. 61–65. The latter mentions only that their election was "unconstitutional."
6 AN C 26, dossier 177³, document 2; AD Gironde 3 L 82, letter of May 8, 1789.
7 François Ménard de la Groye, Correspondance (1789–1791), ed. Florence Mirouse (Mayenne, 1989), p. 25; see also AM Lorient BB 12, no. 2, letter of May 3, 1789. With respect to the latter source, I have actually consulted the microfilm copy of this correspondence in the Archives départementales of the Department of Morbihan, but retaining the original citation makes the reference, even on the microfilm copy, more comprehensible.
8 See the letter of the noble deputies of Roussillon to their constituents in which they note that the Third Estate told the deputies that they recognized in them "only noble deputies

deputies believed – as did many of those who had elected them – that deliberation by order would have the effect of giving the nobility a veto power over the task of reforming and regenerating the nation.[9]

Mutually exclusive positions on the method of deliberation and voting quickly undermined whatever sense of common purpose may have existed and plunged the Estates-General into a deadlock. This stalemate was particularly unfortunate because, as several deputies realized, there was otherwise a fundamental similarity of goals between the orders, but the intensity of feeling on the issue of vote by head or order overshadowed virtually all commonly held beliefs.[10]

The fact that the Third Estate met in the common room gave it a symbolic importance that conferred an enormous moral advantage. Whereas the clergy and the nobility met in closed sessions in their respective chambers, the Third Estate met in the common room, with its sessions open to the public. The meetings were heavily attended; among those most in attendance, according to one deputy, were deputies of the nobility. Ultimately, however, the contrast seemed to indicate that the clergy and the nobility were concerned with their particular interests – especially the preservation of their privileges – while the Third Estate was concerned with the affairs of the nation.[11]

When it became clear that neither of the other two orders would join them, the deputies of the Third Estate had to choose a course of action. Initially, however, chaos hindered their proceedings because there was no established method for deliberation – deputies simply shouted for attention, delegations visited the other two orders without the knowledge of the remaining deputies, and the like.[12] Indeed, it was an early

and not deputies of the order of the nobility" AD Pyreneés-Orientales C 2119, no. 10, letter of June 27, 1789. See also AD Ain 1 Mi 1, letter of June 27, 1789.
9 Duquesnoy, *Journal*, I: 34.
10 See S. Dardy, "Lettres de M. Grellet de Beauregard, député de la Haute-Marche aux Etats-Généraux de 1789," *Mémoires de la Société des Sciences Naturelles et Archéologiques de la Creuse*, 2nd series, 7 (1899), 58–59; R. Herly, "Correspondance du lieutenant-général du bailliage de Sarrelouis de la Salle, député de l'Assemblée Nationale 1789–1790," *Bulletin de la Société des Amis des Pays de la Sarre*, 4 (1927), 195. For a sense of the disappointment on the part of Third Estate deputies at the failure of the clergy and the nobility to join in a spirit of common purpose in the interest of the nation, see AM Bayonne AA 51, no. 1, letter of May 8, 1789; Antoine-François Delandine, *De quelques changemens politiques, opérés ou projettés en France, pendant les années 1789, 1790 et 1791 ; ou discours sur divers points importants de la Constitution et de la nouvelle législation du royaume* (Paris, 1791), pp. 9–14; Ménard de la Groye, *Correspondance*, pp. 23–24.
11 AM Strasbourg AA 2003, fol. 12; AN W 306, dossier 377, fol. 23; AN AB$^{XIX}$ 3494 (13), letter of June 5, 1789; AD Ain 1 Mi 1, letter of June 9, 1789. See also AN AB$^{XIX}$ 3359, dossier 4, document 3; Louis Fauche-Borel, *Mémoires de Fauche-Borel*, 5 vols. (Paris, 1829), I: 66–67; Rivarol, *Mémoires*, pp. 13–14.
12 BN Mss. Fonds Français 10883, fol. 6; Urbain-Réné Pilastre de la Brardière and J. B. Leclerc, *Correspondance de MM. les députés des communes de la province d'Anjou avec leur*

indication of the influence of the Dauphinois delegation that after the failure of an initial plan of deliberation, two Dauphinois deputies, Jean-Joseph Mounier and Pierre-Antoine Barnave, successfully proposed a new method, and the Third Estate then began to plan its response to the failure of the other two orders to join it for verification of credentials.[13]

Although there was a deep conviction within the Third Estate that it represented the nation, there was also a strong sense among most deputies that they should not act precipitately. Most deputies had a strong desire to work in concert with the other two orders.[14] Two contrasting approaches emerged from the initial debate on how to react to the failure of the clergy and the nobility to join them – conciliation or confrontation. The former course, put forward by Jean-Paul Rabaut de Saint-Etienne and seconded by Mounier, sought to exhaust all efforts to reach some kind of agreement with the other orders before undertaking any unilateral action. As a result, Rabaut de Saint-Etienne advocated participating in the conciliatory conferences proposed by the clergy.[15]

The Breton delegation, with Isaac-Guy-Marie Le Chapelier as its principal spokesman, advanced the alternative course of confrontation. The Bretons asserted that the Third Estate should issue a single invitation to the other two orders to verify credentials in common, and that if they failed to respond the Third Estate should immediately proceed on its own. They argued against participation in the conciliatory conferences as a distraction from the objectives of the Third Estate.[16]

The debate reflected the contrasting methods of the two most influential delegations within the Third Estate as the Estates-General opened, those of Dauphiné and Brittany. The delegation from Dauphiné symbolized the aspirations of the Third Estate at the Estates-General – to work on an equal footing with the other two orders for the regeneration

commettants relativement aux Etats-Généraux ... en 1789, 10 vols. (Angers, 1789–1791), I: 17, 20–23; AM Strasbourg AA 2003, fol. 12; BN Mss. Fonds français 13713, fol. 6; Francisque Mège, Gaultier de Biauzat, député du tiers-etat aux Etats-Généraux de 1789; sa vie et sa correspondance, 2 vols. (Paris, 1890), II: 51; Ménard de la Groye, Correspondance, p. 25.

13 BN Mss. Nouv. acq. fr. 12938, fol. 7v°; Pilastre de la Brardière and Leclerc, Correspondance, I: 18–19.

14 See BN Mss. Nouv. acq. fr. 2633, fols. 29–30; BN Mss. Nouv. acq. fr. 12938, fol. 3; AM Strasbourg AA 2003, fol. 11; AD Cantal Fonds J. Delmas 193, document 93; Pilastre de la Brardière and Leclerc, Correspondance, I: 18–19; AN AA 50, dossier 1416–1419, document 67. See also Kenneth Margerison, "The movement for the creation of a union of orders in the Estates General of 1789," French History, 3 (1989), 48–70.

15 See AM Lorient BB 12, no. 4, letter of May 8, 1789; AD Gironde 3 L 82, letter of May 14, 1789.

16 See AM Brest LL 44, p. 4; AM Brest LL 46, no. 3 bis, letter of May 17, 1789; AD Morbihan 1 Mi 240, no. 3, letter of May 15, 1789; AD Eure 5 F 63, pp. 17–18.

of the nation.[17] The Breton deputation, in contrast, was distinguished by the fact that it had already experienced the very situation in which the Third Estate currently found itself – in conflict with the other two orders, which continued to adhere to tradition and prerogative.

The Dauphinois deputation, for its part, worked as a whole to bring about union and harmony among the three orders. They met collectively – clergy, nobility and Third Estate – to decide the best course of action to achieve this goal, and their unmistakable effort to work for the greater good gave them an influence out of all proportion to the small size of their delegation. In the Third Estate, for example, observers considered it significant when Rabaut de Saint-Etienne's proposal to accept the conciliatory conferences gained the support of Mounier and the Dauphinois delegation.[18]

The Bretons, for their part, represented the antithesis of the Dauphinois mode of operation. Whereas the Dauphinois delegation was small and worked unobtrusively, the Breton deputation was the largest in the Third Estate when the Estates-General opened, and it sought openly to maximize its influence and to advance its own agenda for the Third Estate. Even before the Estates-General opened, the Bretons had rented a building in which they met to coordinate their strategy for the Estates-General, and after the meetings began they gathered there virtually every evening in order to achieve a unanimous position on the issues being debated. Although they were by no means the only delegation to meet as a group – those of Provence and Auvergne and doubtless others also did[19] – the seeming imperiousness of the Bretons aroused some resentment. The Bretons, however, forged by their experience prior to the opening of the Estates-General, sincerely believed that they, too, were working for the greater good, but their activities, intolerance and impetuosity generated suspicion in other deputies, preventing the Bretons from achieving the degree of influence they had hoped to have in the early stages of the Estates-General.[20]

17 See BN Mss. Nouv. acq. fr. 12938, fol. 3v°.
18 On the activities of the Dauphinois delegation, see *Journal des Etats-Généraux, tenu par la députation de Dauphiné* (N.p., n.d.) [Newberry Library, FRC 5719.1]; on the Dauphinois endorsement of Rabaut de Saint-Etienne's motion, see BN Mss. Nouv. acq. fr. 12938, fol. 10; AM Lorient BB 12, no. 4, letter of May 8, 1789.
19 See AN AB[XIX] 3359, dossier 4, document 2; AD Bouches-du-Rhône C 1046, letter of Bouche, May 12, 1789; Mège, *Gaultier de Biauzat*, II: 24.
20 On the Breton delegation, see AM Lorient BB 12, no. 1, letter of April 30, 1789; no. 6, letter of May 15, 1789; AM Brest LL 46, no. 3 *bis*, letter of May 17, 1789; no. 7 *bis*, letter of May 21, 1789; BM Versailles Ms. F. 823, fols. 2, 6v°, 10v°. On the suspicion and resentment the Bretons aroused among other deputies, see AD Eure 5 F 63, p. 22; AM Bayonne AA 51, no. 10, letter of June, 14, 1789; BN Mss. Nouv. acq. fr. 12938, fols. 8, 9v°–10, 43; AM Strasbourg AA 2003, fol. 41; Duquesnoy, *Journal*, I: 19; AD Côtes-d'Armor 1 L 389, letter of Palasne de Champeaux and Poulain de Corbion, May 19,

In a reflection of the desire of the vast majority of its members to work in harmony with the other orders, on May 18, the Third Estate concluded the debate on the conciliatory conferences by voting in favor of the proposal of Rabaut de Saint-Etienne to participate in them. At the same time, the Third Estate, seeking to maintain an internal consensus, also attached to the proposal an amendment offered by the Parisian deputy Guy-Jean-Baptiste Target addressing the concerns of the Bretons. The next day the Third Estate elected sixteen members to represent their order in the conferences.[21]

The conciliatory conferences transformed the situation at the Estates-General from a general stalemate among the three orders into a more direct confrontation between the nobility and the Third Estate – the clergy having become at this stage virtually irrelevant as deputies of both the nobility and the Third Estate found the position of the clergy equivocal and ambiguous.[22] In these meetings, the depth of misunderstanding among the orders, especially between those of the nobility and the Third Estate, became apparent. Just as the Third Estate had not sought the abolition of orders in the period preceding the opening of the Estates-General, so, too, the deputies of the Third Estate at Versailles did not seek to abolish orders but simply to have deliberations in common and vote by head.[23] Even in the Breton delegation, the most aggressive and confrontational within the Third Estate, this was the only goal.[24] As Patrice Higonnet has argued, one needs to recognize the distinction between anti-corporatism, which was central to the revolutionary doctrine, and anti-nobilism, which the deputies of the Third Estate sought to avoid.[25] As a result of this stance, then, before the

1789. Much of this correspondence has been published by D. Tempier, "Correspondance des députés des Côtes-du-Nord aux Etats-Généraux et à l'Assemblée Nationale Constituante," *Sociéte d'Émulation des Côtes-du-Nord, bulletins et mémoires,* 26 (1888).

21  See AN C 28, dossier 215[bis], document 4; AD Eure 5 F 63, p. 20; BN Mss. Nouv. acq. fr. 12938, fols. 11v⁰–14. Target's performance attracted attention and marked him as a potential future leader of the Assembly. See AN AB[XIX] 3494 (13), letter of May 26, 1789.

22  For the nobility, see AD Nièvre 1 L 165, entry of June 4, 1789; ADG. A⁴ 56, p. 46; AD Ain 1 Mi 1, letter of June 9, 1789; for the Third Estate, see BM Nantes Collection Dugast-Matifeux, t. 98, letter of June 1, 1789; AN AB[XIX] 3359, dossier 4, letter 1; AM Brest LL 44, p. 4; BN Mss. Nouv. acq. fr. 12938, fol. 20. See also AD Gironde C 4363, document 10; AD Bouches-du-Rhône C 1046, letter of Bouche, May 31, 1789. See also Edmond-Louis-Alexis Dubois de Crancé, *Lettre de M. Dubois de Crancé, député du Département des Ardennes, à ses commettans, ou Compte rendu des travaux, des dangers et des obstacles de l'Assemblée Nationale, depuis l'ouverture des Etats-Généraux, au 27 avril 1789, jusqu'au premier août 1790* (Paris, 1790), p. 4.

23  See Creuzé-Latouche, *Journal,* pp. 13–14; AD Pyrénées-Orientales C 2119, letter of June 27, 1789.

24  See AM Brest LL 44, pp. 22–22v⁰; AM Lorient BB 12, no. 2, letter of May 3, 1789; no. 7, letter of May 19, 1789; no. 25, letter of June 26, 1789.

25  Higonnet, *Class, Ideology, and the Rights of Nobles,* p. 68.

conciliatory conferences opened, the Third Estate adopted for itself the name of "the commons" – a designation carefully chosen to reflect the limited aims of its members. The assumption of the appellation "the commons" was a political tactic designed solely to overturn vote by order – acquiescence to which was inherent in the term "Third Estate" – yet at the same time leaving, to the nobility in particular, a separate honorific social distinction.[26]

The nobility, however, saw in the action of the Third Estate not merely an attempt to subvert vote by order, to which they were committed in any case, but also an effort to abolish orders altogether. Consequently, led especially by Jean-Jacques Duval d'Eprémesnil, the Parisian *parlementaire*, they opposed the position of the Third Estate.[27] Indeed, in a major effort to uphold vote by order, the nobility responded by conditionally linking their renunciation of fiscal privileges with the maintenance of vote by order at the Estates-General, thereby vitiating whatever positive effect the action may have had.[28]

It must be recognized, however, as their renunciation of their fiscal privileges indicates, that the commitment of the nobility to vote by order went beyond simple self-interest or a blind defense of privilege. When the Estates-General opened, the overwhelming majority of the nobility regarded vote by order as central to the constitution, believing that it provided a sense of balance among the orders that a single chamber would not.[29] In yielding their fiscal privileges, then, they believed that they were addressing the financial crisis and assuming their portion of the burden,[30] but their adhesion to vote by order reflected the conviction that it was a deeper issue of constitutional import.[31] The commons, however, believed that vote by head in a single chamber – arranged by order – was imperative for the task of regeneration to be realized. And to retain the term Third Estate would have appeared to acquiesce in vote by order,

26 See Rivarol, *Mémoires*, pp. 11–12; Bombelles, *Journal*, II: 327. The separation between the political and social dimensions of orders is also apparent in Duquesnoy, *Journal*, I: 25.
27 See BM La Rochelle Ms. 21, entry of May 19, 1789; AN AB[XIX] 3562, dossier 1, letter 1; BN Mss. Nouv. acq. fr. 4121, fol. 13; AD Nièvre 1 L 165, entry of May 23, 1789; AD 1 Mi 1, letter of June 14, 1789; AN KK 641, entries of May 28, June 3 and June 5, 1789.
28 See BN Mss. Nouv. acq. fr. 4121, fols. 13, 14, 17; AM Brest LL 46, no. 4, letter of May 23, 1789. See also BN Mss. Fonds Français 10883, fols. 9–9v°.
29 See AN AB[XIX] 3562, dossier 1, letter 1; AD Ain 1 Mi 1, letter of May 30, 1789; on d'Eprémesnil and his commitment to vote by order before the opening of the Estates-General, see Stone, *The Parlement of Paris*, especially pp. 154–178.
30 It should be noted that the nobility was much more willing to yield its fiscal privileges than was the clergy. See AN AB[XIX] 3494 (13), letter of May 26, 1789.
31 See AD Ain 1 Mi 1, letter of June 9, 1789. Many in the nobility, like Garron de la Bévière, believed that the termination of vote by order would signify the abolition of the nobility.

which is why the deputies of the Third Estate had discarded it at the outset.

Not surprisingly, then, the conciliatory conferences opened on May 23 with a long and contentious session, and the incompatibility of positions between the nobility and the commons soon led to an impasse that made their continuation useless.[32] On the evening of May 28, however, as the conferences were about to be abandoned, Louis sent a letter to each of the three orders asking that they resume the conciliatory conferences, now to be held under the auspices of the Keeper of the Seals.[33]

On this occasion the question of whether or not to participate was much more vigorously debated in the commons, and they were especially angered when the nobility, on the eve of the new conferences, decisively reaffirmed its commitment to deliberation by order – apparently foreclosing the key issue that the commons had presumed to be an object of negotiation.[34] Ultimately, the commons, not wanting to put itself in the position of defying the wishes of the monarch, agreed to participate, but only on two conditions. They insisted that they send a delegation to the king and that there be a *procès-verbaux* of the conferences, to be signed by all three orders.[35] Again, however, against the backdrop of discord and continuation of the dispute over the term "the commons," the resumed conciliatory conferences also collapsed within a few days.[36] Indeed, at the

32 For details of the initial conferences see AN C 28, dossier 215[bis], documents 5–15; BN Mss. Nouv. acq. fr. 12938, fols. 17v°–20; BN Mss. Nouv. acq. fr. 17275, fol. 146; for insights into the point of view of the nobility, see BM La Rochelle Ms. 22, fols. 7–9; for the view of the commons, see AM Brest LL 46, no. 5, letter of May 25–26, 1789; no. 6, letter of May 27–29, 1789; AM Lorient BB 12, no. 9, letter of May 24, 1789; no. 10, letter of May 26, 1789.
33 AN AB[XIX] 3359, dossier 4, letter 3; AN C 28, dossier 215[bis], document 16; AD Bouches-du-Rhône C 1046, letter of Bouche, May 29, 1789.
34 On the action of the nobility, see AD Ain 1 Mi 1, letter of May 30, 1789; AN KK 641, entry of May 28, 1789; BN Mss. Nouv. acq. fr. 4121, fol. 25; on the reaction of the Third Estate, AM Brest LL 46, no. 7, letter of May 29, 1789; AD Eure 5 F 63, p. 29; AD Bouches-du-Rhône C 1046, letter of Bouche, May 31, 1789; BN Mss. Nouv. acq. fr. 12938, fol. 22v°.
35 BN Mss. Fonds Français 10883, fol. 74v°; BN Mss. Nouv. acq. fr. 12938, fol. 23.
36 For details of these conferences, see AN C 28, dossier 215[bis], documents 20–122; AN K 679, nos. 71–77; AM Brest LL 46, no. 8, letter of June 1, 1789, no. 9, letter of June 3, 1789, no. 10, letter of June 4–5, 1789, no. 11, letter of June 6, 1789, no. 13, letter of June 8–9, 1789, no. 14, letter of June 10, 1789; AM Lorient LL 12, no. 13, letter of May 30, 1789, no. 14, letter of June 2, 1789, no. 15, letter of June 5, 1789, no. 16, letter of June 7, 1789, no. 17, letter of June 9, 1789, no. 18, letter of June 12, 1789. For the viewpoint of the nobility see AN KK 641, entry of June 3, 1789, entry of June 5, 1789; AN AB[XIX] 3359, dossier 4, document 6; AD Nièvre 1 L 165, entry of June 4, 1789; BN Mss. Nouv acq. fr. 4121, fol. 29; BM Rouen Collection Depetel 425, letter of June 7, 1789. See also *Procès-verbal des conférences sur la vérification des pouvoirs, tenues par MM. les commissaires du Clergé, de la Noblesse et des Communes, tant en la salle du Comité des Etats-Généraux, qu'en présence de MM. les commissaires du Roi, conformément au désir de sa Majesté* (Paris, 1789).

final session, on June 9, the nobility refused to sign the *procès-verbaux* because of their utilization of the designation "the commons."[37]

It was only at this juncture, on June 10, after the failure of all attempts to achieve conciliation and the union of orders, that the influence of the abbé Sieyès, linked in the eyes of some deputies with the Bretons, began to emerge.[38] Under his prodding, the commons now began to consider constituting itself as the nation without the clergy and the nobility. This appropriation of the idea of the nation by the Third Estate was not solely a tactical ploy, however; in its internal operations the Third Estate had deliberately sought to transcend localism and particularism and to realize a broader vision of the polity.[39] Even now, however, the commons continued to adhere to the concept of the union of orders in resisting key elements of Sieyès's program, especially his hostility to the maintenance of orders.[40]

On June 13, during the debate on Sieyès's proposal, three members of the clergy crossed over to the chamber of the commons to have their credentials verified and received an enthusiastic welcome. The development was ironic because both the nobility and the commons had discounted the clergy, believing their stance to be too equivocal. It is little wonder, then, that the *curés* were surprised by the warmth of the welcome given them when they entered the meeting room, receiving applause not only from the galleries, which were full, but also from deputies of the commons, despite a rule against it.[41] Nevertheless, the speech made by the *curés* after their entry into the chamber of the commons left no doubt about the maintenance of orders, for it explicitly noted their identity as "members of the order of the clergy from the province of Poitou" and asserted that they were seeking to establish

37 BN Mss. Nouv. acq. fr. 12938, fol. 32. See also Jean-Sylvain Bailly, *Mémoires d'un témoin de la Révolution*, 3 vols. (Paris, 1821–1822), I : 95.
38 AD Eure 5 F 63, p. 51; on his identification with the Bretons, see BN Mss. Nouv. acq. fr. 12938, fols. 32v°–36v°. See also AD Côtes-d'Armor 1 L 389, letter of Palasne de Champeaux and Poulain de Corbion, June 5, 1789; BM Angers Ms. 1888, p. 128.
39 See *Récit des séances des députés des communes, depuis le 5 mai 1789, jusqu'au 12 juin suivant, époque à laquelle la rédaction des Procès-verbaux a commencé* (Paris, n.d.), p. 135, where, in establishing committees, the Third Estate decided not to place many deputies from the same province in the same committee. See also AN W 306, dossier 377, pp. 7–8; Creuzé-Latouche, *Journal*, p. 104; in their correspondence also deputies revealed a genuine concern for the nation. See, for example, Ménard de la Groye, *Correspondance*, pp. 36–37.
40 See AM Lorient BB 12, no. 20, letter of June 16, 1789; BN Mss. Nouv. acq. fr. 12938, fols. 43–43v°. See also Antoine-Claire Thibaudeau, *Mémoires, 1765–1792* (Paris, 1875), pp. 74–75, and Dumont, *Souvenirs sur Mirabeau*, pp. 47, 70; Emile Queruau-Lamerie, "Lettres de Michel-René Maupetit, député à l'Assemblée Nationale Constituante (1789–1791)," *Bulletin de la Commission Historique et Archéologique de la Mayenne*, 18 (1902), 161.
41 Abbé Jacques Jallet, *Journal inédit* (Fontenay-le-Comte, 1871), pp. 86–87.

peace and harmony "among the orders." Indeed, in a further reflection of the fact that the commons did not seek to abolish orders, in the roll called their presence was recorded geographically – as from Poitou – but they were seated in a separate section designated for the clergy.[42]

On June 17, in an assertion of the primacy of the nation over particularist interests or privileges, the commons assumed the title of National Assembly, after Sieyès amended his motion proposing it.[43] This was clearly a revolutionary measure, converting a traditionally consultative body into a deliberative, policy-making one and it presaged the assertion of national sovereignty. It was, without question, the beginning of what we have come to think of as the French Revolution. At the same time, however, it adhered to the traditional structure, for the statement said nothing about the merging or abolition of orders; indeed, the critical reference to orders – which stated "representation being one and indivisible, none of the deputies, in whatever order or rank he may be chosen, has the right to exercise his duties separately from the Assembly" – clearly envisaged a distinction of orders as long as they met in a single assembly. Without question, the goal continued to be simply voting by head.[44]

By June 19, many members of the clergy had crossed over to join the National Assembly, but again most of those who went over did so in order to break the stalemate that had developed. For most, the idea of going permanently into a national chamber was still an open question; they continued to feel a loyalty both to their order and to the church, and were not seeking in any way to merge their order with the Third Estate.[45] Even after they had their credentials verified in the National Assembly they continued to sit separately as an order, with their *doyen* seated to the right of the president of the Third Estate.[46]

---

42 *Ibid.*, pp. 86–87; Creuzé-Latouche, *Journal*, p. 103; AN W 306, dossier 377, p. 36; *Procès-verbal des séances des députés des communes, depuis le 12 juin jusqu'au 17 juin, jour de la constitution en Assemblée nationale* (Paris, 1789), pp. 100–101, Pilastre de la Brardière and Leclerc, *Correspondance* I: 142–143.

43 See AN 284 AP 4, dossier 1; AM Lorient BB 12, no. 20, letter of June 16, 1789, no. 21, letter of June 20, 1789; AD Eure 5 F 63, p. 73; BN Mss. Nouv. acq. fr. 12938, fols. 43–44v°.

44 For the declaration of the National Assembly, see *Procès-verbal de l'Assemblée nationale*, No. 1 (June 17, 1789), p. 4. Dumont, *Souvenirs sur Mirabeau*, p. 47, reinforces the notion that the Third Estate simply sought a single assembly where it could make itself felt in voting by head; the destruction of distinction of orders was not sought. Finally, see the thoughts of some deputies in Ménard de la Groye, *Correspondance*, pp. 44–45; AN W 306, dossier 377, p. 36.

45 See Maurice Hutt, "The role of the curés in the Estates-General of 1789," *Journal of Ecclesiastical History*, 6 (1955), 205–214.

46 Pilastre de la Brardière and Leclerc, *Correspondance*, I: 205–206; Hutt, "The role of the curés," 213.

Belatedly recognizing the threat that the increasingly autonomous ideal of the nation represented, a threat of which his advisors had sought to apprise him, and of which some noble deputies had been aware,[47] Louis now decided to impose deliberation by order in a royal session. The initial implementation of this decision – the refurbishing of the room in which the commons had been meeting to prepare it for the royal session – produced, of course, the resolution by the commons on June 20 not to disband until they had given France a constitution. Not only did this action provide the commons with even greater unity and resolve, and enable its members to identify potential leaders who emerged during this time of adversity, but by tacitly asserting that France did not have a constitution it weakened the constitutional arguments later used by Louis in the royal session on June 23 to justify deliberation by order.[48]

In the royal session on June 23, Louis offered a program that perhaps would have been acceptable had it been made when the Estates-General had opened; after the actions of June 17 and June 20, which Louis explicitly annulled, it was inadequate. Despite an imperious command by Louis to deliberate by order, the commons remained in the chamber and refused all demands to disband.

The next day the clergy met separately as an order, after which a majority crossed over to the National Assembly. Again, however, those who crossed over continued to sit as an order and were not at all seeking to combine themselves with the Third Estate.[49] When Jean-Baptiste Dumouchel, the rector of the University of Paris and a deputy for the clergy, joined the National Assembly on June 25, for example, he explicitly noted that he had come to join the majority of his order, whose interests, rights and prerogatives, he stated, he would never cease to uphold.[50]

By this time, members of the nobility also began to yield and to join the Assembly. Some were members of the National Party, which had previously favored the doubling of the Third Estate and the idea of the

---

47 Antoine-François de Bertrand-Moleville, *Mémoires particuliers pour servir à l'histoire de la fin du règne de Louis XVI*, 2 vols. (Paris, 1816), I: 77–78; for the realization by a noble deputy, see AN AB^XIX 3562, dossier 1, document 1. The former minister Barentin also wrote that it was only after June 17 that Louis recognized the threat that the actions of the Third Estate represented. See *Mémoire autographe de M. Barentin*, Maurice Champion, ed., (Paris, 1844), p. 169.

48 On the reaction of the commons, see AD Eure 5 F 63, pp. 83–84; for insight into the constitutional question, see Marina Valensise, "La constitution française," *The French Revolution and the Creation of Modern Political Culture: The Political Culture of the Old Regime*, ed. Keith Michael Baker (New York, 1987), pp. 441–467; Baker, "Fixing the French Constitution," *Inventing the French Revolution*, pp. 252–305.

49 Pilastre de la Brardière and Leclerc, *Correspondance*, I: 235–236.

50 Creuzé-Latouche, *Journal*, p. 157.

orders meeting in common. Furthermore, the failure of the Estates-General, the regular convocation of which they also favored, would have precluded it as an alternative to what they regarded as the sterility of court politics.[51] Most went over as a result of concern for the nation arising from the stalemate, which by this time was in its eighth week. The comte de Clermont-Tonnerre, for example, spoke in the chamber of the nobility against continual opposition to all attempts at union and asserted that the greatest act of patriotism that the nobility of France could perform at this moment would be to join the National Assembly in the *Salle des Etats*, thereby ending all debates that were counter to the common good. His speech was greeted with disapproval by many in the chamber, and when it was proposed to put Clermont-Tonnerre's motion up for debate, the chamber tabled it.[52] On June 25, however, a minority of the nobility, forty-seven members, joined the National Assembly as well. As was the case with the clergy, most went over simply in an effort to break the stalemate and were not seeking to abolish the distinction of orders; indeed, one member of the Third Estate noted the aversion that nobles, even the most liberal nobles, had for the term "citizen," which they refused to accept for themselves or to accord to members of the "commons."[53] Like the clergy, the nobles who entered were seated together in a section designated for their order.[54]

Implicitly acknowledging the failure of its policy, the Crown changed tactics. On June 27, in the midst of preparations to dissolve the body,[55] Louis, without ever using the term National Assembly – indeed, his only

51 Daniel L. Wick, "The court nobility and the French Revolution: the example of the society of thirty," *Eighteenth-Century Studies*, 13 (1980), 263–284; Egret, *La Pré-Révolution française*, p. 336.
52 See AN KK 641, entry of June 24, 1789; for more on the motives of the members of the nobility who joined the National Assembly, see *A MM. les citoyens nobles de la ville de Paris* (N.p., 1789); as well as the speech of the duc d'Aiguillon in *Lettre de MM. les députés des communes de Lyon, à leur commettans* (N.p., n.d.) [Newberry Library, FRC 4841].
53 Creuzé-Latouche, *Journal*, p. 157; see also AM Lorient BB 12, no. 7, letter of May 19, 1789. On their unwillingness to abolish the distinction of orders, see Egret, *La Pré-Révolution française*, p. 336.
54 Pilastre de la Brardière and Leclerc, *Correspondance*, I: 238. See also AM Lorient BB 12, no. 25, letter of June 26, 1789.
55 See Jacques Godechot, *The Taking of the Bastille, July 14, 1789* (New York, 1970), especially pp. 178–180. Aside from military movements, the Crown also sought to prepare public opinion by having Louis's speech of June 23 disseminated to the provinces, doubtless to justify dissolving the National Assembly for disobedience. See, for example, AD Dordogne O E DEP 5005, letter to municipal officers of Périgueux from subdelegate, July 21, 1789; AD Ille-et-Vilaine C 1812, letter of Villedeuil to intendant de Rochefort, June 24, 1789; AD Calvados C 6347, letter of Barentin to intendant de Launay, June 24, 1789, letter of Villedeuil to intendant de Launay, June 24, 1789. For an alternative interpretation, arguing that the Crown was not necessarily seeking to dissolve the National Assembly, see Munro Price, "The 'Ministry of the Hundred Hours': a reappraisal," *French History*, 4 (1990), 317–339.

reference in the letter was to the Estates-General – wrote to the recalcitrant members of the clergy and nobility to ask them to join "the other two orders." He did not ask that they recognize vote by head and specifically mentioned that they could join the other two orders but not participate in deliberations until they had received new instructions from their constituents. After an emotional meeting between the presidents of the clergy and nobility and the monarch, late in the afternoon of June 27 the minority of the clergy and the majority of the nobility entered the National Assembly, raising the hopes of deputies already there and producing numerous festivities in both Versailles and Paris. Indeed, the Assembly decided to adjourn for two days in order to allow celebration of the event.[56]

In the period between June 27 and the next meeting of the National Assembly on June 30, however, many recalcitrant deputies held meetings to discuss measures by which they could impede the proceedings of the National Assembly. Several noble deputies, for example, began to prepare a strategy for hindering the Assembly by seeking to have their electoral assemblies reconvened in order to receive new instructions.[57] In fact, the Crown actively discouraged a plan conceived by several noble deputies whereby they would sabotage the National Assembly by going back to their locales, ostensibly to receive new powers, but then not return to the National Assembly.[58] Although the Crown thwarted this effort, it did later authorize deputies to return to their locales for new powers, and several took advantage of the opportunity.[59] More immediately, however, most of these deputies entered the National Assembly still refusing to acknowledge, in any way, voting by head rather

---

56  On the meeting with the king, see AN K 164, no. 4³, entry of June 27, 1789; see also BN Mss. Nouv. acq. fr. 12938, fols. 59–60v°; AM Lorient BB 12, no. 25, letter of June 29, 1789; AM Brest LL 44, pp. 26v°–27; AN AB^XIX 3359, dossier 4, document 8; AN W 306, dossier 377, p. 50. On the reaction to the news, see BN Mss. Fonds Français 13713, fols. 20–20v°.

57  See BN Mss. Nouv. acq. fr. 4121, fol. 50; AN KK 641, entry of June 30, 1789; AN AA 48, dossier 1388–1390, document 87; AN AA 49, dossier 1395–1397, document 102. Deputies of the commons suspected an effort by these deputies to impede the National Assembly. See Ménard de la Groye, *Correspondance*, p. 55.

58  AN M 856, dossier 6⁹, letter of Barentin to Louis, June 28, 1789; see also AN Bᵃ 41, liasse 87, dossier 6, documents 2, 6: AN Bᵃ 49, liasse 114, dossier 7, document 6; AN Bᵃ 76, liasse 176^bis, dossier 3, document 27. Initially, many deputies simply wrote to ask for new powers. See, for example, AN AA 48, dossier 1388–1390, document 87; AN AA 50, dossier 1420–1423, document 24; AN AA 50, dossier 1424–1427, document 49; AN AA 50, dossier 1428–1431, document 82; AN AA 50, dossier 1435–1438, document 82; AN Bᵃ 32, liasse 65, dossier 3, document 2.

59  See, for example, AD Calvados F 780, copy of letter of the duc de Coigny, August 1, 1789; AD Ain 1 Mi 1, letter of July 2, 1789, AD Pyrénées-Orientales C 2119, no. 17, letter of July 6, 1789.

than by order.[60] Indeed, because of his opposition to the idea, as late as July 4 one noble deputy, the duc de Caylus, characterized his presence in the Assembly as "absolutely useless."[61] Similarly, the comte de Helmstatt, asserting that he was "without a voice" until the arrival of new powers, left Versailles altogether to take the waters.[62]

As a result, although the union of the three orders was celebrated locally and hailed throughout France, in reality it did almost nothing to ameliorate the stalemate for, as a totally artificial construct, the National Assembly had little sense of cohesion or purpose during its early existence.[63] This lack of identity manifested itself immediately in the first joint meeting on June 30. The meeting was scheduled to begin at 9.00 a.m., but the minority of the clergy and the majority of the nobility did not appear. The president of the Assembly, Jean-Sylvain Bailly, delayed the start of the meeting for an hour, but they still did not arrive; only at 11.00 a.m. did they enter the Assembly. By what was presumed to be a prearranged strategy, many of these deputies then attempted to maintain vote by order by claiming that they could not deliberate in common without receiving new powers from their constituents, an enterprise that would have impeded the operations of the Assembly indefinitely. The reading of these protests – forty-four according to one deputy – consumed most of the first meeting, much to the chagrin of the Assembly. Indeed, the protests ended only when a deputy – apparently Rabaut de Saint-Etienne – noted that men whose credentials were not verified did not have the right to protest to an Assembly to which they did not yet belong.[64]

60 BN Mss. Nouv. acq. fr. 4121, fols. 50–51; Duquesnoy, *Journal*, I: 137–138; Mège, *Gaultier de Biauzat*, I: 149.
61 AN B[a] 41, liasse 87, dossier 6, document 4. See also AN B[a] 49, liasse 114, dossier 7, document 6; AD Ain 1 Mi 1, letter of July 2, 1789.
62 AN AA 50, dossier 1424–1427, document 50.
63 On the welcome given to the union of orders, see Ménard de la Groye, *Correspondance*, p. 54; AN C 86, dossier 1, document 2; AN C 88, dossier 48, document 2; AN C 91, dossier 71, document 44. For an insight into the lack of cohesion amidst the celebration, see *Mémoire autographe de M. de Barentin*, pp. 244–245.
64 See AM Bayonne AA 51, unnumbered letter of June 30, 1789; AN K 164, no. 4[3], fol. 122; AD Eure 5 F 63, pp. 98–99; AD Loire-Atlantique C 626 (2), no. 137; AD Gironde 3 L 82, letter of June 30, at 5.00 p.m.; AN KK 641, entry of June 30, 1789; AM Brest LL 46, no. 21, letter of June 30, 1789; AM Lorient BB 12, no. 27, letter of June 30, 1789; BN Mss. Fonds Français 10883, fol. 61; BN Mss. Nouv. acq. fr. 4121, fol. 51; AD Bouches-du-Rhône C 1380, fol. 169; *Journal de Versailles*, July 1, 1789; *Journal des Etats-Généraux, aujourd'hui Assemblée nationale permanente. Par M. Le Hodey de Saultchevreuil*. 35 vols. (Paris, 1789–1791), (hereafter *Journal des Etats-Généraux*), I: 267, 271–272, 277; *Suite des nouvelles de Versailles, du 30 juin 1789, publiées le premier juillet*, July 1, 1789. See also Nicholas Jean Hugou de Basseville, *Mémoires historiques, critiques et politiques de la Révolution de France, avec toutes les opérations de l'Assemblée Nationale*, 4 vols. (Paris, 1790), III: 87–89; Armand Louis de Gontaut Biron (duc de Lauzan), *Lettres sur les Etats-*

The incident made deputies aware of the problem of imperative mandates as an issue that would have to be addressed quickly. And while the Assembly functioned relatively smoothly the next day, giving at least one deputy cause for hope, the lack of unity of purpose became abundantly apparent on July 2, when cardinal de la Rochefoucault, speaking for the minority of the clergy, explicitly attempted to reserve the right of the clergy to continue to meet and to vote separately as an order. Threatening, as it did, to undo the crucial achievement of the formation of the National Assembly, his action produced a tumult in the Assembly.[65] Undaunted, however, a majority of the nobility reassembled separately as an order the following evening and drafted a similar, more strident, declaration, which they sent directly to the king.[66] Furthermore, many of the deputies in these groups boycotted meetings of the subcommittees (*bureaux*) of the Assembly in the evening in order to meet separately as an order, usually to support grievances against the Assembly, and this subsequently culminated in their withdrawal from the Assembly altogether.[67] In addition, on July 4, in the first voice vote by head in the National Assembly, a substantial number of noble and clerical deputies refused to participate; when called, most sat in silence or else left the hall just before their name was called.[68]

The National Assembly, after largely completing verification of credentials, struggled to achieve a sense of purpose, and decided on July 6 to devote itself to drawing up a constitution; to expedite the task, it chose to establish a committee of thirty members to study preliminary questions involved in drafting one.[69] The Assembly elected the committee that evening, and the results of the balloting were announced the

*Généraux de 1789 ou Détail des Séances de l'Assemblée de la Noblesse et des Trois Ordres du 4 mai au 15 novembre* (Paris, 1865), p. 11; Honoré Gabriel de Riqueti, Comte de Mirabeau, *Lettres à ses commettans* (Paris, 1791), pp. 341–342. For a brief description of the nature of the various objections to meeting in common, see *Le Point du Jour*, July 1, 1789.

65  *Procès-verbal de l'Assemblée nationale*, No. 12 (July 2, 1789), pp. 3–4; *Le Point du Jour*, July 3, 1789; BN Mss. Nouv. acq. fr. 4121, fols. 54–55; Bombelles, *Journal*, II: 339. On the hopes of one deputy the previous day, Mège, *Gaultier de Biauzat*, I: 153.

66  See BM La Rochelle Ms. 21, entry of July 3, 1789 at 7.00 p.m.; BM Versailles Ms. F. 823, fol. 49 v°; *Supplément au procès-verbal de l'ordre de la noblesse aux Etats-Généraux* (Paris, 1792), pp. 359–362. See also Bailly, *Mémoires*, I: 282–285; marquis Charles-Elie de Ferrières, *Mémoires du marquis de Ferrières*, 3 vols. (Paris, 1821), I: 73.

67  *Supplément au procès-verbal de l'ordre de la noblesse*, pp. 365–376; AD Bouches-du Rhône C 1046, letter of Bouche, July 7, 1789; ADG. A⁴ 56, p. 155; Dardy, "Lettres de M. Grellet de Beauregard," 68.

68  AD Ain 1 Mi 1, letter of July 7, 1789; BN Mss. Nouv. acq. fr. 4121, fol. 57; AM Brest LL 46, no. 24, letter of July 7, 1789; AM Le Havre D³ 38, no. 6; Mège, *Gaultier de Biauzat*, I: 160. Again, see the comments of the deputy duc de Caylus on that date in AN Bᵃ 41, liasse 87, dossier 6, document 4.

69  BN Mss. Nouv. acq. fr. 12938, fols. 67–67v°; R. K. Gooch, *Parliamentary Government in France: Revolutionary Origins 1789–1791* (Ithaca, 1960), pp. 21–22.

next day, but in the process an incident occurred that betrayed the manner in which the Assembly still operated primarily in terms of orders. After the balloting, several deputies noted that not a single member of the clergy had been chosen, prompting an outcry from the commons to name six additional clerical members to the thirty originally selected. For their part, the clergy responded that they had participated in the selection process and were satisfied with the outcome. Nevertheless, the commons renewed their effort, and the nobles joined them, but the clergy continued to refuse the offer, to the acclaim of the Assembly. Although perhaps relatively minor, the episode highlights not only the intention of the deputies to continue to maintain distinction of orders but also the tentativeness and lack of cohesion of the Assembly early in its existence.[70]

Immediately afterward, however, the deputies addressed the issue of imperative mandates by opening a debate on representation, the resolution of which would prove critical in the evolution of the National Assembly. In yet another effort to retard the work of the Assembly and to assert vote by order rather than by head, several noble and clerical deputies returned to the issue that had been so troublesome to the Assembly when it had begun the joint verification of credentials on June 30 – the issue of mandates. The issue had not been addressed before the verification of credentials had begun, and these deputies, now that they were a part of the Assembly, argued that they were merely *mandataires*, bound strictly by an imperative mandate to reflect the wishes of their electors and the views expressed in the *cahiers*, which in most cases specified vote by order.[71] The danger that imperative mandates posed to the operation of a deliberative body had long been recognized, even before the opening of the Estates-General,[72] and during the Estates-General/National Assembly they had been treated inconsistently. In the royal session on June 23, Louis had sought to disallow imperative

70 *Procès-verbal de l'Assemblée nationale*, No. 17 (July 7, 1789), pp. 7–8. See also Duquesnoy, *Journal*, I: 167–168, 173; Bailly, *Mémoires d'un témoin de la Révolution*, I: 290–291. This episode led one deputy to believe that "much union and cordiality" existed among the members of the Assembly; see Ménard de la Groye, *Correspondance*, p. 57. See also AM Bayonne AA 51, no. 16, letter of July 7, 1789. Underscoring the fact that the commons had sought only to overturn the political dimension of orders, the National Assembly at this time, in terms of its seating, was still divided into orders. See Pilastre de la Brardière and Leclerc, *Correspondance*, II: 48–49; Ménard de la Groye, *Correspondance*, p. 58.

71 *Procès-verbal de l'Assemblée nationale*, No. 17 (July 7, 1789), pp. 7–8. For a good account of the debate, see Creuzé-Latouche, *Journal*, pp. 195–201, and Duquesnoy, *Journal*, I: 169–170. On the competing theories of representation, see Eric Thomson, *Popular Sovereignty and the French Constituent Assembly 1789–1791* (Manchester, 1952), pp. 48–49.

72 See, for example, AD Gironde 3 L 82, letters of January 13, 1789, February 4, 1789, April 25, 1789.

mandates, but on June 27, in a transparent maneuver, he seemed to approve of them. The attempted use of imperative mandates on June 30 and afterward to impede the work of the Assembly clearly indicated that their status had to be settled.[73] Talleyrand initiated the debate on July 3 by offering a motion that annulled any imperative clause forbidding deputies to vote in the National Assembly or ordering a deputy to withdraw from it. Reports on subsistence and other matters delayed further discussion until July 7, when it consumed the remainder of the meeting and continued the next day, July 8, when the Assembly, amidst much confusion, rejected the doctrine of binding mandates by approving a motion by Mirabeau that there was nothing to debate. The motion carried by a wide margin because the opposing sides had each interpreted it in its own favor. The commons and its supporters among the clergy and the nobility believed that the issue had been settled on June 17 when the National Assembly had been proclaimed and that there was therefore no need to go over it again. For their part, however, a majority of the nobility and a minority of the clergy believed that their binding mandates on the form of deliberation remained valid even after they joined the National Assembly and, evidently believing that the idea that there was nothing to debate applied to Talleyrand's motion or to their situation, believed it favored their position. As a result, they were initially quite happy when it passed, until they realized its true significance.[74]

Rejection of imperative mandates, in whatever manner it came about, represented a critical step, for not only did it endow the National Assembly with an independence that could serve as the basis for a new sense of identity, it also established the conditions that made possible the momentous night of August 4, although the latter development could not, of course, have been foreseen at the time. Indeed, although the decision attracted little attention when it occurred, and has been relatively neglected since, members of the Assembly subsequently judged

---

73 When nineteen members of the nobility of Bourg-en-Bresse wrote to their deputies in early July to inform them that they had decreed that their mandate for vote by order was not imperative, the assembly of the nobility at the National Assembly overruled that decision and deemed the mandate imperative. Since the purpose of the imperative mandate was to reflect faithfully the view of the constituents, and since the constituents had unmistakably indicated their view, this was a subversion of it and was clearly being used to retard the Assembly. See AD Ain 1 Mi 1, letter of July 7, 1789.

74 On the confusion that surrounded the vote of July 8, see BN Mss. Nouv. acq. fr. 4121, fol. 64; BN Mss. Fonds Français 10883, fol. 65v°; *Etats-Généraux. Journal de la Correspondance de Nantes*, 10 vols. (Nantes, 1789–1791), I: 101–102; AM Strasbourg AA 2005, fol. 17; Duquesnoy, *Journal*, I: 174. See also *Procès-verbal de l'Assemblée nationale* No. 18 (July 8, 1789), p. 2. In effect, the rejection of imperative mandates meant that deputies were free to exercise their own judgment and to reach their own conclusions in the Assembly. See AN AB[XIX] 3359, dossier 4, document 9.

it one of the most significant acts in the initial stages of the Revolution.[75] On July 14, the Assembly elected a Committee of the Constitution to expedite the drafting of the constitution.[76] Once again, however, it is indicative of the primacy accorded to achieving vote by head and the intention to continue a distinction of orders that on this occasion its members were not chosen at large, but in strict accordance with orders – two from the clergy, two from the nobility and four from the commons. Selection of the committee was all but overshadowed, of course, by the popular rising in Paris, but there is a certain symmetry in the fact that both occurred on the same day. On the one hand, the Committee of the Constitution would take the lead in defining the Revolution in juridical terms. On the other hand, the rising in Paris, as well as the municipal revolutions that followed in the provinces, assured that the Revolution would not be simply an abstract legal exercise, but an event that would engage the energies of much of the populace, which had mobilized to preserve and defend the revolution of the commons. The interconnection between the National Assembly and the rest of France was an enduring feature for the remainder of the Assembly's existence.[77]

Even the Assembly's deliverance from threatened dissolution, however, did little to instill in it any sense of cohesion or identity. The insurrection did lead the deputies who had withdrawn from the Assembly to return to it and to agree to deliberate by head, but they were not warmly received. In addition, during the following days, responses of the Assembly to homages paid to it, many of which, significantly, came only after July 14, had a stilted quality that betrayed the absence of any strong sense of coalescence.[78]

75 See BM Nantes Collection Dugast-Matifeux, t. 12, fol. 49. A clerical deputy opposed to the Assembly's rejection of binding mandates believed that it was this rejection that truly marked the change from the Estates-General to the National Assembly; see AN AD[XVIIIc] 135, *Première lettre de M. l'abbé de Bonneval, député du clergé de Paris, à ses commentans*, pp. 81–82. See also Pierre-Victor Malouet, *Mémoires de Malouet, publiés par son petit-fils le Baron Malouet*, 2 vols. (Paris, 1868), I: 299–301.
76 See AM Bayonne AA 51, no. 19, letter of July 14, 1789.
77 See Godechot, *The Taking of the Bastille*. On the Committee of the Constitution, see Keith Michael Baker, "Fixing the French constitution," *Inventing the French Revolution*, pp. 252–305; Michael P. Fitzsimmons, "The committee of the constitution and the remaking of France, 1789–1791," *French History*, 4 (1990), 23–47.
78 On the return of the deputies to the Assembly, *Procès-verbal de l'Assemblée nationale*, No. 25 (July 16, 1789), pp. 4–6; AD Pyrénées-Orientales C 2119, no. 23, letter of July 16, 1789; BM Dijon Ms. 2074, fols. 429–430; Bailly, *Mémoires d'un témoin de la Révolution*, II: 38–39; de Ferrières, *Mémoires*, I: 150–151. For the attitude encountered by the deputies who returned, see especially AM Bergerac, fonds Faugère, carton I, no. 6, letter of July 17, 1789; Creuzé-Latouche, *Journal*, pp. 238–239; for an example of the stilted quality of responses to homages, see the reply to the homage offered by the *Parlement* of Paris, in the *Procès-verbal de l'Assemblée nationale*, No. 30 (July 23, 1789), pp. 7–8. The pervasive unease was noted by Dumont, *Souvenirs sur Mirabeau*, p. 94.

At the time of its formation, the Committee of the Constitution had been given a mandate to draft a plan for the new constitution and to present it to the Assembly. It is indicative of how limited this task was perceived to be that on July 24, only ten days after the committee's formation, a member of the Assembly proposed that the committee be required to present a report on its work immediately.[79] Other members supported the suggestion, and the Assembly decided that the committee should present an account of its deliberations on July 27. It also specified that the committee should condense its proposals into a form that would allow for discussion of them.

The presentation of July 27 is of particular interest because it reveals how limited the initial aspirations of the National Assembly were. Jean-Baptiste-Marie Champion de Cicé, the archbishop of Bordeaux, began by reading a report summarizing the committee's deliberations; he indicated that the committee had felt itself obliged to take account of the views of their constituents as expressed in the *cahiers*, on which Clermont-Tonnerre would report immediately afterward. Champion de Cicé presented the first chapter of the constitution, on the principles of French government, and invited members of the Assembly to submit their ideas on such issues as administrative organization, judicial power, public education, the military and the legislature, with particular emphasis on the last.

Clermont-Tonnerre then followed with his report summarizing the *cahiers* on the question of a constitution. He noted that although the *cahiers* were unanimous in their desire to see a regeneration of the realm, they were divided on the extent of this regeneration. Some asked simply for a reform of abuses and a repair of the "existing constitution", while others desired a new constitution. After summarizing the sentiments of some *cahiers* on selected questions, Clermont-Tonnerre put forward two sets of propositions, one consisting of accepted principles and the other of questions arising from the lack of uniformity among the *cahiers*. Among the latter issues, issues that the Assembly would have to decide, were whether or not laws would be submitted to sovereign courts for registration and whether *lettres de cachet* would be abolished or merely modified.[80]

79 See BM La Rochelle Ms. 21, entry of July 24, 1789. For more on the sense of imminence concerning the constitution, see *Le Point du Jour*, July 22, 1789; Mercy-Argenteau, *Correspondance secrète*, II: 258.
80 *Procès-verbal de l'Assemblée nationale*, No. 33 (July 27, 1789), p. 8. The *procès-verbal* mentions that the Assembly ordered the printing of the reports, so I have utilized the texts found in J. Mavidal and E. Laurent, eds., *Archives parlementaires de 1787 à 1860*, 1st series, 82 vols. (Paris, 1862–1913), (hereafter *AP*), VIII: 280–285. See also BN Mss. Nouv. acq. fr. 4121, fol. 90.

The presentation by the Committee of the Constitution illustrates how limited the initial objectives of the National Assembly were; indeed, there was a perception among deputies that the drafting of the constitution would be only a matter of weeks.[81] Although the committee recognized the latitude that had been provided by the decision of July 8, it intended to adhere as closely as possible to the *cahiers*. The committee was so restrained, in fact, that it did not preclude the possibility of seating by various forms of orders in future legislatures. The readiness of the Assembly to maintain traditional – and even, in the *lettres de cachet*, some of the worst – features of the kingdom is apparent. Under such a standard of prescriptive tradition, it is clear that alterations in the essential configuration of the state would have been of a very limited character. Since the *cahiers* had been concerned especially with equality of taxation, and since the clergy and nobility had already conceded this, the fiscal system clearly would have been amended. Beyond that, however, the fundamental, privileged, corporate structure of the polity would have remained largely undisturbed.[82]

Shortly afterward, however, the Assembly totally abandoned such restraint as a result of the night of August 4; in the aftermath of that historic meeting the National Assembly undertook to remake the French nation virtually in its entirety. Inspired by the new ideal of the polity attained during the session, the Assembly moved well beyond such matters as whether to reform or abolish *lettres de cachet* or whether laws would be submitted to sovereign courts for registration to reshape completely the institutions of the nation and to redefine altogether civic relations between Frenchmen.

The proposals initially advanced that evening apparently began as a prearranged strategy to stem the violence associated with the Great Fear,[83] but other deputies put forward succeeding resolutions, which

81 See, for example, AD Bouches-du-Rhône C 1337, letter of Verdolin, July 6, 1789; AD Ain 1 Mi 1, letter of July 22, 1789; M. Leroux-Cesbron, "Lettres de Lofficial, député à l'Assemblée constituante, sur la Révolution de 1789," *Nouvelle Révue rétrospectif*, 38 (1897), 100, in which, after the report of July 27, Lofficial told his wife that the drafting of the constitution would take at least a month if they worked twelve hour days. See also AD Côtes-d'Armor 1 L 389, letter of Champeaux-Palasne and Poulain de Corbion, July 21, 1789.
82 On the recognition of the broader latitude available and the possibility of meeting by some system of orders, see *AP* VIII: 283–285. One contemporary noted that the report was scarcely innovative in its proposals, and would, in fact, leave the monarch in an extremely favorable position. BM Dijon Ms. 2522, no. 3, letter of July 30, 1789. The report seems to have produced some sense of purpose among the deputies for the first time. See BN Mss. Fonds français 10883, fol. 80vº; Pilastre de la Brardière and Leclerc, *Correspondance*, II: 48–49.
83 See Georges Lefebvre, *The Coming of the French Revolution*, (Princeton, 1967) pp. 157–158. There is also an allusion in AM Brest LL 46, no. 36, letter of August 5, 1789. The

were heartily applauded. However contrived or premeditated the initial renunciations of that evening may have been, they electrified the Assembly. A wave of emotion overtook the deputies and launched them into an unrelenting condemnation of privilege, producing a new ideal of a polity that could be sublime – a belief that the nation should henceforth be a source of equity and the focus for the highest ideals and conduct of its members.[84]

Out of this meeting the nation emerged as a unifying ideal, transcending the paradigm of privileged corporatism that had hitherto prevailed. The Assembly discarded the inequity of privilege for the equity of laws common to all, which in turn would form the basis for a fraternal community of citizens. Although calculation and jealousy may have characterized some actions that evening, the sense of renewal and altruism was far stronger, as the letters and recollections of deputies and observers attest.[85]

most comprehensive study of the night of August 4 is Patrick Kessel, *La Nuit du 4 août 1789* (Paris, 1969). See also Jean-Pierre Hirsch, *La Nuit du 4 août* (Paris, 1978); Carl Christophelsmeier, *The Fourth of August, 1789* (Lincoln, 1906).

84 The word "sublime" was used frequently by both members and observers of the National Assembly. The spirit of generosity and altruism that redefined the idea of the nation on August 4 led contemporaries to ascribe the quality of sublimity to the constitution, leading to frequent references to the "sublime constitution." See especially AN F$^1$c III Maine-et-Loire 9, letter of administrators comprising directory of department to Louis, September 21, 1791; AN F$^1$c III Doubs 1, dossier 2, *Procès-verbal* of patriotic festival celebrated at Nancray, August 4, 1791; AN C 126, dossier 412, document 31; AN C 129, dossier 441$^2$, document 89. There were also other similar usages. See, for example, AN 284 AP 2, dossier 15, notebook 4, part 1, in which Sieyès described the members of the Assembly on June 23 as "full of sublime love of the fatherland." For other examples of the use of the term, see AN C 125, dossier 408, document 10; AN C 126, dossier 412, document 3; AN C 129, dossier 437, document 22; AN C 129, dossier 439, document 33; AN C 129, dossier 440, document 47; AN C 129, dossier 442, document 31; AN C 129, dossier 442, document 36. See also Michael P. Fitzsimmons, *The Parisian Order of Barristers and the French Revolution* (Cambridge, Mass., 1987), p. 41, in which the term "sublimity of the nation" was used as a shorthand for these various usages.

85 Ménard de la Groye, *Correspondance*, pp. 78–79; AD Orne C 1227, document 183; AD Bouches-du-Rhône C 1380, fols. 235–236; BN Mss. Fonds Français 10883, fol. 84; BN Mss. Fonds Français 13713, fol. 114. The deputy Duquesnoy, who was frequently scathing in his judgments, was rapturous, while the deputy Gaultier de Biauzat wrote to his constituents immediately afterward that he was embarrassed by the difficulty of conveying the "grandeur and beauty" of the evening and said that he was tempted to take after the poet. Similarly, Rabaut de Saint-Etienne complained that only those who were present could understand it. Duquesnoy, *Journal*, I: 267; Mège, *Gaultier de Biauzat*, I: 224; Rabaut de Saint-Etienne, *Précis de l'histoire de la Révolution française*, p. 201. See also Queruau-Lamerie, "Lettres de…Maupetit," 19, 216–217. Even the clerical deputy François Chevallier, who despised the Revolution, which he portrayed as a Protestant plot, and who particularly detested the night of August 4, conceded the genuine sense of generosity of spirit among those there that night. See BM Nantes Collection Dugast-Matifeux, t. 12, fol. 69. The unfavorable, even cynical, interpretation of the night of August 4, including the notion that the bishop of Chartres retaliated for the abolition of tithes in

For several hours deputies from all estates and orders, and virtually every province, spontaneously relinquished a wide variety of rights and privileges. After renunciations made by the nobility and the clergy, the provinces and towns followed, with the juxtaposition between Dauphiné and Brittany, one of the leitmotifs of the period preceding the opening of the Estates-General, once again manifesting itself. The deputies of Dauphiné renounced the privileges of their province and agreed to accept the regime that the National Assembly would determine; they were followed by the Breton deputies who provisionally offered the privileges of their province, pending the consent of its inhabitants.[86] Several other provinces and towns renounced their privileges in turn.[87] Indeed, it is indicative of how deliberately and self-consciously the deputies repudiated privilege and its divisiveness as an instrument of government that they made a pact of association of all the provinces against any effort by the monarch to reimpose privilege.[88] According to the deputy Jacques-Bernardin Colaud de la Salcette, the pact was directed against the Crown, particularly the ministry, and it is likely that, in order to preserve harmony and in seeking to associate Louis with its actions, the Assembly did not want to risk alienating him by emphasizing the pact, which had potential implications of insubordination or seditiousness. The pact is not explicitly mentioned in the *procès-verbal*, but its essence – without the vow to resist the reimposition of privilege, of

kind by renouncing hunting rights, seems to stem chiefly from de Ferrières, *Mémoires*, I: 187–190. These memoirs were composed many years later and were refracted through the bitterness of the Terror and, given his contemporary sentiments, to be quoted below, should be treated with caution and accorded somewhat less credibility.
86  AM Lorient BB 12, no. 47, letter of August 5, 1789; AM Strasbourg AA 2003, fols. 120–121; AD Pyrénées-Atlantiques C 1377, letter of August 7, 1789. See also [F. M. Kerverseau and G. Clavelin], *Histoire de la Révolution de France ... par deux amis de la liberté*, new edn., 20 vols. (Paris, 1792–1803), II: 223–224. The Breton deputies immediately and privately assured their colleagues that their renunciation would be ratified. See AM Bordeaux D 220, no. 13, letter of Lafargue to electors of Bordeaux, August 5, 1789.        87  AD Pyrénées-Atlantiques C 1377, letter of August 7, 1789.
88  The most explicit references to the pact are found in J. de Font-Réaulx, "Lettres de J. Bern. Colaud de la Salcette, chanoine de Die, député aux Etats-Généraux en 1789," *Bulletin de la Société d'Archéologie et de Statistique de la Drôme*, 69 (1944), 149; Camille Looten, "Lettres de François-Joseph Bouchette, avocat à Bergues, membre de l'Assemblée Nationale constituante," *Annales du Comité flamande de France*, 29 (1908–1909), 238; and AM Lorient BB 12, no. 47, letter of August 5, 1789. More oblique allusions to it are found in AM Arles AA 23, fol. 537; AD Bouches-du-Rhône C 1046, letter of Bouche of August 5, 1789; AD Bouches-du-Rhône C 1337, letter of Verdolin of August 7, 1789; AD Bouches-du-Rhône C 1380, fol. 228; R. Hennequin, "La nuit du 4 août 1789 racontée par le constituant Parisot," *La Révolution Française*, 80 (1927), 16–22, with the reference on 20; *Journal de Versailles*, August 8, 1789; *Etats-Généraux. Bulletin de la correspondance de la députation du tiers-état de la sénéchaussée de Brest* (Brest, 1789–1790), p. 235, and *Nouvelles Ephémérides de l'Assemblée Nationale, ou correspondance d'un député à l'Assemblée Nationale, avec un Membre du Parlement d'Angleterre*, August 8, 1789.

course, which doubtless remained an unwritten agreement among the members of the Assembly – appears in article X of the August decrees.

A national constitution and public liberty being more advantageous to the provinces than the privileges that some enjoy, the sacrifice of which is necessary for the intimate union of all parts of the Empire, it is declared that all the particular privileges of the provinces, principalities, *pays*, cantons, towns and communities, whether pecuniary or of any other type, are permanently abolished and will be merged into the common rights of all Frenchmen.

As one contemporary noted, the meeting marked "the first time that all these provinces created their act of union and association."[89] After several hours of what one deputy called a "combat of generosity," and another observer termed "a sublime struggle of justice and generosity," the Assembly concluded the emotional session by proclaiming Louis "the restorer of French liberties."[90]

In discussing the night of August 4, scholars – with the notable exception of Georges Lefebvre – have often concentrated on the qualifications that vitiated the bold opening assertion of the August decrees that the feudal regime had been destroyed in its entirety and have considered only secondarily its other elements.[91] The weakening of the initial generous spirit is undeniable[92] but, however regrettable, it is only one aspect of the night of August 4, which should be viewed in a context wider than its implications with respect to peasants.[93]

Most immediately, the unifying effect that the night of August 4 had on the National Assembly cannot be overestimated; it changed the spirit of the Assembly completely, as well as the scope of its deliberations. No longer feeling a sense of resentment toward the nobility, most members of the commons now felt a sense of admiration for the spirit of sacrifice

---

89 BN Mss. Fonds Français 10883, fol. 84v°.
90 The characterizations are from BM La Rochelle Ms. 21, entry of August 4, 1789 and BN Mss. Fonds Français 10883, fol. 84; see also *Procès-verbal de l'Assemblée nationale*, No. 40 *bis* (August 4, 1789), pp. 14–42.
91 A representative example of this tendency would be Albert Soboul, *The French Revolution 1787–1799* (New York, 1974), pp. 148–150, which devotes much greater attention to the deficiencies of the decrees before briefly characterizing them as "of the very utmost importance" and noting that the National Assembly had destroyed the Ancien Régime. Lefebvre, by contrast, was much more balanced in his treatment. Although noting the shortcomings of the decrees, he asserted that the session "destroyed the feudal system and aristocratic domination over rural areas" and "achieved in principle the legal unity of the nation." See Georges Lefebvre, *The French Revolution*, 2 vols. (New York, 1962–1964), I: 130.
92 See P. M. Jones, *The Peasantry in the French Revolution* (Cambridge, 1988), pp. 81–85.
93 This has briefly been suggested by D. M. G. Sutherland, *France 1789–1815: Revolution and Counterrevolution* (London, 1985), p. 79; Keith Michael Baker, *Inventing the French Revolution*, p. 58.

that they had shown and a sense of gratitude for leading the way to the new ideal of the polity that the Assembly had achieved.[94] Out of this meeting emerged an overwhelming sense of union and singularity that dissolved all variations of orders, provinces or other differentiations. There was a pervasive sense that there were no longer clergy, nobles or *roturiers*, nor Bretons, Burgundians or Provençals – there were only Frenchmen, united in a sense of common purpose now that privilege had been proscribed.[95] Indeed, several deputies of the clergy and nobility who had not been present at the meeting began the next day and in following days to adhere to the actions of that evening, often citing "the public good" as their motivation.[96] Across the spectrum, from strong-willed Breton deputies to conservative noblemen, there was a belief that all differences had either disappeared or could be resolved.[97]

This sense of unity underlay a consensus formed that evening that enormously expanded the Assembly's task and had an incalculable impact on the nature of the state. The National Assembly, a recognized representative body, had freely renounced the privileges that had divided the polity and, in the pact of association forged that evening, had rejected privilege as an instrument of government or as a superintending principle of society. In proclaiming Louis "the restorer of French liberties," it had sought to associate the Crown with its action, an action that the Crown itself could never have accomplished without opening itself to charges of despotism. The intense emotion and general exaltation present at the conclusion of the meeting, then, is not difficult to understand. In supplanting privilege with the more unifying higher ideal of the nation, and in associating the Crown with that endeavor, the Assembly had, in its view, resolved all anomalies in the polity and fused the state and society.

94 AD Orne C 1227, document 183; Ménard de la Groye, *Correspondance*, p. 78; AD Bouches-du-Rhône C 1380, fol. 235. See also AM Strasbourg AA 2003, fols. 120–121; AM Bergerac, fonds Faugère, carton I, no. 11, letter of August 7, 1789; AM Bordeaux D 220, no. 13, letter of Lafargue to electors of Bordeaux, August 5, 1789; AD Pyrénées-Atlantiques C 1377, letter of August 7, 1789 and, although not from a deputy, AD Pyrénées-Atlantiques C 1601, letter of Polverel to Estates of Béarn, August 7, 1789.
95 See AD Morbihan 1 Mi 240, no. 20, letter of August 4, 1789. Because of a defect in the departmental microfilm, this letter must be supplemented by the copy published by Gustave Bord, "Ouverture des Etats-Généraux de 1789," *Revue de la Révolution*, documents section 14–16 (1889), 20–26. See also AD Dordogne O E DEP 5004, letter of Fournier de la Charmie to municipal officers of Périgueux, August 9, 1789; BM Versailles Ms. F 823, fol. 91v°; Queruau-Lamerie, "Lettres de ... Maupetit," 19, 218–219.
96 See, for example, AN C 30, dossier 251, documents 1, 2, 9, 10, 11, 12, 15, 19; see also AM Bayonne AA 51, no. 23, letter of August 5, 1789.
97 See, for example, AM Lorient BB 12, no. 47, letter of August 5, 1789; AM Brest LL 46, no. 36, letter of August 5, 1789 for Breton reactions; BM La Rochelle Ms. 21, entry of August 4, 1789 and AN AB^XIX 3562, dossier 1, letter 2, for the reactions of conservative nobles.

Henceforth, state and society would be one in the nation, which was itself a fraternal community of citizens; the individual's relationship with the state would no longer be mediated by privilege and corporate bodies. The Assembly subsequently proceeded to reorganize the kingdom in accordance with this vision. No longer confining itself, as it had on July 27, to the standard of prescriptive tradition, the National Assembly now set out to remake the nation totally in a more equitable manner.

Not only did the night of August 4 immeasurably expand the magnitude of the Assembly's task, it also served to infuse the Assembly with a powerful sense of identity, vision and purpose. Up until this time, the Assembly had attempted to strike a delicate balance between tradition and reform in its proceedings. Although it was a functioning institution, its uncertain origins had given its deliberations a timidity and tenuousness that had done little to satisfy hopes for the regeneration of France. In the rarefied atmosphere at the conclusion of that meeting, however, the renunciations made that evening seemed to represent fulfillment of the regeneration that was so desired but which had proven to be so elusive. Its realization gave the National Assembly a sense of cohesion and confidence that enabled it to assume an identity of its own. The galvanizing effect of August 4 can be seen particularly in the person of the marquis de Ferrières, a conservative noble deputy representing Saumur, who had been one of the recalcitrant deputies whom Louis had had to ask to join the National Assembly on June 27. On August 7, as the Assembly sought to transform its pledges into a formal decree, he wrote to a constituent about the significance of the meeting. He stated that it had produced something that twelve centuries of the same religion, the same language and the habits of common manners had not been able to achieve – the reconciliation of interests and the unity of France toward a single objective, the common good of all. Then, without mentioning the pact of association or the National Assembly explicitly, but unmistakably referring to them, he told his correspondent of the session " fashioning, so to speak, a solemn new covenant, and, from this very moment, acquiring an irresistible strength, and a might that will necessarily prevail over other forces."[98]

---

98 On de Ferrières' original recalcitrance, see AN AD[XVIIIc] 135, *Compte rendu par M. le marquis de Ferrières à Messieurs les gentilhommes de la sénéchausée de Saumur*, p. 72. On the letter of August 7, see marquis Charles Elie de Ferrières, *Correspondance inédite (1789, 1790, 1791)*, Henri Carré, ed., (Paris, 1932), p. 115. He went on to warn his correspondent that it would be useless and dangerous to oppose the will of the nation and asked the nobility not to censure publicly the Assembly's decree. De Ferrières, *Correspondance inédite*, pp. 116–117. His entire letter is indispensable for a full understanding of the impact of August 4. See also AN AB[XIX] 3562, dossier 1, document 2, for the reaction of another conservative noble deputy.

This same sense of mission is also evident in a letter of another deputy, Ménard de la Groye. On August 21 he wrote to his wife:

It is ... a great and arduous undertaking, that of reforming the outdated laws of a great empire, and of changing almost entirely its constitution. It is necessary to battle with a multitude of particular interests, and to compel to give in to reason prejudices sanctified by the course of centuries and which have acquired the most imposing authority ... Doubtless bitter plaints will be raised against us, and our operations will be harshly criticized, but we would scarcely be worthy of the august duties that we have to fulfill if this consideration was capable of weakening our fortitude and of lessening our efforts. The sublime quality of legislators, which is entrusted to us, ought to make us cast our glance toward a distant future; and we ought to make ready for future races the happiness which it will perhaps not be possible for us to allow the present generation to enjoy.[99]

The vision that opened before the National Assembly as a result of August 4 was one of a society virtually without conflict. Its abolition of the institutions of privileged corporatism was directed toward this end, as were those it created in their place. Members of the Assembly envisioned a society in which particular interests, aspirations and beliefs would operate in almost total harmony under the benevolent auspices of the nation, which itself would be dedicated to the greater good of all.[100] It was a unitary vision of France – not unitary in the old absolutist sense of *un roi, une loi, une foi*, a unity that the members of the Assembly knew perhaps better than anyone had been illusory – but unitary in a more fundamental and fraternal sense in which all would work together in a spirit of concord and goodwill for the common good out of love of the nation. It was a tangible and compelling vision, as the letters of de Ferrières and Ménard de la Groye attest, and although the effort to

---

99 Ménard de la Groye, *Correspondance*, pp. 88–89. The same characteristics appear in the letters of the deputy Gaultier de Biauzat. In a letter to his constituents on August 8, he wrote that the Assembly had on August 4 "roughed out ... the foundations for the public happiness". Later, in warning against impatience, he told them "Keep in mind that we are performing a task made difficult by more than eight hundred years of injustice or folly". Mège, *Gaultier de Biauzat*, II: 233–235. I particularly disagree here with the comment of Furet, *Interpreting the French Revolution*, pp. 94–95, that the night of August 4 was not "a battle-front rallying all classes of society to the common interest, but the means to gloss over a disagreement or at least a radical misunderstanding." If that were the case, it is difficult to understand how the National Assembly could have reshaped the polity to the extent that it did. It would seem, however, that he has since amended this position, for in a more recent treatment he termed it "an extraordinarily modern event ... that revealed a deep emotional investment in the belief that an Assembly could, through its political will, change the course of a nation's history." See François Furet, "Night of August 4," *A Critical Dictionary of the French Revolution*, ed. Furet and Ozouf, pp. 107–114, with the quotation from p. 109.

100 Indeed, as Patrice Higonnet has argued, one cannot understand the zeal of the Revolutionaries if the genuineness of their convictions is brought into question. Higonnet, *Class, Ideology and the Rights of Nobles*, p. 33.

achieve it was not altogether harmonious, the sense of identity, purpose and vision that emerged from the night of August 4 was nevertheless so strong that in its aftermath a body of men that had been able to agree on little for the previous three months proceeded in the following twenty-four to reorganize the French nation in its entirety.

In doing so, it codified a new language of politics and a new political imagery based on the new ideology of the nation for, with the traditional political structure of the kingdom swept away, the existing political lexicon, which had acquired its meaning and connotation within that structure, was now also outmoded. Keith Baker has recently traced three currents out of which political culture emerged in late eighteenth-century France – discourses of reason, justice and will. The discourse of reason represented the replacement of the disorder of "feudalism" with a rational social order based on, among other precepts, property, public welfare and the rights of man. The discourse of justice achieved realization in the elaboration of an ideal of government by the rule of law through a constitutionally defined system of representative government. The discourse of will manifested itself with the nation declaring itself "one and indivisible in the assertion of its inalienable sovereignty."[101] All three of these currents – which Baker notes competed with rather than complemented one another – were in evidence on the night of August 4, but the crystallization of them that occurred that evening was less a cognitive experience than an emotional one. Indeed, several deputies had written letters attempting to explain what had occurred that evening and seeking to describe the principles that would hereafter guide the Assembly, but the inadequacy of words to convey what had occurred was evident.[102]

The only terminology broad enough to encompass all three discourses and to fill the lacuna was that of the Enlightenment and, with deputies aware of the need for a new ascription for the enterprise that the Assembly was to undertake,[103] Enlightenment phraseology became the underpinning for the new political language of the Revolution.[104] In a

101 Baker, "On the Problem of the Ideological Origins of the French Revolution," *Inventing the French Revolution*, pp. 24–27.
102 Once again, see Mège, *Gaultier de Biauzat*, I: 224. See also AM Bergerac, fonds Faugère, carton I, no. 11, letter of August 7, 1789; AM Bordeaux D 220, no. 13, letter of Lafargue to electors of Bordeaux, August 5, 1789, and AD Orne C 1227, document 183, in which the deputy Guillaume-Gabriel Leclerc wrote in terms of happiness and joy, but could give little import beyond specific renunciations.
103 See, for example, the letter of Gaultier de Biauzat in Mège, *Gaultier de Biauzat*, II: 268.
104 Both Lynn Hunt and Keith Baker have emphasized the importance of new language and imagery in the Revolution. See Lynn Hunt, *Politics, Culture and Class in the French Revolution* (Berkeley, 1984), especially pp. 19–119, much of which extends chronologically

new context, albeit one broadly linked to Enlightenment and Physiocratic traditions of reform that were hostile to privilege, irrationality and inequity, the Assembly appropriated Enlightenment rhetoric to legitimate its vision as it remade the polity.[105]

A final consequence of the night of August 4 was to increase enormously the importance of the constitution. To be sure, the constitution had been the reason that the National Assembly had come into existence in the first place, but the night of August 4 enhanced its significance as the logical vehicle to realize the new ethos of the nation. There was little expectation that the promulgation of the constitution was imminent, as had been the case in late July; the deputies now knew that the task before them would be of much longer duration. For many members of the Assembly the night of August 4 symbolized the cutting of the Gordian knot blocking reform and regeneration, allowing the National Assembly to undertake the task for which, as the Estates-General, it had originally been convened.[106] The constitution became the central element of the new political framework and the focal point of the effort by the National Assembly to remake the French nation altogether in a more equitable manner,[107] an effort that it now began in earnest.

beyond the period under discussion here; and Baker, *Inventing the French Revolution*, pp. 18–20, 272–274. As Baker noted in another essay, the common "ideological arsenal" of all groups had been history, but history, in the form of prescriptive tradition, had been obliterated. See Baker, "Controlling French history: the ideological arsenal of Jacob-Nicolas Moreau," *Inventing the French Revolution*, pp. 59–85. Even new pejorative political language emanated from the Revolution as well. See Patrice Higonnet, "Aristocrate," "Aristocratie": language and politics in the French Revolution," *The French Revolution 1789–1989: Two Hundred Years of Rethinking*, ed. Sandy Petrey, (Lubbock, 1989), pp. 47–66.

105 To some extent, this harmonizes with the argument of Taylor, "Revolutionary and nonrevolutionary content in the *cahiers* of 1789," 500–501, but I believe greater allowance needs to be made beyond the *cahiers* for continuity between the Old Regime and the Revolution. On such continuity see, for example, Baker, *Inventing the French Revolution*; Dale Van Kley, "The Jansenist constitutional legacy in the French Prerevolution 1750–1789," *Historical Reflections/Réflexions Historiques*, 13 (1986), 393–453; Dale Van Kley, "New wine in old wineskins," *French Historical Studies*, 17 (1991), 447–465, and the useful essay by Thomas E. Kaiser, "Strange offspring of philosophie: recent historiographical problems in relating the French Enlightenment to the French Revolution," *French Historical Studies*, 15 (1988), 549–562.

106 See AM Lorient BB 12, no. 47, letter of August 5, 1789; BN Mss. Nouv. acq. fr. 12938, fols. 107v°–108; AM Bergerac, fonds Faugère, carton I, no. 11, letter of August 7, 1789; Rabaut de Saint-Etienne, *Précis de l'histoire de la Révolution française*, p. 202; Bailly, *Mémoires d'un témoin de la Révolution*, II: 215–218; Pilastre de la Brardière and Leclerc, *Correspondance*, II: 85–88; Pierre L. Roederer, *L'Esprit de la Révolution de 1789* (Paris, 1831), pp. 80–81; Dumont, *Souvenirs sur Mirabeau*, p. 100; Queruau-Lamerie, "Lettres de ... Maupetit," 19, 227–228.

107 See Dubois de Crancé, *Lettre de M. Dubois de Crancé*, p. 9, which traces all of the subsequent actions of the Assembly to the night of August 4. Similarly, Choiseul d'Aillecourt, who heartily disapproved of August 4, began his discussion of the constitution

Initially, the effort went very well, with deputies feeling that the spirit of unity and harmony achieved on August 4 still animated the discussion, even during the most difficult portion, dealing with the tithe.[108] In addition, several deputies and deputations began to contact the inhabitants of their locales to explain and to help realize the new vision, an endeavor that will be more closely examined later.

The Assembly completed the drafting of the decrees on August 11 and, in a reflection of the collective sense of pride and accomplishment that inspired the deputies, the Assembly as a whole presented them to Louis at noon, on August 13, Indeed, it was an indication of the new ideal envisioned by the Assembly – entailing the end of the corporate paradigm – that the deputies met with the king without following any distinctions of rank or birth.[109] The Assembly presented the decrees to Louis, who explicitly accepted the title "Restorer of French Liberties," and there was widespread expectation that they would quickly be promulgated.[110] The sense of confidence and hope that characterized the Assembly in the aftermath of August 4 is evident in a letter written by the deputy Charles-François Bouche to his constituents on August 17. Alluding to the violence of the Great Fear, he compared the situation of the Assembly to a climber resting high on a mountain with a calm breeze around him as he gazes at a clear and calm sky. Beneath him, however, he can hear wind engulfing and roaring through valleys and caverns.[111] The assuredness and equanimity of the metaphorical climber despite the chaos around him captured the mood of the Assembly in August, 1789. Many deputies believed that dissemination of the decrees would enable

with it. AN AD[XVIIIc] 136, *Compte rendu par M. Choiseul d'Aillecourt, député de la noblesse du bailliage de Clermont-en-Bassigny, à ses commetans,* pp. 237–240. See also Thibaudeau, *Mémoires 1765–1792,* pp. 96–97; AN BB[30] 21, dossier 4, state of constitutional decrees, May 26, 1790, in which the first item listed is the August decrees.

108 AM Bayonne AA 51, no. 24, letters of August 11 and 12, 1789; AD Bouches-du-Rhône C 1046, letter of Bouche of August 5, 1789, letter of Bouche of August 10, 1789; AM Lorient BB 13, no. 50, letter of August 12, 1789; BN Mss. Nouv. acq. fr. 12938, fol. 108v°; AN M 788, dossier 2[17], document 8.

109 See AM Bergerac, fonds Faugère, carton I, no. 14, letter of August 14, 1789; *Le Point du Jour,* August 16, 1789; *Journal de Versailles,* August 18, 1789; [Kerverseau and Clavelin], *Histoire de la révolution de 1789* (new edition), II: 286. See also Louis Henry Charles, comte de Gauville, *Journal du baron de Gauville, député de l'ordre de la noblesse aux Etats-Généraux depuis le 4 mars 1789 jusqu'au 1er juillet 1790* (Paris, 1864), p. 19. For more on the abolition of the distinction of orders after August 4, see AD Bouches-du-Rhône C 1046, letter of Bouche of August 15, 1789; AM Le Havre D[3] 38, no. 46, letter of September 10, 1789; BM Versailles Ms. F 823, fol. 147.

110 See AN K 679[2], no. 238; BN Mss. Nouv. acq. fr. 12938, fol. 118v°; AD Gironde 3 L 82, letter of August 7, 1789. For a draft of Louis's response to the deputies, see Harvard University, Houghton Library b MS 167 (35).

111 AD Bouches-du-Rhône C 1046, letter of Bouche of August 17, 1789. See also Ménard de la Groye, *Correspondance,* p. 93, for another indication of the attitude of deputies at this time.

harmony and concord to succeed the unrest then convulsing France, ensuring a happy future.[112]

Also on August 17 the bold new direction of the National Assembly became evident in a report on the judiciary offered by Nicolas Bergasse for the Committee of the Constitution. Whereas the report of July 27 had envisaged the possibility of submitting laws to sovereign courts for registration, the report of August 17 implicitly endorsed the abolition of the *parlements*. Furthermore, conforming with renunciations made on August 4, the report proposed termination of venality and proprietary rights in the judiciary. Noting that the influence of judicial power was constant and that it affected the lives of citizens the most, and stating that judicial power would be badly organized if it depended on a will other than that of the nation, the committee recommended election of judges and the use of juries in criminal cases. As envisioned by the committee, justice would henceforth be an obligation of society dispensed freely by the nation through elected judicial officers. Bergasse acknowledged that the report endorsed a system that was unprecedented, but it was, in fact, an outline that revealed the new direction in which the Assembly would take the polity – repudiating privileged corporatism as a superintending principle of society and replacing it with the new organizing principle of the sovereignty of the nation.[113] The report imparted to the Assembly a strong sense of the grandeur of the task before it and left many feeling optimistic about its prospects.[114]

At the time that Bergasse presented the report on the judiciary, the National Assembly was debating the Declaration of the Rights of Man. Many deputies, especially Mirabeau, wished to defer action on the Declaration and to move ahead directly with the constitution, believing that time spent on the Declaration would detract from the larger task of the constitution itself, the urgency of which was increasingly felt because popular unrest had not yet subsided.[115] The Assembly, however, defeated

112 AM Angoulême AA 19, no. 1, letter of August 14, 1789; AM Le Havre D³ 38, no. 31, letter of August 5, 1789; AD Loire-Atlantique C 626 (2), no. 151; AM Arles AA 23, fol. 547.

113 The substitution of "organizing" for "superintending" is deliberate, for the fusion of state and society redefined the relationship between them. The new concept of the nation was best captured by the deputy Gaultier de Biauzat, who described the basis of the constitution to his constituents in the following manner: "All the French are joining together to form a single national body, a single sovereign authority, of which our king believes himself the leader, whereas his predecessors believed themselves the masters." Mège, *Gaultier de Biauzat*, II: 241.

114 AM Lorient BB 13, no. 52, letter of August 20, 1789; BN Mss. Nouv. acq. fr. 4121, fol. 121; BN Mss. Fonds Français 10883, fols. 102vº–103; AN M 788, dossier 2¹⁷, document 109.

115 BN Mss. Fonds Français 10883, fols. 104vº–105; BN Mss. Nouv. acq. fr. 12938, fol. 122; AM Angoulême AA 19, no. 2, letter of August 22, 1789, no. 3, letter of August 26,

Mirabeau's proposal and continued working on the Declaration of Rights, which was of great importance in the mind of many deputies. Indeed, like the constitution which it was to precede, the Declaration of Rights had also had its importance significantly enhanced by the night of August 4. That night had destroyed the Old Regime, but there was as yet nothing to fill the void that had been created. In both its maxims and language, the Declaration now served to occupy that vacuum – as Aulard noted, it was "to settle the principles from which the Constitution should issue" and "to consecrate, to ratify the Revolution."[116] Furthermore, the vocabulary of the Declaration provided the language of the Revolution. It is little wonder, then, that despite the amount of time taken to complete the Declaration, about which they were occasionally defensive, deputies continued to defend its value.[117]

The Assembly completed the Declaration of Rights on August 26 and immediately returned to consideration of the constitution. On August 27 there were renewed calls for the Committee of the Constitution to present an account of its work immediately.[118] As a result, the next day, Mounier, in the name of the Committee of the Constitution, proposed to decree preliminarily six fundamental articles of the constitution. Many deputies believed, however, that one of the articles put forward by the committee prejudged the issue of the royal veto in according to the nation alone the right to make the law.[119]

As a result of this disagreement, on August 29 the Assembly discussed at length a motion by the vicomte de Noailles, who believed it necessary to clarify the matter of the royal veto. He proposed that the Assembly decide, above all, the nature of the royal veto and whether the legislature would be divided into two chambers or remain in a single chamber. After a sharp debate, the Assembly decided to defer reorganization of the judiciary and give immediate priority instead to these two questions.[120] Consequently, on August 31, Lally-Tollendal, speaking for the Com-

1789; AM Le Havre D³ 38, no. 37, letter of August 12, 1789; AD Ain 1 Mi 1, letter of August 22, 1789.
116 François Victor Alphonse Aulard, *The French Revolution: A Political History 1789–1804*, reprint edition, 4 vols. (New York, 1965), I: 146. See also Marcel Gauchet, *La Révolution des droits de l'homme* (Paris, 1989).
117 AD Pyrénées-Atlantiques C 1377, letter of August 28, 1789; AN W 12, no. 34, letter of Barnave of August 27, 1789; BN Mss. Nouv. acq. fr. 12938, fol. 125v°; AD Côtes-d'Armor 1 L 389, letter of Champeaux de Palasne and Poulain de Corbion, August 29, 1789.                    118 BN Mss. Nouv. acq. fr. 12938, fol. 132v°.
119 *Ibid.*, fols. 134v°–135.
120 On this important turn of events, which is treated in barest form in official records, see AN C 30, dossier 249, document 18; AN KK 642, entry of August 28, 1789; BN Fonds Français 10883, fols. 119–121; BN Mss. Nouv. acq. fr. 4121, fols. 133–134; BN Mss. Nouv. acq. fr. 12938, fols. 136v°–137; BM La Rochelle Ms. 21, entry of August 29, 1789;

mittee of the Constitution, recommended an absolute veto for the monarch and a bicameral legislature, and the important debate that followed on these issues produced an erosion of the consensus formed on August 4.[121]

The split that developed in the Assembly was reflected in the Committee of the Constitution, which itself was divided on the project.[122] Some members of the committee, especially Mounier and the monarchical element, still adhered largely to a pre-August 4 idea of the Revolution and had misgivings about the direction in which it was moving.[123] For them, the Revolution entailed reform of the existing order rather than a complete restructuring of the polity. At issue was whether sovereignty would be exercised chiefly by the nation, which was understood to mean the National Assembly, or by the monarch, and the debate on the veto and the structure of the legislature crystallized these differences. Indeed, one scholar has recently argued that this debate, by forcing the Assembly to define the nature of the constitution, led to the articulation of the implications of the principle of national sovereignty, thereby transforming "understanding of the nature of the relationship between French society and its form of government."[124]

Many deputies viewed an upper house as a reversion to the society of orders – obviated by the night of August 4 – and as a potential impediment to reform. Furthermore, if the king gained an absolute power to veto acts of the Assembly, many members believed it would enable him to delay or even to prevent regeneration of the nation.[125] The discussion was both heated and prolonged, and deputies were distressed

BM Versailles Ms. F. 823, fols. 128–128vᵒ; AD Ain 1 Mi 1, letters of August 28, and August 30, 1789; AM Brest LL 46, no. 48, letter of August 30, 1789; Pilastre de la Brardière and Leclerc, *Correspondance*, II: 283–288.

121 AM Bergerac, fonds Faugère, carton I, no 19, letter of September 1, 1789.

122 BN Mss. Nouv. acq. fr. 12938, fol. 139.

123 As early as August 12 one deputy had noted that the Committee of the Constitution had strayed from its aim and that members were permitting themselves to present their individual work as the opinion of the committee. See Duquesnoy, *Journal*, I: 286. This grievance seems to have become particularly acute in September. See the comments of Mirabeau in *Courier de Provence*, September 28, 29, 30, 1789. On Mounier's alienation from the night of August 4, see BM Grenoble Ms. R 6314 (14), III, fols. 57–59. For more on divisions within the committee and on the monarchical element in the National Assembly, see Jean Egret, *La Révolution des Notables: Mounier et les Monarchiens 1789* (Paris, 1950), and Robert Griffiths, *Le Centre perdu: Malouet et les « monarchiens » dans la Révolution française* (Grenoble, 1988), especially pp. 62–63. For a consideration of those opposed to the ideas and course that the National Assembly was taking, see Sullivan, "Defenders of Privilege."

124 Baker, "Fixing the French Constitution," *Inventing the French Revolution*, pp. 271–272. The entire essay is pp. 252–305.

125 AN W 13, no. 247, no. 248; AN ABˣᴵˣ 3562, dossier 1, letter 3; AM Le Havre D³ 38, no. 46, letter of September 10, 1789; BN Mss. Nouv. acq. fr. 12938, fol. 141vᵒ.

at the unravelling of the consensus of August 4 brought about by the debate, with several believing that many within the clergy and the nobility were seeking to reclaim their former privileges.[126] Mounier attempted to allay the concerns that were raised, but with little success.[127] On September 10, the Assembly decisively rejected the concept of an upper house and voted to form a unicameral legislature. The next day it vested the king with a suspensive rather than an absolute veto.[128]

Rejection of the committee's proposals by the Assembly was a clear sign that it accorded supreme importance to implementation of the ideals of August 4 and to the new ethos of the nation that it had produced. Several deputies had seen in the absolute veto and bicameral legislature a threat to the new ideal of the polity formed and the sacrifices made on that historic night; some believed that Louis would use an absolute veto to veto them.[129] Defeat of the absolute veto clearly strengthened the pact of association made on the night of August 4, in which the Assembly had explicitly stipulated that it would resist any effort by the monarch to reimpose privilege. Indeed, the two votes, both of which passed by substantial margins, served to reaffirm the sense of identity, vision and purpose that had infused the Assembly on August 4 and indicated its steadfastness in asserting its new ideal.[130]

The failure of their program led the monarchical element of the committee – Mounier, Bergasse, and Lally-Tollendal – to resign on September 12, and the other members, on learning of their action, resigned as well,[131] requiring formation of a new committee on September 15. Four original members – Sieyès, Talleyrand, Lally-Tollendal and Le Chapelier – were reelected, and were joined by Jacques-Guillaume Thouret, Jean-Paul Rabaut de Saint-Etienne, Jean-Nicolas

126 See AD Nièvre 1 L 165, letter of August 31, 1789; AD Bouches-du-Rhône C 1046, letter of September 2, 1789; Ménard de la Groye, *Correspondance*, p. 102; AD Puy-de-Dôme F. 141, no. 1, letter of Gaultier de Biauzat, September 3, 1789; AD Ain 1 Mi 1, letter of September 20, 1789; AM Strasbourg AA 2004, fol. 7; Font-Réaulx, "Lettres de ... Colaud de la Salcette," 151–152.
127 BN Mss. Nouv. acq. fr. 4121, fols 142–143; BN Mss. Nouv. acq. fr. 12938, fols. 141–142v°; AM Brest LL 44, fol. 69v°.
128 AN C 31, dossier 254, documents 22, 24; *Procès-verbal de l'Assemblée nationale*, No. 71 (September 10, 1789), pp. 3–4; *Procès-verbal de l'Assemblée nationale*, No. 72 (September 11, 1789), pp. 3–6.
129 AM Arles AA 23, fol. 558; BM Lyon Ms. 5430, no. 13; AD Seine-Maritime LP 8454, letter of September 19, 1789; AD Nord L 10. 316, extract from letter written to Bertrant by Merlin, September 22, 1789; [Jacques-Samuel Dinochau], *Histoire philosophique et politique de l'Assemblée nationale, par un député des communes de B***.* 2 vols. (Paris, 1789), II: 58.
130 See AD Ain 1 Mi 1, letter of September 15, 1789, in which the deputy Garron de la Bévière advised his wife to give up all hope of returning to the old order, which, he said, was impossible.
131 BN Mss. Fonds Français 10883, fol. 141; BN Mss. Fonds Français 13713, fol. 290.

Démeunier and Guy-Jean-Baptiste Target.[132] These choices again emphasized the preeminence that the National Assembly attached to the ideals of August 4, for nearly all, especially Rabaut de Saint-Etienne and Thouret among the new members, had distinguished themselves in the constitutional debates of August and early September.[133]

Furthermore, in the wake of the votes on the legislature and the veto, the Assembly renewed its commitment to the pact of association by seeking to impel Louis to approve and promulgate the decrees of August 4–11, which he had not yet done. Beginning on the evening of September 12, the Assembly discussed having the decrees of August 4 carried to Louis in order to be promulgated in the provinces.[134] On September 14, on the eve of the formation of the new Committee of the Constitution, Barnave proposed that the Assembly suspend discussion on the length of the suspensive veto until Louis ordered the promulgation of the decrees of August 4. His motion was put aside, but in the evening session there was further discussion of the manner in which the decrees should be presented to the king; the Assembly decided to charge its president to present himself to Louis in order to ask him to sanction the decrees.[135]

Louis, however, equivocated and on September 18 sent the Assembly some personal observations rather than a promulgation or a sanction. The response clearly annoyed many deputies, who found it totally inadequate, especially since many believed that Louis had tacitly approved the decrees when he had accepted the title "Restorer of French Liberties" when the decrees were presented to him on August 13.[136] The

132 AN C 31, dossier 254, document 32.
133 On Rabaut de Saint-Etienne and Thouret, see BN Mss. Fonds Français 13713, fols. 255–255v°. Those reelected had stood apart from the monarchist element and their reelection amounted to a vote of confidence. Indeed, although a rupture clearly occurred, one should not allow a focus on Mounier and the monarchical element to exaggerate its extent. Other conservative deputies who were not in accord with the new ideal of the nation nonetheless conceded the good intentions of the deputies. See marquis de Laqueville, *Lettre écrite à mes commettans* (N.p., n.d.) [BN Lb[39] 2897], pp. 4–5.
134 AM Lorient BB 13, no. 2, letter of September 13, 1789; AM Le Havre D[3] 38, no. 48, letter of September 13, 1789; AM Strasbourg AA 2004, fol. 7; BN Mss. Nouv. acq. fr. 4121, fol. 15.
135 AN KK 642, entry of September 14, 1789; AM Brest LL 44, entry of September 14, 1789; AM Angoulême AA 19, no. 8, letter of September 14, 1789; BN Mss. Nouv. acq. fr. 12938, fol. 157; BM Versailles Ms. F. 823, fol. 143; AM Bergerac, fonds Faugère, carton I, no. 26, letter of September 14, 1789.
136 On the reaction of deputies, see AD Seine-Maritime LP 8454, letter of September 19, 1789; AD Loire-Atlantique C 626 (2), no. 157; AM Angoulême AA 19, no. 9, letter of September 17, 1789; BN Mss. Nouv. acq. fr. 4121, fols. 158–160; BN Mss. Nouv. acq. fr. 12938, fols. 161v°–163; AM Bergerac, fonds Faugère, carton I, no. 26, letter of September 18, 1789; AD Pyrénées-Atlantiques C 1377, letter of September 21, 1789. On the belief that Louis had tacitly accepted the decrees, see, for example, AM Bayonne AA 51, no. 29, letter of September 18, 1789; Antoine C. Thibaudeau, *Correspondance inédite du constituant Thibaudeau*, ed. Henri Carré and P. Boissonnade, (Paris, 1898), p. 15; BN Mss. Fonds

president of the Assembly was once again charged to return to Louis and to tell him that his views would be considered in the drafting of laws, but that all that was called for now was to sign and promulgate the decrees because they were constitutional. The National Assembly also delayed setting the length of the suspensive veto until the decrees were approved.[137]

On September 21, Louis notified the Assembly that he would agree not to the promulgation but to the publication of the decrees. Although even a conservative noble deputy characterized this response as "a little Jesuitical," the Assembly, very much wanting to believe in the king and desiring to work with him, seized on a rather diffident expression of goodwill by Louis and pronounced itself satisfied with this response. It then immediately set the term of the suspensive veto.[138]

Almost seven weeks after the National Assembly had conceived its new ideal of the polity, it had, with difficulty, obtained the adhesion of the monarch to that vision. Several deputies believed that the effort expended to gain the acquiescence of Louis had consumed time that could otherwise have been spent drafting the constitution in order to realize the new ideal, so the Assembly felt a sense of urgency to begin the task.

The central tenets that the National Assembly would subsequently follow had an internal logic that had arisen only in the course of events in the Estates-General/National Assembly itself. The proceedings continued to reshape the outlook and goals of deputies, and culminated on the night of August 4, when the Assembly achieved its own new concept of the polity. Jettisoning the precepts of society as expressed in the *cahiers*, to which it had adhered until this time, the National Assembly now began to enact its new ideal of the polity, an ideal completely unrelated to the events preceding the opening of the Estates-General. The evolution of this distinct dynamic is evident in the comments of the deputy François-Joseph Bouchette, from Bergue, in the autumn of 1789:

When we left our homes there was not one of us who did not believe he was going to work principally for the particular interests of his compatriots; but since the time of the formation of the National Assembly, June 17, the sphere of our

Français 10883, fol. 143; Ménard de la Groye, *Correspondance*, pp. 86–87. See also Harvard University, Houghton Library Fr 1380.20\*, fol. 387.

137  AM Le Havre D³ 38, no. 49, letter of September 18, 1789, no. 50, letter of September 20, 1789; AM Lorient BB 13, no. 4, letter of September 18, 1789.

138  For the characterization of Louis's response, see BM La Rochelle Ms. 21, fol. 90vº; see also AM Arles AA 23, fols. 567–568; AD Gironde 3 L 82, letter of September 22, 1789; AM Bergerac, fonds Faugère, carton I, no. 27, letter of September 21, 1789; AD Pyrénées-Atlantiques C 1377, letter of September 21, 1789; BN Mss. Nouv. acq. fr. 4121, fols. 163–164; BN Mss. Nouv. acq. fr. 12938, fols. 166–166vº; Harvard University, Houghton Library Fr 1380.20\*, fols. 390–391. On the distress that these events caused some deputies, see Font-Réaulx, "Lettres de ... Colaud de la Salcette," p. 157.

operations was substantially enlarged, since all particular interests were set aside, especially after the famous night of 4–5 August, during which all privileges, preeminence and particular rights were given up. Since then each [of us] has contented himself only with the propitious point where fate and nature have placed it and undoubtedly the town of Bergue will have nothing to be sorry for, but it is necessary, like everyone, to have a little patience yet. Nothing can be forced.[139]

Similarly, the deputy Pierre-Louis Roederer wrote many years later that the Constitution of 1791 had been drafted in an effort to realize the principles of August 4.[140]

Indeed, when he had yielded the presidency of the National Assembly on August 17, Le Chapelier, who had presided over the meeting of August 4, spoke of the meeting, in what was unquestionably an allusion to the pact of association forged that evening, as a "family compact."[141] There can be little doubt that the majority of deputies regarded it in such terms as they reshaped the nation in the following two years.

139 Looten, "Lettres de ... Bouchette," p. 292. For a similar, but less explicit example, see AM Strasbourg AA 2003, fol. 5, fol. 122; AM Strasbourg AA 2004, fol. 70. See also AN M 788, dossier $2^{17}$, document 109.
140 Roederer, *L'Esprit de la révolution de 1789*, p. 189.
141 See *Le Point du Jour*, August 18, 1789; AN KK 642, entry of August 17, 1789; *Etats-Généraux. Journal de la Correspondance de Nantes*, I: 309–310.

# 3    The achievement of the new ideal of the polity

> No blot of personal interest has yet sullied the decrees of the Constituent
> Assembly; even our enemies grant us this fairness.
>
> Duport to the National Assembly, March 29, 1790

The pact of association forged on the night of August 4, with its repudiaton of privilege, created a vacuum in the governance of the kingdom. As a result, the task before the National Assembly was a comprehensive one encompassing all of society, and any attempt to analyze it risks presenting an incomplete or fragmentary picture of the effort to attain it.[1] At the same time, however, although its members wrestled with a myriad of issues such as the debt, the powers of the monarch, the composition of future legislatures, taxation, the restructuring of the military and the Church and other matters, there were two undertakings that the National Assembly regarded as of fundamental importance in establishing its new ideal of the polity – the reorganization of administration and of the judiciary. These two spheres were the areas in which the privileged corporate paradigm had been most evident – and a point of tension – under the Old Regime.[2] Although other matters were of great significance, the deputies regarded these issues as critical not only for realizing the goals of the Assembly for the nation, but also for ensuring the continuation of its ideals into the future after it had disbanded. The reorganization of the administration offered the National Assembly the opportunity to institutionalize the new ethos for governance of the nation – the ideal of a fraternal community of citizens working together for the common good – into the indefinite future. The reform of the judiciary was likewise of fundamental concern, for law was central to the new ideal of the polity advanced by the National Assembly. Laws common to all were to be the source of equity and justice in the nation as well as the unifying bond among citizens, so that law became paramount

---

1 Frédéric Braesch, *1789, L'Année cruciale* (Paris, 1941) offers, however, a useful overview.
2 See Keith Michael Baker, "Representation," *The Political Culture of the Old Regime*, ed. Baker, pp. 469–492; Bossenga, *The Politics of Privilege*, pp. 35–46.

in the new regime's definition of itself. As a result, these two fields – administration and justice – became the foundation of the effort by the National Assembly to refashion the polity.[3]

For several months, however, the Crown and its agents sought to impede and to discredit the National Assembly as it attempted to enact its new ideal for the nation. This obstruction of the efforts of the National Assembly continued until February, 1790, when Louis made an unscheduled visit to the Assembly. Louis's visit made an enormously favorable impression and produced such a sense of common purpose that, thereafter, the Assembly was able to proceed with its program without significant difficulty, much to the dismay of its opponents in the nation. The sense of common purpose that emerged from Louis's visit to the Assembly culminated in the *Fête de la Fédération* in July, 1790, and continued until the time of Louis's flight from Paris in June, 1791.

In late September, 1789, having spent several weeks defining the authority of the monarch and gaining what it believed was his assent to the August decrees, the Assembly now moved to realize the new ideal that it had conceived on August 4. The day after Louis agreed to the publication of the decrees – thereby leading to the settlement of the question of his powers – Rabaut de Saint-Etienne, one of the newly-elected members of the Committee of the Constitution, spoke of the need to establish new municipal and provincial administrations. He cited the irregular patchwork of municipal governments then in existence and warned the Assembly that its efforts to produce a constitution would be futile if there were no well-established and uniform administrative base on which it could be built.[4]

Clearly, a new administrative structure offered several advantages. Most immediately, it would stabilize an irregular situation, particularly in the municipalities, where municipal revolutions had produced a conglomeration of governing bodies, nearly all of which professed loyalty to the National Assembly.[5] Furthermore, a new administration would also enable the National Assembly to abolish those bodies that might obstruct the implementation of its new vision of the polity – municipal oligarchies, provincial estates and the like.

Ultimately, however, the National Assembly intended that the new

3 See especially the ideograph by Sieyès in AN 284 AP 2, dossier 15, notebook 4, part 3, p. 32.
4 *Le Point du Jour*, September 23, 1789; BM La Rochelle, Ms. 21, fol. 92v°, *Etats-Généraux. Journal de la Correspondance de Nantes*, II: 122.
5 For an insight into the different municipal revolutions and structures in existence, see Daniel Ligou, "A propos de la révolution municipale," *Revue d'Histoire Économique et Sociale*, 38 (1960), 146–177; Lynn A. Hunt, *Revolution and Urban Politics in Provincial France: Troyes and Reims, 1786–1790* (Stanford, 1978).

administration be more than a tactical device to regularize the unsettled condition of localities or to overcome bodies that might be hostile to its new goals for France. The preeminent purpose of the new administration was to be a linchpin of the new ideal of the polity devised by the Assembly – to encompass the sovereign power of citizens in the nation and to realize the new ideals that underlay that sovereignty. Not only would all citizens of a given locality come together to deliberate on the greater interests of the nation, but in so doing would be bound together with citizens of all other areas of France through the medium of the nation. In contrast to the Old Regime, when provinces had had to compete with each other for the acquisition or maintenance of privileges through the sovereign Crown,[6] the new administrative structure would inaugurate the pact of association by emphasizing the fundamental unity of the nation. Indeed, the primacy given to making the new administration the vehicle for realizing the new ideal of the nation – as opposed simply to utilizing it as an opportunity to destroy rival bodies – can be seen in the expectation of the Assembly that members of existing administrations would carry out their duties until their replacements were created and would then graciously yield before the self-evident superiority of the new institutions.[7]

On September 29, then, Thouret, in the name of the "new" Committee of the Constitution, delivered a report outlining the committee's plan for a new administration.[8] Drafted primarily by Thouret and Sieyès, the report of the committee asserted that representation should be based as much as possible on territory, population and wealth. Since the constitution was seeking to establish an entirely new order, the committee did not want to adhere to the imperfections of the past. As a result, it proposed the creation of eighty departments, each of which would be 324 square leagues in size. Each department would be subdivided into nine communes of thirty-six square leagues, and each commune would be further subdivided into nine cantons of four square leagues. In addition, the committee sought to achieve a parity of population and wealth within this structure.[9] Although unrealistic, the

6 See, for example, AD Côte d'Or C 3367, fols. 150 v°, 156 v°.
7 See, for example, AD Orne C 1227, document 196, letter of Leclerc to deputies at Argentan, September 22, 1789, document 199, letter of Leclerc to deputies at Argentan, September 25, 1789; BN Mss. Nouv. acq. fr. 4121, fol. 295; Dardy, "Lettres de M. Grellet de Beauregard," 75–76.
8 *Procès-verbal de l'Assemblée nationale*, No. 87 (September 29, 1789), pp. 2–3; Jacques-Guillaume Thouret, *Rapport du nouveau comité de constitution, fait à l'Assemblée nationale le ... 29 septembre 1789, sur l'établissement des bases de la représentation proportionelle* (Paris, 1789). See also Ménard de la Groye, *Correspondance*, p. 111.
9 AM Le Havre, D³ 38, no. 58; AN 284 AP 2, dossier 15, notebook 4; AN 284 AP 3, dossier 2 (3); AN 284 AP 4, dossier 2, dossier 3.

determination to impose uniformity reflected the antipathy for the irrationality and inequity of privilege that had gripped the National Assembly on August 4 – just as it had earlier motivated Physiocratic reformers in the royal ministry since the mid-1770s. The committee offered a map reflecting the new division of the kingdom to deputies and stated that the maps would also be sent to the provinces.[10]

In the following week, however, the removal of the royal family from Versailles to Paris on October 5–6 not only altered the confidence and perceptions of some members of the National Assembly, but also delayed the opening of debate on the new administration. Although it secured the pure and simple assent of the king to the August decrees and the Declaration of Rights, and although the National Assembly subsequently followed the monarch to Paris, numerous deputies were shaken by the October Days, and some, including Mounier, who had been a member of the original Committee of the Constitution, left the Assembly to return to their native region. At the same time, however, many other deputies did not become disillusioned and remained committed to the new ideal of the polity developed by the National Assembly and continued to be inspired by a strong sense of purpose. In a letter to his wife on October 13, for example, the deputy Ménard de la Groye wrote:

The present revolution against which so many people struggled and hardened themselves with obstinacy will complete itself, and it will render France more successful and flourishing than ever. The current misfortunes were inevitable; it is necessary to endure them. It is also necessary to put up with the grumbling of all the malcontents, who are not lacking for numbers.

The uneasiness of the people will calm itself; they will recover in duty and subordination, and when a new order of things is perfectly established it is then that they will do justice to us and will praise the National Assembly. As for now, whatever the outcries of the ill-intentioned may be, it is necessary for us to act, and were we to perish in the midst of our noble endeavors, we must never abandon them.[11]

Indeed, shortly afterward, on October 15, the National Assembly once again avowed its unity of purpose with two actions. The vicomte de Beauharnais told the Assembly that allowing the election of replacement deputies by separate orders at the local level would be contrary to the principle of the joining together of the Assembly, and he therefore

10 See AN CP NN 50/6 and 50/7 for the early cartographic efforts of the committee. The comments on the former indicate that the committee realized this initial effort was too idealized. On the administrative reorganization, see Marie-Vic Ozouf-Marignier, *La Formation des départements: la représentation du territoire française à la fin du 18ᵉ siècle* (Paris, 1989); Ted W. Margadant, *Urban Rivalries in the French Revolution* (Princeton, 1992).     11 Ménard de la Groye, *Correspondance*, p. 124.

proposed that in the future no deputy nor alternate to the National Assembly be elected by separate orders. Another deputy, Louis-Simon Martineau, supported the motion and chided those members who had left the Assembly at the moment that their mission seemed perilous. He suggested a moratorium on the issuance of any further passports authorizing deputies to leave the Assembly temporarily. The Assembly received Martineau's idea favorably and, under a proposal put forward by Démeunier, sought to recall those deputies who had left. Seeking to reinforce the ideal of the unity of the nation, the National Assembly passed both motions and also went on to abolish all distinctions of costume and seating for deputies in the Assembly, even on ceremonial occasions.[12] These actions represented a reaffirmation by the deputies of the aspirations of the National Assembly. By summoning back members who had left, the Assembly indicated the primacy of its purpose over any personal or particular considerations. Furthermore, on its final day in Versailles, the National Assembly, by eradicating the last vestiges of orders, unmistakably asserted the unitary ideal of the nation and definitively destroyed the corporate, hierarchical society of orders with which Versailles was synonymous. Henceforth, the polity was to be comprised only of citizens equal before the law.[13] As one scholar has underscored, the program of the National Assembly from 1789 to 1791 was the result of a consensus, in which the nobility had a particularly strong role, and these decrees were an extraordinary avowal of that sense of common purpose.[14]

When the National Assembly reconvened in Paris four days later, there were, in fact, more members present than deputies had expected.[15] But while the National Assembly reaffirmed its unity of purpose, the

12 AN C 31, dossier 258, document 41; BN Mss. Nouv. acq. fr. 12938, fols. 203–203v°; AD Gironde 3 L 82, letter of October 20, 1789; AD Côtes-d'Armor 1 L 389, letter of Palasne de Champeaux and Poulain de Corbion, October 16, 1789. See also Pilastre de la Brardière and Leclerc, *Correspondance*, II: 585–586; *Le Point du Jour*, October 16, 1789. Louis-Henri-Charles, comte de Gauville, *Journal*, p. 31. For an indication of the link between these actions and the night of August 4, see AD Gironde 3 L 82, letter of November 3, 1789; for an insight into the way in which the measures galvanized and inspired the Assembly, see especially *Courier de Provence*, October 14–15, 1789; *Lettre d'un député de la sénéchaussée de Toulouse* (Paris, n.d.) [Newberry Library, FRC 4737]. For a commentary on the seating shortly before the abolition, see *Chronique de Paris*, October 5, 1789. For more on the sense of duty and purpose felt by members of the Assembly, even those of the Right, see Timothy Tackett, "Nobles and Third Estate in the revolutionary dynamic of the National Assembly," *The American Historical Review*, 94 (1989), 271–301, especially 290.
13 AM Bayonne AA 51, no. 37 (4), letter of October 31, 1789; AM Arles AA 23, fol. 613; BM Nantes Collection Dugast-Matifeux, t. 98, letter of November 2, 1789.
14 Alison Patrick, "The Second Estate in the Constituent Assembly, 1789–1791," *The Journal of Modern History*, 62 (1990), 223–252.
15 AM Angoulême AA 19, no. 18, letter of October 20, 1789.

events of October caused uneasiness throughout France and led to undertakings that the Assembly came to view as threatening to itself and especially to its new ideal of France. In Dauphiné, for example, the Intermediate Commission met in mid-October to seek the convocation of the provincial Estates in Romans on November 2 to advise its deputies on how to respond to the removal of the monarch to Paris and, because of an insufficient number of alternates, to elect additional deputies to represent the province in the National Assembly.[16] While the original purpose of the meeting may have been relatively benign, the threatened convocation soon became a vehicle for Mounier, along with several deputies from the clergy and the nobility, to express their personal opposition to the course of events in the National Assembly.[17] Those deputies from Dauphiné who remained in the Assembly were dismayed at the convocation of the Estates and responded with a public letter to the Intermediate Commission assuring it of the safety of the king and of the Assembly and warning that convening the Estates would result in a usurpation of powers that belonged to the National Assembly. They pointed out that the distinction of orders under which the Estates would meet had been abolished and was no longer recognized. They also argued that such gatherings could become a means for advancing particular interests against the general interest and could become a source of disunity, and they therefore asked the commission to revoke the convocation as soon as possible.[18] The National Assembly clearly had its own ideal that it intended to pursue, unfettered by any local or regional preferences, even from Dauphiné, the very symbol of the aspirations of the nation only a year earlier.

The decision to convene the Estates divided the province, and the town of Saint-Marcellin wrote to the Assembly to ask for advice in a letter that revealed the manner in which the Assembly had become the focal point of civic and political life in France. The town observed that the Estates sought to convene under the form they had followed the previous year – with double representation for the Third Estate. Noting that the form of 1788 had been "the most perfect" at that time, the town stated that it was now contrary to the abolition of orders decreed by the National Assembly. After an allusion to the night of August 4, the town

16 AD Isère C III 5*, fols. 390–393; AN Bª 75, liasse 175, dossier 1, document 29.
17 See *Chronique de Paris*, October 28, 1789; on Mounier, see Egret, *La Révolution des notables*, pp. 192–202; and William Doyle "La pensée politique de Mounier," *Terminer la Révolution : Mounier et Barnave dans la Révolution française*, ed. François Furet (Grenoble, 1990), pp. 25–41. For a subsequent indication of sentiment toward Mounier's struggle with the National Assembly, see *L'Observateur*, July 15, 1790.
18 AN C 95, dossier 109, document 92; see also AN W 12, no. 24; AN W 13, no. 227, no. 238.

of Saint-Marcellin sought the guidance of the Assembly, saying that it desired only the view and the orders of the National Assembly.[19] The reading of the letter prompted the deputy Adrien Duport to propose that all assemblies by order at any level be banned and that any meeting of provinces, except at the *bailliage* level to elect alternates to the National Assembly, also be forbidden. Jean-Denis Lanjuinais supported Duport's motion, pointing out that the nobility of Languedoc had gathered as an order to inveigh not only against the situation of the king, whom they wished to restore to "his legitimate authority," but also to oppose the abolition of the rights and franchises of the provinces and of the towns – a resolution that another member of the Assembly privately characterized as "directed entirely against the National Assembly."[20] The first of Duport's motions – that forbidding assemblies by order at any level – passed with little difficulty.

The second, prohibiting the meeting of provinces, encountered more opposition. In a statement that in some ways prefigured the federalist revolt years later, the marquis de Blacons, a deputy from Dauphiné, argued that if political assemblies in the provinces were to be banned then the districts of Paris should also be included in the proscription. Clermont-Tonnerre opposed the motion and asserted that the decree would impinge on the right of assembly of citizens, and also that it interfered with the right to present petitions to the Assembly, a right the Assembly had recently confirmed when it had provided local authorities with the right to declare martial law.

Proponents of the measure argued that there ought not to be provincial assemblies because the National Assembly had been formed and every province was represented in it. Other advocates asserted that to allow provinces to meet would endanger completion of the constitution. In the end, supporters of the motion carried the day and the Assembly voted to forbid convocations of provincial Estates.

At the same time that its authority was being challenged from outside, the Assembly, much to its dismay, also found itself being undermined from within by the Crown. On October 20, the Assembly learned that its decrees of August 4–11 and other critical decrees, such as that on provisions, had not been sent to all of the provinces, while others had perhaps been altered before being sent. Nowhere, the Assembly believed,

19 BN Mss. Nouv. acq. fr. 4121, fols. 226–227; *Procès-verbal de l'Assemblée nationale*, No. 108 (October 26, 1789), p. 2; *AP*, IX: 552–555. For other examples of how the decision divided the province, see AN C 95, dossier 107, documents 14–15; dossier 108, documents 1–2; dossier 109, documents 10–11, 25–28. See also Egret, *La Révolution des notables*, pp. 202–203.

20 *Procès-verbal de l'Assemblée nationale*, No. 108 (October 26, 1789), pp. 2–5; AN KK 645, fols. 350–352; for the private comment, see BN Mss. Nouv. acq. fr. 4121, fol. 228.

had the promulgation of the decrees of August 4–11 that had been ordered taken place, nor had there been any transcription of them in the registers of courts and municipalities, as had also been ordered. Indeed, the only item that had been widely disseminated was an earlier long letter from the king in which he had discussed his reservations about the decrees of August 4–11 and why he refused to accept them.

The meaning and significance of the failure to publish the decrees was clear to the National Assembly. Not only would the perception of sluggishness and inaction produce a reaction against the Assembly, but it also left its central ideal and major accomplishments imperfectly understood or possibly altogether unknown.[21] On a motion introduced by Le Chapelier, the Assembly ordered that the decrees of August 4–11 and all others accepted by the king be sent to the courts, municipalities and other bodies without any additions, changes or observations so that they could be transcribed on the registers without modification or delay. In addition, they were also to be read, published and posted. Furthermore, the Keeper of the Seals was ordered to appear before the Assembly to give an account of the reasons for the tardiness of the publication and promulgation of the different decrees, to explain the additions, modifications and changes that had been made and to give the reasons for the publication of the observations sent, in the name of the king, on the decrees of August 4–11.[22]

The threats from within by the Crown and from without in the provinces produced a sense of siege in the Assembly[23] and prompted a sharp change of attitude, leading it to assert its new ideal more forcefully. In originally naming Louis "the restorer of French liberties" on August 4, the Assembly had sought to associate him with its new conception of the nation and, utterly convinced of its validity and confident that he would share it, had been prepared to trust him and to work with him. The tortuous seven-week effort to gain his assent to the decrees of August 4–11, however, led many deputies to suspect his motives, and the fact that they had not been disseminated weeks after he had agreed to publish them engendered a deep sense of betrayal and mistrust.

Similarly, in dealing with society at large, the Assembly had initially been so certain of the integrity and momentousness of the new ideal to which it had given birth that its members had contented themselves with

21 See AM Bayonne AA 51, no. 37 (4), letter of October 31, 1789.
22 BN Mss. Nouv. acq. fr. 4121, fol. 213; AD Morbihan 1 Mi 240, no. 34, letter of October 23, 1789; Pilastre de la Brardière and Leclerc, *Correspondance*, III: 14–15; *Procès-verbal de l'Assemblée nationale*, No. 103 (October 20, 1789), pp. 6–9.
23 On the sense of siege that developed, see AM Lorient BB 13, no. 23, letter of October 28, 1789; AN M 788, dossier 2[17], documents 99, 108; AM Brest LL 46, no. 74, letter of October 26, 1789.

belief in the self-evident worth of the new vision or, at most, gentle persuasion.[24] With the revelation of apparent duplicity and malfeasance on the part of the Crown, as well as the challenge posed by traditional bodies, the Assembly changed its attitude and assumed a more aggressive stance. During the course of the debate on October 20, for example, the Assembly rejected all efforts to soften the wording of its decree ordering the Keeper of the Seals to appear before it.[25] The granting to municipalities of authority to declare martial law the next day was another manifestation of the strength of resolve of the Assembly.[26] In addition, later in the month the Assembly displayed a new vigilance in ensuring that its orders were carried out, particularly the diffusion of the decrees of August 4–11 that it had ordered on October 20.[27] The difficulties of October unquestionably strengthened the sense of mission of the National Assembly.[28]

Indeed, the new determination and strengthened sense of purpose of the National Assembly became most evident in its meeting of November 3. On that day the Assembly began debate on the new plan of administration, which it regarded as a cornerstone of its new ideal of the polity. Believing this new ideal to be much more in jeopardy from traditional bodies than it had thought in August and September, when it had been convinced that its new vision would be universally accepted and shared, the Assembly now struck preemptively at what it believed to be one of the most formidable of its adversaries among traditional bodies, the *parlements*. Because these had customarily viewed themselves as representatives of the nation, because they could be an obstacle to the new administration, and because of a belief within the Assembly that the *parlements* were scheming against it, Alexandre Lameth proposed that the Assembly order the *parlements* to remain on vacation rather than

24 See, for example, AD Orne C 1227, document 199, letter of Leclerc to deputies at Argentan, September 25, 1789; Ménard de la Groye, *Correspondance*, p. 93.
25 On the intent of the Assembly to send a clear message, see AD Ain 1 Mi 1, letter of October 20, 1789.
26 See, for example, AN AB[XIX] 3562, dossier 1, document 5. In part, the decree on martial law was also a reaction to the lynching of a baker in the neighborhood of the National Assembly. See AD Ain 1 Mi 1, letter of October 22, 1789; AN 291 AP, dossier 2, liasse 13, letter of Conzie to d'Aine, October 25, 1789. At the same time, however, the Assembly was aware of the vacuum in government created by the night of August 4, and its new firmness was a clear recognition that it could no longer rely on benevolent good will – as it had heretofore sought to do – until it could enact a new administrative structure.
27 See Thibaudeau, *Correspondance inédite*, ed. Carré and Boissonnade, p. 32; *Le Point du Jour*, October 29, 1789, November 22, 1789. Despite the suspicions exhibited on the latter occasion, the Crown had, in fact, begun to circulate the decrees of August 4–11 by early November. See, for example, AD Seine-Maritime C 2, letters-patent of king, November 3, 1789; AD Bouches-du-Rhône C 102, fol. 146v°.
28 See Ménard de la Groye, *Correspondance*, pp. 130–131; *Courier de Madon*, November 2, 1789.

reassemble for their new session.[29] After a brief discussion in which deputies paid homage to the *parlements* for their past services, the Assembly passed the measure, viewing the *parlements* as "incompatible with the new order of things."[30] The action was a remarkable demonstration of the resolution and firmness of purpose of the Assembly as it moved to enact its new ideal of the polity.

For most deputies, in fact, a major element in the realization of their goal had been the new plan of administration, which would lay the foundation for translating the ideals of August 4 into the reality of workable governance.[31] In the interval between the initial presentation on September 29 and the beginning of debate on November 3, the formulation of a new administrative structure took on even greater importance for the Assembly, in part because its new ideal of the polity had come to seem imperiled during that period.[32] Yet for all the urgency that the Assembly felt, there was little consensus on how to achieve it, for during this same interval much opposition had developed to the plan put forward by the Committee of the Constitution.[33]

Speaking for the Committee of the Constitution on November 3, Thouret presented the committee's rationale for its proposed plan, in a speech stamped by the influence of August 4, especially in its break with prescriptive tradition and its aspirations to forge deeper bonds among Frenchmen in a France devoid of privileged corporatism. Thouret noted that, for the Assembly, to establish the constitution meant to reconstruct and regenerate the state. He exhorted deputies not to hold themselves to the old order by routine or timidity when it was possible to establish better bases and when it was necessary to prepare the structure of government to obtain the results the Assembly desired. He urged the members of the Assembly not to despair of the day when, with the

29 See AM Bayonne AA 51, no. 39, letter of 7 November 1789; Lameth, *Histoire de l'Assemblée constituante*, I: 243–244; Sallier, *Annales françaises mai 1789 – mai 1790*, II: 45; *Procès-verbal de l'Assemblée nationale*, No. 115 (November 3, 1789), pp. 12–13.
30 AD Gironde 3 L 82, letter of November 10, 1789; Pilastre de la Brardière and Leclerc, *Correspondance*, III: 83. See also BM Lyon Ms. 2191, letter of November 7, 1789.
31 Lameth, *Histoire de l'Assemblée constituante*, I: 202. See also Dardy, "Lettres de M. Grellet de Beauregard," 79.
32 For the importance that the Assembly attached to the new plan of administration, see AD Orne C 1227, document 215, letter of Leclerc to deputies at Argentan, October 26, 1789; Ménard de la Groye, *Correspondance*, pp. 127, 136–137.
33 See, for example, BM Lyon Ms. 2193, no. 2; BN Mss. Nouv. acq. fr. 4121, fol. 247; BN Mss. Nouv. acq. fr. 12938, fols. 205v°–206; AM Strasbourg AA 2004, fol. 31; *Etats-Généraux. Journal de la Correspondance de Nantes*, II: 251. During the interval between its initial presentation and the opening of discussion, the committee had changed its position and agreed to respect provincial boundaries in the configuration of departments. It should also be noted that nearly all those who opposed the committee nevertheless recognized the need for change. They simply believed that the plan proposed by the committee was too extreme or impractical.

national spirit better formed, all Frenchmen would be joined together in a single family, having only a single law, a single form of government and would renounce all prejudices resulting from a corporate or local outlook. The constitution, he asserted, should expedite this impulse. In a passage that underscored the central tenet of the National Assembly, expressed in the pact of association forged on August 4, Thouret said:

To establish the constitution, is to bring in the name of the nation, in pursuance of the most powerful of its powers that exists only in it, and not in any of its parts, the supreme law that binds and subordinates the different parts of the State to the *whole*. The interest of this *whole*, that is to say the nation as a body, can alone determine the constitutional laws; and nothing that would ensue from systems, from prejudices, from habits, from local claims, can come into the balance ... If such sentiments could exist among us, show themselves and attain acceptance, how can we dare think of drafting a constitution?... Let us recall again what we thought of imperative mandates, when they made a claim against our reunion. "A *bailliage*, a province," we said, "simple members and parties subject to the nation, cannot dictate laws to it, make their particular opinions prevail, nor prevent the public good, because [of what] they believe to be their particular interest. There are no representatives of *bailliages* or of provinces, there are only representatives of the nation." If these truths are beyond doubt, it is especially so on the matter of the constitution, the first maxims of which are those of political union of all members of the State in a single body, and the subordination of all parties to the great national whole.[34]

Thouret went on to deal with objections raised to the committee's project, in the course of which he dismissed the resistance of public opinion, which he claimed would be won over to the plan, and he concluded by asking that the Assembly approve the committee's recommendation of eighty departments. The Assembly ordered that Thouret's presentation be printed and that three copies be given to each deputy for consideration and distribution to constituents.[35]

In addition to Thouret's presentation, another member of the Committee of the Constitution, Rabaut de Saint-Etienne, offered his ideas on the new administrative structure, and they provide additional insight into the Assembly's ideals and ambitions. Rabaut de Saint-Etienne stated that the new division of the kingdom was as much a moral action as a physical one. He asserted that an initial objection to the committee's plan – that it did not respect natural boundaries or traditions of provinces – had already disappeared. He then directed his attention to

34 *AP*, IX: 655.
35 *Procès-verbal de l'Assemblée nationale*, No. 115 (November 3, 1789), pp. 11–12; Jacques-Guillaume Thouret, *Discours de M. Thouret ... fait à l'Assemblée nationale sur la nouvelle division territoriale du royaume. Séance du ... 3 novembre (1789)* (Paris, 1789). See also Thibaudeau, *Correspondance inédite*, ed. Carré and Boissonnade, p. 25; *Etats-Généraux. Correspondance de Bretagne*, 5 vols. (Rennes, 1789–1790), II: 382.

other issues, especially privilege. Rabaut de Saint-Etienne argued that the greatest difficulty facing the plan of the committee was that some persons, including some deputies, believed that one privilege of provinces was to remain in existence as provinces. These deputies believed that they would break faith with their constituents if they consented to the division of their province, arguing that only the provinces themselves could consent to their dismemberment. Even though several of these deputies considered themselves representatives of the entire nation – a status that the Assembly had formally accorded to its members – many nonetheless felt that they had been sent by a province and that their constituents would judge them disloyal if they sanctioned its destruction or partition.

Responding to these concerns, Rabaut de Saint-Etienne alluded to the pact of association sworn on the night of August 4, reminding deputies of *pays d'états* that they had exchanged the system of privilege for a better arrangement, believing that the sacrifice of provincial privileges had been a real benefit. He recalled the actions of representatives of Dauphiné, Brittany, Provence, Languedoc, Burgundy and other provinces on that evening and, referring to the many overlapping jurisdictions of the Old Regime, he argued that the new regime decreed by the National Assembly replaced five or six defective regimes. There were no longer different nations in the kingdom, he said, there were only French. Rabaut de Saint-Etienne maintained that just as Louis XIV had once stated, of an ordinary family pact, that the Pyrénées no longer existed, the 1,200 deputies of the nation could say of the solemn pact that they had sworn that provinces no longer exist.

In a reflection of the troubles the Assembly was experiencing, Rabaut de Saint-Etienne offered one additional observation – that no province had the right to convoke itself when it had given its deputies the right to represent it, particularly at a time when the National Assembly was sitting and occupying itself with the interests of that province. For a province to convene would be to declare itself independent, thereby separating itself from the nation. Noting that the National Assembly was preparing legal and uniform usages that should be followed everywhere, Rabaut de Saint-Etienne asked citizens not to attend any such provincial convocations and to choose instead the common good.[36]

Both communications were well received and, as the first elaboration of the grand design of the Assembly, served for some deputies to proclaim its sense of purpose and to reassert the ascendancy of its ideal

36  *AP*, IX: 669. See also *Procès-verbal de l'Assemblée nationale*, No. 115 (November 3, 1789), pp. 11–12; Jean-Paul Rabaut de Saint-Etienne, *Réflexions sur la nouvelle division du royaume et sur les privilèges et les assemblées des provinces d'Etats* (Paris, 1789).

over competing considerations, including the sensitivities of constituents. The deputy Antoine-René-Hyacinthe Thibaudeau, for example, who had misgivings about the new division of the kingdom – he even told his constituents he would have preferred to preserve the administration of the province as it was – nevertheless recognized and acknowledged the primacy of the Assembly's objectives in the overall interest of the nation.[37]

Although the plan put forward by the Committee of the Constitution was politely received, it was not widely accepted.[38] Indeed, there were several projects for the division of the realm circulating in the National Assembly, ranging from one dividing the kingdom into thirty departments to a proposal calling for it to be divided into 203 departments. As a result, the Assembly seemed to lack a clear sense of direction,[39] although it did give priority to the plan of the committee. The project that ultimately emerged as the chief alternative to that presented by the committee was one offered by Mirabeau – almost immediately after Thouret had presented the plan of the committee – that called for the creation of 120 departments and providing for no administrative structure between the towns and the department. Believing that the plan submitted by the committee was excessively harsh toward former provincial identities, Mirabeau's project nevertheless also reverted more toward the ideal of uniform departments by establishing them on the basis of equality of population and taxable wealth, but within the framework of historic provincial boundaries.[40]

The comments of the deputy Adrien-Cyprien Duquesnoy the next day reflect the support that the project of the committee enjoyed. Noting that any plan should especially dissolve local or particularist outlooks in favor of a national one and make all inhabitants feel French rather than Provençal, Norman or Parisian, he claimed that the proposal advanced by the committee offered all these advantages. He asserted that he did not see any of the difficulties cited by Mirabeau when he had put forward his plan. Duquesnoy exhorted the Assembly not to be timid or dissuaded by resistance in the provinces and pointedly reminded deputies that they had nullified imperative mandates.

37 Thibaudeau, *Correspondance inédite*, ed. Carré and Boissonnade, pp. 30–31. Similarly, the deputy Duquesnoy said that Thouret had made the Assembly aware of the overwhelming need for a new division. See Duquesnoy, *Journal*, II: 14. See also BN Mss. Nouv. acq. fr. 4121, fol. 243.
38 See AM Bayonne AA 51, no. 39, letter of November 7, 1789; Duquesnoy, *Journal*, II: 17.       39 See *Journal des Etats-Généraux*, V: 31.
40 BN Mss. Nouv. acq. fr. 4121, fol. 244; BN Mss. Nouv. acq. fr. 12938, fols. 224–225v°; AN KK 645, fols. 362–363; AN C 32², dossier 273, document 2; BM Lyon Ms. 2191, letter of November 7, 1789. For a detailed exposition of Mirabeau's differences with the plan of the committee, see *Courier de Provence*, November 3, 1789.

Duquesnoy's support of the committee's plan was a minority position, however, for Mirabeau's project had many adherents, and consideration of the division of the realm continued for several days, during which time, despite criticisms of their plan, the members of the Committee of the Constitution said little.[41] On November 9, however, Thouret vigorously defended the plan of the committee against other proposals, especially the one offered by Mirabeau. Obviously frustrated with the desultory discussion, he concluded his speech by urging the Assembly to hasten the reconciliation of opinions since it was already united in its intention and views. Thouret's remarks made a deep impression on the Assembly, leading many members to demand that the division of the kingdom be put to a vote.[42]

Mirabeau, however, demanded an opportunity to respond, a request to which the Assembly acceded. The following day, on November 10, he replied forcefully to the points raised by Thouret, arguing that the new division ought to be based only on population and taxable capacity. The Assembly warmly applauded his presentation, and immediately afterward Thouret asked to reply to some of Mirabeau's objections, to which the Assembly again consented.[43]

When the meeting began the next day, however, in what was an apparent effort to save the project put forward by the Committee of the Constitution, another member of the committee, Target, spoke first instead. Target, whose considerable rhetorical skills had been developed as a pleading barrister at the *Parlement* of Paris, aggressively defended the plan of the committee, frequently citing opponents of the plan by name and rebutting their position. Target reproached the Assembly for losing sight of the totality of the committee's plan and for concentrating only on individual points. He also defended the committee's plan against all others and articulated many of the considerations that underlay it. He noted, for example, that the figure of eighty departments was not an arbitrary one, but one based on the calculation that any individual should

---

41 On Duquesnoy's position, see *Journal des Etats-Généraux*, V: 344. On the debate, see BN Mss. Nouv. acq. fr. 4121, fols. 245–246. See also *Recueil des travaux de la Société académique d'Agen*, 3e série, tome I. *Correspondance des députés de la sénéchaussée d'Agen aux Etats-Généraux et à l'Assemblée nationale (1789–1790)* (Nérac, 1967), pp. 64–65; *Lettres de MM. les députés des communes de la ville de Marseille à l'Assemblée nationale, à MM. les échevins & membres du comité de correspondance* (Marseille, 1789) [Newberry Library, FRC 4999].

42 *Procès-verbal de l'Assemblée nationale*, No. 120 (November 9, 1789), p. 3; BN Mss. Nouv. acq. fr. 4121, fol. 257; *Journal des Etats-Généraux*, V: 420; Poncet-Delpech, *Bulletins*, p. 144; AD Gironde 3 L 82, letter of November 13, 1789. See also Margadant, *Urban Rivalries*, pp. 100–107.

43 *Procès-verbal de l'Assemblée nationale*, No. 121 (November 10, 1789), p. 6; BN Mss. Nouv. acq. fr. 4121, fols. 260–261; Poncet–Delpech, *Bulletins*, p. 145.

be able to arrive at the administrative center of a department within one day of travel.

Target also defended the criteria utilized by the committee – the combination of size, population and taxable wealth – to determine departments. To those who wanted them to be based on population, he argued that the population was constantly changing, which would require a continual redrawing of boundaries. To illustrate the difficulty of equalizing population, he noted that to give Landes a population equal to that of Flanders it would be necessary to give Landes territory comprising nearly ten percent of the realm. To those who wanted the departments to be based on population and wealth, Target argued not only that population varied, but that with industry increasing and diminishing and with commerce expanding and contracting, the sources of wealth were in "perpetual agitation," which would also require a redrawing of boundaries. Target argued that the plan put forward by the committee offered greater stability than did projects based on other criteria.

In a clear allusion to Mirabeau's plan, which provided only for municipalities and departments, Target defended the committee's plan establishing an intermediate jurisdiction between them. In part, it was based on a desire not to have towns dominate the countryside; indeed, Target stated that the countryside would have more deputies than the towns. More important, however, the Committee of the Constitution wanted to ameliorate historic antagonisms between town and country and to bring them together. In a passage that clearly reveals the new ideal of the nation that guided the committee, Target argued against separating towns from the countryside, saying that hatreds were born of separation. Rather, town and country should reach out to each other in union and, in working together for the common good, they would learn more about each other. Then, and only then, Target asserted, would France form a nation. Just as the mixing of men in conversations destroys prejudices, Target said, so, too, the blending of citizens in political assemblies would temper their aversion for each other and reconcile their interests. Alluding to the pact of association, Target contended that the sacrifice of privileges in the interest of the nation would be meaningless unless sentiments of personal interest – egoism, as he also called it – were destroyed as well. He realized that this would be a more difficult task, but stated that political institutions ought to aspire to this goal. Far from separating citizens, as Target implied that Mirabeau's plan would in effect do, the Committee of the Constitution sought to blend them in patriotic assemblies, hoping ultimately that military men, men of the Church, men of law, businessmen, cultivators and others would put aside their prejudices in the interest of the nation and henceforth be only citizens.

Target went on to tell the Assembly that once the division of France into eighty parts was decreed, it remained only to choose the capitals and to chart the boundaries of each department. He stated that the committee would give primacy to rivers, mountains and other natural features in determining the new division, but that it would also take into consideration and respect historic frontiers of provinces. Target noted that the subdividing of departments would be done by the deputies from each region, who were more familiar with localities and who could combine their knowledge of taxable capacity and local tradition to designate sites for assemblies.

Target demonstrated impatience with the majority of deputies who had argued for the necessity of preserving ties to the provinces because inhabitants would only gradually come to love of the nation. He stated that such considerations had no place in the plan of the committee. He noted that having already abandoned their privileges, it was now necessary for the provinces to abandon arrogance, rivalries and jealousies as well. Henceforth, Target asserted, the happiness of all would lie in the union of all. To underscore the ideal that infused the committee, he referred to ancient Sparta. On public monuments in Sparta, he noted, the inscription read "a Spartan did such or such a memorable deed." The Spartans did not want the name of the citizen engraved and known to others so that self-interest would not be elevated above the fatherland. Although modern peoples were far from such virtue, Target asked why, in a moment of rebirth, should the National Assembly not seek to bring people together through the new institutions. He ended by observing that he believed he had answered all objections and invited the deputies to conclude their consideration of a project that had been awaited with impatience for several months and on which the well-being of the kingdom depended.[44]

After presentations by two other deputies, Thouret delivered his response to Mirabeau, which had been postponed at the beginning of the meeting. Stating that the Committee of the Constitution had on the previous day reexamined the project submitted by Mirabeau, he asserted that most of the principles it included had been rejected by the Assembly after serious consideration. Rather than attempt a detailed refutation,

44 *AP*, IX: 744–749. See also *Procès-verbal de l'Assemblée nationale*, No. 122 (November 11, 1789), pp. 7–10; *Etats-Généraux. Correspondance de Bretagne*, II: 430; *Etats-Généraux. Journal de la Correspondance de Nantes*, II: 458; *Journal de la ville et des provinces, ou le Modérateur, par une société de gens de lettres*, November 12, 1789; *Suite des nouvelles de Paris, du 11 novembre 1789, publiées le 12*, November 12, 1789.

Thouret said he wanted to reestablish basic postulates that led the committee to favor the plan that it had submitted. He repeated some of the points made by Target, noting that the committee's proposal offered fixed and permanent boundaries, whereas Mirabeau's project would require periodic readjustment of them. In addition, the attempt to equalize population would lead to great disparities in the size of departments. Inhabitants of sparsely populated areas would be placed at a severe disadvantage by being far from the *chef-lieu*, and administrators of such departments would have a territory too extensive to govern effectively. Conversely, densely populated departments would in effect be "overgoverned" because administrators in such departments would have only a small amount of territory to govern. He reiterated that the committee had not arrived at the figure of eighty arbitrarily nor as a figure of geometric harmony.

Thouret reaffirmed many of the fundamental positions of the committee by rebutting putative objections to them. He concluded by observing that no plan could be free of flaws or not be improved upon, but that if the Assembly continued to seek the perfect project, it would never adopt any plan. He stated that the moment had arrived when the Assembly should have the courage and moderation of reason not to sacrifice the common good, to which all subscribed and were currently bringing about, to the vain, deceptive and exaggerated hope of something better.

Thouret's presentation significantly affected the National Assembly, for as soon as he finished many deputies asked that the issue be decided. As a result, the Assembly framed two questions to be submitted to a vote, despite the objections of many deputies who still wished to speak, some in an effort to delay passage in order to try to achieve a lesser number of departments than was called for in the committee's plan. The first question was whether or not there would be a new division of the kingdom, and the Assembly voted affirmatively for a new division. The second question was whether the number of departments would be "around" eighty. Démeunier, a member of the Committee of the Constitution, argued that the word "around" was too vague and offered an amendment specifying that the number of departments would be between seventy-five and eighty-five. With Démeunier's amendment attached, the Assembly again voted in favor of the article.[45]

45 *Procès-verbal de l'Assemblée nationale*, No. 122 (November 11, 1789), pp. 7–10; BN Mss. Nouv. acq. fr. 4121, fols. 262–263; *Etats-Généraux. Correspondance de Bretagne*, II: 430; *Etats-Généraux. Journal de la Correspondance de Nantes*, II: 459; AM Brest LL 46, no. 81, letter of November 11, 1789. For an insight into how one deputy became persuaded of the utility of the plan of the comittee, see Adam-Philippe Custine, comte de, *Cinquième*

It is a measure of the enhanced stature and respect achieved by Thouret and the Committee of the Constitution that on the following day, November 12, Thouret was elected president of the National Assembly, even though he had not been a leading candidate until then.[46] Indeed, with the fact of a new division of the realm and its basic structure established, much of the remaining discussion was far less extensive, even anticlimactic.

After a report by Rabaut de Saint-Etienne on the state of the work of the Committee of the Constitution on the new division of the kingdom, the Assembly began to debate the different jurisdictions. After a change in terminology from commune to district, the Assembly decreed that each department would be divided into districts, but not necessarily the nine districts called for in the committee's plan. Instead, the number of districts would not necessarily be uniform for all departments, although the number of districts in each would be ternary. The number of districts for each department would be fixed by the National Assembly after having heard the deputies of each province concerning local traditions or principles and the needs of each department.

On November 16, the Assembly decided that each district would be divided into cantons, each of which would be approximately four square leagues in size. There would be one primary assembly in each canton, as close as possible to six hundred members in number, but with no more than nine hundred. The Assembly also decided that there would be an intermediate jurisdiction between the primary assemblies, and national and administrative assemblies.

Finally, the next day, the Assembly voted in favor of the committee's proposal to base representation on the national level on a combination of population, territory and taxable wealth. With this vote, the success of the Committee of the Constitution was complete.[47] Virtually every major element that it had considered necessary to realize the new ideal of the polity in the new administration had been accepted by the Assembly

compte rendu par le comte de Custine à ses commettans, de ses opinions dans les délibérations de l'Assemblée Nationale du 27 octobre jusqu'au 9 janvier 1790 (Paris, 1789 [sic]), p. 38.
46 On Thouret's election, see Procès-verbal de l'Assemblée nationale, No. 123 (November 12, 1789), p. 1. Earlier, however, he had trailed the Archbishop of Aix in the balloting. See Procès-verbal de l'Assemblée nationale, No. 121 (November 10, 1789), p. 7; AN C 32², dossier 276, document 9. On the adoption of the plan as a triumph for Thouret, see AM Arles AA 23, fol. 601. Mirabeau also paid tribute to Thouret in Courier de Provence, November 9–10, 1789. For more on the increase in Thouret's stature, see Journal de la ville et des provinces, ou le Modérateur, par une société de gens de lettres, November 12, 1789.
47 Procès-verbal de l'Assemblée nationale, No. 127 (November 17, 1789), p. 6; Poncet-Delpech, Bulletins, pp. 148, 153–155. On the ease with which the committee's plan passed after the critical vote of November 11, see BN Mss. Nouv. acq. fr. 4121, fols. 283, 292–294; AN KK 645, fols. 396–401, 408–410; BN Mss. Nouv. acq. fr. 12938, fols. 245–245v°, 249–250v°, 251–252.

despite strong initial opposition. Under the tutelage of the committee, the Assembly had forged a system that it believed could translate the abstract belief in the nation as a sublime entity into a practical mechanism for the citizenry. At least one deputy was clearly heartened by the debate and its outcome.[48]

A week later, on November 24, the Committee of the Constitution presented a project outlining the duties of departmental administrators. After a brief discussion, the Assembly approved the proposals of the committee.[49]

The next day the Assembly opened consideration of the formation of municipal governments, and on this topic the Assembly followed the recommendations of the committee much more readily and with far less debate. In order to make the transition to the new system more orderly, the first article presented by the committee provided that, although all municipalities were suppressed, municipal officers currently in power were to continue in office until they were replaced. In subsequent articles, however, the goal of the new administration once again became evident – to eradicate privileged corporatism and to replace it with a common devotion to the nation. Understanding privilege in its Old Regime sense of rights enjoyed by some that were not enjoyed by others, the Assembly sought to make municipal government more uniform and to provide for equivalent administrations throughout France by structuring it according to population. Thus, for towns of 500 or fewer inhabitants, there would be three municipal officers, for those with 500 to 3,000 inhabitants there would be six municipal officers, nine for those of 3,000 to 10,000 inhabitants, twelve for those of 10,000 to 25,000, fifteen for those of 25,000 to 50,000, eighteen for those of 50,000 to 100,000 and twenty-one for cities of 100,000 or more. Indeed, one of the few difficulties that the committee encountered in presenting its plan was that it sought to make the municipal government of Paris the object of separate legislation, which struck some members of the Assembly as granting Paris "privilege," a point to which the committee successfully responded, so that ultimately Paris was governed under a separate set of laws.

The effort to abolish corporatism was evident in the Assembly's replacement of municipal officers whose positions had been venal with elected representatives. It was even more apparent in the article specifying that municipal assemblies could not form themselves by trade, profession or corporations, but only by neighborhoods or arrondisse-

48  See BM Lyon Ms. 5430, no. 16, letter of November 16, 1789.
49  *Procès-verbal de l'Assemblée nationale*, No. 133 (November 24, 1789), pp. 7–10; BN Mss. Nouv. acq. fr. 12938, fols. 259–259v°.

ments.[50] Although the Assembly completed most of the legislation on municipalities by December 3, it was not issued until December 14 and that on the departments was not promulgated until December 22. Nevertheless, the attainment of the new administrative structure by early December greatly encouraged the Assembly and once again reaffirmed its sense of mission and purpose.[51]

The framing of the new administrative structure was the first major action taken by the National Assembly in pursuit of its new ideal of the polity that would directly affect the lives of all Frenchmen. The Declaration of the Rights of Man had proclaimed the new governing precepts of the polity; the new administration was now to be the structure within which those precepts would operate. Henceforth, administrative duties and leadership at every level – from the smallest bourg or village to the departmental level and the national legislature – would be exercised by men elected by assemblies comprised of individuals concerned with the welfare of the nation rather than with corporate or particular interests.[52] Ultimately, the administrative structure was to be the basis of the passage from privileged corporatism to the new ideal of the polity, offering French society the opportunity to realize the possibilities envisioned by the National Assembly. Indeed, with the enactment of the new administrative structure, some in the Assembly saw its work as largely completed, with the establishment of a new judiciary as the other major element to complete its grand design.[53] As the deputy Ménard de la Groye wrote to his wife:

50 *Procès-verbal de l'Assemblée nationale*, No. 134 (November 25, 1789), pp. 5–8, especially p. 7; BN Mss. Nouv. acq. fr. 4121, fols. 295–296, 311–313, 327; on the ease with which the articles of the committee were accepted, see AM Bayonne AA 51, no. 41, letter of November 28, 1789; AM Bergerac, fonds Faugère, carton I, no. 45, letter of November 28, 1789; no. 46, letter of December 1, 1789; AD Ain 1 Mi 1, letter of November 26, 1789. See also *Journal de Versailles*, November 28, 1789.
51 See Ménard de la Groye, *Correspondance*, pp. 149, 157–158. See also BN Mss. Nouv. acq. fr. 4121, fol. 327; AD Puy-de-Dôme 4 J 6, copy of letter of Huguet, November 28, 1789; AM Bayonne AA 51, no. 41, letter of November 28, 1789; AD Ain 1 Mi 1, letter of November 26, 1789; *Journal de Versailles*, November 22, 1789; BM Lyon Ms. 5430, no. 16, letter of November 16, 1789; Duquesnoy, *Journal*, II: 81, 88; Rabaut de Saint-Etienne, *Précis de l'histoire de la Révolution française*, p. 232. Again, for more on the formation of departments, see Ozouf-Marignier, *La Formation des départements*; Margadant, *Urban Rivalries*. See also Mona Ozouf, "Département," *A Critical Dictionary of the French Revolution*, ed. Furet and Ozouf pp. 494–503.
52 Ménard de la Groye, *Correspondance*, pp. 155–156; BM Angers Ms. 1888, pp. 161–162.
53 See Ménard de la Groye, *Correspondance*, p. 161. The letters of Ménard de la Groye comprise one of the single most valuable sources for insight into the National Assembly. His letters are those of an obscure back bencher confiding his innermost thoughts to his wife, and as such are more candid than those generally found. Many letters of deputies were to municipal authorites or electors and were intended for dissemination or publication, and therefore often sought to influence opinion or to purvey a point of view. The letters of Ménard de la Groye were purely private and therefore have greater value. See also BM Lyon Ms. 2191, letter of February 3, 1790.

I will be very glad when we have completed this task, and even more when the new judicial power is organized. Then one will begin to be conscious of the benefit that should be the outcome of our actions: at that time our political system, to which all parties subscribe and are ultimately bound, will rise as a majestic edifice that offers to the astonished eye the most beautiful and exact proportions. Without a doubt the present revolution will long have its detractors; but I would like to know if, among those who criticize it, there are many who have thought deeply on the most momentous and most difficult of all arts, that of reforming the ways of a people by their laws; of making love of the nation and the public interest succeed indifferent egoism, and finally to set on a firm base the freedom of citizens. Despite all the sacrifices that it is necessary to make, who will be sorry for us if we attain a proper and sensible constitution?[54]

The deputies underestimated the time necessary to form departments, so that consideration of the judiciary did not begin until March, 1790.[55] Nevertheless, the sense of confidence, pride and accomplishment felt by the National Assembly at this time was considerable, and is perhaps best reflected in yet another letter from Ménard de la Groye to his wife:

The National Assembly presents to the entire universe a great and magnificent sight. In putting aside the different prejudices that are now very much blunted, I see only a genuine patriotism, an ardent zeal for the common good impelling the very great portion of the members who form it, whether in the clergy, whether in the nobility, whether among the Third Estate. Thus, my dear wife, everything will be fine, I am certain: the spirit that directs us at Paris will propagate itself little by little in the provinces; one will become accustomed to a new order of things of which one will be aware of the wisdom and usefulness; and our work, open now to so much criticism, will conclude by being generally approved. I do not know when it will be completely consummated, this task, but I very much hope that it could be next spring.

Then, justifying their separation, he wrote a passage that clearly reveals the ethos of the new ideal of the polity that animated many members of the Assembly – particularly the subordination of all personal or private considerations to the good of the nation – and the heightened significance it lent to their acts, he wrote that "the great interest of the fatherland must elevate my mind, interrupt my private attachments and absorb all my thoughts." Telling his wife that he was continually occupied and questioning whether he merited the honor of being chosen a deputy, he

54 Ménard de la Groye, *Correspondance*, p. 165; see also BM Lyon Ms. 2191, letter of December 6, 1789.
55 In December, 1789, for example, one deputy wrote that he thought the framing of departments, districts and cantons would take at most three weeks. See BM Nantes Collection Dugast-Matifeux, t. 98, letter of December 24, 1789. On the issues and difficulties that the Assembly encountered in the formation of departments, see Margadant, *Urban Rivalries*, pp. 178–274, 287–321.

observed that he was "aware every day how much it is great indeed, this honor of which I was so little worthy."[56]

Although the formation of the new administrative structure instilled a sense of pride and accomplishment in the Assembly, these months were also a difficult period for the National Assembly.[57] To be sure, during the summer and autumn of 1789 the Assembly received a torrent of protestations of loyalty from municipalities all over France, virtually all of which endorsed the actions it had taken.[58] From the outset many members of the Assembly had attached great significance to them, for these addresses enabled deputies legitimately to believe that they were operating in accord with the wishes of the nation.[59] Such expressions of support were gratifying, for at the same time there was much discontent in France – occasionally fanned by the Crown against the National Assembly[60] – and this discontent at times grew into open confrontation between the Assembly and such traditional bodies as the *parlements* or intermediary commissions of provinces.

In addition to the previously mentioned episodes of the Estates of Dauphiné and the nobility of Languedoc, one of the conflicts that gained the most attention was that between the Assembly and the Intermediate Commission of Cambrésis in November, 1789. On November 9, 1789, members of the commission convened and, after denouncing various decrees of the National Assembly as leading to the ruin of the kingdom, called for the revocation of the powers of the deputies from the province.[61]

56 Ménard de la Groye, *Correspondance*, p. 154. For more on the high-mindedness and busy schedule of the deputies, see Theodore de Lameth, *Mémoires*, ed. Eugène Welvert (Paris, 1913), pp. 74–76. Again, Lemay, *La Vie quotidienne des députés aux Etats-Généraux 1789*, provides an extraordinary insight into the routine of the deputies.
57 See BM Nantes Collection Dugast-Matifeux, t. 98, letter of December 24, 1789; AM Arles AA 23, fol. 634.
58 See, for example, AN C 87, dossier 44², document 70; AN C 91, dossier 72², document 1; AN C 96, dossier 115, document 11; AN C 97, dossier 117, document 25.
59 See, for example, Dardy, "Lettres de M. Grellet de Beauregard," 67; Ménard de la Groye, *Correspondance*, p. 69; AN 291 AP 1, dossier 2, liasse 13, letter of November 27, 1789. Occasionally deputies solicited such addresses from their constituents. See AD Côtes-d'Armor 1 L 389, letter of Palasne de Champeaux and Poulain de Corbion, June 30, 1789; Leroux-Cesbron, "Lettres de Lofficial," 107.
60 See AD Somme C 731, letter of intendant D'Agay to comte de Saint-Priest, December 17, 1789, letter of comte de Saint-Priest to D'Agay, December 20, 1789, letter of D'Agay to Keeper of the Seals, Necker and others. The casual attitude of the Crown to a situation that the intendant regarded as alarming reflected the lack of common purpose between the Crown and the National Assembly, and the letter of December 20, clearly reveals an effort to place any onus for civil unrest on the National Assembly.
61 See *Extrait du Procès-verbal de l'Assemblée renforcé des Etats de Cambrai & du Cambrésis. Arrêté unanime de l'Assemblée du 9 novembre 1789* (n.p., n.d.). For a response by deputies in the National Assembly, see *Lettre de plusiers membres de l'Assemblée nationale à leurs commettans de provinces de Flandres & de Cambrésis* (N.p., 1789) [Newberry Library, FRC 4870].

While other bodies had gathered to disparage the Assembly and its work, or had sought to instruct their representatives, this was the first instance of a province attempting to recall its deputies. The incident encouraged those opposed to the Revolution, who hoped that other provinces would follow the example of Cambrésis and thereby destroy the Assembly.[62]

The action of the Intermediate Commission represented a significant threat to the National Assembly because, according to one observer, it was an "established principle" in the Assembly that whatever the privileges of the different regions that had sent deputies to the Assembly, the deputies had renounced those privileges from the moment that they had taken their seat. In a reflection of the primacy that the Assembly accorded to the pact of association, it asserted that whatever protest deputies might make or receive, their presence alone was an acquiescence to everything that the Assembly would bring about.[63] The hopes of opponents of the Assembly that the revocation of powers might destroy the National Assembly were not exaggerated, so that it required the attention of the Assembly, which dealt with it in three meetings that month.

Discussion began on November 17, and the proposed responses ranged from a suggestion by Le Chapelier to send the members of the commission before the Châtelet, to one by Barnave that the Assembly content itself with suspending the members of the commission from office. Ultimately, on November 24, the Assembly concluded by declaring that the Intermediate Commission did not represent the inhabitants of the province and that the convocation of the board (*bureau renforcé*) – and the deliberation that it had taken on November 9 – were null and damaging to the sovereignty of the nation and to the rights of citizens. The Assembly decreed that it would ask the king to recall the members of the commission to their duties and to implement the decrees of the National Assembly in that province.[64]

Although some saw this response as timid,[65] it reflected not only the desire of the Assembly to work with the king, but also the devotion of the Assembly to law and moral suasion that was inherent in the new ideal of the polity conceived by the National Assembly. Although its members

62 See Antoine-François Bertrand de Moleville, *Annals of the French Revolution*, 9 vols. (London, 1809), II: 207–208.
63 AD Pyrénées-Atlantiques C 1601, register of decrees of committee of correspondence, August 4, 1789. See also AM Arles AA 23, fol. 544, in which the deputies mention that the Assembly would not admit any protest at the abolition of privileges from individual deputies or groups of deputies.
64 *Procès-verbal de l'Assemblée nationale*, No. 133 (November 24, 1789), pp. 15–19; BN Mss. Nouv. acq. fr. 4121, fols. 280, 284–285, 295; AD Ain 1 Mi 1, letter of November 19, 1789.        65 See Bertrand de Moleville, *Annals*, II: 209.

felt strongly about the actions of the intermediate commission – one moderate deputy characterized them as "criminal" and "seditious"[66] – the National Assembly consciously refused to resort to violence or coercion to gain obedience to its decrees. Concerned with the good of the nation, and expecting citizens to embrace that ideal, the Assembly believed that its decisions ought to be accepted solely on their merit and not through force, which would compromise the moral authority of the Assembly[67] and vitiate the new ideal of the polity. In late October, 1789, when one of the Dauphinois deputies who had left the Assembly was arrested at Montélimart, the president of the Assembly had been charged to write to the municipality to remind it that "the principles of the National Assembly are irreconcilable to all violence," and this precept was followed not only with the intermediate commission of Cambrésis but also to *parlements*, particularly those of Rouen, Metz and Rennes, that refused to yield.[68] Far from being a sign of weakness or timidity, the restraint of the Assembly was one of the most significant affirmations of its central principle as well as a striking demonstration that the Assembly itself would submit to the fundamental ideal it had established – the unity of the nation in the free acceptance of laws common to all.

The National Assembly wished to be respected rather than feared and, buttressed by a total belief in the validity of its ideals, it could act in a confident, unwavering and nonviolent manner. Indeed, the most forceful action of the National Assembly before June, 1791, was that which it took against the magistrates of the *Parlement* of Rennes who defied it in January, 1790. After summoning them to the Assembly to explain their conduct, it deprived them of the right to participate in primary assemblies until they swore loyalty to the new constitution.[69] There was no logic of violence implicit in the Revolution of 1789, nor are the origins of the Terror to be found in that year; the political culture to which the Revolution of 1789 gave birth was representative, broad-minded, pacific and tolerant.[70] The inability of these values to endure did not stem from any inherent deficiency in the work of the National Assembly so much as

66 See Ménard de la Groye, *Correspondance*, pp. 144, 146.
67 One deputy had written privately to his wife that the power of the Assembly was purely moral. See AD Ain 1 Mi 1, letter of August 18, 1789.
68 See AD Ain 1 Mi 1, letter of October 29, 1789; *Etats-Généraux. Journal de la Correspondance de Nantes*, II: 361. On the *parlements*, see *Correspondance inédite de J. M. Pellerin*, ed. Gustave Bord (Paris, 1883), p. 134; AN W 12, undated memo of Barnave on the *parlement* of Brittany. On the basic precept of avoiding coercion, see AM Strasbourg AA 2005ᵃ, fol. 58.
69 See *Courier de Madon*, February 1, 1790, for the benevolent attitude of even a left-wing member of the Assembly, Jacques-Samuel Dinochau.
70 This point is also made in a different context by Margadant, *Urban Rivalries*, pp. 452–453.

it did from the behavior of the king, a point that will be more fully developed later.

The last months of 1789 were a particularly trying time for the National Assembly, for deputies did not always feel confident that their new course for the polity was gaining acceptance in the nation.[71] On December 22, for example, the deputy Joseph-Michel Pellerin wrote to his constituents asking them to reconcile themselves with the National Assembly.[72] As the year 1790 began, however, many deputies took on a more optimistic outlook, believing that the completion of work on the administration laid the foundation for the new polity envisioned by the Assembly and believing also that the Assembly had truly joined together in a renewed unity of purpose.[73]

In the meantime, however, the undercurrents of tension that were present in late 1789 found a catalyst in the arrest of the marquis de Favras on December 24, 1789. Favras was accused of seeking to assemble a royalist force, to assassinate Bailly and Lafayette and to take the king and queen to Metz, where they would dissolve the National Assembly and convene a new Estates-General. Favras's activities seemed to implicate the comte de Provence, who hastily appeared before a special meeting at the Hôtel de Ville to deny any connection with the conspiracy and to swear allegiance to the Revolution. Favras's trial at Paris was closely followed and was the occasion for some mysterious and obscure political maneuvers. Ultimately, Favras was convicted and executed on February 19, 1790, and he is remembered virtually as much for the manner of his execution as for the crime of which he was convicted.[74] Yet in the winter of 1789–1790 his arrest and trial became the point of convergence for widespread suspicion and mistrust of the king.[75]

In an effort to ameliorate the tension, Louis sent a note to the Assembly on February 4, 1790, stating that he intended to visit, but without ceremony. The Assembly received the message enthusiastically and made some hasty preparations to receive him. The king soon arrived

71 See, for example, AM Strasbourg AA 2005ᵃ, fols. 31, 38, 49.
72 *Correspondance inédite de J. M. Pellerin*, ed. Bord, p. 132. See also AM Strasbourg AA 2004, fol. 81.
73 On the sense of unity felt by the Assembly as the new year began, see Ménard de la Groye, *Correspondance*, pp. 166–167; BN Mss. Nouv. acq. fr. 4121, fol. 368; Henri-Joseph Jessé Levas, baron de, *Lettre de M. le baron de Jessé, député de la sénéchaussée de Béziers, à ses commettans* (Paris, 1790) [BHVP 954420].
74 In a macabre aspect of the new principle of laws common to all in place of privilege, Favras was the first nobleman to be executed by hanging, as there was no longer any distinction between noble executions – beheading – and common executions. For more on Favras, see AN BB³⁰ 82.
75 BN Mss. Nouv. acq. fr. 4121, fols. 423–424; Mercy-Argenteau, *Correspondance secrète*, II: 292–293.

accompanied only by his ministers and, wearing a plain black suit and speaking uncovered, quickly began a remarkable address. After alluding to the unrest and tension in France, Louis declared that the time had come when it was in the interest of the state that he associate himself more explicitly and more clearly with all that the Assembly had proposed for the welfare of France. He therefore promised to defend and maintain the constitutional liberty whose principles were sanctioned by the will of the nation and by him. Later, promising to do more, he averred that along with the queen, who shared his sentiments, he would educate his son in accordance with the new order of things and teach him that a wise constitution would save him from the dangers of inexperience. Finally, he concluded his lengthy speech by stating "Let us all, from this day forward, following my example, be moved by one opinion, one interest, one purpose – attachment to the new constitution and ardent desire for the peace, happiness and prosperity of France."[76]

Six months to the day after its formulation, the king had, at last, clearly and unambiguously aligned himself with the new ideal of the polity; he had, in effect, assumed the role bestowed on him on August 4 – "restorer of French liberties." Louis's speech was heartily applauded and set off a wave of emotion among deputies and spectators similar to the one that had seized the Assembly on August 4. A motion proposing that the members of the National Assembly should follow the example of the king and promise loyalty to the constitution quickly passed. The oath that was devised perfectly reflected the new ethos of the nation, with clear primacy accorded to the nation and the rule of law, as well as the union of the National Assembly and the king: "I swear to be faithful to the nation, the law and the king, and to uphold with all my might the constitution decreed by the National Assembly and accepted by the king." The president of the Assembly first took the oath and then each deputy individually went to the tribune to say "I swear it." The scene was compelling, and after the deputies had taken the oath those present in the galleries of the Assembly – alternate deputies, spectators and others – also asked to take it.[77] It was a solemn occasion for the Assembly, fulfilling the aspiration of August 4 – the Assembly and the king working together harmoniously in the greater interest of the nation.

There can be little doubt that the National Assembly considered the speech to be not a mere gesture, but a statement of principle, even a binding covenant. Deputies believed that Louis had solemnly accepted the constitution and allied himself so clearly with the new order that all

76 For Louis's speech, see *Procès-verbal de l'Assemblée nationale*, No. 192 (February 4, 1790), pp. 8–19.
77 *Ibid.*, pp. 21, 23; see also BN Mss. Nouv. acq. fr. 4121, fols. 425–426.

dissent in France would soon cease and union and concord would ensue.[78] The deputy Jean-Antoine Huguet, for example, told his constituents:

It will no longer be allowed to enemies of the public good to cast doubts on the intentions of the king: he has just shown them in a most positive manner in a speech that he made in the middle of the deputies of the nation, a speech that produced tears of joy in all those who heard it. It is thus no longer possible to doubt the consent that the king gives to a constitution of which he declares himself the head. How much this wonderful day should hasten our task! It should disconcert all the senseless plans of those who still keep in their heart the hope of seeing destroyed a work that should give happiness to France; it should reestablish calm and tranquility everywhere.[79]

Similarly, Ménard de la Groye wrote to his wife that Louis's visit to the Assembly "was a day of happiness and joy, a day forever memorable in which the king again won claims to the love of his people; in which the bases on which French liberty ought to rest have been affirmed by his august hands; in which finally the enemies of the public good ought to lose all hope of sowing new troubles and of succeeding in overturning the constitution."[80] Likewise, another deputy noted in his journal that "the meeting today cannot help but have a considerable influence on subsequent events and the destinies of France."[81] There was a deep conviction in the Assembly that Louis's visit was a milestone that guaranteed the success of the Revolution.

These perceptions were not confined to the Assembly alone; they were shared by the nation at large. Even relatively radical newspapers were enthusiastic; the *Révolutions de Paris*, for example, wrote "it is impossible in such moments to give oneself over to any reflections: it is

78 AM Bergerac, fonds Faugère, carton I, no. 61, letter of February 6, 1790.
79 AD Puy-de-Dôme 4 J 6, copy of letter of Huguet, February 6, 1790.
80 Ménard de la Groye, *Correspondance*, p. 187.
81 BN Mss. Nouv. acq. fr. 4121, fol. 423. For the perspectives of other deputies, see AM Le Havre D³ 39, no. 83, letter of February 4, 1790; BN Mss. Nouv. acq. fr. 12938, fols. 325v°–327; AM Brest LL 46 (1790), no. 17, letter of February 4, 1790; AD Loire-Atlantique C 627 (2), no. 289, letter of February 6, 1790; AN KK 643, entry of February 4, 1790; Thibaudeau, *Correspondance inédite*, ed. Carré and Boissonnade, pp. 68–73; Poncet-Delpech, *Bulletins*, pp. 231–233; Rabaut de Saint-Etienne, *Précis de l'histoire de la Révolution*, pp. 238–240; *Correspondance des députés de la sénéchaussée d'Agen*, pp. 131–133; Lameth, *Histoire de l'Assemblée constituante*, I : 316–326; Duquesnoy, *Journal*, II : 349–352; Pilastre de la Brardière and Leclerc, *Correspondance*, IV: 76–84; *Considérations adressées par M. d'Eymar, député de Forcalquier, à ses commettans, sur la nouvelle division du royaume et la formation prochaine des assemblées de districts et de départmens. Du 4 février 1790* (Paris, n.d.), pp. 14–15. See also Thomas Lindet, *Correspondance de Thomas Lindet pendant la Constituante et la Législative (1789–1792)*, ed. Armand Montier (Paris, 1899), pp. 62–65. Lindet was the brother of a deputy.

necessary to feel it all. We will then say only, and from the bottom of our heart: may this day stifle the discord that prevails among citizens, and to bring round to the nation those who did not want to recognize its rights."[82] Furthermore, as will be seen in the next section, there were spontaneous celebrations of the event throughout France – from cities such as Paris, Rouen, Dijon and Bordeaux to the smallest provincial villages – as a general sense of elation pervaded the nation.[83]

The National Assembly, seeking to convey this unity of purpose to the nation, charged Talleyrand with preparing an address to the French, which he presented to the Assembly in two readings on February 10 and 11. After reciting the accomplishments of the Assembly, the address discussed the criticisms raised against it, but asserted that the Assembly would not be discouraged. After briefly outlining its remaining goals, the address asked citizens to associate themselves with those goals by ignoring the Assembly's detractors. Noting Louis's appearance in the Assembly, it called for all citizens to join together in a spirit of common purpose and told them that they had nothing to fear. Talleyrand's effort was vigorously applauded, and the Assembly ordered that it be printed and sent to the provinces, where it would be posted and read from the pulpit by curés.[84] Indeed, reflecting the newfound unity between the Crown and the Assembly, and in complete contrast to the situation only a few weeks earlier, ministers and intendants alike made every effort to carry out the wishes of the Assembly and to ensure that the address was disseminated to every corner of France.[85]

It was in this atmosphere of general accord and agreement that the

82 *Revolutions de Paris*, January 30–February 6, 1790. See also *Revolutions de France et de Brabant*, No. 12. For the reactions of other papers, see *Le Point du Jour*, February 5, 1790, February 6, 1790. On the circulation of the news throughout the kingdom by the newspapers, see Bertrand de Moleville, *Annals*, II: 288. For the reaction of another contemporary outside of the Assembly, a member of the *Parlement* of Paris, see Sallier, *Annales françaises mai 1789 – mai 1790*, II: 89, in which he said that Louis "contracted a solemn alliance with the revolution." On the goodwill generated between the Crown and the people, see *Courier Provincial*, May, 1790.

83 See Edmond Géraud, *Journal d'un étudiant (Edmond Géraud) pendant la Révolution, 1789–1793*, ed. Gaston Maugras, 2nd edn., (Paris, 1890), pp. 44–45; AM Rouen Y 1, fols. 973–975; BM Dijon, Ms. 1660, fol. 31; AN F¹c III Gironde 11, letter of inhabitants and citizens of Bordeaux to Louis, February 16, 1790. See also Bertrand de Moleville, *Annals*, II: 277–279.

84 See *Procès-verbal de l'Assemblée nationale*, No. 192 February 4, 1790), p. 22; No. 198 (February 10, 1790), p. 4; No. 199 (February 11, 1790). See also BN Mss. Nouv. acq. fr. 4121, fols. 435–436, 447; *Le Point du Jour*, February 11, 1790, February 12, 1790, February 14, 1790; Pilastre de la Brardière and Leclerc, *Correspondance*, IV: 121–122.

85 See, for example, AD Hérault C 5959, dossier 326, dossier 329; AD Ille-et-Vilaine C 3901, letter of Intermediate Commission of Estates of Brittany to commissars of eight dioceses, March 12, 1790; AD Côte d'Or C 3359, no. 128; AD Seine-Maritime C 3, letter of intendant to comte de Saint-Priest, February 9, 1790.

Assembly began consideration of the judiciary in March, 1790. Originally, as indicated in Bergasse's report of August 17, the judiciary had served as a starting point for the Assembly's break with prescriptive tradition in the aftermath of the night of August 4. A few days after Bergasse presented his report, however, the Assembly gave precedence to completing the Declaration of the Rights of Man and then, following its determination of basic principles in August and September, rearranged its agenda, giving first priority to the reorganization of the administration of the kingdom. The Assembly decided the structure of the new administration by mid-December, 1789, and, in anticipation of soon moving on to consideration of the judiciary, Thouret, speaking for the Committee of the Constitution, offered a revised report on the judiciary on December 22, 1789.[86]

The task of defining the boundaries and determining *chefs-lieux* and districts of the departments took much longer than expected, thereby delaying consideration of the judiciary until late March.[87] While the process of demarcating the departments was largely uneventful, two episodes that occurred during this period merit attention for the insights they offer into the frame of mind of the National Assembly and the spirit of its operations. On February 26, 1790, the Committee of the Constitution, seeking to destroy all vestiges of provinces, proposed to give each department a name corresponding to its most prominent natural feature, such as rivers or mountains. Furthermore, to eradicate the "aristocracy of towns" and to foster complete equality among them, the committee recommended that no department could take the name of its *chef-lieu*.[88] Several deputies resisted the first proposal in particular, but after some debate both measures passed. Furthermore, the Assembly charged the Committee of the Constitution to name each department.[89] The action was another notable example of the determination of the

86 *Procès-verbal de l'Assemblée nationale*, No. 157 (December 22, 1789), pp. 18–19; *Projet de l'organisation du pouvoir judiciaire proposé à l'Assemblée Nationale par le Comité de Constitution, dont l'annexe a été ordonné au procès-verbal du 22 décembre 1789* (Paris, n.d.); BN Mss. Nouv. acq. fr. 4121, fols. 353–355; Ménard de la Groye, *Correspondance*, p. 161; Poncet-Delpech, *Bulletins*, p. 191. The committee offered another element of its plan for the judiciary on February 2, 1790; see *Procès-verbal de l'Assemblée nationale*, No. 190 (February 2, 1790), pp. 3–4; Ménard de la Groye, *Correspondance*, p. 185; Poncet-Delpech, *Bulletins*, p. 230.
87 On the expectation that the judiciary would be treated earlier, see AD Bouches-du-Rhône C 1337, letter of February 10, 1790; Ménard de la Groye, *Correspondance*, p. 182; Queruau-Lamerie, "Lettres de Maupetit," 20, 176; *Courier de Madon*, February 1, 1790, February 4, 1790.
88 This measure, as Ted Margadant has noted, also served to disguise urban rivalries in many departments. Margadant, *Urban Rivalries*, pp. 255–256.
89 *Procès-verbal de l'Assemblée nationale*, No. 213 (February 26, 1790), pp. 2–3; BN Mss. Nouv. acq. fr. 4121, fols. 460–461.

Assembly to abolish *l'esprit de province* that had been central to privileged corporatism. By effacing even the former names of the provinces in designating the departments, the Assembly highlighted the new beginning for all and underscored the spirit of total unity and equality in the nation.[90]

The second incident occurred on March 15, when the Assembly elected Rabaut de Saint-Etienne as its president. The fact that the Assembly could elect a Protestant minister as president – succeeding, in fact, a Catholic priest, the abbé de Montesquiou – struck several deputies and observers. Indeed, the Assembly had entrusted its presidency, and by extension the destinies of France, to a man who only a few years previously would not have been recognized as a member of the polity. Presiding as he did over a large number of bishops as well as *curés*, his election demonstrated clearly and unequivocally that the Assembly had itself realized the ethos that it sought to impart to France at large. Rabaut de Saint-Etienne became the personification of the ideal of subsuming all other qualities – profession, place of birth, social origin or religious persuasion – to the grander ideal of the nation. In his brief acceptance speech, Rabaut de Saint-Etienne alluded to this fact, stating that in his person the Assembly had strengthened its principles.[91]

In creating the new administration the National Assembly had levelled provinces and towns, not only eliminating privilege as an instrument of government, but even abolishing the provinces, formerly one of the chief repositories of privilege. The Assembly next sought to establish the mechanism for the new governing ideal – laws common to all – by instituting a new judiciary. Due to the unexpectedly long time it took to form the departments, consideration of the judiciary did not occur until March 24, 1790, with a report by Thouret.

After cataloging abuses of the Old Regime, including proprietary rights in judicial office and the confusion of legislative and judicial powers, Thouret inveighed against the central role of privilege under the

90  See *Courrier de la Révolution, ou Journal des municipalitiés, et des corps administratifs et militaires du Département d'Indre-et-Loire*, April, 1790 [BN L° 9. 126]; *Courier de Madon*, February 26, 1790.
91  *Procès-verbal de l'Assemblée nationale*, No. 230 (March 15, 1790), p. 1; BN Mss. Nouv. acq. fr. 4121, fol. 489; AM Brest LL 46 (1790), no. 36, letter of March 15, 1790; Faulcon, *Correspondance*, II: 157; *Journal de Versailles*, March 17, 1790; *Courier de la Patrie, ou Journal des Municipalités, assemblées administratives, districts, tribunaux et garde nationale de France*, March 18, 1790 [Newberry Library, FRC 5.289]; *Chronique de Paris*, March 16, 1790. On the particular pride of the Assembly on the matter of making citizenship independent of religious affiliation, see BM Nantes Collection Dugast-Matifeux, t. 98, letter of December 24, 1789. Furthermore, the selection of Rabaut de Saint-Etienne was another sign of the regained confidence of the National Assembly. On this resurgent confidence, see AM Douai D³ 1, letter of Champeaux, April 3, 1790.

Old Regime, denouncing privileged tribunals and privileged forms of procedure for certain kinds of privileged litigants. He mentioned that there had been a distinction made in criminal law between a privileged crime and a common crime. He also noted that privileged defenders of the cases of others possessed the exclusive right of pleading, even for those who were able to do without their help, and observed that it was remarkable that no law in France recognized the natural right of each citizen to defend himself in civil law and that criminal law deprived him of a defender for the protection of his life. He told the Assembly that a sensible organization of judicial power ought to make it impossible in the future for these injustices, which destroyed the civic equality of citizens, to manifest themselves in a part of public administration where this equality ought to be the most inviolable. Thouret then informed the Assembly that the plan of the committee would entail "the necessary destruction" of all existing tribunals, which would be replaced by new institutions, a condition necessary for regeneration to be achieved.

He then presented a plan under which there would be a justice of the peace for each canton and a tribunal for each district. The justice of the peace could adjudicate, without appeal, any case in which the amount at issue was up to fifty *livres*, and because its purpose was to render justice quickly, expeditiously and without expense, no legal practitioners were to be allowed to practice before them. They would also judge cases in which the amount at issue was up to one hundred *livres*, and in some cases an even greater amount, particularly in rural areas. Judgments in this category were eligible for appeal, which would take place at the district court and could not be carried beyond it.

The jurisdiction of the district court began where that of the justice of the peace ended, and completed what Thouret called the first degree of jurisdiction in the judiciary. The committee wanted the Assembly to determine the number of tribunals for each district, the number of judges in each tribunal and the extent of their competence up to a value of 250 *livres*. Finally, although Thouret did not discuss them specifically, his plan also envisaged courts of appeal, but he wished to defer consideration of them until after the first degree of jurisdiction was completed.[92]

After Thouret's presentation, however, his report did not emerge as the focus for discussion, which centered instead on the scope of the reform itself, for some deputies were extremely reluctant to break completely with several hundred years of legal development and tradition. They argued that a major reform of the existing judicial system

---

92 *AP*, XII: 344–349; *Procès-verbal de l'Assemblée nationale*, No. 239 (March 24, 1790), p. 9.

was sufficient and that it was not necessary to destroy it altogether. Jacques-Antoine-Marie de Cazalès, for example, spoke immediately after Thouret and defended the existing judiciary, particularly the *parlements*. He put forward a motion by which the Assembly would decide whether the existing judicial order would be destroyed or only reformed and asked that the Assembly spend at least three days considering the issue. His motion produced a tumult in the Assembly and Cazalès withdrew it when the president of the Assembly, Rabaut de Saint-Etienne, pointed out that the constitutional aspects, rather than the structure of the judiciary, had to be considered first. But as soon as Cazalès withdrew his motion, Roederer said that the Assembly ought to decide immediately whether or not the current judicial system would be restructured entirely. This led to an angry exchange during which another deputy asked for a reconsideration of Cazalès's motion, and the session ended with the Assembly defeating it and decreeing the complete reconstruction of the judicial system.[93] For the judiciary, then, it was this vote, as much as the night of August 4, that was the death knell of the Old Regime.

The decision reflected the paramount importance that the National Assembly accorded to the judiciary as a critical element in its regeneration of France. Justice was now to be dispensed by the nation, guided by a sense of equity through the medium of laws common to all. Realizing that one of the greatest influences that a nation could have over its citizens was through the administration of justice, the deputies wanted the judiciary to reflect faithfully the new values of the nation.[94] Indeed, along with the new administration, the National Assembly considered the judiciary a linchpin of its new ideal of the polity.[95]

Furthermore, with the spirit of union that was central to the new ethos of the nation, the National Assembly sought to promote harmony and consensus among its citizens. Aware of the litigious nature of Old Regime society, the Assembly did not seek merely to administer justice freely, fairly and expeditiously; as it formulated its new ideal for the polity the National Assembly, particularly through the institution of the justice of the peace, sought to discourage litigation altogether and to promote goodwill among citizens as much as possible. Ultimately, the Assembly sought to transform the judiciary in such a way that recourse to litigation would be only an action of last resort. In order to achieve its goals, then,

93 *AP*, XII: 349; *Procès-verbal de l'Assemblée nationale*, No. 239 (March 24, 1790), pp. 9–10; BN Mss. Nouv. acq. fr. 4121, fols. 508–509; AN KK 643, entry of March 24, 1790; AM Brest LL 46 (1790), no. 43, letter of March 24, 1790.
94 AN T 643, undated memoir on organization of new judiciary.
95 AM Arles AA 23, fol. 634.

reform of the judiciary was insufficient; it had to be restructured in its entirety, which is what the Assembly proceeded to do.

Following the decision to reorganize the judiciary, discussion did not resume until March 29. As had been the case with the debate on the administration, between the time of its presentation in December and the beginning of consideration in March, the project put forward by the committee had been heavily criticized,[96] so when deliberation began alternative plans began to emerge. The first one advanced was by Adrien Duport, whose project called for a judiciary similar to that of England, with juries in civil as well as criminal cases and travelling judges on a circuit holding sessions in different departments of the kingdom. It also called for "*grands juges*" for the entire kingdom, who would hear cases on appeal and be empowered to revise judgments if necessary. The reading of Duport's plan occupied the remainder of the March 29 meeting and continued into that of the next day.[97]

After Duport completed the reading of his plan on March 30, Charles Chabroud, a barrister from Vienne who was little known in the Assembly, rose to speak. He began by stating that he had not been presumptuous enough to build a system, and chided his colleagues for their propensity to set up a judiciary similar in structure to the old one, a series of ascending jurisdictions. Confessing a sense of unease over the similarities between the old judiciary and the proposed plans for the new one, he told his colleagues that it was not worth the trouble of changing decorations if the scene was to remain the same. Like Duport, Chabroud opposed permanent, fixed courts, particularly courts of appeal, which he saw as bastions of a corporate frame of mind inimical to the general interest. He went well beyond Duport, as well as the Committee of the Constitution, however, in denouncing permanently established courts not only because of their narrow corporate outlook, but also because, in his view, their existence would encourage litigation, which in turn would promote discord among citizens. Chabroud argued that one goal of the Assembly in establishing the new judiciary should be fewer barristers, fewer attorneys, fewer consultations, fewer summons and fewer lawsuits. He contended that neighbors would reconcile themselves once they had had time to reflect, implying that the new judiciary ought to seek to discourage litigation as much as possible. He also asserted that permanent tribunals were more likely to give rise to corruption, but he believed all of these dangers would disappear with circuit courts.

96 See Ménard de la Groye, *Correspondance*, p. 182; Faulcon, *Correspondance*, II: 142–143; Duquesnoy, *Journal*, II: 199–200, 503.
97 *Procès-verbal de l'Assembleé nationale*, No. 244 (March 29, 1790), p. 8; No. 245 (March 30, 1790), p. 10; BN Mss. Nouv. acq. fr. 4121, fols. 518–519.

Chabroud also went on to argue for the periodic election of judges, only a single degree of jurisdiction, that the king have no role in the nomination of judges and that the people have no role in the nomination of *procureurs du roi*. He then submitted his own plan for the judiciary to the Assembly.

Chabroud's speech made a powerful impression on the Assembly.[98] Under the Old Regime the administration of justice had been chaotic, with the jurisdiction of courts often unclear and frequently disputed.[99] As a result, most of the plans submitted to the Assembly had been concerned as much with the structure of the judiciary as with the dispensation of justice; based on the new administrative framework just decreed by the Assembly, they were rational – even elegant – constructs in which their authors took great pride. Chabroud, however, did not wish the mandate of August 4 interpreted so narrowly and challenged the Assembly to do more. Looking beyond merely the dispensation of justice to such broader concerns as the reduction of litigation, he wanted the new judiciary to be a vehicle for realizing the new ideal of the polity by promoting fellowship, union and concord among citizens. More concerned with the spirit than with the structure of the new judiciary, this heretofore obscure back bencher excited the Assembly with his aspirations for using the new judicial order to achieve a fraternal community of citizens.[100]

By the next day, however, the Assembly was beginning to feel overwhelmed by a surfeit of plans for the judiciary. Although the observation by one member of the Assembly that 200 to 300 deputies had projects on the judiciary that they wished to present was doubtless an exaggeration, there were several plans circulating – that of the committee, those of Duport and Chabroud, as well as projects submitted by other deputies.[101] After a desultory discussion on March 31,[102] the deputy Bertrand Barère took the floor in order to attempt to provide a better focus for the discussion of the judiciary than that of simply considering various competing plans. Rather than concentrating on one project or another, Barère suggested a set of propositions that the

98 See *Journal des Etats-Généraux*, X: 61–62; BN Mss. Nouv. acq. fr. 4121, fols. 518–519.
99 See C. B. A. Behrens, *Society, Government and the Enlightenment: The Experience of Eighteenth-Century France and Prussia* (New York, 1985), p. 94.
100 BN Mss. Nouv. acq. fr. 4121, fols. 518–519; Duquesnoy, *Journal*, II: 504–505; *Journal des Etats-Généraux*, X: 60–62; Faulcon, *Correspondance*, II: 165; Poncet-Delpech, *Bulletins*, p. 258; *Courier de Madon*, April 5, 1790. For a contemporary assessment of Chabroud's influence on the judiciary, see Eustache-Antoine Hua, *Mémoires d'un avocat au Parlement de Paris* (Poitiers, 1871), pp. 28–31, 181.
101 See Faulcon, *Correspondance*, II: 143, for the mention of hundreds of projects on the judiciary. See also *Etats-Généraux: Journal de la Correspondance de Nantes*, IV: 264.
102 BN Mss. Nouv. acq. fr. 4121, fol. 520.

Assembly should decide before formulating a new judiciary. His agenda, which the Assembly adopted, concerned itself with the use of juries, whether there would be sedentary tribunals or whether justice would be rendered by judges travelling a circuit, the number of jurisdictions in the new judicial system, whether judges would have lifetime appointments or whether they would be elected for a fixed term, whether judges would be elected by the people or appointed by the king, whether the public prosecutor would be appointed by the king only, whether or not a high court of review would be established and how its duties should be distributed.[103]

Adhering largely to the outline offered by Barère, the Assembly debated and decided most matters concerning the new judicial system throughout the spring and much of the summer of 1790. It then awaited the new project from the Committee of the Constitution incorporating them, which the committee distributed in late June and presented on July 5.[104] Many deputies believed that the new judiciary was the single most important element of its remaking of French society – indeed, one predicted in a letter shortly before consideration began that there would be more debates on the judiciary than they had ever had on any other subject,[105] and the discussion frequently revealed the new ideal of the nation that infused the Assembly. It is the effort to realize and instill this ethos that will be examined more than the entire course of the restructuring of the judiciary, which has been ably treated elsewhere.[106]

Over the following months much of the debate was, of course, often legal and technical in nature, but from the outset it was apparent that the discussions were also informed by the new ideal of the polity. One underlying assumption of the Assembly throughout its consideration of the judiciary, for example, was a totally new conception of the citizenry that derived from its new ideal. In accordance with its belief that citizens would make the nation the focus for their highest ideals and conduct, the Assembly did not view the populace as an inert mass that needed to be policed; instead, the citizenry was the conscience of the nation and the upholder of its moral sense. This tenet manifested itself in the first days

103 *Procès-verbal de l'Assemblée nationale*, No. 246 (31 March 1790), pp. 3–4; AN KK 645, fol. 610.
104 See AD Charente-Maritime 4 J 1523, letter of June 25, 1790; *Procès-verbal de l'Assemblée nationale*, No. 340 (July 5, 1790), p. 6.
105 See Faulcon, *Correspondance*, II: 142–143.
106 See Edmond Seligman, *La Justice en France pendant la Révolution*, 2 vols. (Paris, 1901–1913); Jean-Paul Royer, *La Société judiciaire depuis le XVIIIᵉ siècle* (Paris, 1979); Robert Badinter, ed., *Une Autre justice. Contributions à l'histoire de la justice sous la Révolution française*, (Paris, 1989). In addition, Ted Margadant discusses another aspect of the debate on the judiciary, which was to foster greater equality between towns. See Margadant, *Urban Rivalries*, pp. 327–346.

of discussion, on the use of juries in the new judiciary, and was perhaps best captured by Thouret in a speech on April 6. Contrasting the indifference and callousness of a criminal court judge after ten years on the bench, who would, said Thouret, be so cynical that he would have difficulty making a distinction between an accused and a guilty individual, he asserted that only the institution of the jury could prevent such a scandal from developing in the new judiciary.[107] This belief also made itself felt in the unanimous decision of the Assembly that judges would be elected by the people exclusively.[108]

While much of the debate on the new judicial system revolved around the resolution of the issues approved by the Assembly on March 31, there was also an underlying agenda devoted to realizing the new ideal of the polity through the new judiciary, an agenda to which Thouret had briefly alluded in his speech of April 6 when he exhorted the Assembly not to despair of diminishing and abbreviating the number of cases. French society under the Old Regime had been extremely litigious, and the Assembly viewed the destruction of privileged corporatism as but a first step in addressing the problem. In its restructuring of the judiciary, the National Assembly also devised several institutions designed specifically to discourage litigation and to foster the spirit of harmony and union that was an indispensable element of the Assembly's new ideal.

One such institution, modeled especially after analogues in England and Holland, was that of the justice of the peace, which the Committee of the Constitution presented to the Assembly on July 7. Thouret introduced the project by noting that it was an institution known in several other nations. Its goal was to provide, especially for rural inhabitants, justice that would be prompt, easy to obtain and, perhaps most important, local. It was not to be encumbered by formal legal procedure and would be governed less by law than by common sense – a great benefit, Thouret said, for citizens who had long been duped by practitioners. The holder of the office would not be required to have any legal background; the major criteria were to be the wisdom of experience and sound judgment, and he would act as a mediator or a judge. In order to make justice readily accessible to citizens, the committee proposed that there be a justice of the peace for at least each canton. Indeed, as they were intended and as they evolved, the justices of the peace have

---

107 *Procès-verbal de l'Assemblée nationale*, No. 251 (April 6, 1790), pp. 8–9; Jacques-Guillaume Thouret, *Second discours de M. Thouret à l'Assemblée nationale sur l'organisation du pouvoir judiciaire ... Séance du 6 avril 1790 : discussion sur l'établissement des jurés* (Paris, n.d.).
108 The Committee of the Constitution had recommended that the king choose between two individuals elected for each judgeship. On the unanimity, see *Journal des débats*, May 4–5, 1790. See also AN KK 645, fols. 644–645; de Ferrières, *Mémoires*, II: 46–47.

correctly been described as "a sort of flying squadron of legal order and social peace" who were "to be permanently available, even to judge, arbitrate, and conciliate in homes, cafés, wine shops, ateliers, on the streets, at the very sites and moments of disputes,"[109] and to this one might add that rural justices were likewise to be available in the field, in barns and other such sites. No legal counsel of any kind was permitted in any hearing for fear that they would impair the process of conciliation. The cost of such justice was to be quite low; justices could charge no more than twelve *livres* in total costs. Furthermore, as "offices of charitable jurisprudence," the justice of the peace and his assistants were also to provide the poor with free legal advice. The Assembly enthusiastically approved the office without major debate and it became a cornerstone of the new judiciary that the National Assembly established.[110]

Whereas the new administration, in eliminating anomalies or partiality and instituting uniform government, had represented the macro-effort to repudiate privilege in the overall governance of the kingdom, the new judiciary was a micro-effort designed to realize the new ideal of the polity in the daily life of citizens. In an effort to attract good candidates, in fact, the National Assembly established generous salaries for administrative and judicial posts, particularly the latter, which some thought excessive but which highlighted the desire of the National Assembly to realize its vision as fully as possible.[111] No longer would justice be a preserve of special interests nor characterized by undue expense and aggravation; instead, it would be the source of equity and fairness in the polity. In a fraternal community of citizens – in which all were equal before the law and in which rights were therefore equal and universal rather than exclusive, as they had been under the Old Regime – justice would be

109 Richard M. Andrews, "The justices of the peace of revolutionary Paris, September 1792–November 1794 (frimaire year III)," *Past and Present*, 52 (August 1971), 56–105. Although the focus of this article is the period of the Convention, it captures well the intent of the National Assembly in founding the institution. Indeed, one newspaper in 1790 indicated that the justice of the peace ought to be accessible at all hours of the day or night every day of the year. See *Journal du Département de l'Allier*, December 10, 1790 [BN 8° Lᶜ 10.12]. For a contemporary insight into the idea of the justice of the peace, see *Journal des décrets de l'Assemblée nationale, pour les habitans des campagnes*, July 10–16, 1790.

110 For the perspective of deputies on the institution of the justice of the peace, see Queruau-Lamerie, "Lettres de ... Maupetit," 22, 220–221; AD Côtes-d'Armor 1 L 389, letters of Baudouin, October 16, 1790, October 19, 1790; AN DIV* 2, fol. 163; AN T 643, undated memoir on organization of new judiciary. See also [Kerverseau and Clavelin], *Histoire de la Révolution de France*, new edition, V: 70–71; *Journal de correspondance de Paris à Nantes, et du Département de la Loire-Inférieure*, 10 vols. (Nantes, 1789–1791), X: 219.

111 See Thibaudeau, *Correspondance inédite*, ed. Carré and Boissonnade, p. 134; BM Lyon Ms. 2191, letter of August 30, 1790, letter of September 4, 1790; AN DIV 67, dossier 2030, document 2.

administered in a rational and totally disinterested fashion.[112] And because its disinterestedness and equitability would be apparent to all, it would promote and reinforce harmony and concord. It is little wonder, then, that members of the National Assembly viewed the judiciary as a foundation of their remaking of the polity, extending impartial and enlightened judgments to all. Indeed, underscoring the centrality of the judiciary to the new ideal of the polity, the populace was, through the institutions of the justice of the peace and the jury respectively, to be both a beneficiary and a source of the new conception of the nation. Justice would consist of the rendering of sound, intelligent decisions and not the adversarial and illogical process that it had been under the Old Regime.[113]

The aspirations of the National Assembly, however, were not limited simply to the equitable dispensation of justice. In the course of the discussion on justices of the peace, the deputy Louis-Pierre-Joseph Prugnon had alluded to the ideal first advanced by Chabroud on March 30, when Prugnon asserted that rendering justice was only the second obligation of society; the first, he said, was to prevent litigation. Prugnon said that society had to tell parties that in order to arrive at the temple of justice it was necessary to pass through that of harmony. This imperative, directly derived from the new ideal of the polity, underlay a more original institution devised by the National Assembly to realize that ideal, the bureau of peace and conciliation, the proposal for which was presented by Thouret to the Assembly, along with the family court, on August 5. Thouret said the purpose of the bureau would be to calm the passions of those who entered too rashly into litigation. Noting that there were many motives that impelled litigants, he asserted that it was necessary to balance such malign influences with a beneficial institution. There was some opposition to the bureau, chiefly from deputies who believed it would infringe on the justices of the peace. Chabroud, however, came out strongly in favor of the bureau, stating that it was the institution designed to lessen litigation and asserting that it would approach and fulfill the constitution. Following a brief discussion, the Assembly voted in favor of establishing them.

The deputies then went on, with little discussion, to require that, before a case could proceed to a district court, the litigants had to present a certificate attesting that they had attempted arbitration in a bureau of peace and conciliation. The Assembly also decreed that in each town in

112 See Delandine, *De Quelques changemens politiques*, p. 166; Jean-Baptiste-Joseph-Innocent-Philadelphie Regnault-Warin, *Mémoires pour servir à la vie du général Lafayette et à l'histoire de l'Assemblée constituante*, 2 vols. (Paris, 1824), II: 145–146.
113 For an insight into the legal system of the Old Regime, see Steven G. Reinhardt, *Justice in the Sarladais 1770–1790* (Baton Rouge, 1991).

which a district court was situated there would be a bureau of peace made up of six members, chosen from among citizens known for their patriotism and probity, of whom two had to be men of law, who would serve a two year term. Likewise, the family court sought to settle disputes without publicity or expensive, cumbersome legal procedures.[114]

A final aspect of the effort of the National Assembly to attain its new ideal of the polity stemmed from a criticism that Thouret had made when he presented the report of the Committee of the Constitution on March 24 – the impediments to personal defense under the Old Regime. Thouret had asserted that civil equality ought to be the most inviolable in the judicial sphere, and the Assembly moved to realize this goal in September, 1790. On September 2, in complementary legislation on the judiciary, the National Assembly dissolved the Orders of Barristers in France, thereby abolishing the legal profession in France. In granting each citizen the right to defend himself, the Assembly opened the law to all equally, not allowing it to be dominated by any group. If a litigant wished to retain a person trained in the law to handle a lawsuit, he or she could do so, but the practitioner was clearly a servitor rather than an oracle, as had been the case under the Old Regime. Law and justice in the new judiciary would be so self-evident that professional legal practitioners would be unnecessary and superfluous. Indeed, several weeks later, on January 29, 1791, the Assembly made access of citizens to the law complete by establishing the office of *défenseur officieux*. The law authorized a citizen to ask any other citizen to act as a *défenseur officieux*, empowering him to argue a case, whether orally or in writing. Once again, these actions of the National Assembly emanated directly from the new ethos of the nation and the central place of law in it. Law was the chief source of equity and equality in the nation, and if laws common to all were to be the basis of society, they could not be the preserve of a few; it was imperative that each citizen have untrammeled access to it. The degree of consensus on this question within the National Assembly is clear, for both measures passed without debate.[115]

Through these institutions and actions, as well as others, the National Assembly sought to put the judiciary in the service of its new ideal of the nation. Law was no longer partial or synonymous with rights or privileges

114 *Procès-verbal de l'Assemblée nationale*, No. 371 (August 5, 1790), pp. 7–13. See also *Courier de Madon*, August 5, 1790. For more on the bureaus of peace and conciliation, see Jacques Godechot, *Les Institutions de la France sous la Révolution et l'Empire* (Paris, 1968), pp. 148–149; on the family courts, James F. Traer, *Marriage and the Family in Eighteenth-Century France* (Ithaca, 1980), pp. 143–144.
115 On changes within the legal profession during the Revolution, see Lenard Berlanstein, *The Barristers of Toulouse in the Eighteenth Century (1740–1793)* (Baltimore, 1975); Fitzsimmons, *The Parisian Order of Barristers and the French Revolution*.

and thereby divisive, as it had been under the Old Regime; rather, as the Declaration of Rights stated, law was the expression of the general will. Consequently, adjudication was not to be disputatious or adversarial, but conciliatory and a search for equity. Henceforth, justice would no longer be the arcane, legalistic, interminable and occasionally biased procedure that it had been under the Old Regime; it was to be prompt, disinterested and easily accessible to all. It was to be a justice of the people, by the people, for the people under the benevolent auspices of the nation.

From the institutions of the justices of the peace to the use of juries in criminal cases, the National Assembly sought as much as possible to realize the new ideal of the polity. A scholar of the justices of the peace has aptly stated that the post was responsible for bolstering the moral unity and preserving the social continuity of society, and that the justices were "defending the rule of law itself and on its first line of defense."[116] The rule of law that they were defending was the idea of law as the very fabric of the nation, the source of equality, fraternity, equity and union. In the judiciary established by the National Assembly, any resort to litigation was perceived as nothing less than a societal failure.[117] Indeed, Richard Andrews's description of the office of justice of the peace as "a totally revolutionary institution, a radical breach with the past, in conception, structure and implications for local collective existence"[118] could be equally applied to most of the institutions and measures of the National Assembly concerning the judiciary. The repudiation of privileged corporatism and the effort to realize the new ideal of the nation totally redefined the structure, scope and role of justice in the nation.[119] The restructuring of the judiciary was a task that the deputies found much more difficult than their other major undertaking, the reorganization of the administration, but it was an achievement in which they took enormous pride.[120]

116 Andrews, "The justices of the peace," 61. I obviously disagree somewhat with his assertion that however benevolent and sentimentally generous the role of the office may have been, it was also a more subtle and effective means of social control. This was much truer for the period of the Convention that Andrews analyzes; for the period of the National Assembly I would argue that the emphasis was far more on benevolence.
117 See the comment of Thouret on August 16 in Pilastre de la Brardière and Leclerc, Correspondance, IV: 194. It occurred during discussion of arbitration. See Procès-verbal de l'Assemblée nationale, No. 382 (August 16, 1790), pp. 6–8.
118 Andrews, "The justices of the peace," 57.
119 See, for example, Duquesnoy, Journal, II: 501–502. See also BM Grenoble Ms. R 5949, document 10; Isser Woloch, "The fall and resurrection of the Civil Bar, 1789–1820s," French Historical Studies, 15 (1987), 241–262.
120 On the difficulties, see Duquesnoy, Journal, II: 503. On the pride of the Assembly in the new structure, see Ménard de la Groye, Correspondance, pp. 214–215; BM Lyon Ms. 2191, letter of August 19, 1790; Rabaut de Saint-Etienne, Précis de l'histoire de la Révolution, p. 260; Faulcon, Correspondance, II: 308–309.

It was during the course of discussions on the new judiciary that the National Assembly saw the most tangible realization of its new ideal. In the evening session of June 7, a deputation from the Commune of Paris appeared before the Assembly. Noting that various federations had formed spontaneously in different parts of France, the members of the delegation proposed that all of the newly formed or forming departments be invited to send representatives to Paris so that, in the name of all of France, they could, in the presence of the National Assembly, swear to defend and maintain the new constitution to the death. The deputation proposed July 14 as the date for the event. The Assembly enthusiastically welcomed the proposal and charged the Committee of the Constitution with preparing a decree on having National Guards of all the departments send representatives to Paris.[121]

In this way the *Fête de la Fédération* evolved, culminating in the grand ceremony on July 14, 1790, the original and perhaps the grandest of all the national festivals.[122] Despite heavy rain, representatives of National Guards of all eighty-three departments drew up before the king, queen and National Assembly in a moving and imposing demonstration of national unity. Those assembled took an oath of fidelity to the nation, the law and the king, while Louis swore to maintain the constitution and Talleyrand said Mass on an "altar of the fatherland" specially built for the occasion.[123] The entire ceremony seemed to represent the apotheosis of the new ideal of the polity conceived by the Assembly: Crown and society, as one in the nation, to which all other personal values, interests or beliefs – political, social, economic, religious, regional – were subordinated in a spirit of union and goodwill.[124]

Without question, the *Fête de la Fédération* marked the zenith of the National Assembly's existence; deputies and observers from across the entire political spectrum were moved by the spectacle.[125] The sense of unity and civic spirit descended from the night of August 4 and consolidated on February 4 was magnificently realized in a spirit of common purpose felt throughout the realm, as the king, the National Assembly and the nation seemed completely unified in expectations and

121 *Procès-verbal de l'Assemblée nationale*, No. 312 (June 7, 1790), p. 10; Ménard de la Groye, *Correspondance*, pp. 227–228. See also Mona Ozouf, *Festivals and the French Revolution* (Cambridge, Mass., 1988), p. 44.
122 On the festivals, see Ozouf, *Festivals and the French Revolution*; Hunt, *Politics, Culture, and Class in the French Revolution*.
123 For good descriptions of the festival, see Bertrand de Moleville, *Annals*, II: 518–534; *Description fidèle de tout ce qui a précédé, accompagné et suivi la cérémonie de la confédération nationale du 14 juillet 1790* (Paris, n.d.).  124 See BM Angers Ms. 1888, p. 175.
125 See, for example, *Révolutions de Paris*, No. 53; *Révolutions de France et de Brabant*, No. 34, No. 35.

outlook.[126] Indeed, the collective goodwill of the *Fête de la Fédération* carried the National Assembly through the following months, as the end of its term seemed in sight.[127]

Without question, it now appeared that the aspirations of the National Assembly would unquestionably be attained and that Louis and the Assembly were joined in a partnership dedicated to advancing the cause of the nation through the constitution. Indeed, Mirabeau, who was in the service of the king as a secret advisor at this time, compellingly argued in secret correspondence that the destruction of powerful privileged corporations in the kingdom was advantageous to the Crown and that the achievements of the National Assembly – particularly the creation of what he called "just one class of citizens," of which, he said, Richelieu would have approved – could clearly work in the Crown's favor.[128]

The spirit of harmony and common purpose generated by the *Fête de la Fédération* extended well beyond July, 1790, and continued throughout the following year.[129] By June, 1791, the National Assembly, confident of the support of the nation and the assent of the king, had begun to conclude its work. The Committee on Revision was helping the Committee of the Constitution to draw up the Constitutional Act by separating laws that were not constitutional from those that were, and elections to the Legislative Assembly were in progress. Suddenly, however, the National Assembly had its existence artificially and painfully prolonged by the departure of the king from Paris.

126  See AN F¹c III Gard 10, letter of administrators of Department of Gard to Louis, July 19, 1790; AN F¹c III Vosges 8, letter of mayor, municipal officers and *procureur* of commune of Saint-Die to Louis, July 20, 1790; AN F¹c III Var 9, letter of mayor, municipal officers and notables of Toulon to Louis, July 30, 1790; AN F¹c III Gers 9, undated letter of administrators of Department of Gers to Louis; Ménard de la Groye, *Correspondance*, pp. 244, 246–247. See also Ozouf, *Festivals and the French Revolution*, p. 54.
127  On the degree of consensus that existed in the National Assembly, see Patrick, "The Second Estate in the Constituent Assembly," especially 231, 235, 241–242, 246, 249 and 251. As the title of his work indicates, Norman Hampson, *Prelude to Terror : the Constituent Assembly and the Failure of Consensus, 1789–1791* (Oxford, 1988), chooses to emphasize quarrels that arose in the remaking of the polity, but argues that these disagreements came about because both the Left and the Right in the Assembly were seeking to build a new and perfect society. It was, in fact, this commitment to a new and more perfect society – embodied in the pact of association forged on the night of August 4 – that was the object of consensus. Disagreement arose over how to achieve this new ideal, to be sure, but the differences that ensued did not, in my opinion, constitute "hatred."
128  See Honoré-Gabriel Riquetti Mirabeau, *Correspondance entre le comte de Mirabeau et le comte de la Marck pendant les années 1789, 1790 et 1791*, ed. Adolphe Fourier de Bacourt, 3 vols. (Paris, 1851), II: 74–79, with the quotation on II: 75. See also II: 120, 192–198, 225–227, 268–270, 431–432.
129  See, for example, AM Toulon L 104, dossier D⁴ 2, letter of Ricard to municipal officers of Toulon, December 3, 1790, in which this deputy asserted that the king was entirely in favor of the Revolution and that France was fortunate to have such a monarch.

I accept, then, the Constitution; I will promise to maintain it ... I declare that, informed of the adhesion that the great majority of the people give to the Constitution, I will renounce at the meeting what I asked for in the work and, being responsible only to the nation, no one else, when I renounce it, will have the right to complain.

Letter of Louis to the National Assembly, September 13, 1791

On Tuesday, June 21, 1791, as the secretary prepared to read the *procès-verbal*, the president of the National Assembly, Alexandre de Beauharnais, took the floor to announce to its astonished members that at eight o'clock that morning the mayor of Paris had appeared at Beauharnais's residence to apprise him of the departure of the king and the royal family. Thus began an episode that would become one of the finest hours of the National Assembly, yet would also precipitate some of its least defensible actions. The crisis provoked by the king's flight cast a pall over the completion of the constitution, vitiated somewhat its grandeur – if not its moral force – and resulted in an awkward and anticlimactic conclusion to the Assembly's work.

The National Assembly had good reason to be puzzled and surprised. The sense of common purpose arising from the *Fête de la Fédération* had generated a strong sense of affection for the monarch and maintained belief in a unity of outlook that Louis had only recently reaffirmed. The fondness and respect accorded to Louis had been apparent during a serious illness he experienced during the spring of 1791. When his recovery became evident, a number of *Te Deums* were offered and expressions of relief arrived from all parts of France.[1] More significant in reinforcing the sense of common purpose, however, had been Louis's

1 AN F¹c III Oise 7, undated letter of municipal officers and notables of Compiègne to Louis; AN F¹c III Côtes-du-Nord 1, letter of mayor and municipal officers of Saint-Brieuc to Louis, March 23, 1791; AN F¹c III Hérault 10, letter of administrators of Department of Hérault to Minister of the Interior, March 28, 1791; AN F¹c III Seine-Inférieure 14, undated letter of administrators of Department of Seine-Inférieure to Louis; AN F¹c III Seine-et-Oise 11, extract of deliberations of commune of Louvres, March 25, 1791; BM Lyon Ms. 2191, letter of March 20, 1791. The scope of such events is especially evident in AM Toulon L 614, dossier K 47, list of attendees at the *Te Deum*, March 25, 1791.

handling of a war scare shortly after his recovery from his illness. A deep sense of unease had arisen in many parts of France about possible intervention by foreign powers to suppress the Revolution; indeed, as tensions increased, Louis received several requests to clarify the situation.[2] He finally responded clearly and forcefully through a communication that the Minister of Foreign Affairs revealed to the National Assembly during the evening session of April 23. In a letter that was to be sent to all ambassadors and ministers of France in foreign countries, who in turn were to communicate it to their host governments, Louis recounted the actions undertaken by the National Assembly and asserted that the Revolution represented the abolition of a number of abuses accumulated over centuries. He stated that he accepted, without hesitation, an auspicious constitution that simultaneously regenerated his authority, the nation and the monarchy. He particularly criticized those who sought to cast doubt on his intentions, and recalled his visit to the National Assembly on February 4, during which he had promised to uphold the constitution and the *Fête de la Fédération*, where he had sworn to do so before the assembled kingdom. He also alluded to the night of August 4, noting how honored he was by the title given to him that evening.

Refuting rumors that the king was not happy, that he was not free and other such assertions, rumors that he observed had now reached foreign courts, the letter instructed ambassadors or ministers to leave no doubt with their host governments that Louis intended to uphold with all of his power the constitution which, in assuring the liberty and equality of citizens, founded national prosperity on the steadiest foundations, affirmed royal authority by laws and would make him happy. It stated that the chief task of the envoys was to justify, to defend and to take as a guide to their conduct the constitution. The Assembly interrupted the reading of this letter by its president several times with applause, and it produced enormous satisfaction in the Assembly, which ordered a copy sent to all departments, the army, the navy and the colonies. The Assembly further ordered that the letter be read from the pulpit of each parish in France.[3] The letter eased tensions

2 AN F¹c III Ille-et-Vilaine 9, letter of administrators and *procureur-général-syndic* of Department of Ille-et-Vilaine to Louis, April 26, 1791; AN F¹c III Côte d'Or 8, dossier 3, letter of administration of Department of Côte d'Or to president of National Assembly, April 18, 1791; AN F¹c III Finistère 1, letter of administrators of directory of Department of Finistère to Louis, April 25, 1791. See also *Etats-Généraux. Journal de la Correspondance de Nantes*, VIII: 422–423.
3 *Procès-verbal de l'Assemblée nationale*, No. 630 (April 23, 1791), pp. 29–30. For more on the effect of the letter on the Assembly, see [Kerverseau and Clavelin], *Histoire de la révolution de 1789*, new edn., VI: 83; *Journal des Etats-Généraux*, XXIV: 423–430.

considerably and restored confidence and a sense of partnership with Louis.[4]

In addition, in June, shortly before his flight, Louis had written an urgent letter to Condé, urging him to return to France, and it was rumored that Artois had paid his debts in Paris and was preparing to return to France before July 14 in order to attend the anniversary of the *Fête de la Fédération*.[5] However much the notion that Louis had been kidnapped later became a convenient fiction, it must be recognized that the initial belief that Louis may not have been acting on his own free will was not at all unwarranted.

When he fled, Louis left behind a letter that indicated that he was unhappy with the new political arrangements stipulated in the constitution, but his disaffection with the Revolution extended more deeply than that. A major source of Louis's estrangement was the religious policy of the National Assembly. The ideal of the National Assembly – the repudiation of privileged corporatism and the realization of the new ideal of the polity – was comprehensive, and the effort to realize it therefore took the Assembly into the sphere of religion. Having destroyed the corporate identity and independence of the Catholic Church in France by confiscating its lands, the Assembly sought to integrate the Church fully into the nation by making the clergy civil servants.[6] Aside from paying them salaries for the positions to which they were elected, the law of February 23, 1790, for example, made the clergy the chosen agents of the nation in the dissemination of new laws and decrees, which would be read by them from the pulpit.[7] The religious policy of the National Assembly was not the work of deputies hostile to religion or the Church – in fact, members of the clergy were eligible for all civic posts, including mayor or member of the directory of a department – but a consistent application of its new ideal of the polity within the new administration. Unfortunately, however, the Church was not merely a

4 AN F¹c III Ille-et-Vilaine 9, letter of administrators and *procureur-général-syndic* of Department of Ille-et-Vilaine to Louis, April 28, 1791; AN F¹c III Gironde 11, letter of administrators of Department of Gironde to Louis, April 30, 1791; AD Côte d'Or L 368, address of directory of Department of Côte d'Or to the king, April 28, 1791; AN C 125, dossier 407, documents 23–24; Ménard de la Groye, *Correspondance*, pp. 372–373.

5 *Etats-Généraux. Journal de la Correspondance de Nantes*, IX: 409, 441–442.

6 On the reorganization of the Church, which has a rich historiography, see John McManners, *The French Revolution and the Church* (New York, 1969); Bernard Plongeron, *Conscience religieuse en Révolution* (Paris, 1969). Good local studies include John McManners, *French Ecclesiastical Society under the Ancien Régime: A Study of Angers in the Eighteenth Century* (Manchester, 1960); Timothy Tackett, *Priest and Parish in Eighteenth-Century France: A Social and Political Study of the Curés of a Diocese in Dauphiné* (Princeton, 1977) and *Religion, Revolution and Regional Culture in Eighteenth-Century France: The Ecclesiastical Oath of 1791* (Princeton, 1986).

7 Tackett, *Priest and Parish*, p. 277.

national institution, but a supranational one, and it was this fact that led to difficulties. Louis, intensely religious and uncertain of the reaction of the pope, believed that his own salvation was at stake and delayed giving his approval to the Civil Constitution of the Clergy until late December, 1790. Furthermore, Louis himself continued to attend Mass in the chapel of the Louvre with refractory priests.

The approach of Easter, 1791, placed Louis in a dilemma. It was expected that he would attend Easter Mass at the parish of Saint-Germain l'Auxerrois, in which case he would receive communion from a constitutional priest. If he were in Paris and did not attend Mass at Saint-Germain l'Auxerrois, he would be vulnerable to the accusation that he had been disrespectful toward the constitution.[8] In order to avoid being caught in this quandary, Louis sought, on April 18, the Monday before Easter, to go to a summer palace at Saint-Cloud, but as the royal family attempted to leave a crowd of Parisians blocked their carriage, forcing cancellation of the trip. The incident produced a special meeting of the council of the Department of Paris, which drew up an address asking the monarch to dismiss advisers hostile to the constitution and to announce to foreign powers his free acceptance of the changes wrought by the Revolution.[9]

On April 19, the king reluctantly received a deputation delivering the address to him and offered only a curt response to it before he left for the National Assembly to protest what had happened. The statement of the administrators of Paris garnered support from other areas of France and the Assembly was hardly sympathetic in its reaction, with the president characterizing the incident as inseparable from the progress of liberty.[10] The episode heightened tension and suspicion on all sides, and although Louis's letter to his ambassadors a few days later did much to defuse the disquietude, Louis's religious concerns – to which he obliquely alluded in his statement to the National Assembly – now became compounded by a sense of personal affront.

Although there were other points of friction between Louis and the Assembly, this incident, according to the deposition that Louis gave after

8  See Bertrand de Moleville, *Annals* IV: 17–26.
9  AN F⁷ 3688¹, letter of administrators of Department of Paris to Minister of Interior, April 18, 1791; extraordinary session of council of Department, April 18, 1791. For more on the reaction of Paris, see BN Mss. Nouv. acq. fr. 2671, fols. 293–294, 295.
10  See AN C 184, dossier 115, document 6; AN F⁷ 3688¹, extraordinary session of council of department, April 19, 1791; *Procès-verbal de l'Assemblée nationale*, No. 626 (April 19, 1791), pp. 11–12. On the support the address of the Department of Paris received, see AD Côte d'Or L 347², extract from *procès-verbaux* of meetings of directory of district of Arnay-le-Duc, evening meeting of April 27, 1791; AN F¹c III Aude 7, dossier 1, letter of members of directory of Department of Aude to Louis, April 30, 1791; AN F¹c III Indre 7, extract from deliberations of directory of Department of Indre, April 22, 1791.

his return, was the chief catalyst in his decision to flee Paris. Preparations for the flight began to be made, and on the night of June 20 Louis and his family slipped out of the Tuileries, resulting in Beauharnais's disclosure to the stunned Assembly on June 21.[11] When Beauharnais finished his announcement, the deputy Charles Regnault took the floor to remind the Assembly of the courage and calm it had shown two years earlier, during the rising in Paris, and he encouraged it to offer the same spectacle once again. Furthermore, he proposed asking the ministers to come to the Assembly in order to receive orders from it, and to send couriers to all the departments with orders to arrest any members of the royal family not holding an authorization from the National Assembly. These motions were passed, as was one by Le Chapelier proposing that the National Assembly meet continuously day and night in order to prevent disorder, and that this decision be posted throughout Paris.[12]

The Assembly decided that the ministers, who were provisionally authorized to attend meetings, would be placed together in a nearby office to receive precise orders for the execution of decrees of the Assembly and to provide necessary information. In addition, the Assembly ordered its Diplomatic Committee to coordinate measures concerning foreign powers. It also authorized the promulgation of decrees without the approval of the king; provisionally, only the seal of state, which was delivered to the Assembly despite a putative prohibition by Louis, and the signature of the ministers would be necessary.[13] From this point, the National Assembly began to take charge, thereby reassuring the Parisian populace and the nation at large.[14]

The belief in a shared consensus with the king had been so strong that deputies had difficulty believing that Louis had fled. Indeed, the initial references to kidnapping or abduction do not appear to have been a ruse.[15] Soon afterward, however, the Minister of Justice, Duport du

11 For a sense of the shock with which the news was received in the Assembly, see BHVP Ms. 805, fol. 162.
12 *Procès-verbal de l'Assemblée nationale*, June 21, 1791, pp. 1–6. Because this session became permanent, it was not numbered. See also *Procès-verbal très-exact de la séance permanente de l'Assemblée Nationale, ouverte le mardi matin, 21 juin 1791, et levée, le dimanche 26, à quatre heures après-midi* (Paris, 1791), pp. 2–3.
13 *Procès-verbal de l'Assemblée nationale*, June 21, 1791, pp. 8–9; *Procès-verbal très-exact*, pp. 14–16, 20–21. See also AM Brest LL 46 (1791), no. 75, letter of June 21, 1791.
14 See AD Nord L 792, anonymous letter of June 22, (1791) by a deputy; François Hue, *Dernières années du règne et de la vie de Louis XVI* (Paris, 1814), p. 217.
15 See AD Meurthe-et-Moselle L 212, letter of Duquesnoy, June 21, 1791; on the sense of surprise, see, for example, AM Le Havre D³ 39, no. 150, letter of June 22, 1791; the letter of June 21 by the deputy Roger, in R. Rumeau, "Lettres du constituant Roger," *La Révolution française*, 43 (1902), 70–71. Similarly, a reference to abduction appears in a resolution of Barnave, who was at this time scarcely a friend of the royal family. *Procès-verbal très-exact*, p. 10.

Tertre, one of the first ministers to report to the Assembly, notified it of the discovery of an important document by a valet, who had turned it over to Laporte, Intendant of the Civil List. The Assembly summoned Laporte, and the document, a manifesto written in Louis's hand, was read to the Assembly.[16]

The manifesto was churlish in tone, complaining of the contraction in royal power that had occurred since July 14, 1789. To buttress his contentions Louis outlined the changes that had taken place in different areas of his authority, and it is indicative of their centrality to the Assembly's new ideal of the polity that the first two topics he addressed were justice and administration. It concluded with a paternalistic appeal that was hopelessly anachronistic, particularly in comparison with the grandeur of the new idea of the nation. At the completion of the reading, there was no tumultuousness in the Assembly, although there could no longer be any doubt about the Louis's intentions. Instead, Beauharnais calmly proposed that the Assembly pass to the order of the day and that the memoir of the king be sent to the Committee of the Constitution in order to prepare a proclamation, and both measures were approved. The moment symbolized the sense of union and resolve of the Assembly.[17]

Many deputies also sent private communications to the administrators of their department exhorting them to carry out their duties and to reassure the populace. It is clear that despite the public demeanor of calm by the Assembly, many deputies felt a deep concern about civil disorder or even civil war and also felt profoundly betrayed by Louis.[18] The most significant factors in allaying the uneasiness of deputies were the calm

16 *Procès-verbal de l'Assemblée nationale*, June 21, 1791, pp. 9–10; *Procès-verbal très-exact*, pp. 7–19. For the manifesto, see *I$^{ère}$ suite du procès-verbal de la séance permanente du 21 juin*, pp. 5–23.
17 See Ménard de la Groye, *Correspondance*, pp. 395–396; *I$^{ère}$ suite du procès-verbal de la séance permanente*, p. 23; *Procès-verbal très-exact*, p. 68. See also Thibaudeau, *Correspondance inédite*, ed. Carré and Boissonnade, pp. 143, 147. Even those hostile to the Assembly acknowledged the impressiveness of its conduct. See Hue, *Dernières années du règne et de la vie de Louis XVI*, pp. 220–221. See also Marie-Joseph-Paul-Yves-Roch-Gilbert du Motier, marquis de Lafayette, *Mémoires, correspondance et manuscrits du général Lafayette, publiés par sa famille*, 6 vols. (Paris, 1837), III: 80.
18 AD Loire-Atlantique L 176, no. 3, letter of Baco to administrators of Department of Loire-Inférieure, June 22, 1791; AD Puy-de-Dôme L 543, letter of Andrieu to administrators of Department of Puy-de-Dôme, June 23, 1791; AD Côte d'Or L 346², letter of Navier to administrators of directory of Department of Côte d'Or, June 22, 1791, and letter of deputies of Department of Côte d'Or to administrators of Department of Côte d'Or, June 22, 1791; AD Nord L 792, letter of anonymous deputy to his brother, June 23, 1791, 6.00 a.m.; AD Nord L 792, letter of deputies of Department of Nord to administration of department, June 22, 1791; Ménard de la Groye, *Correspondance*, pp. 395–396; AD Côtes-d'Armor 1 L 389, letter of Baudouin, June 21–22, 1791. See also BM Angers Ms. 1888, pp. 190–191.

that reigned in Paris and the way in which the city rallied to the National Assembly. As one deputy wrote:

It caused a great sensation at first, and everyone was in distress, but everything became calm after the shops closed, the horse-drawn carriages were sent back to their stables, [there were] no plays, [and] that evening everyone illuminated their home. It was never ordered that this be done; the least thing that there was one lit up. The Assembly is [held] in the greatest veneration, the people in the streets believe that we no longer have a king; it is the Assembly that is our king.[19]

Indeed, the quiet of the city and the resolve of the National Assembly were symbiotic; the tranquility of Paris gave the Assembly greater confidence, and the determination of the Assembly reassured the populace, allowing life to return to normal quickly.[20]

It is uncertain precisely what Louis was seeking to achieve by fleeing Paris. Some of his antagonists, attributing the worst motives to him in order to weaken his position, accused him of attempting to obtain the aid of foreign powers to restore his authority. This interpretation has gained some acceptance, and cannot in any way be dismissed, but other sources suggest that Louis did not seek to leave France nor did he desire a forcible solution, but sought to go to Montmédy in order to negotiate changes in the constitution from a more favorable position than was possible in Paris.[21] Because work on the constitution was nearing its conclusion Louis had to act before the constitution became final in order not to have to accept it in its then-current form.

In his longest letter to the court, Mirabeau had warned that it was imperative to seek revisions in the constitution before the National Assembly disbanded, at which time its prestige and that of the constitution would be at their zenith. He went on to suggest various projects to influence public opinion in favor of the Crown, but Louis

19 AD Nord L 792, letter of anonymous deputy to his brother and sister, June 22, 1791. See also AM Le Havre D³ 39, no. 150, letter of June 22, 1791; AD Marne 1 L 369, dossier June 25, letter of Prieur to municipal officers of Châlons-sur-Marne, June 25, 1791; AM Bordeaux D 227, no. 18, copy of letter of Nairac and de Sèze to directory of Department of Gironde, midnight, June 22, 1791; AM Toulon L 338, dossier H³ 13, letter of Ricard to municipal officers of Toulon, June 27, 1791; Queruau-Lamerie, "Lettres de Maupetit," 22, 474–475.
20 See, for example, Le Moniteur universel, June 24, 1791 and June 25, 1791 for the resumption of plays. Also on the situation at Paris, BHVP Ms. 805, fols. 201–217.
21 The duc de Choiseul, for example, asserted that Louis's determination not to leave France was well-known. Bouillé also stated that Montmédy was the goal, but noted that Louis was considering such plans as early as late January, 1791 – before the April incident at the Tuileries. See le duc de Choiseul-Stainville, Relation du départ de Louis XVI, le 20 juin 1791 (Paris, 1822), p. 53; see also pp. 53–56. On Bouillé, see François-Claude-Arnou Bouillé, Mémoires du marquis de Bouillé (Paris, 1822), pp. 191–193. Also supporting the case that Louis sought to negotiate, J. H. Clapham has observed that even after his return from Varennes and his suspension, in July, 1791, he preferred negotiations to force. See J. H. Clapham, The Causes of the War of 1792, reprint edn. (New York, 1969), p. 91.

apparently responded only to the admonition to act before completion of the constitution. The timing of Louis's flight, the memoirs of persons close to him and the tone and content of the manifesto he left behind all support such an explanation.[22]

Whatever Louis's intentions were, Mirabeau had also warned the court that in any confrontation between the Crown and the constitution, the nation would invariably choose the latter, and the correctness of his counsel on that issue was now borne out. A deputation from the various administrative bodies of the Department of Seine-et-Oise appeared before the Assembly on the evening of June 21 to express their loyalty and confidence in the National Assembly, and to reaffirm their oath to maintain the constitution of the kingdom.[23] This was the first of many protestations of loyalty that flooded the Assembly in the following days, leaving absolutely no doubt about the support it enjoyed from the nation.[24] In fact, on June 22, the Assembly approved an address to the French, written by the Committee of the Constitution, reassuring the nation that government would not cease with the flight of the king.[25]

A few hours later, at approximately ten o'clock in the evening, an exhausted courier arrived at the National Assembly amidst great commotion to announce that the king had been stopped at Varennes.[26] The Assembly decided to take measures for the king's security, to return him to Paris and to move against General de Bouillé. It also decreed that no one could leave Paris that night without a passport from the National

22 See Mirabeau, *Correspondance entre le comte de Mirabeau et le comte de la Marck*, II: 414–504. See also Bertrand de Moleville, *Annals* IV: 11; Hue, *Dernières années du règne et de la vie de Louis XVI*, p. 221. The manifesto appears to be more of a basis for negotiation, and follows Mirabeau's advice of attacking the constitution rather than the Revolution.

23 AN C 71, dossier 696, document 30; AN C 70, dossier 689, document 3. *II^ème suite du procès-verbal de la séance permanente*, pp. 12–13. Somewhat more improbably, but nevertheless reassuring to the Assembly as a reaffirmation of its ideals, was a deputation of "former Bretons," who extolled the principles of the nation and the law. See AN C 71, dossier 697, documents 19–21; *IV^ème suite du procès-verbal de la séance permanente*, pp. 5–8; *Procès-verbal très-exact*, pp. 110–112.

24 See, for example, AN DIV 27, dossier 641, document 17; AN C 127, dossier 428, document 74; AN F¹c III Gironde 8, copy of letter written to National Assembly by directory of Department of Gironde, June 26, 1791; AN F¹c III Morbihan 11, proclamation of June 24, 1791; AN F¹c III Finistère 9, document 35; AN C 71, dossier 702, document 23; *VI^ème suite du procès-verbal de la séance permanente*, pp. 3–4. On the manner in which these addresses encouraged the deputies, see AM Toulon L 338, dossier H³ 13, letter of Ricard to municipality of Toulon, June 28, 1791.

25 AN C 71, dossier 697, document 22; *IV^ème suite du procès-verbal de la séance permanente*, pp. 8–9; *Procès-verbal très-exact*, pp. 112–115. On this occasion, of course, the reference in the address to kidnapping was misleading; in fact, according to the latter source Roederer protested that the king had deserted his post when kidnapping was mentioned. *Procès-verbal très-exact*, p. 113.

26 *IV^ème suite du procès-verbal de la séance permanente*, p. 15; *Procès-verbal très-exact*, pp. 129–134.

Assembly. After a one hour suspension from eleven o'clock until midnight, the Assembly reconvened and decided to send three deputies – Barnave, Latour-Maubourg and Pétion – to accompany the monarch back to Paris and to suspend Bouillé from his military duties. Finally, it passed a motion commending the city of Paris for the calm that had reigned there and expressing the desire to see it continue. It then suspended its meeting at one o'clock in the morning.[27]

Louis soon began his return journey to Paris, a voyage that could not have left any doubt in his mind about the loyalty of the populace to the nation, the National Assembly and the constitution before the sovereign. Nowhere in France had the people mobilized in support of the king – everywhere the constitution had been given priority. Indeed, the deputies sent to meet Louis reported or recalled that on the way to Varennes the reaction everywhere was the same as in Paris and that they had encountered nothing but confidence and respect for the Assembly.[28] And, as his carriage made its way back to Paris, Louis experienced this reality personally as the nation, the constitution and the National Assembly – but never the king – were cheered in his presence.[29] There could be no doubt about the resentment that the betrayal of his oath had provoked. At one stop during Louis's return, a man turned his back on the king and left his hat on; when the deputy Pétion – of the three accompanying Louis, the one least sympathetic to the monarch – upbraided him, the man replied that one did not salute or look at a king in flight.[30] Furthermore, when Louis reentered Paris there were large crowds, but they remained silent and every man kept his hat on.

A final reminder for Louis of his position, relative to the National Assembly and the constitution, came at the end of his return to Paris. When the entourage returned to the royal apartments, a group of deputies arrived to escort the royal family. According to Barère, who was among them, the crowd hurled insults at the queen, causing the deputies great concern about the situation. Barère noted, however, that the deputies hoped that the high regard of the populace for the National Assembly would work to the benefit of the deputies. Their hopes were met, for he said the deputies had only to give their names and show their medals, "which acted like a talisman," and the crowd opened before

27 *II^ème suite du procès-verbal de la séance permanente*, p. 23. The Commune of Paris similarly took precautions for Louis's security. BHVP Ms. 805, fol. 209.
28 AN W 13, no. 312; AN F$^7$ 4385$^1$, dossier 5, pp. 2, 4. For a similar assessment, see AN C 71, dossier 702, document 23.
29 Louise Elisabeth Félicité Françoise Armande Anne Marie Jeanne Joséphine Tourzel, *Mémoires de madame la duchesse de Tourzel, gouvernante des enfants de France pendant les années 1789, 1790, 1791, 1792, 1793, 1795*, 2 vols. (Paris, 1883), I: 334; AN F$^7$ 4385$^1$, dossier 5, p. 11.     30 Tourzel, *Mémoires*, I: 340–341, 344.

them, allowing them to reach the carriages of the king and his family. Despite further difficulties with the crowd, the royal family was seen safely to its apartments.[31]

With Louis's return, the National Assembly now faced the pivotal issue of the role of the monarch in a constitutional order which he had repudiated. The Assembly directed the Committee of the Constitution to prepare a decree, and Thouret introduced the project by noting that it was impossible to allow the original relationship between the monarch and the Assembly to continue to exist, and that the Assembly could not permit its decrees to be jeopardized by submitting them to a sanction that could be subject to disavowal. He also asserted that the Assembly could not allow executive power to reside in an entity hostile to the constitution.[32] Thouret introduced seven articles that provided for a guard to be placed on Louis, as well as on the heir presumptive and the queen; that those who had accompanied the royal family would be arrested; and that the king and queen would give depositions to three deputies chosen by the Assembly, the results of which would determine the future role of the monarch in the polity. An additional article further stipulated that, in the meantime, the decree of June 21, which authorized decrees to be implemented without the approval of the king, would continue to be in effect.[33]

The recommendations met with opposition from deputies who claimed that the dispositions sought to change the nature of the government. These deputies asked that the Assembly form a large committee to deliberate on the proposed decrees, or at least that the Committee of the Constitution listen to different views that might be offered to it. During the discussion that followed, deputies Amable de Brugier, baron de Rochebrune and Pierre-Victor Malouet argued that Louis would be a prisoner, while Roederer, Antoine-Balthazar-Joseph d'André, Duport and Alexandre-Théodore de Lameth, in the casuistical judgment of one contemporary source "proved that the decree did not say that."[34] After some discussion, the proposed decrees were adopted in their entirety. As a result, Louis remained suspended from his position as monarch pending a full debate by the National Assembly.

---

31 Barère, *Mémoires*, I: 334. See also Bertrand de Moleville, *Annals*, IV: 183–184.

32 Bertrand de Moleville, *Annals*, IV: 173–175.

33 AN C 70, dossier 690, document 8; *VIII^{ème} suite du procès-verbal de l'Assemblée nationale*, p. 7; *Procès-verbal très-exact*, pp. 249–250. On the strictness of Louis's guard, see AN M 664, no. 31.

34 The quote is from *Procès-verbal très-exact*, p. 250; see also AN C 70, dossier 690, document 8; AN C 71, dossier 699, document 13; and *VIII^{ème} suite du procès-verbal de l'Assemblée nationale*, p. 8, which offer only an oblique distillation of the discussion. See also *AP*, XXVII: 519–521.

The three deputies chosen by the National Assembly to take the depositions, d'André, Duport and François-Denis Tronchet spoke with Louis on June 26 and with the queen on the morning of June 27.[35] As noted earlier, in his meeting with the deputies, Louis cited what he called the "outrage" of April 18 as the motivation for his flight because, he claimed, many writings after that date had sought to provoke violence against him, as well as his family. He asserted that he had never sought to leave the kingdom, and that he had not acted in coordination with foreign powers, with his relatives or any other émigrés. He also stated that he had intended to go to Montmédy and that he had not made any protestations other than the one he had left behind in his apartment. He had recognized in the course of his voyage that public opinion heavily supported the constitution and he was prepared to make personal sacrifices for the happiness of his people.[36]

Although some of his deposition may have been somewhat disingenuous, Louis does, in fact, seem to have recognized his standing relative to the constitution. Shortly after his return to Paris he mentioned to Lafayette that he had long believed that the marquis had surrounded him with a host of people who shared Lafayette's opinions, but Louis had felt that these were not the opinions of France. Now, however, as a result of his journey, he had discovered that he was mistaken.[37] However belatedly he had come to recognize the strength of loyalty to the constitution, his action had placed the Assembly in a difficult and virtually unresolvable dilemma. The Assembly had already declared that France was a hereditary monarchy and that the monarch was inviolable, but his inviolability had clearly been breached by his suspension so that Louis was, in fact, a virtual prisoner – although government continued to be carried out in his name, it was the work of the National Assembly alone. Furthermore, having all but accused Louis of perjury in its declaration to the nation, the Assembly now had to confront the problem of dealing with a king who had sought to overturn, virtually in its entirety, the constitution encapsulating the grand design for the polity, a constitution that he had solemnly sworn to uphold before the assembled French nation.[38]

In addition to the constitutional problem, the Assembly also faced the

---

35 On the choice of the three deputies, see AN C 70, dossier 690, document 11. The essence of Louis's deposition appears to have been known in advance. See AM Brest LL 46 (1791), no. 78, letter of June 26, 1791.
36 Procès-verbal de l'Assemblée nationale, No. 687 (June 27, 1791), pp. 32–39; Procès-verbal très exact, pp. 291–296.
37 Lafayette, Mémoires, correspondance et manuscrits du générale Lafayette, III: 91.
38 See AM Brest LL 46 (1791), no. 77, letter of June 24, 1791; Faulcon, Correspondance, II: 441.

extraordinarily difficult mission of attempting to reestablish political equilibrium and consensus. Louis's flight had angered much of the nation, particularly because it had revealed the utter insincerity of his past actions with respect to the constitution. Despite the provisions of the constitution relating to the inviolability of the king, provisions to which much of the Assembly felt bound, during his flight a distinction had begun to be drawn between the nation, the constitution and the law on the one hand and the king on the other.[39] To attempt to make the king a continuing, integral part of the government while maintaining support and respect for the constitution was the critical and fundamental mission facing the Assembly. Unfortunately, however, the complete unity that had characterized the Assembly at the time of Louis's flight quickly eroded, further complicating the Assembly's task. On June 29, a group of 290 conservative deputies issued a declaration in which they denounced the substance of the decree of June 25 and stated that they regarded the king as a prisoner. They announced that, solely out of loyalty to the king, they would remain in the Assembly so as not to appear to abandon him but, while they would attend the sessions of the National Assembly, they would not participate in debate – in effect, boycotting the proceedings – and they tried unsuccessfully to read their statement in the meeting of July 5.[40]

Several committees of the Assembly that had been jointly charged with preparing a report on Louis's flight presented it on July 13, and the equivocal approach of the report reflected the predicament that the National Assembly faced. The committees began by noting that the monarchy had been created for the nation and not for the king, and that the hereditary throne and the inviolability of the king were both also in the interest of the nation. The report went on to single out Bouillé, whom

39 See, for example, AD Orne L 140, fol. 78; AN F¹c III Gironde 8, copy of *procès-verbal* of June 23, 1791 of directory of Department of Ille-et-Vilaine; AD Loire-Atlantique L 45, fols. 161–161v°.

40 This incident does not appear in the *procès-verbal*, nor is it recorded in the archives of the meeting for that day. See AN C 74, dossier 716, document 8; AN C 74, dossier 722. On February 15, 1790, the National Assembly, acting on the conviction that the Assembly was a body representing all of France, had decided that protests of individual towns or provinces would not be included in the *procès-verbal*. This principle was now clearly applied to the protest of the deputies. The incident is treated in *Le Spectateur national et le Modérateur*, July 6, 1791; *Assemblée nationale. Journal des débats et des décrets*, 5 July 1791, 9.00 a.m.; *Journal des Etats-Généraux*, XXIX: 168. It is mentioned briefly in *AP*, XXVII: 752. See also AM Brest LL 46 (1791), no. 82, letter of July 6, 1791; AD Seine-Maritime LP 8454, letter of July 8, 1791; AD Puy-de-Dôme F 141, no. 72. For the original statement, see *Déclaration de deux cent quatre-vingt-dix députés sur les décrets qui suspendent l'exercice de l'autorité royale, et qui portent atteinte à l'inviolabilité de la personne sacrée du Roi* (Paris, 1791). Again, the best insight into those deputies opposed to the course of the Assembly is Sullivan, "Defenders of Privilege."

it compared to Benedict Arnold, and those who had aided Louis's flight, and sought to prosecute them. The committees observed that since the constitution had rendered the king inviolable, and because he had not left the country his flight did not violate any law, the question of guilt did not apply to him. Nevertheless, the report sought to clarify the position of the king and his inviolability, and it did not lift the suspension that had been approved at the time of his flight. It also asserted that although Louis was free to refuse the constitution, it would be enacted without him – in effect, he would lose his throne.[41]

The inconsistencies of the report clearly indicated the quandary confronting the Assembly. Externally, the Assembly was buffeted by disparate forces. The flight of the king had given greater impetus to republicanism in Paris, and it gained additional strength from deteriorating economic conditions.[42] In addition, fear of foreign invasion was a constant concern of deputies, particularly after the war scare of the spring. The monarch was the chief bulwark against both threats.

Internally, within the Assembly, the irreconcilable tenets of the report were obvious. If Bouillé and the others were to blame, and the question of guilt did not apply to Louis, his suspension made little sense, but the committees did nothing to lift it. Furthermore, the report reaffirmed the king's inviolability even as it implicitly threatened him with the loss of his throne. The contradictions of the report, however, revealed the deeper concerns of the Assembly. It had already proclaimed the inviolability of the king, and the suspension enacted against Louis on his return had produced a rupture, with many conservative deputies refusing to participate in the debate.[43] On the one hand, then, the Assembly sought not to contradict itself and to maintain, as much as possible, the consensus that had sustained it since August, 1789. On the other hand, not to have acted against the king would virtually have invited him to tamper with the edifice constructed by the National Assembly. Recognizing the lack of any acceptable alternatives, much of the Assembly simply decided to maintain the constitution, which entailed leaving the king in power.[44]

Debate on the report began immediately and lasted three days. The

41 See AN C 74, dossier 717, document 10; *Procès-verbal de l'Assemblée nationale*, No. 703 (July 13, 1791), pp. 15–16; *Le Point du Jour*, July 14, 1791; *AP*, XXVIII: 231–242.
42 See George Rudé, *The Crowd in the French Revolution* (Oxford, 1959), pp. 87–88; Gary Kates, *The Cercle Social, the Girondins, and the French Revolution* (Princeton, 1985), pp. 158–164.
43 See the comment of the deputy Salle in *AP*, XXVIII: 322. This refers, of course, especially to the 290 deputies mentioned above.
44 Faulcon, *Correspondance*, II: 442–444. See also AM Brest LL 46 (1791), no. 90, letter of July 24, 1791; BM Grenoble Ms. R 5949, document 9. See also *Mes Collègues* (N.p., n.d.). For the dilemma of the Assembly, especially members of the left, see Kenneth

speeches reflected the wide range of opinion in the Assembly which, according to one deputy, ranged from wanting to try Louis to allowing him to accept or refuse the constitution.[45] The debate, which was quite contentious, centered especially on the issue of inviolability. Several deputies argued in favor of revoking the inviolability of the king and trying him. Others argued that he should not benefit from a constitution against which he had protested and wanted to abolish. One such deputy, the abbé Grégoire, seemed to speak for virtually all of the deputies when he said that the king would doubtless accept the constitution, but could his oath be accepted?[46] Those who favored the constitution also spoke eloquently, although the Assembly was at times confused about some of the ramifications of the debate.[47] Ultimately, however, a compelling speech by Jean-Baptiste Salle, who spoke in favor of the plan of the committees, set the stage for a decisive oration by Barnave that settled the questions.[48]

Clearly impatient with the narrowness of the discussion, Barnave stated that he wanted to leave the constitution aside and to speak on the Revolution. He then delivered an impassioned address that focused not on the issue of inviolability, but on the majesty of the Revolution itself. He pointed out that if the Assembly defied the constitution once, at what point would it, or especially its successors, stop? Arguing that any further change would be disastrous, he asked the Assembly if it was going to conclude the Revolution or whether it was seeking to start it again. Asserting that those who make revolutions did not make them with metaphysical maxims, he extolled the night of August 4, stating "all of you know [that] the night of August 4 gave more strength to the Revolution than all the constitutional decrees; but for those who would want to go further, what night of August 4 remains to do, if it is not laws against property?"[49] Barnave urged the Assembly to recognize that the

Margerison, *P.-L. Roederer: Political Thought and Practice During the French Revolution* (Philadelphia, 1983), pp. 63–74.
45 On the range of opinions in the Assembly, see Faulcon, *Correspondance*, II: 440–441. See also AD Puy-de-Dôme F 141, no. 72, letter of July 14, 1791.
46 For Grégoire's comment, see *AP*, XXVIII: 270. An echo of that sentiment by another deputy is found in Faulcon, *Correspondance*, II: 441.
47 Some deputies, for example, were uncertain whether the debate superseded the suspension imposed on Louis on June 25 as recommended by the Committee of the Constitution and approved by the Assembly. The committee said that it did not and the suspension remained in force. See AN C 74, dossier 717, document 11; *Procès-verbal de l'Assemblée nationale*, No. 704 (July 14, 1791), pp. 7–8. See also AN C 74, dossier 726, document 16.
48 For the speech by Salle, see *AP*, XXVIII: 320–324. On the sense of urgency felt by the Assembly, see AD Seine-Maritime LP 8454, letter of July 15, 1791.
49 *AP*, XXVII: 330. See also Patrice Gueniffey, "Terminer la Révolution: Barnave et la révision de la constitution (Août 1791)," *Terminer la Révolution*, ed. Furet, pp. 147–170.

common interest required that the Revolution be concluded and, telling them that they had previously shown their ability to put in place beneficial institutions, he exhorted them to prove that they had the strength and wisdom to protect and maintain them. He went on to note that the nation had just provided a great example of strength and courage and urged the Assembly, after it had received accolades for being courageous and powerful, to be wise and moderate.[50]

Barnave's speech was a brilliant effort that overwhelmed all previous discussion. Rising above such issues as inviolability or the question of whether Louis "deserved" to be left on the throne, Barnave successfully portrayed the Revolution as larger than the person of the king, recalling for the Assembly that the new institutions it had created were of far greater importance. It was an unassailable theme that overshadowed all the arguments that had preceded his speech. The deputies of the left could not attack it without appearing to denigrate or trivialize the magnificence of the Revolution. At the same time, however, his speech reminded the members on the right that Louis had been an integral part of the new institutions, so to attack Barnave's presentation would merely highlight the perfidy and deceit of the king. Finally, by invoking the night of August 4 and appealing to the disinterestedness of deputies, Barnave brought back a mythic moment when they had transcended their differences and implied that they could do so once again.

Barnave's speech appears to have genuinely moved the Assembly; it responded with prolonged applause and ordered that it be printed and sent to all the departments.[51] It was a further measure of its success that the Assembly then voted to close discussion. It approved articles proposed by Salle specifying that a king who placed himself at the head of an army to move against the nation would be regarded as having abdicated, as would any monarch who retracted his oath to the constitution. Any monarch who abdicated would become an ordinary citizen and would be answerable for all acts subsequent to his abdication.

50 See *Procès-verbal de l'Assemblée nationale*, No. 705 (July 15, 1791), pp. 7–12; *AP*, XXVIII: 326–331, *Le Point du Jour*, July 17, 1791. On its decisiveness, see Queruau-Lamerie, "Lettres de Maupetit," 22, 478–479.
51 See AD Meurthe-et-Moselle L 212, letter of Duquesnoy, July 19, 1791, in which he observed that the speeches of Duport, Salle and Barnave expressed the sentiments of the Assembly and revealed "the real motives for its conduct in the difficult circumstances in which it finds itself." On its circulation, see AM Le Havre D³ 39, no. 156, letter of July 20, 1791; AN F¹c III Creuse 9, letter of administrators comprising directory of Department of Creuse to de Lessart, September 3, 1791; AN F¹c III Indre 7, letter of administrators and *procureur-général-syndic* of directory of Department of Indre to de Lessart, July 20, 1791; AN F¹c III Mayenne 8, letter of administrators of Department of Mayenne to de Lessart, July 29, 1791; AN F¹c III Nièvre 7, dossier 2, document 11; AN F¹c III Oise 10, letter of administrators comprising directory of Department of Oise to de Lessart, July 27, 1791.

It then adopted the report of its committees, ordering the arrest of Bouillé and others whom it believed involved in seeking to overthrow the constitution and ordering them to be tried before the provisional High National Court in Orléans.[52] The following night, in the evening session of July 16, the Assembly confirmed Louis's suspension until the constitution could be presented to him in its entirety for acceptance or rejection.[53]

The decision of the National Assembly to retain Louis led to a call for a protest in a petition drawn up by the Cordeliers Club on July 16. Their action was initially supported by the Jacobin Club but, in what is an indication of the consensus that existed in the National Assembly, the Jacobins, on a motion by Robespierre, retracted their endorsement.[54] The Cordeliers then drafted a more radical petition that it placed on the altar of the fatherland asking the National Assembly to annul its decree, to consider the monarch as having abdicated and to organize a new executive power. It also requested that the decision of the National Assembly be submitted to a plebiscite in the departments. In its reorganization of France, the Assembly had never referred any of its actions to a plebiscite, so such a course was completely unprecedented, and in any case deputies feared that it could lead to a civil war. The discovery of two men under the altar resulted in their murder, which in turn provoked a strong response from the municipality. It declared martial law and, after the crowd at the Champ de Mars did not disperse, the National Guard fired into it, causing a significant loss of life.[55]

The members of the National Assembly were distressed by the agitation, as well as its outcome, which they nevertheless believed justified. One of the best insights into the matter from the perspective of the National Assembly comes from a letter of Duquesnoy. He believed that republicans were trying to intimidate the National Assembly and to advance principles contrary to those that the Assembly had established. In seeking to have the king dethroned and tried, Duquesnoy argued that

---

52 *AP*, XXVIII: 331–336. At the same time, however, it declined to indict several individuals. See AN C 74, dossier 725, document 33; *Procès-verbal de l'Assemblée nationale*, No. 705 (July 15, 1791), pp. 10–12.

53 *Procès-verbal de l'Assemblée nationale*, No. 706 (July 16, 1791), p. 28; *AP*, XXVIII: 337. For the perspective of one deputy, see Rumeau, "Lettres du constituante Roger," 75–77. See also AN C 74, dossier 726, document 16.

54 Again, on the dilemma of the left, see Margerison, *P.-L. Roederer*, pp. 63–74.

55 See Rudé, *The Crowd in the French Revolution*, pp. 88–89. The Assembly had anticipated trouble in Paris and had asked the municipality to take all necessary steps to preserve order, but it is difficult to discern a premeditated plan, as Rudé, following Mathiez, asserts. See AN C 74, dossier 726, document 12. The Champ de Mars episode is still underinvestigated, but see AN W 294, dossier 235, documents 14, 45, 69 bis, 78. On the fear of civil war by deputies, see Looten, "Lettres de ... Bouchette," 617.

the republicans had not considered how the king would be replaced, and he asked how one could replace an institution sanctioned by the national will. Duquesnoy asserted that, however mistaken their view may have been, the republicans had the right to advance it, but only up until the moment the law was promulgated. After that, it became an act of rebellion against the law, particularly when it was supported by a mob that threatened the freedom of the Assembly to deliberate. The representatives of the people, he stated, should not suffer such outrages against national sovereignty, and they had asked the public authorities to repress disorders. Duquesnoy concluded by observing that

the National Assembly is firmly determined to have respected and executed the sovereign will of the nation, of which it is the organ and interpreter ... The patriot members of the Assembly, for too long divided among themselves on various matters, have joined together on this important issue, [and] I am indeed assured that efforts to disunite them again will be in vain.[56]

The Champ de Mars episode did, in fact, serve to discredit republicanism, which became associated with lawlessness, and led to renewed support for the Assembly.[57]

At the same time, however, the incident sullied supporters of the constitution and made Barnave's appeal to make France a nation in which all patriotic citizens could live in peace irrespective of their opinions ring hollow, as did the following wave of arrests, instigated by the Assembly.[58] Indeed, an outcome more antithetical to the ideal of August 4 invoked by Barnave could scarcely be imagined.

Outside of Paris the decision produced no unrest and was almost universally endorsed. Departmental, district and municipal administrators, as products of the National Assembly and generally attuned to its outlook and attitudes, almost unanimously acclaimed the resolution. Much like the National Assembly, the administrators were aware of the consequences for governance that were inherent in the decision and therefore showed considerable forbearance and understanding for the Assembly's action.[59]

---

56 AD Meurthe-et-Moselle L 212, letter of Duquesnoy, July 19, 1791. See also AM Toulon L 80, dossier 37, letter of Ricard to municipal officers of Toulon, July 19, 1791.
57 See AN F¹c III Ain 7, extract from register of deliberations of directory of district of Saint-Rambert, August 2, 1791; AN C 128, dossier 429, document 1.
58 On the situation after the Champ de Mars, see Ran Halévi, "Les feuillants," *Terminer la Révolution*, ed. Furet, pp. 171–180.
59 See, for example, AN C 124, dossier 404², document 38; AN C 125, dossier 408, document 112; AN C 126, dossier 414, document 21; AN C 126, dossier 422, document 7; AN C 129, dossier 414², document 87; AN C 130, dossier 442, document 20; AN C 130, dossier 443, document 6. See also AD Cantal L 76, entry 2440; AD Isère L 103, fols.

What dissonant reaction there was came from a small number of Jacobin clubs. It was almost invariably muted and, while expressing disagreement, also acknowledged acceptance, making themselves a sort of loyal opposition.[60] Overall, however, the overwhelming majority of Jacobin clubs concurred with the decision,[61] and the firmness of the Assembly amidst the agitation that culminated at the Champ de Mars increased admiration for it. The Jacobin club of Agen, for example, praised the decision of the National Assembly as destroying "forever the hopes of despots and factions."[62] Similarly, the Jacobin club and National Guard of Abbeville told the Assembly:

Already the malcontents have succeeded in exciting some movements, but we count always on your courage. Those who could not be frightened by the bayonets of despotism will not allow themselves to be intimidated by threats from the factions. The ship of state is struck by furious tempests. Continue to guide the government with a firm hand. Save France a third time.[63]

Indeed, some Jacobin clubs asserted that the decision underscored the integrity of the constitution.[64] Ultimately, the decision served to reassure the nation, but the National Assembly still faced the formidable task of completing the constitution.

Political life was, in fact, frozen, awaiting completion of the constitution and the decision of the king to accept or reject it. Furthermore, as Michael Kennedy observed, as long as the fate of the monarch remained unresolved, the entire constitution was in question.[65] As it continued work on the constitution, however, the National Assembly did have several factors in its favor. Aside from the obvious fact that there was little alternative to retaining the king, there was a nascent willingness to forgive the king for his transgression. Furthermore, many deputies in

143–144; AN F¹c III Ain 7, extract from register of deliberations of directory of district of Saint-Rambert, August 2, 1791; AN F¹c III Loir-et-Cher 8, document 481; AN F¹c III Lot-et-Garonne 12, dossier 2, document 237; AN F¹c III Marne 8, dossier 2, document 253. The Assembly had, in fact, counted on their support. See AM Toulon L 80, dossier 37, letter of Ricard to municipal officers of Toulon, July 19, 1791.
60 See AN C 124, dossier 404¹, documents 20, 58; AN C 124, dossier 405, documents 1, 67; AN C 125, dossier 408, document 60.
61 Some representative examples among the numerous declarations of support are AN C 124, dossier 404², documents 60–61, 78; AN C 125, dossier 409, document 20; AN C 126, dossier 411, documents 65–66; AN C 126, dossier 413, document 36; AN C 127, dossier 427, document 52.          62 AN C 124, dossier 404¹, document 10.
63 AN C 124, dossier 404¹, document 4.
64 AN C 125, dossier 408, document 120; AN C 129, dossier 438, document 9; AN C 129, dossier 441¹, document 22. See the survey of reactions outside of Paris in Michael L. Kennedy, *The Jacobin Clubs in the French Revolution: The Early Years* (Prineton, 1982), pp. 270–277, although he overemphasizes the disagreement of clubs with the Assembly, especially after the decision in July.
65 Kennedy, *The Jacobin Clubs in the French Revolution*, p. 274.

the Assembly deeply believed in the validity of the constitution and wanted to bring it to fruition.[66]

On August 5, Thouret, in the name of the Committee of the Constitution, went before the Assembly to present the constitution for consideration. In his opening remarks he reminded the Assembly that the previous evening had been the anniversary of the immortal time when many abuses had been overturned and, in an allusion to the decrees concluded on August 11, 1789, and following the theme adduced earlier by Barnave, he said that the current meeting marked the anniversary when the National Assembly had begun to lay the foundation for the magnificent edifice that was nearing completion. At the exact expiration of the second year, he said, their committees came to present deputies with the result of their work. Because the Assembly had set aside only two hours for reading the proposed constitution, without providing for any discussion immediately afterward, Thouret stated that he did not wish to offer any kind of explanation. Instead, a simple unveiling would allow more private consideration by deputies so that they could form a careful opinion on the effect that the constitution would have on the French nation. Thouret then read the proposed constitution to the Assembly, which greeted its completion with warm applause.[67]

At the conclusion of the reading the president of the National Assembly recognized Lafayette. Noting the advantages to be gained from completion of the constitution, Lafayette proposed that the Committee of the Constitution be charged with preparing a bill stipulating the manner in which the constitution, as soon as it was completed, would be presented for full consideration and unqualified acceptance by the king. The Assembly again responded with applause and adopted the motion by acclamation.[68]

Beginning on August 8, and continuing for the remainder of the month, the Assembly began a comprehensive consideration of the constitution. In a prefatory speech, Thouret, speaking for the Committees of the Constitution and on Revision, noted that the Assembly had not established the constitution for a new people, nor for a virgin land, but that France for many centuries had groaned beneath a host of institutions incompatible with a true and generous constitution. Consequently, he asserted, the civic heading of abolitions that necessarily

66 On the willingness to forgive the king, see AD Rhône 1 L 259, no. 269, entry of July 12, 1791; AN C 184, dossier 115, document 57; on the feelings of deputies, see AM Le Havre D³ 39, no. 157, letter of August 6, 1791; Rumeau, "Lettres du constituant Roger," 77.
67 Procès-verbal de l'Assemblée nationale No. 726 (August 5, 1791), p. 45; XXIX: 207–217; AM Le Havre D³ 39, no. 157, letter of August 6, 1791.
68 Procès-verbal de l'Assemblée nationale No. 726 (August 5, 1791), pp. 45–46; AP, XXIX: 217–218.

preceded the implantation of liberty and equality – contained in the preamble – ought to be regarded as constitutional. He then went on to explain the rationale used by the committees in presenting the constitution and suggested a method for consideration thereof.[69] Despite a protest by deputies of the right, the Assembly immediately began work examining the constitution clause by clause.[70]

The discussion of the constitution, conducted in a somber atmosphere as the war scare of the spring now seemed compounded by Louis's flight, was a difficult period for the National Assembly. In addition, the nascent Jacobin–Feuillant schism also increased the sense of tribulation, for the constitution was one of the main arenas of this struggle.[71] The Committee on Revision, which had been formed in September, 1790, to separate ordinary statutes from constitutional principles and to present a coherent constitutional document to the Assembly for final approval, had a heavy representation of Feuillants, including Barnave, Duport and Alexandre de Lameth. Although the two committees, the Committee of the Constitution and the Committee on Revision, worked closely together and shared a similar political outlook, they should not be thought of as synonymous. The members of the Committee of the Constitution accorded political primacy not to the king, but to the constitution, of which the king was a part. Ultimately, imbued as they were with the new ideal of the polity, the members of the Committee of the Constitution wanted the constitution to be above politics and partisanship. Unfortunately, however, the consensus that was indispensable to this aspiration had been undermined by Louis's flight, so the Assembly now, more than previously, had to deal with political issues where recourse to high ideals of the nation did not always provide a clear direction for action, especially as the Feuillants sought to utilize the Committee on Revision to safeguard the king's position. To be sure, the inclination of the Feuillants toward the king obviously harmonized better with the established principle of constitutional monarchy, but this coalition led to hostility toward the committees.

It is not surprising, then, that sections of the constitution relating to the king provoked controversy, and this discord was compounded in the initial days of review by resentment against the committees for what

---

69 *Procès-verbal de l'Assemblée nationale* No. 729 (August 8, 1791), p. 12; *AP*, XXIX: 262–263.

70 Deputies did not anticipate much difficulty in this process. See AM Arles AA 23, fol. 774; AM Toulon L 80, dossier 37, letter of Ricard to municipal officers of Toulon, July 19, 1791; AM Toulon L 104, dossier D⁴ 2, letter of Ricard to municipal officers of Toulon, August 11, 1791.

71 Again, on the Jacobin-Feuillant conflict, see Bradby, *The Life of Barnave*, especially II: 197–229; Michon, *Essai sur l'histoire du parti Feuillant: Adrien Duport*, pp. 286–343.

many deputies believed was their imperious and unilateral presentation of the constitution. In the discussion of public powers, for example, the definition of sovereignty led to much debate, resulting in the approval of an amendment adding the words "inalienable" and "imprescriptible" to the statement of sovereignty advanced by the committees. Similarly, article two of the section on public powers, which declared the king representative, also produced sharp debate, although it passed without amendment.[72]

Tension between the committees and the Assembly continued to mount, however, with Robespierre, during discussion on August 11 of the conditions necessary to be an elector, accusing the committees of seeking to change the spirit of the constitution with their proposed requirements for qualification as an elector. Indeed, on August 12 the Assembly twice overruled the committees to reinsert articles in the constitution that the committees had omitted.[73]

The next day, in what may have been a fit of pique, Thouret asserted that he was too exhausted to continue his presentation of the constitution and asked to be replaced by one of his colleagues from the committee. The ire of some in the Assembly continued unabated, however, as the deputy Louis-Marie Guillaume observed that "the agitation that has reigned in this Assembly since the beginning of the discussion of the constitutional act comes from many serious omissions that true friends of the constitution have been able to perceive in the project submitted to us." The committees reacted angrily but, with discontent against them rising, Guillaume reiterated that the turmoil had been caused by the omissions by the committees, although he noted that these had almost all been restored.[74] It is, in fact, a measure of the level of exasperation with the committees that the deputy Jean-François-Pierre Poulain wrote to his constituents, asking who was more infallible than the pope and the Committees of the Constitution and on Revision.[75]

On August 14 Thouret opened consideration of the constitution with a conciliatory speech. He defended the position of the committees – which he said had met until midnight after having their previous recommendations rejected – but acknowledged that the constitution was a common responsibility. Indeed, he told the deputies that rather than compromise the Revolution out of resentment toward the committees,

---

72 *AP*, XXIX: 323–324; Margerison, *P.-L. Roederer*, pp. 68–69.
73 *Procès-verbal de l'Assemblée nationale*, No. 732 (August 11, 1791), p. 13; *Procès-verbal de l'Assemblée nationale*, No. 733 (August 12, 1791); *AP*, XXIX: 359–360, 391–396; Margerison, *P.-L. Roederer*, p. 70.
74 *Procès-verbal de l'Assemblée nationale*, No. 734 (August 13, 1791), p. 8; *AP*, XXIX: 405–407.    75 AD Côtes-d'Armor 1 L 389, letter of Poulain, August 15, 1791.

they should instead consider the common good.[76] The exchange seems to have had a salutary effect, for the remainder of the examination of the constitution did not produce the acrimony that characterized the early stages of consideration of the document. Indeed, in the final analysis, the conflict over the constitution should not be exaggerated. Bertrand Barère, one of the deputies opposed to the revisions proposed by the committees, noted that there were only about thirty-five deputies willing to oppose the revisions, and Barère, along with others, believed that, with the restorations they achieved, they had gained most of what they had sought.[77]

It was no coincidence that it was the issue of the conditions necessary to be an elector that became the catalyst for the anger and resentment of the Assembly against the committees for, along with the wave of repression following the Champ de Mars killings, the revision of the electoral requirements comprised one of the least defensible actions of the National Assembly. The amended requirements to be an elector were perhaps not anti-democratic, as is often presumed, for the conditions for primary assemblies remained unchanged. Clearly, however, it subverted the ideals of 1789, when the original requirements had been formulated, and left the constitution open to criticism, by contemporaries as well as historians, even though these standards were never utilized. Indeed, the revised conditions for electors appears to be the major element that those opposed to revisions believed that they had not gained.

Indeed, of far greater consequence is the fact that the examination of the constitution gave the National Assembly an opportunity to reaffirm its controlling principles and fundamental vision, thereby beginning to reestablish the constitution as an object of consensus. At the outset, after making a minor change in the Declaration of Rights, the Assembly began consideration of the preamble. The framing of the preamble generated discussion because it summarized the actions of the Assembly over the past two years, restating the precepts that had governed it. The preamble ultimately passed with only minor revisions.[78]

76 *Procès-verbal de l'Assemblée nationale*, No. 735 (August 14, 1791), p. 8; *AP*, XXIX: 429.
77 Barère, *Mémoires*, I: 330–331, and the aforementioned comments of Guillaume in *AP*, XXIX: 405–407. See also AD Côtes-d'Armor 1 L 389, letter of Poulain, August 15, 1791; Queruau-Lamerie, "Lettres de Maupetit," 23, 88–89, 92–95, 97–98, 100, 102–103; Edmond-Louis-Alexis Dubois-Crancé, *Analyse de la Révolution française depuis l'ouverture des Etats-Généraux jusqu'au 6 frimaire an IV de la république*, ed. Th. Iung (Paris, 1885), p. 67. See also Margerison, *P.-L. Roederer*, p. 68, in which he astutely observed that the deputies of the left acted in an individual fashion and did not coordinate their actions. Instead, each acted simply on what interested him most.
78 *AP*, XXIX: 269–270. For an example of the manner in which the review served to reaffirm the basic vision of the Assembly, see Lindet, *Correspondance*, p. 305.

In fact, the ideals of the Assembly were evident throughout the examination of the constitution. In defining citizenship, for example, the deputies strengthened the provisions to decree that French citizenship could be lost not only through such means as naturalization in foreign countries or conviction of crimes, but also through affiliation with any order or foreign body that demanded proof of nobility, distinctions of birth or religious views.[79] The nation was a unitary association, and one's membership in it could not be vitiated by any corporate loyalty or tie. Similarly, when a deputy from the former province of Dauphiné sought to fulfill his mandate by asserting the desire of the province to preserve all of its former rights, he drew a rebuke from Chabroud, one of his colleagues in the delegation from Dauphiné. Stating that in view of the consent of the people of the province and believing that he would not be disavowed by any of his colleagues, he averred that there was no longer a province of Dauphiné, that there were now only French – a statement that drew applause from the Assembly.[80]

Also, near the end of the review, on August 29, an allusion by Malouet to "the scum of the nation" provoked an uproar in the Assembly, with the president telling him that he was offending the principles of the Assembly with such an expression. Another deputy observed that there were no "scum" in the nation since all citizens were equal.[81] Indeed, so seriously did the Assembly treat the task of review that at one point Barère rebuked a fellow deputy for making a joke.[82]

The dissension that arose during review of the constitution had largely disappeared by late August, and at the completion of the review the deputy Bon-Albert Briois-Beaumetz, a member of the Committee on Revision, speaking jointly for the Committee of the Constitution and the Committee on Revision, gave a conciliatory speech. He opened by telling his fellow deputies that their oath was now fulfilled, that their task was now concluded and that after twenty-eight months of hard work they had completed the constitution that was going to rule the destinies of France. He observed that, from the beginning, obstacles had presented themselves and the Assembly had overcome all of them, and went on to highlight the night of August 4 in the course of events.

Briois-Beaumetz was complimentary to Louis, reflecting the desire of much of the Assembly for union and harmony under the new constitution. He said the moment had come when the Assembly was going to ask the king of the French to undertake the most serious and solemn obligation imaginable and that he hoped it would be preceded by a deep

79 *Procès-verbal de l'Assemblée nationale*, No. 731 (August 10, 1791), p. 5; *AP*, XXIX: 321–322.          80 *AP*, XXIX: 430.          81 *Ibid.*, XXIX: 446.
82 *Ibid.*, XXIX: 41.

reflection proportionate to the grandeur of the occasion. After ardent applause, Briois-Beaumetz went on to propose a procedure for presenting the constitution to the king, which the Assembly adopted.[83] For much of the Assembly, the speech served to restore the sense of purpose and achievement that had been so debilitated by the flight of the king.[84]

The next day, September 2, Thouret began reading the constitution, with all the corrections, additions and deletions that had been decreed by the Assembly, a task he concluded the following day. Immediately after the reading, deputies from all shades of the political spectrum put forward various motions. The conservative d'André asked that the constitution be carried to the king that very day, a suggestion that the Assembly greeted with warm applause. Another deputy, Lavie, proposed that sixty deputies be named by the president to present it to the king. This, in turn, precipitated a suggestion from Roederer that underscored the unique status of the National Assembly. He proposed that instead of sixty members the Assembly should designate eighty-three, one for each department. His suggestion produced murmurs in the Assembly and Barnave, Le Chapelier and Alexandre de Lameth observed that the National Assembly did not have representatives by department. They announced their opposition to the motion, leading Roederer to withdraw it, and the Assembly adopted the motions of d'André and Lavie.[85]

Next, in response to a letter from the printer Baudouin, reporting that there were forged copies circulating, the Assembly moved to protect the integrity of the constitution. The younger Choiseuil-Praslin moved that the Assembly order that a definitive edition of the constitutional act be printed and that all necessary measures be taken to prevent the fabrication of any specious editions. The deputy Pierre-Louis Prieur proposed that the Assembly also order that as soon as the definitive edition was printed it should be sent immediately to all of the departments, where mayors would read it to assembled communities. The Assembly approved both measures. Finally, the deputies decided that no speech would be made when the constitution was presented to the king.[86]

At nine o'clock in the evening of September 3, then, a delegation of sixty deputies, accompanied by an honor guard, left for the Tuileries to present the constitution to the king. Louis, accompanied by his ministers, received the deputation courteously, and Thouret made a brief pres-

83 *Ibid.*, XXX: 135–137, 140–141; *Procès-verbal de l'Assemblée nationale*, No. 753, (September 1, 1791), pp. 12–15. See also Bertrand de Moleville, *Annals*, IV: 293–294.
84 See, for example, AM Brest LL 46 (1791), no. 107, letter of September 3, 1791.
85 *Procès-verbal de l'Assemblée nationale*, No. 755 (September 3, 1791), pp. 18–20; *AP*, XXX: 189–190; AN C 77, dossier 763, documents 3–5. See also Faulcon, *Correspondance*, II: 456–457.        86 AN C 77, dossier 763, documents 3–5; *AP*, XXX: 190.

entation offering the constitution to him. The delegation then returned to
the meeting hall, where many deputies had remained, along with a large
number of citizens, hoping to learn the results of the presentation.[87]

The presentation instilled in deputies a sense of hope and optimism.
Most expected that Louis would accept it quickly and, in a reflection of
the hope for a new beginning, Louis's guards were removed and he was
permitted to leave Paris to consider the constitution, although he did not
do so.[88] At the same time, however, during this period of Louis's
consideration of the constitution, on September 10, a group of conservative deputies denounced it, especially the remaking of the administration and judiciary that it encompassed. Their declaration even
extolled the virtues of privilege in governance, revealing not only how
removed they were from the ideal forged by the Assembly and accepted
by most of the nation, but also indicating their unwillingness to accept
virtually any constitution.[89]

It was not until ten days after its presentation, on the evening of
September 13, that Louis notified the Assembly, through the Minister of
Justice, of his acceptance of the constitution.[90] In a courteous and
conciliatory letter he stated that he accepted the constitution as the will
of the nation and, in a section almost certainly directed at the conservative
deputies, he asserted that once he had accepted it no one else would have
the right to complain. In another passage that revealed his understanding
of the Assembly's grand design, he asked all Frenchmen to come together
to respect laws and to reestablish order and union, asserting that the
common enemies now were anarchy and discord. He wrote that from this
point there should be an effort to forget the past and that he hoped all
accusations and indictments for events arising from the Revolution could
be annulled in a general reconciliation. In a postscript he noted that he
believed he ought to pronounce his acceptance in the place where the
constitution had been drafted and announced that he would therefore
come to the Assembly at noon the next day.

The reading of Louis's letter had been punctuated with warm
applause, and at the conclusion of it there was a strong sentiment in favor
of the king. Lafayette immediately proposed freeing all those arrested in
connection with Louis's flight and charging the Committee of the
Constitution and the Committee on Jurisprudence with presenting a

87 *AP*, XXX: 194; AN C 77, dossier 763, document 4.
88 AD Cantal Fonds J. Delmas, dossier 160, document 15; AM Brest LL 46 (1791), no.
108, letter of September 5, 1791; Looten, "Lettres de Bouchette," 634; BM Angers Ms.
1888, p. 206.
89 AN AD[XVIIIc] 133, *Compte rendu par une partie des députés à leurs commettans*. See also,
for an individual example, Jean-François Laroque de Mons, comte de, *Lettre à mes
commettans* (N.p., n.d.) [BHVP 605774].        90 AN C 77, dossier 769, document 22.

project for a general amnesty for all offenses arising from the Revolution. The Assembly quickly passed the motion by acclamation. It was reflective of the general desire for a new beginning that the amnesty that was ultimately proclaimed excused not only those implicated in Louis's flight, but also those arrested in connection with disturbances after the Champ de Mars massacre.[91]

The spirit of the National Assembly was tolerant – one might even say magnanimous – and the attitude that produced the amnesty is evident in a letter from Robert-Thomas Lindet, a bishop and a deputy in the National Assembly, to his brother. After noting that the duty of citizens and of Christians was to be forgiving toward, among others, those who are victims of their own prejudices, he wrote:

At the moment when the constitution is completed, when the fate of France is irrevocably cast, the duty of good citizens is to perceive the least [number] of victims as possible, to see return the greatest number of those who were opposed to the new established order. The benevolent fatherland opens its arms to them, it is ready to receive them. Their repentance is a new triumph for the constitution, and the forbearance they will have experienced will be a guarantee of their future patriotism.[92]

The next day, on September 14, Louis visited the Assembly to profess formally his acceptance of the constitution, signing it in the presence of the Assembly amidst a strong spirit of reconciliation. Following the signing, the entire Assembly accompanied Louis back to the Tuileries, producing an amusing incident in which the deputy Louis-Jean-Henri Darnaudat, the secretary to whom the constitution had been given after its signing, returned afterward to the meeting hall of the Assembly to find the signed constitutional act left unattended. He then learned, to his consternation, that the meeting had been adjourned, as had the morning session of September 15. A flustered Darnaudat approached several other deputies and asked them where to deposit the signed constitution, only to be told by them that he was personally responsible for it. As a result, the disconcerted Darnaudat never separated himself from the constitution, clutching it constantly and even, he said, sleeping with it in his bed that night! With evident relief, he finally presented the constitutional act to the Assembly on September 15.[93]

91 *Procès-verbal de l'Assemblée nationale*, No. 765 (September 13, 1791), pp. 12–20; *AP*, XXX: 620–621. The details of this amnesty seem to have been worked out in advance. See AD Côtes-d'Armor 1 L 389, letter of Poulain, September 10, 1791. See also Faulcon, *Correspondance*, II: 458; BM Angers Ms. 1888, p. 208; AN BB[30] 16, dossier 6, letter of minister of Justice to Bailly, September 13, 1791.
92 AN AB[XIX] 3327, dossier 1, letter of September 8, 1791.
93 *AP*, XXX: 635–636, 644. See also *Journal des décrets de l'Assemblée Nationale, pour les habitans des campagnes*, September 15, 1791.

As the meeting of September 15 began, deputies sought to share with the nation the sense of fulfillment and harmony felt within the National Assembly. Guillaume-François-Charles Goupil-Préfeln asked that, before passing to the order of the day, the Assembly consider an appropriate manner to commemorate Louis's acceptance of the constitution, which he called "the base of our public law and the eternal guarantee of our national prosperity." The Assembly greeted Goupil-Préfeln's proposal with applause, leading another deputy to recall the ceremony that had traditionally been utilized to celebrate the signing of peace treaties. He noted that the National Assembly had decreed that there would be public festivals to celebrate the great events of the Revolution and, calling the constitutional act a new alliance between the French and their leader, said that he believed that no circumstance more commanding could occur. As a result, he asked that on the next Sunday, September 18, in Paris, and on the following Sunday in the rest of the kingdom, Louis's acceptance of the constitution be solemnly proclaimed, that a *Te Deum* be sung in thanks and that the municipalities order whatever festivities they might find appropriate. The Assembly quickly passed the motion.[94]

Despite Louis's assertion that once he had accepted the constitution no one else would have the right to complain, a group of conservative deputies drafted a protest against the acceptance of the constitution by the monarch. On September 15, the very day the Assembly decided to celebrate Louis's acceptance, the group of deputies denounced Louis's acceptation, which they did not regard as a free act. Their isolation, however, was particularly evident in their reference to themselves, in September, 1791, as "deputies to the Estates-General of France."[95] Such anachronistic views had little influence either in the National Assembly or in society at large.[96]

Elsewhere within the Assembly, including, among them, deputies of the left, there was a general willingness to forgive the king and to rally to the constitution as the guarantor of the nation's future. Furthermore, the reservoir of goodwill toward Louis present in the Assembly was mirrored in the larger body politic, so that the constitution was an object of pride

---

94 *Procès-verbal de l'Assemblée nationale*, No. 767 (September 15, 1791), pp. 3–4; *AP*, XXX: 645. See also AN C 77, dossier 770, document 11.

95 AN AD$^{XVIIIc}$ 132, *Declaration d'une partie des députés aux Etats-Généraux de France, sur l'acceptation donnée par le roi à l'acte constitutionnel*. See also Faulcon, *Correspondance*, II: 460.

96 See AN C 130, dossier 453, document 9, which refers to the protest of the 290 deputies. Lest the degree of consensus achieved be overlooked, it should be noted that this protest, the largest, was nonetheless subscribed to by less than one quarter of the Assembly, meaning that the constitution commanded a wide margin of support.

and consensus and not simply a benighted creation of the National Assembly.[97] A letter to the monarch from Evreux illustrates the spirit of goodwill:

You have just sealed the treaty of alliance between the French people and their monarch. You have yielded to the wishes of the great family of which you are the head. You have consulted public opinion, this incorruptible sentinel of the fatherland, this sacred guarantee of social peace.

You have just given, Sire, a great example to kings, in accepting the constitutional charter. It will soon be that of all nations, since it is based on the sacred and imprescriptible rights of man. Sooner or later peoples will be governed only by kings who will exert only the empire of the law on them, and from the entire universe confederated nations will celebrate the triumph of liberty that the French have taught them to conquer.

May this memorable epoch be the happy signal for universal peace! And may the oath of fidelity taken by the king of the French be the guarantee of a reciprocal confidence.[98]

Indeed, it is an indication of the sense of accomplishment, consensus and union that the celebrations of the constitution, both in Paris and in outlying departments, were not perfunctory, but major events. One deputy compared the celebration in Paris to the *Fête de la Fédération* in 1790, and the royal family was hailed everywhere in the city.[99] Most of the nation clearly welcomed the end of uncertainty and heartily embraced the new constitution. Amidst this spirit of consensus, the Assembly

97 On the Assembly, see AM Brest LL 46 (1791), no. 112, letter of September 14, 1791, no. 116, letter of September 24, 1791; AD Côtes-d'Armor 1 L 389, letter of Couppé, September 13, 1791, letter of Baudouin, September 17, 1791; Queruau-Lamerie, "Lettres de Maupetit," 23, 109; Rumeau, "Lettres du constituant Roger," 77–79; Barère, *Mémoires*, I: 334–335; Faulcon, *Correspondance*, II: 459; Bertrand de Moleville, *Annals*, IV: 335, 337–339. On the willingness of the body politic to forgive the king, see AD Rhône 1 L 259, no. 269; AD Rhône 1 L 371, address of administrators to all citizens, September 17, 1791. See also AN F¹c III Ain 8, document 69; AN F¹c III Aveyron 8, letter of administrators of directory of Department of Aveyron to Louis, September 26 1791; AN F¹c III Bouches-du-Rhône 8, undated letter of citizens of Saint-Chamas to Louis; AN F¹c III Eure 9, letter of mayor and municipal officers of Gisors to Louis, September 16, 1791; AN F¹c III Gironde 8, deliberation of mayor and municipal officers of city of Bordeaux, September 17, 1791.
98 AN F¹c III Eure 9, letter of administrators comprising directory of Department of Eure to Louis, September 19, 1791.
99 See AM Brest LL 46 (1791), no. 114, letter of September 19, 1791; see also BN Nouv. acq. fr. 308, fols. 140–143; Queruau-Lamerie, "Lettres de Maupetit," 23, 109; Rumeau, "Lettres du constituant Roger," 79–80; Célestin Guittard de Floriban, *Journal 1791–1796*, ed. Raymond Aubert, (Paris, 1974), pp. 92, 94–96. On celebrations elsewhere, to be examined more closely in the next section, see BM Dijon Ms. 1660, fol. 90; AD Côte d'Or L 36, fol. 123v°; AD Indre-et-Loire L 82, fol. 23; AD Loiret 2 Mi 3114. There were also spontaneous demonstrations; see, for example, AD Seine-Maritime L 14, fol. 207; AD Seine-Maritime L 225, document 128; AD Nord L 111*, fols. 135–138v°; AD Nord L 1245, document 3; AD Nord L 5874, dossier 2, letter of administrators comprising directory of district of Berguès, September 17, 1791.

moved to protect its work and to implant its new ideals in society. In an effort to protect the constitution from subversion, on September 23, the Assembly passed a series of articles prohibiting individuals who signed protests against the constitution from fulfilling any duties specified by the constitution. And, although the National Assembly had to defer the plan on national education that it had hoped to develop, it did, in an effort to impregnate the ideals of the constitution in society, mandate that each School of Law offer students a course on the French constitution, beginning with the term that would soon open in October.[100]

Then, on September 30, after a speech by Louis in which he again pledged to maintain the constitution, and after receiving a tribute from the city of Paris, the National Assembly disbanded.[101] After Louis had departed, the president of the Assembly, Thouret, declared the mission of the Assembly completed and announced that it now concluded its sittings. The deputies left the Manège to enter the new society that they had created.

It is occasionally noted that the Paris crowd acclaimed Pétion and Robespierre at this moment, but this reflected little more than the latest turn in Paris opinion. Rather, the spirit of the era was much better captured by another contemporary observer, Mme. de Staël, who, in recalling the period of the National Assembly, wrote that "ideas reigned at this time and not individuals."[102] The reigning idea from 1789 to 1791, the new ideal of the polity, was the achievement of the Assembly as a whole rather than any individual or group within it, and it is the reception by society of the institutions designed to realize this idea that will next be considered.

100 AN C 77, dossier 765, document 12; AN C 78, dossier 776, document 6; AP, XXXI: 245, 340.
101 See AN C 78, dossier 780, document 4; AN C 77, dossier 765, document 20.
102 Mme. de Staël, *Considérations sur les principaux événements de la Révolution*, I: 381.

# 5    The reception of the new ideal of the polity

> It seems that one is taken up with destroying, as much as the remains of prejudices will put up with it, these former divisions of France into dioceses, governments, *généralités* and *bailliages*, which are no longer suitable to the representative order and could only maintain seeds of scission and ideas of *corps* and *ordres*.
>
> *Journal d'Etat et du Citoyen*, October 29, 1789

As the year 1789 began, and a sense of the nation began to crystallize, France was gripped by the imminent convening of the Estates-General, which was universally viewed as the forum for solving the problems facing the country. The level of enthusiasm was partially sustained, however, by a misapprehension on the part of the clergy and the nobility on the one hand, and the Third Estate on the other. For their part, many within the clergy and nobility, especially the latter, interpreted the December 27, 1788, decision by the Crown to double the representation of the Third Estate as an independent action that did not necessarily amend the traditional method of voting by order. The Third Estate, however, believed that vote by head was implicit in the doubling of its representation, and most elements within it felt a sense of gratitude toward Louis for the action.[1]

The drafting of *cahiers* in preparation for the opening of the Estates-General particularly encompassed many of the contradictory currents circulating in France during the early months of 1789. In *cahiers* of all three orders an ideal of the nation, as distinct from the monarch, was evident, but at the same time there were widely differing conceptions of its complexion.[2] The vast majority of the nobility, while acknowledging

---

1 See, for example, AN B$^a$ 80, liasse 191, dossier 1, document 21; AN F$^1$c III Seine 26, undated (but January 8, 1789) message of members of Third Estate of Paris to Louis. On the hopes raised by the convening of the Estates-General, see AD Seine-Maritime C 2185, fol. 108.

2 On the idea of the nation in *cahiers* of the clergy, see Hyslop, *French Nationalism in 1789*, pp. 65–71; AN B$^a$ 47$^{b2}$, liasse 111, dossier 5, document 2; BN Mss. Fonds Français 20706, fols. 50–50v$^o$; for the nobility, see AN B$^a$ 20, liasse 28, dossier 6, document 3; AN B$^a$ 27, liasse 45, dossier 6, document 3; for the Third Estate, see AN B$^a$ 26, liasse 128, dossier 3,

that there would no longer be fiscal privileges in the nation, nevertheless clearly viewed the distinction of orders as total and an integral component of the social and political structure of the polity. The Third Estate was willing to accept social distinctions by order and to accord numerous honorific privileges to the clergy and nobility, but it refused to recognize orders as a political institution, especially as a basis for voting at the Estates-General. Although these differing perceptions resulted in a profound disagreement, this political quarrel did not translate into a deep sense of social conflict before the Estates-General met.[3] Indeed, on the local level, the renunciation of fiscal privileges frequently generated a sense of goodwill that raised hopes and tended to obscure deeper political differences, for the issue of vote by order seemed abstract and a problem that could be more properly resolved at the Estates-General itself.[4]

After hopes and expectations had been raised, the stalemate that ensued at the Estates-General proved to be a severe disappointment. As was the case in the mind of most deputies, politically aware elements in society also viewed the deadlock largely as a contest between the nobility and the Third Estate.[5] As will be seen, however, many members of the nobility in the provinces were at variance with their counterparts in the Estates-General, viewing the solution of the problems facing the nation as more important than the issue of vote by order. Indeed, this common desire of the nobility and the Third Estate in the provinces to see the problems of the nation addressed accounts for the widespread joy that greeted news of the union of orders in the National Assembly on June 27.[6] The event also produced greater enunciation of the idea of the nation, for there was a widespread belief that the difficulties confronting the nation would finally be addressed.[7]

The Crown, however, obviously unaware of the backing enjoyed by the National Assembly in the nation, began to make preparations to

document 5; AN B[a] 29, liasse 48, dossier 7, document 3. See also Hampson, "The idea of the nation in revolutionary France."

3  See, for example, AN B[a] 11, liasse 5, dossier 12, document 6; AN B[a] 25[1], liasse 42, dossier 2, document 2; AD Charente-Maritime 4 J 1574 (28), *cahier* of third estate of *sénéchaussée* of Saintonge seated at Saint-Jean d'Angély; AD Seine-Maritime C 2185, fol. 116.

4  See, for example, AN AA 49, dossier 1391, document 52; AN B[a] 27, liasse 45, dossier 6, documents 1, 3.

5  See, for example, AN AA 48, dossier 1380–1381, documents 1–2; *La Nation à ses représentans* (N.p., n.d.); AM Lorient BB 12, no. 12, letter from Lorient, June 3, 1789.

6  See especially AM Strasbourg AA 2003, fol. 74; AM Le Havre D[2] 1, fol. 85v[o]; AM Aurillac II[7], no. 15, fol. 1v[o]; AM Toulon L 107, dossier D[4] 15, letter of July 15, 1789; AN B[a] 16, liasse 17, dossier 2, document 36; *Journal de Provence, dédié à M. le Maréchal prince de Beaveau*, July 11, 1789.

7  AM Le Havre D[2] 1, fol. 88; AD Bouches-du-Rhône C 1383, fol. 266; AM Aix BB 5, fols. 134–135.

dissolve it, including an effort to prepare public opinion for the action.[8] Even a *cahier* of the nobility had asserted that the deputies should be inviolable and should not "under any pretext" be disturbed in their duties, and it was clear to all concerned that the deputies had not yet had the opportunity to make any substantial progress toward the paramount task of drafting a constitution with which their constituents had charged them.[9]

Emulating their Parisian counterparts, inhabitants of many provincial towns staged municipal revolutions in support of the National Assembly during July and August. There was no uniform pattern; in some towns the municipalities were taken over completely while in others traditional bodies had to share power with *ad hoc* groups.[10] These revolutions, while usually precipitated by such fundamental issues as grain supply or security, nevertheless also had a political content in that they represented a reaction against old oligarchies that were viewed not merely as ineffectual, but also as more loyal to the Crown than to the nation. The deliverance of the National Assembly was widely acclaimed, and admiration for the courage of the deputies increased its stature.[11] Indeed, the new bodies that established themselves in municipalities not only moved to address problems that had been the catalyst for the risings, but almost invariably expressed their unswerving devotion to the National Assembly, confirming the loss of royal control over the kingdom.

Just as important as the expressions of support, however, was the tone in which they were put forward. In a society heavily defined by localism and tradition, inhabitants of these municipalities, in superseding or supplementing local authority, had clearly broken with both and now sought a new focus in the ideal of the nation, embodied by the National Assembly. Furthermore, by pledging virtually unlimited support to

---

8 The Crown ordered the text of the king's speech of June 23 to be disseminated urgently, apparently in an effort ultimately to justify the dissolution of the National Assembly. See, for example, AD Ille-et-Vilaine C 1812, letter of Villedeuil to Rochefort, June 24, 1789; AD Calvados C 6347, letter of Barentin to de Launay, June 24, 1789 and circular of Villedeuil to de Launay; AD Dordogne O E DEP 5005, letter of subdelegate to municipal officers of Perigueux, July 21, 1789. Again, for the argument that the Crown was not necessarily seeking to dissolve the National Assembly, see Price, "The 'Ministry of the Hundred Hours': a reappraisal."

9 For the *cahier* of the nobility asserting the inviolability of deputies, see AN B^a 14, liasse 10, dossier 4, document 2; on the primacy accorded to drafting a constitution, see AN H^1 148, dossier 2, documents 40, 53, 60, for the Third Estate; AN H^1 149, dossier 1, documents 7, 8, 11.

10 Again, see Ligou, "A propos de la révolution municipale"; Hunt, *Revolution and Urban Politics*.

11 See AD Calvados C 6354, letter of Courage du Parc to intendant, July 21, 1789; AM Lorient BB 12, message from Lorient, July 22, 1789; AM Toulon L 107, dossier D^4 15, letter of July 28, 1789.

whatever measures the National Assembly might choose to undertake, the new bodies effectively ratified the decision on imperative mandates that the Assembly had recently made. Earlier, constituents had sought to guide the Estates-General closely in its deliberations,[12] but now they began to give the National Assembly a larger – indeed, almost exclusive – determining role. This metamorphosis was evident in a letter written by the commissioners of the commons of Provence. Professing admiration for the depth of knowledge of the deputies, the sublimity of their ideas and their assiduousness, the commissioners averred that all Frenchmen ought to be imbued with the same spirit as the deputies and to watch over and consolidate their work. They then stated that "all Frenchmen, disdaining in these circumstances the unfortunate precaution of limited powers, ought to grant the most blind confidence to an assembly so worthy of fulfilling the august duties confided to it, and join his individual view, to give the most extensive and solemn adhesion to all the decrees that it has published." In this way, they asserted, France would assure itself of a sage and solid constitution.[13] Similar sentiments arrived from elsewhere in France as well.[14] Indeed, messages that came in from all parts of France deeply affected the deputies, greatly increasing their confidence and sense of mission.[15]

The flood of communications to the National Assembly demonstrated the crystallization of the ideal of the nation that occurred during the stalemate at the Estates-General. Arising as a negative reaction to the narrow and self-interested ethos of privileged corporatism, the emerging ideal of the nation had at its core a sense of high-mindedness and disinterestedness. A characteristic example of frustration with the circumscribed outlook of privileged corporatism occurred in Normandy in early June when the *procureurs-syndics* of the province of Normandy, responding to an internal administrative problem, wrote to the *bureau* of Pont l'Evêque that they hoped "that a new order of things will stop all these conflicts of which you so rightly complain and that there will come a day when in order to do good, it will suffice to want to do it."[16] Throughout France, from May through July, 1789, an amorphous concept of the nation began to gain greater definition, albeit in varying

---

12  See, for example, AD Bouches-du-Rhône C 1046, letter of May 16, 1789, in which the deputy Bouche noted that in the three weeks that he had been at Versailles, he had received 111 letters, memoirs, pamphlets or instructive advice through the mail.
13  AN C 88, dossier 52, document 7.
14  AD Marne E supp. 4812*, fols, 269v°–270; AN C 87, dossier 44², document 70.
15  See, for example, Ménard de la Groye, *Correspondance*, pp. 69, 71.
16  AD Seine-Maritime C 2152, letter of provincial *procureurs-syndics* to *bureau* of Pont l'Evêque, June 6, 1789.

manners, but ultimately centering on and being systematized by the National Assembly.

In other areas of France the emerging ideal of the nation went beyond a mere yearning for change. In Burgundy, for example, the town of Saint-Jean-de-Losne – in a reflection of the antithesis between privilege and the nation that developed in the months preceding the opening of the Estates-General – offered to yield its fiscal privileges, awarded during the Thirty Years' War, to the nation. Although the Estates of Burgundy, as a result of the construction of a bridge near the town, had been attempting since 1786 to breach some of these privileges, a number of its other fiscal privileges remained untouched, and the renunciation of them by the town gained the attention of deputies when it was announced to the National Assembly on July 7. While the renunciation made by Saint-Jean-de-Losne attracted the most notice, it was not the only town to offer to yield its privileges; among others, Sarlat and Soubise did so as well.[17]

Yet another example of the manner in which the emerging ideal of the nation began to establish itself at the expense of privileged corporatism during this period occurred in Aix-en-Provence. Following a proposal by a group of citizens on July 25 to send a message to the king and to the National Assembly, a member suggested the election of eight commissioners to compose it, and proposed that they be chosen according to orders – two from the clergy, two from the nobility and four from the Third Estate. In response, d'Albert de Bornes, the president of the *Cour des Comptes*, said that the city was one, like the nation. Stating that the present assembly was made up only of citizens, and of citizens animated by the same spirit, he said that no distinction existed, so that it was not necessary to observe a difference of orders. He proposed that the eight commissioners be chosen indistinctly rather than on the basis of orders and expressed the hope that Provence could serve as an example to all of France. His suggestion was immediately and enthusiastically adopted.[18]

All of these stances reflected a more advanced position than that held by the National Assembly; indeed, at the time of the gathering in Aix-en-Provence the National Assembly was still sitting by orders and dividing its committees in precisely the manner rejected by the inhabitants of Aix. But these were local developments that could not influence events at the

---

17 On Saint-Jean-de-Losne, see AD Côte d'Or C 2987[6]*, message of Saint-Jean-de-Losne to Estates of Burgundy, November 19, 1787; AD Côte d'Or C 3367, fols. 133v°, 144v°, 150v°, 156v°, 189v°; AD Côte d'Or C 2987[6], fols. 114v°–117v°; AD Côte d'Or C 3843, fols. 114v°–117, 165–168. On the attention it gained in the Assembly, see *Procès-verbal de l'Assemblée Nationale* No. 17 (July 7, 1789), pp. 3–6; AN C 28, dossier 222, document 8; AN C 28[2], dossier 224, document 4. On Sarlat, see AN C 88, dossier 51, document 42; on Soubise, AD Charente-Maritime 4 J 1574 (28), letter of Sozeau to deputies at National Assembly.          18 AM Aix BB 115, p. 7.

national level. At the same time, however, it is clear, given the existence of such sentiments, why the initiatives emanating from the National Assembly after the night of August 4 were able to strike such a responsive chord in much of France.

Indeed, where the inroads made by the emerging ideal of the nation, as well as the fact that inhabitants of the provinces were in many cases more advanced in their thinking than were their representatives in the National Assembly, can be seen most vividly is in the response of provincial nobility to the rejection of imperative mandates and to the requests by their representatives in the National Assembly for new powers. Almost immediately after the recalcitrant members of the clergy and the nobility joined the National Assembly, several of the noble deputies wrote to their constituents to ask for new powers.[19] It is clear, however, that in most instances this was less a matter of conscience than yet another effort to hinder the functioning of the National Assembly.[20] Indeed, some who sought to return to their localities ostensibly to ask for new powers were, in fact, planning to sabotage the National Assembly by not returning, so the Crown, aware of their plan, initially dissuaded deputies from going back to their home districts.[21] Many of the noble deputies hoped that the National Assembly would fail or be dissolved.[22]

Indeed, seeking as they were to use the issue of imperative mandates to retard the work of the National Assembly, the noble deputies could only have been surprised by the replies that their requests for new powers produced.[23] In what was occasionally a tacit disavowal of the views or a rebuke of the judgment of their representatives, provincial nobility throughout France abrogated the imperative mandates of their deputies and gave them unlimited powers in an effort to have the problems of the nation addressed.

The day after the reunion of orders, on June 28, the duc de Caylus had pronounced himself as absolutely opposed "to the new order of things which prepares itself," but the nobility of Saint-Flour, whom he

19 See, for example, AN AA 48, dossier 1388–1390, document 87; AN AA 49, dossier 1395–1397, document 102; AN AA 50, dossier 1424–1427, document 50; AN AA 50, dossier 1428–1431, document 82; AN AA 50, dossier 1435–1438, document 82; AN B$^a$ 38, liasse 81, dossier 4, document 8; AN B$^a$ 41, liasse 87, dossier 6, document 2.

20 In one instance, noble deputies inverted the entire premise of imperative mandates by overruling their constituents on the issue of whether their mandates were imperative after their constituents had said they were not. See AD Ain 1 Mi 1, letter of July 7, 1789.

21 AN M 856, dossier 6$^9$, letter of Barentin to Louis, June 28, 1789; see also AN B$^a$ 41, liasse 87, dossier 6, documents 4, 6; AN B$^a$ 49, liasse 114, dossier 7, document 6; AN B$^a$ 76, liasse 176$^{bis}$, dossier 3, document 27.

22 ADG A$^4$ 56, p. 154; AN K 164, no. 4$^3$, fol. 122.

23 On the evident surprise of noble deputies at the response of their constituents, see, for example, AD Ain 1 Mi 1, letter of July 7 1789.

represented, responded to his request for new powers with the observation that it was only by general accord of the deputies of the different orders that comprise the Estates-General that the deputies could accomplish the task with which they were charged, and that the nobility of Saint-Flour had greeted the news of the reunion of orders with joy. They stated that they had broken and annulled all of the imperative and limited powers that they had earlier given to their deputies at the National Assembly and replaced them with general powers in order to cooperate with the assembled nation, whose interests were theirs, for the common good. To eradicate any doubt about the intentions or the disinterested sentiments that animated them, they also decided unanimously that each member present would sign the declaration.[24]

The nobility of the *sénéchaussée* of Saintonge opened their assembly with an affirmation that they were dedicated to the happiness of the nation and, fully convinced that the greatest of all titles was that of citizen, they ordered their deputies to cooperate with other representatives of the French people to accelerate the great work of regeneration of the state. The nobility of Saintonge then annulled their previous mandate with the comment that they desired "to cement the precious union that has always reigned among the three orders of the province accustomed to regarding each other as brothers."[25] In similar fashion, the nobility of Loudon released their deputy from his imperative mandate with the admonition to "consent to all that he will believe necessary for the well-being of the state."[26]

The nobility of the *bailliage* of Alençon, which had strongly prohibited its deputies from meeting in common, reconvened early in August and, citing its attachment to the monarch and its desire for the tranquility of the fatherland, gave them general powers without any limitation or restriction, and charged them to work for the common good of all.[27] The nobility of the *sénéchaussée* of Condom had mandated vote by order rather than by head and had demanded that if the latter occurred, their deputy was to protest and to retire. On July 9, however, when they reconvened to give the deputy unlimited powers, the nobility stated that its interests were inseparable from those of the nation.[28]

---

24 AN B$^a$ 41, liasse 87, dossier 6, documents 2, 10.
25 AN B$^a$ 77, liasse 179, dossier 5, document 6.
26 AN B$^a$ 49, liasse 115, dossier 6, document 9. See also AN B$^a$ 14, liasse 11, dossier 3, document 3; *Le Point du Jour*, July 29, 1789.
27 On the original mandate, see AN AB$^{XIX}$ 3258, *cahier* of order of nobility of *bailliage* of Alençon, pp. 10–11; on the reconvening, see AN C 127, dossier 426, document 35.
28 AN AB$^{XIX}$ 3258, *cahier* of order of nobility of *sénéchaussée* of Condom, p. 6; AN B$^a$ 33, liasse 68, dossier 5, documents 4–8, especially 6.

To be sure, there were occasional instances of reluctance to provide new powers, but these were rare. One such instance was that of the nobility of the *sénéchaussée* of Castres, which had insisted on vote by order and had instructed its deputy, the comte de Toulouse-Lautrec, to receive new instructions before voting definitively on any proposal contrary to those prescribed in his mandate. Indeed, his instructions stated that if he varied from any of the clauses in his mandate he would be judged forever unworthy of their confidence.

As a result, the comte de Toulouse-Lautrec wrote for new powers on June 28, and the nobility of the *sénéchaussée* reconvened on July 23. Although they endorsed the statement drawn up by the recalcitrant members of the nobility in the National Assembly on July 3, they voted new powers to their deputy, urging him to "propose, advise and consent to all that he will judge useful to the well-being of the State."[29]

Conversely, the nobility of Autun, noting that despite the imperative mandate their deputy had carried, he had attended and deliberated in the National Assembly, asserted that the welfare of the nation was the supreme law to which all considerations ought to yield due to the importance of reestablishing close concord among all citizens. They observed also that no obstacle could henceforth delay the fortunate effects that the nation expected from the voluntary reunion of the three orders of the state in the National Assembly. They went on to approve of the conduct of their deputy, to revoke the imperative mandate with which he had been charged, and to authorize him to deliberate in common and to vote by head in the National Assembly. They also urged him to consider the public good and the happiness of the nation in his conduct.[30]

One of the most remarkable exchanges between noble deputies and their constituents in the provinces – revealing the gulf between them – was that between the comte de Helmstatt and the comte de Gomer and their constituents in the *bailliage* of Sarreguemines. When the former wrote to the *bailliage* on July 11 to request new powers, he stated that, because of his mandate and because of his personal opposition to joining the National Assembly, he intended to take advantage of the interval

29 On his instructions, see AN AB[XIX] 3958, dossier 5; on his request for new powers, AN AA 50, dossier 1435–1438, document 82; on the reconvening of his electoral assembly, AN B[a] 30, liasse 53, dossier 5, document 11.
30 AN B[a] 16, liasse 16, dossier 4, document 2. For other revocations of imperative mandates, see AN B[a] 11, liasse 5, dossier 8, document 2; AN B[a] 29, liasse 49, dossier 11, documents 3, 4, 11; AN B[a] 38, liasse 81, dossier 4, document 8; AN B[a] 43, liasse 92, dossier 4, documents 5–6; AN B[a] 47[B2], liasse 111, dossier 6, document 15; AN B[a] 57, liasse 140, dossier 5, document 5; AN B[a] 66, liasse 156, dossier 5, documents 2, 6; AN T 1108/3, document 548.

provided by the need for new powers to go to take the baths to reestablish his health. For his part, the comte de Gomer returned to his residence at Dieuze.

When the nobility of Sarreguemines reconvened on August 3 they sharply upbraided both deputies. They stated that it was against the grain of all the members of the *bailliage* that their deputies, under a pretext of illness, had left the National Assembly. They ordered both men to return to Versailles in order to carry out the duties that had been confided to them. They pointedly added that they had not elected them in order to confer some sort of honorific title on them and made clear that they expected the two men to cooperate in working toward the well-being of the state.[31]

Furthermore, although the Crown had initially discouraged noble deputies from returning to their localities for new powers, it later relented, and some took advantage of the opportunity to return during the month of July. In the course of their visit, they personally encountered the sentiments that had been expressed in the new mandates sent to noble deputies in the Assembly. On July 27, for example, after his return from Caen, the duc de Coigny reported to the National Assembly that his constituents had specially charged him to bring about concord, to cooperate in the well-being of the fatherland and the regeneration of the public welfare, and he mentioned that he, along with his two colleagues who represented the nobility of Caen, considered themselves obligated to do all that they could to concur in the good that the National Assembly would bring about. He added as a personal reflection that the provinces, including his own province of Normandy, were in agitation and that nothing was more important than that the National Assembly occupy itself with the constitution.[32] Similarly, when the comte de Mont-Revel returned to his *bailliage* of Maconnais to receive new powers, his assembled constituents acknowledged the reservations he had made for their rights and privileges and noted that he had followed their desires but, in what was yet another indication of the resolution of the tension between privilege and the nation, they now declared themselves more concerned with "the happiness of all French citizens." Consequently, they revoked their imperative mandates and gave him a new mandate to participate fully in all of the deliberations of the National Assembly according to "his mind and conscience."[33] As a result of both written

31 AN AA 50, dossier 1424–1427, document 50; AN B^a 77, liasse 177, dossier 4, documents 3, 4, 6.
32 AD Calvados F. 780, copy of declaration made to National Assembly, July 27, 1789, copy dated August 1, 1789. For a description of the situation at Caen, see Paul R. Hanson, *Provincial Politics in the French Revolution: Caen and Limoges, 1789–1794* (Baton Rouge, 1989), pp. 31–35.        33 AN B^a 49, liasse 114, dossier 7, document 8.

communications and personal encounters, then, by early August many noble deputies had come into contact with the new ideal of the nation that was beginning to develop in society at large.

This crystallization of the ideal of the nation in society and the growing awareness of it by the National Assembly came together, however fortuitously, on the historic night of August 4. Although the prearranged renunciation for that evening went awry, it nevertheless struck a resonant note with the nobility, who led the way in the avalanche of relinquishments of privilege to the nation that followed.[34] This elevation and articulation of the idea of the nation, breaking as it did with prescriptive tradition, was obviously far more comprehensive and total than expected. The National Assembly had, in fact, repudiated history and tradition and sealed France off from its past. As a result of the pact of association forged that night – the "new covenant" of which the marquis de Ferrières wrote and the "family compact" to which Le Chapelier alluded – the nation now had to be built *de novo* and, with the deputies possessing unlimited mandates, it was almost universally recognized that the task of redefining the nation lay exclusively with the National Assembly through the medium of the new constitution.[35]

After weeks of stalemate at the Estates-General and the initial slow pace of the National Assembly, and amidst the unrest convulsing many parts of France, the actions of August 4 resounded across France. At municipal gatherings that assembled all over France, speakers noted the way in which the decrees, by effacing the divisiveness of privileged corporatism, had suddenly reconciled the nation and produced the consensus that was a necessary precondition to an effective constitution.[36] Even at a distance, the reaction in society was occasionally as rhapsodic as it had been in the Assembly itself. In Tonnerre, for example, an inhabitant named Heuvrard composed a poem in honor of what one municipal officer had called "this sublime decree."[37]

The event struck a responsive chord in much of France; as the commissioners of the Third Estate to the communities of Provence replied to the letter of their deputies informing them of it, the news "was received here with an astonishment mixed with admiration and surprise. One cannot conceive that you have covered so much road in such a short time; you march on the path of giants, and one must acknowledge that

34 AM Strasbourg AA 2003, fol. 120.
35 See, for example, BHVP Ms. 737, fol. 14; AD Gironde 3 L 82, letter of August 22, 1789.
36 See AM Nevers BB 46, fols. 83v°–84v°; AM Laon BB 46, fols. 32v°–33v°. See also AD Gironde 3 L 82, letters of August 14 and 24, 1789.
37 AD Yonne L 191, deliberation of the town and commune of Tonnerre, August 13, 1789.

your success surpasses the hopes of the nation."[38] But several deputies, particularly Third Estate deputies from *pays d'états*, had been concerned about the reaction of their constituents and had, in some instances, made their renunciations provisional, pending approval of their constituents. In fact, however, what now occurred was that the process that had begun in July of entrusting the National Assembly with an exclusive, determining role in the redefinition of the nation was strengthened and affirmed. Indeed, the effort by deputies to gain the consent of constituents fostered enthusiasm for, and even a sense of participation in, the endeavor of remaking the nation.

This was most evident in Provence, where a vicarious sense of partaking in the renunciation of privilege resulted from management of the issue by its deputation to the National Assembly. On August 6 the entire group of deputies from the province, including those of the clergy and the nobility, met to plan a strategy by which the privileges of Provence could be willingly yielded by its inhabitants, a particularly delicate issue since their constituents had heretofore been aggressively advancing a project for a new constitution for Provence, which they had just completed in late July.[39]

The tension between the imperative of the pact of association and local privileges particularly concerned the deputies from Arles, who informed their constituents of the abolition of all the privileges of provinces and towns. They anxiously solicited a renunciation by Arles of its privileges, sending several letters to this end, one of which indicated their inability to prevent their abolition. On August 13, before the arrival of two of the most urgently worded letters, written August 12 and 13, the town reluctantly abandoned its privileges and gave its deputies new powers.[40] With evident relief, the deputies from Arles offered the privileges of the town to the National Assembly on September 12.[41]

The misgivings of Arles, however, appear to have been atypical, for on August 14, following an assembly of all three orders, commissioners of the communities of Provence indicated to the deputies that the province welcomed the measures and no longer felt any need to pursue its own constitution. The commissioners further notified the deputies that the province renounced its special sovereign status and would register, without protest, all decrees of the National Assembly, which would be

38 AD Bouches-du-Rhône C 1380, fol. 240.
39 AD Bouches-du-Rhône C 1337, letter of August 7, 1789; AD Bouches-du-Rhône C 1380, fols. 228–229; AD Bouches-du-Rhône C 1383, fols. 172–197. See also AD Bouches-du-Rhône C 1241, undated letter of deputies of Provence to National Assembly to unnamed addressee. On the completion of it, see AM Arles AA 23, fols. 485–486.
40 AM Arles AA 23, fols. 536–537, 540–541, 543, 544–545, 547; AM Arles BB 56, fol. 150.
41 AM Arles AA 23, fol. 558; AN C 30, dossier 251, document 19.

fully and freely executed.[42] On August 16, the deputies, obviously unaware of this development, sent their own letter to the province telling it that the project for a constitution for Provence was dead and seeking the approval of the towns and communities of Provence for the actions of the National Assembly on August 4, while warning that the opposition of Provence or any other province would not stop execution of the decrees.[43]

After further correspondence and coordination between the deputies and commissioners of the commons of Provence, on August 27 the latter convoked the different communities of the province to ratify formally and collectively the decrees of August 4.[44] Over the next month, throughout Provence, gatherings took place in scores of cities and towns and an extraordinary wave of enthusiasm for the new ideal of the polity advanced by the National Assembly on August 4 swept over the region. In a long and remarkable speech in Aix prior to ratification of the decrees, for example, a municipal officer told assembled inhabitants of the town that "August 4 will become as celebrated among us as the year 1689 in England."[45] In Saint-Maximin, M. de Benoît, the chief municipal official, exhorted his fellow townsmen to "abdicate, then, all personal and particular privileges and glorify ourselves by sharing with the French citizens, our brothers, some rights we had, in order to acquire those that the French nation is going to enjoy."[46] By unanimous consent Provence dropped its project for a special constitution and fully empowered the National Assembly to chart the future course of the nation.[47] By late September, the commissioners of the commons of Provence sent adhesions from at least eighty-five towns to deputies of the province; in addition, there were many others that had been sent directly to the National Assembly itself.[48]

Provence may have had the most systematic method for ratifying the decrees of August 4 and for investing the National Assembly with the task of determining the future of the nation, but these two tendencies were also present almost everywhere else in France. In fact, in the letter

42 AD Bouches-du-Rhône C 1380, dos. 250–251; AD Bouches-du-Rhône C 1383, fol. 198v°–201.          43 AD Bouches-du-Rhône C 1337, letter of August 16, 1789.
44 AD Bouches-du-Rhône C 1241, letter of August 22, 1789; AD Bouches-du-Rhône C 1383, fol. 272v°–273; Newberry Library, FRC 10160, notice of convocation of assemblies, August 27, 1789.          45 AM Aix BB 114, fol. 58v°.
46 AN C 93, dossier 86, documents 13–14.
47 AD Bouches-du-Rhône C 1383, fols. 198v°–201; to give but one example of the latitude given to the National Assembly, see AN C 93, dossier 86, document 15.
48 See AD Bouches-du-Rhône C 1381, fol. 91; see also AN C 93, dossier 86, documents 16–25; dossier 87, documents 7–14; dossier 88, documents 6–7; dossier 89, documents 36–62; dossier 90, documents 10, 16–19. For a good account of one such meeting, see Thomas F. Sheppard, *Lourmarin in the Eighteenth Century: A Study of a French Village* (Baltimore, 1971), pp. 179–180.

of August 16 to the commissioners of the commons of Provence, the deputy Jacques Verdollin had noted that the city of Rennes and all the municipalities of Brittany, which had, he wrote, "seemed to hold more strongly than any other province of the kingdom to its privileges, to its capitulations with its particular princes and with France," were daily sending adhesions and renunciations of privileges to the National Assembly.[49] Indeed, Brittany, as the most privileged of all the provinces, became a barometer of the success of the new ideal of the polity, for quick acceptance of that ideal by Brittany did much to advance it at a critical time.

As in Provence, presentation of the issue by deputies to the National Assembly played some role in its acceptance, but there was a much greater degree of spontaneity in actions in Brittany. This was especially true among the nobility, and it lent greater credibility to the new ideal advanced by the Assembly, especially because after the events of late 1788 and early 1789, and the initial refusal to send deputies to the Estates-General, there was a widespread belief that if the new ideal of the polity was going to meet resistance it would be among the nobility of Brittany.

On August 9, however, the nobility of Nantes came together in order to adhere to the decrees of the National Assembly, to renounce their privileges and their loyalty to the Breton constitution and to pledge their loyalty to the nation.[50] After a change of municipal government on August 18, the nobles reaffirmed their pledge on August 27, even changing the wording of their pledge slightly in order to make it more acceptable to the new municipality, which had assumed office on August 22.[51] The document was then circulated throughout the bishopric for confirmation by the remainder of the nobility before being forwarded to the Intermediate Commission of Brittany.[52] Likewise, the nobility of Quimper, shortly after the meeting of August 4, gathered to pledge adhesion to the decrees that the National Assembly had taken and to all those that it would take.[53] With the Breton nobility and the Breton constitution in particular having been for so long the symbols of privilege in opposition to the ideal of the nation, such actions were regarded to be of great significance.[54]

49 AD Bouches-du-Rhône C 1337, letter of August 16, 1789.
50 AM Nantes AA 82, document 15.
51 AM Nantes AA 82, document 46; on the changes in the municipal government, see AM Nantes BB 112, fols. 97–98v°; 99–99v°.
52 AM Nantes AA 82, documents 17–45, 47–69; AD Ille-et-Vilaine C 3842, entry of September 1, 1789.          53 Le Point du Jour, August 22, 1789.
54 Ibid. See also AM Brest LL 46, no. 43, letter of August 14, 1789; AM Lorient BB 13, no. 51, letter of August 15, 1789.

Although adhesions of the nobility attracted the most attention, the reaction of the Third Estate was also of great consequence. On the night of August 4 Breton deputies in the National Assembly had made their renunciation conditional on the approval of their constituents, and they broached the issue with them carefully.[55] The deputies from Nantes, for example, wrote to their constituents only on August 29 and noted that "conforming to the almost general view of the inhabitants of the kingdom," the National Assembly had, on August 4, destroyed the privileges of all the provinces and towns of the kingdom. They observed that they had been able to take part in this decree only under the reservation of obtaining the acquiescence of their constituents, and they asked that the inhabitants of Nantes be assembled in order to indicate their attitude.[56] As a result, an extraordinary assembly of the inhabitants of Nantes gathered at 8.00 a.m. on September 14 and tacitly approved of the sacrifice of their privileges by deciding unanimously by acclamation to retire the imperative mandates of the deputies. The assembly empowered them with absolutely free and unlimited powers "in order to cooperate for the well-being of the state," although they still expected them to take into account the interests of the province.[57] Renunciation of privileges soon followed in outlying areas of the bishopric as well.[58]

Elsewhere in Brittany, the inhabitants of Lorient initially reacted in a cautiously favorable fashion, but only a few days later fully approved of the conduct of their deputy. Indeed, the municipality later sent him an expression of unqualified support and a full reaffirmation of its re-nunciation of its privileges.[59]

The *pays d'états*, in particular, of which Provence and Brittany were two of the most important, had a decisive role in the system of privilege under the Old Regime and, as a result, their responses are of fundamental

55 The deputies had, however, privately assured their colleagues that they would secure approval for the renunciation. See AM Bordeaux D 220, no. 13, letter of Lafargue to electors of Bordeaux, August 5, 1789.

56 AD Ille-et-Vilaine C 1807, copy of letter of deputies of Nantes to Bellabre, August 29, 1789, copy dated September 5, 1789.

57 AD Ille-et-Vilaine C 1807, letter of Bellabre to mayor and aldermen of Nantes, September 7, 1789; AM Nantes BB 112, fols. 100–101. The issue of unlimited powers had previously been discussed and they had been granted, but without specific reference to the decrees of August 4. The earlier discussion may have been in response to the decision of the National Assembly in July to invalidate all imperative mandates. See AM Nantes AA 82, document 70; AM Nantes II 151, document 30.

58 *Etats-Généraux. Journal de la Correspondance de Nantes*, II: 163–164, 250, 312.

59 AM Lorient BB 12, letters from Lorient, August 10, 1789, August 12, 1789, August 17, 1789; AM Lorient BB 12, no. 51, letter of August 15, 1789; AM Lorient BB 13, letters from Lorient, September 24, 1789, September 28, 1789. See also AD Côtes-d'Armor 1 L 576, letter from Pontrieux, August 15, 1789.

importance in understanding the degree to which French society delegated the task of redefining the polity to the National Assembly and relinquished any guiding role for itself. Provence, for example, had originally sought to determine its own future in the National Assembly through its advocacy of a constitution for the province, but after August 4 it gave up the effort and entrusted its destiny entirely to the National Assembly. Likewise, in Brittany most of the deputies had been sent to the Estates-General with imperative mandates specifying that the privileges of the province would be surrendered only after the completion of a constitution and only after each province had obtained a uniform regime.[60] By renouncing its privileges Brittany yielded its surety, and by retiring its imperative mandates the province gave up all influence and explicitly ceded its status to the National Assembly as a whole rather than to its own deputies. Although virtually all of France did this, its significance was most extraordinary in Brittany because it was the most privileged of all provinces and because its delegation, as the formation of the Breton Club indicated, was among the most influential. Henceforth, most of the inhabitants of Brittany, both noble and non-noble, recognized that, as one of their deputies indicated, they would be more French than Breton, and it was the National Assembly that would lay the foundations for that new identity.[61]

Not all of the *pays d'états* were as willing to surrender their privileges as readily as Provence and Brittany, although this was occasionally due in part to the timidity or political ineptitude of their deputies in the National Assembly. The deputies from Béarn were taken aback by the renunciation of privileges on August 4, and exhibited no leadership or initiative in presenting them to their constituents. The letter of the deputies was largely descriptive, whereas that of an extraordinary deputy who formed part of a committee of correspondence offered a more comprehensive account of the goals of the Assembly.[62] Although they did not oppose outright the abolition of privileges, the deputies in the Assembly nevertheless sought some sort of exemption due to the special status Navarre had with the monarch. Indeed, mindful that the National Assembly considered presence at meetings

60 AM Lorient BB 12, no. 47, letter of August 5, 1789.
61 AD Morbihan 1 Mi 240, no. 20, letter of August 4, 1789, supplemented by Bord, "Ouverture des Etats-Géneraux de 1789," 20–26.
62 For the letter of the deputies in the Assembly, see AD Pyrénées-Atlantiques C 1377, letter of August 7, 1789; for that of the extraordinary deputy, AD Pyrénées-Atlantiques C 1601, register of commissioners comprising committee of correspondence, August 4, 1789. At the same time, at least one deputy of the clergy of Béarn in the National Assembly quickly aligned himself with the renunciations of August 4. See AN C 30, dossier 251, document 12.

tantamount to yielding privileges, the deputies initially refused to attend.[63]

A few days later, the deputation asserted that it was not clear that all the principles and operations of the National Assembly applied to Navarre. The deputies determined that the best course was to seek a solemn declaration of independence from France that would allow it to keep its own constitution, without giving up the hope of one day adopting that of France, "if it was good and solidly established." The deputies believed this act was all the more essential due to the determination of the National Assembly to abolish the rights and constitutions of all regions in order to have them ruled equally by the laws that it had made and was going to make.[64]

The extraordinary deputy for Béarn at Versailles was less anxious or alarmed than the deputies in the National Assembly about the ramifications of August 4. He wrote that the province would have to consider the price it would have to pay to be more closely tied to France, but that it would equally have to weigh what means of resistance it would have to oppose the French nation, even if it could put off sacrificing its privileges until the time that the French constitution was complete. He then went on to endorse the new constitution taking shape in the Assembly.[65]

The Estates, in fact, although apprehensive, were not as opposed to giving up the privileges of the province as the deputies in the Assembly believed. In an initial response, representatives of the Estates observed that they were not necessarily against yielding their privileges to a common rule. They observed that a close union with France could, in fact, be seen as an advantage rather than a sacrifice. Their chief concern was that the new constitution for France was obviously unknown, and they believed that a renunciation of their own constitution might be premature.[66] Some days later, inhabitants of Pau and other towns asked

63 AD Pyrénées-Atlantiques C 1601, extract from register of deputation of Navarre to Estates-General, August 6, 1789.
64 *Ibid.*, August 10, 1789. From the beginning, the participation of Béarn and Navarre in the Estates-General had been problematical, for they did not consider their *pays* to be a province of France, but an independent kingdom, so their position in August was not a radical departure. See *Très-humbles et très-respectueuses rémontrances des Etats-Généraux du royaume de Navarre* (N.p., 1789) [Newberry Library, Case FRC 5758]; *Copie de la lettre de MM. les députés de la Province de Béarn, à M. de Luxembourg, président de l'ordre de la noblesse* (N.p., n.d.), pp. 4–5, [Newberry Library, Case FRC 2492].
65 AD Pyrénées-Atlantiques C 1601, register of commissioners comprising committee of correspondence, August 14, 1789.
66 AD Pyrénées-Atlantiques C 1377, letter of d'Assant, Mallon, Vergès, *et al.* to deputies at National Assembly, August 17, 1789.

for a convening of the Estates to consider the decrees because of their obvious importance.[67]

The deputies in the National Assembly had, in fact, been working toward this goal, and in late August the Crown authorized the convocation of the Estates of Navarre in order to deliberate on adhesion or nonadhesion to the decrees of the National Assembly.[68] Shortly afterward, however, the Crown cautioned the deputies on any notion of pursuing independence from France.[69]

Indeed, increasingly concerned about the potential outcome of deliberations by the Estates, the Crown began to treat the convocation more cautiously and to manage it in order to avoid a conflict with the National Assembly over its abolition of privilege.[70] The monarch placed strict limits on the matters that could be addressed and emphasized his desire to see a closer union of Béarn and France. The Keeper of the Seals further recommended that two deputies from Béarn in the National Assembly attend the meeting of the Estates "to enlighten their constituents on the dispositions of the National Assembly and on the true state of things" – a clear allusion to the imperative of the pact of association. The Keeper of the Seals asked the comte de Saint-Priest to inform the syndic of the Estates, the marquis de Lons, of the purpose of the trip by the deputies and to notify him that it would please the monarch if the marquis guided the convocation in a manner that would produce a prompt and favorable result.[71] Furthermore, before the Estates met, the town of Oloron, in a direct communication to the National Assembly, unilaterally renounced its privileges and adhered to the August decrees.[72]

The Estates of Navarre opened before the marquis de Lons received the letter from the comte de Saint-Priest, and as the meeting progressed it appeared that the clergy and the nobility of Navarre would reject the decrees of the National Assembly. The marquis abruptly suspended the Estates and went to Pau, where he opened the Estates of Béarn. The Crown sought to prevent the Estates of Navarre from reopening by citing the custom that the Estates of Béarn traditionally met before the Estates of Navarre did.[73]

---

67 AD Pyrénées-Atlantiques C 1377, extract of register of deliberations of *Hôtel de Ville* of Pau, August 29, 1789.

68 AD Pyrénées-Atlantiques C 1601, extract from register of deputation of Navarre to Estates-General, August 29, 1789.          69 *Ibid.*, September 11, 1789.

70 AN B$^a$ 60, liasse 147, dossier 7, document 4.

71 AD Pyrénées-Atlantiques C 1377, copy of letter written by Keeper of Seals to comte de Saint-Priest, September 21, 1789.

72 AD Pyrénées-Atlantiques C 1377, letter of Mourot to Estates of Béarn, September 7, 1789.          73 AN B$^a$ 60, liasse 147, dossier 7, documents 6–7.

At this juncture, the deputies from Béarn in the National Assembly, aware of the irreversibility of the pact of association, became more assertive. They wrote to their constituents that the National Assembly was unshakable on the matter of administrative uniformity.[74] On October 26 the National Assembly banned any meetings of provincial estates and the matter ended. If the new ideal of the polity did not advance as readily in Béarn as it had in Provence or Brittany, for example, it is nevertheless evident that the inhabitants of Béarn were more receptive to that ideal than the deputies believed. The tentative course of the new ideal in Béarn is attributable as much to a failure of leadership on the part of its deputies in the National Assembly as to any misgivings by the populace.

In other areas of France, less privileged than the *pays d'états*, the reaction to the new ideal of the polity, while perhaps less significant, was also quite enthusiastic. The town of Châlons-sur-Marne, for example, which earlier had agreed to respect all of the decrees of the National Assembly, now demonstrated its willingness to honor that commitment by celebrating the operations of the National Assembly with a *Te Deum* on August 16 and by formally renouncing all of its privileges on September 8.[75] Likewise, after meeting on August 16 to adhere to the decrees, the municipality of Laon reassembled the next day to consider them further. Stating that it saw in the decrees the constitutional bases of French liberty, the regenerating principles of happiness and public prosperity and an unlimited devotion on the part of the deputies of the nation to the happiness and interests of all citizens and all regions without distinction, the municipality assured the deputies that the town felt a sense of gratitude toward the Assembly. Furthermore, the gathering informed the Assembly that it could rely on the "ardor of its zeal to conserve, with all of its might, the regenerating principles" contained in the August decrees and asked the Assembly to accept the abandonment of the particular privileges of Laon.[76] The municipality of Le Havre, after receiving and publicizing the decrees, hailed them as "an excellent work" that they "would never have dared to ask for in their *cahiers*."[77] In Nevers, a gathering of citizens "of all ranks and conditions without distinction of orders," met on August 9 and warmly endorsed the actions taken by the Assembly at the meeting of August 4. It assured the Assembly of the homage and devotion of the entire commune and observed that union and concord reigned among the citizens of all the

74 AD Pyrénées-Atlantiques C 1377, letter of Pémartin and Noussiton to Estates of Béarn, October 13, 1789. On the determination of the National Assembly with respect to Navarre, see AD Ain 1 Mi 1, letter of October 12, 1789.
75 AD Marne E supp. 4812*, fol. 287; AN C 93, dossier 86, documents 27–28; for the earlier declaration, see AD Marne E suppl. 4812*, fols. 269v°–270.
76 AM Laon BB 46, fols. 31v°, 32v°–33v°.        77 AM Le Havre D² 1, fol. 99v°.

orders of the town, all of whom adhered to the measures announced by the Assembly.[78] In Paris and Bourges, too, the decrees were favorably received.[79]

To be sure, the reaction to the new ideal of the polity was not uniformly enthusiastic; in other regions the response ranged from treating the decrees as a matter of course to indifference to doubt and even to outright hostility. The Intermediate Commission of the province of Maine, for example, simply registered and promulgated the decrees without comment, treating them as if they were any other ordinance.[80]

Beginning in late July and continuing into August, many regions in France were convulsed by turmoil associated with the "Great Fear," which had been the catalyst for the night of August 4 in the National Assembly.[81] In some locales the agitation overshadowed the August decrees, so that their reception met with indifference. In Dauphiné, for example, which had led the way in 1788 by offering to yield its privileges to the nation in a new constitution, the night of August 4, corresponding as it did to that ideal, should have been especially well-received, perhaps more than elsewhere in France. But the authorities of the region, consumed as they were with public order, clearly did not want to allow gatherings of any sort, even to celebrate or to acknowledge the August decrees. Indeed, one inhabitant found the unrest and violence so distressing that in the summer of 1789 he regarded the Dauphinois ideals of 1788 almost as a chimera.[82] As a result, in Dauphiné, amidst the disorder, the decrees were barely noticed.[83] In Alençon the Intermediate Commission seized much more on the dissemination of the proclamation of the National Assembly of August 10 on public tranquility than on the simultaneous circulation of the August decrees.[84] Similarly, although La Rochelle was unaffected by the Great Fear, a provisioning crisis nevertheless overshadowed the August decrees.[85]

It must be remembered, however, that the Great Fear was not directed

78 AM Nevers BB 46, fols. 83v°–84.
79 See BHVP Ms. 736, fols. 29–30; Ms. 737, fol. 14; BN Mss. Fonds Français 10883, fols. 84–84v°; *Journal d'Etat et du citoyen*, August 13, 1789; Harvard University Fr 1380.20*; Joachim Heinrich Campe, *Eté 89: Lettres d'un Allemand à Paris* (Paris, 1989), pp. 51–53.
80 AD Sarthe C 90, fol. 179v°.
81 Georges Lefebvre, *The Great Fear of 1789: Rural Panic in Revolutionary France* (New York, 1973), remains the definitive study. See also the recent local study by Clay Ramsay, *The Ideology of the Great Fear: The Soissonnais in 1789* (Baltimore, 1992).
82 BM Grenoble R 6314 (8), no. 7.
83 On the disorders, see AD Isère C III 4*, fols. 395–405, 417–436; AM Grenoble BB 128, fols. 144–146v°. See also Pierre Conard, *La Peur en Dauphiné (Juillet–Août 1789)*, (Paris, 1904). On the virtual *pro forma* reception of the decrees in Dauphiné, see AM Grenoble BB 128, fols. 149v°–150; AD Isère C III 4*, fols. 406–413.
84 AD Orne C 1183, entry of August 17, 1789.
85 AM La Rochelle BB 33, fols. 7v°, 8, 16v°–17v°, 18–19v°, 31v°–32, 37–38.

against the Revolution nor the National Assembly. As a result, despite the turmoil, the new ideal of the polity continued to engage much of the populace, particularly in cities and towns. Indeed, Tonnerre, Aix-en-Provence, Châlons-sur-Marne and Nevers, where the decrees had been received with such enthusiasm, were all in areas affected by currents of the Great Fear. Far from impeding progress of the new ideal of the polity, in fact, the Great Fear may actually have accelerated or reinforced it, for even avowedly Marxist scholars have acknowledged that the Fear produced an extraordinary social cohesion.[86]

Sentiments of doubt were more amorphous, but stemmed in part from uncertainty about the future because of the suddenness and magnitude of the change. While perhaps recognizing the utility and value of the decrees, there was also a sense of apprehension about the ability of the Assembly to bring about such an entirely new situation.[87] The town of Nancy and the province of Lorraine, another *pays d'états*, sent a delegation to Versailles in early October that met with the deputies from Nancy, Claude-Amboise Regnier and Pierre-Joseph Prugnon. Reflecting the imperative of the pact of association, the deputies informed the emissaries that it was crucial for the province to renounce all of its privileges, and they later reiterated that this renunciation was not merely hypothetical. Although the purpose of their mission had clearly been to attempt to safeguard some of the privileges of the town and the province, the members of the delegation came away from the meeting recognizing the inevitability of change. Indeed, the final recommendation of the envoys to the province was to establish a correspondence with the deputies of the National Assembly to have a role in the "most delicate and most alarming circumstances in which we have ever been."[88]

Moreover, much concern arose among members of the clergy, who viewed the decrees somewhat ominously because of the abolition of the tithe. Despite occasional reassurances from their deputies,[89] it caused them much concern. In fact, the municipal officers of Cambrai wrote to the National Assembly to ask it to reconsider the abolition of the tithe.[90]

The single strongest negative reaction, however, one of outright hostility, came from the city of Strasbourg and the province of Alsace, a

86  See Lefebvre, *The Great Fear of 1789*, p. 203; Ramsay, *The Ideology of the Great Fear*, p. xviii. The latter argues that this solidarity was only momentary, but I would agree with Lefebvre that its influence lasted much longer.
87  See, for example, AD Indre-et-Loire L² 692, dossier 2, document 3.
88  AN AB^{XIX} 3319, dossier 2. The town of Metz also sought initially to retain its privileges. See *Extrait des registres des délibérations des trois-ordres de la ville de Metz. Du 21 août 1789*. (Metz, n.d.) [Newberry Library, Case Folio FRC 9971].
89  See Font-Réaulx, "Lettres de J. Bern. Colaud de la Salcette," 149.
90  AN F¹c III Nord 13, letter of municipal officers of Cambrai to National Assembly, September 25, 1789 and attached *mémoire*.

*pays d'état*, and this region seems to have been the only locale to respond in this manner. In two separate letters, deputies from Strasbourg provided a detailed account of the meeting of August 4 to their constituents. In one letter the deputy noted the generous spirit of other provinces, especially Brittany, and emphasized that Strasbourg ought not to pit itself against the national will by attempting to maintain its privileges.[91] The other letter indicated the regret that the delegation had felt at not being able to present to the nation any homage from the town, but they had remained faithful to their mission and to their *cahiers* and had made only a conditional declaration. He made a veiled allusion to the pact of association and pointed out that it was absolutely necessary for Strasbourg to ratify the renunciation of its privileges. To this end, he also enclosed a proposed text for renunciation. He went on to warn that, after the relinquishments that had been made, it would be difficult, if not impossible, for Strasbourg and Alsace to seek to conserve their privileges and to stand alone in what would be a uniform regime.[92]

Despite the viewpoint and counsel of its deputies, the town and the province reacted negatively from the start. The municipal government of Strasbourg had begun a memorandum defending the town's rights and privileges, and a subsequent municipal revolution did not alter the determination of the city to defend its exemptions.[93] Initially its defense was rather modest in tone, but as the dimensions of the proposed changes and the determination of the National Assembly to realize them became clearer, the city, as well as the nobility and clergy of the province, became more aggressive in their assertions.[94] Clearly torn by a personal sense of commitment to the new ideal of the National Assembly and the refusal of his constituents to subscribe to it, one of the deputies, Jean de Turckheim, resigned on September 22, warning the city that its continuing adhesion to privilege could have unfortunate consequences.[95] Undeterred, however, in late September the city aligned itself with the clergy and the nobility of the province in seeking to maintain its

91 AM Strasbourg AA 2003, fols. 120–121. The deputies had been cautious in their renunciation on the night of August 4. See *Procès-verbal de l'Assemblée nationale*, No. 40 bis (August 4, 1789), p. 32. At the same time, however, deputies of the clergy and nobility of Alsace in the National Assembly had quickly adhered to the renunciations of August 4. See AN C 30, dossier 251, document 1.
92 AM Strasbourg AA 2003, fols. 122, 123; the *cahier* for Strasbourg did, in fact, contain numerous injunctions that the rights and privileges of Alsace be preserved. See AM Strasbourg AA 2002, fols. 1–5.
93 See Franklin L. Ford, *Strasbourg in Transition, 1648–1789* (Cambridge, Mass, 1958), pp. 249–250.
94 AM Strasbourg AA 2003, fols. 126–127; AN C 93, dossier 89, document 35; AN C 94, dossier 91, document 18.
95 AM Strasbourg AA 2004, fols. 11–13, 16, 19, 21; AN AA 50, dossier 1435–1438, document 93.

privileges.[96] Indeed, in early October it sent a letter to its deputies in the National Assembly stating that the decrees of August 4–11 seemed unable to distinguish "simple privileges and concessions from the rights that are an emanation of the territorial superiority that the town of Strasbourg enjoyed before its voluntary reunion to France." The city enclosed a declaration in which it put forward its observations and reservations concerning the August decrees.[97]

The recalcitrance of Strasbourg and Alsace, more recently incorporated into France and where, as a result, a sense of the nation was less developed, was virtually unique at this time. Indeed, the entire range of less enthusiastic responses was far less representative of opinion in the nation as a whole which, after weeks of stalemate, was elated by the sense of progress and movement. From mid-August until well into September, much of the nation was optimistic and receptive to the changes that would be forthcoming and eager to have them codified in a new constitution. Perhaps this attitude is best captured in a brief letter from an inhabitant of Issoire to the deputy Jean-François Gaultier de Biauzat on August 21, in which he wrote "we have seen, Tuesday, the different decrees of the National Assembly; we await their sanction. Nothing is more beautiful than this spirit of generosity; it ought to produce forever the most complete union of all citizens of the kingdom. Send us a constitution quickly"[98]

Unfortunately, however, the National Assembly, by continuing to devote itself to the formulation of the Declaration of Rights, by falling into disagreement over how comprehensively to carry out the new ideal of August 4, and as a result of its struggle to gain the sanction of the king for the decrees, squandered the opportunity to take advantage of the high degree of hope and expectation present in the nation. Indeed, the optimism and faith of the nation in the new ideal of the polity conceived by the National Assembly began to yield initially to a sense of impatience and subsequently to one of misgiving. Before August 4, the nation had had, in many instances, as progressive an outlook as the National Assembly, and the two points of view had fused on August 4. Thereafter, however, the inability of the Assembly to work harmoniously in pursuit of its new ideal left some in the nation impatient, especially because in several locales the three orders were working in concert for the common good.[99] With the apparent sanction of the August decrees delayed until

96 AM Strasbourg AA 2004, fol. 25.
97 AN Bª 80, liasse 193, dossier 4, documents 4–5, with the quotation from the former.
98 AD Puy-de-Dôme 4 J 2, letter of d'Estaing to Gaultier de Biauzat, August 21, 1789.
99 The example of Angoulême is illustrative; on the ability of the different orders to work together, see AM Angoulême BB 20 (liasse), declaration of committee of town of Angoulême, August 7, 1789, declaration of curés, August 9, 1789; AM Angoulême BB 20

September 20,[100] and with the deputies not deciding until after that to initiate the new ideal with administration, the Assembly did not actively begin to implement its new ideal of the polity until the report of Thouret on September 29. As a result, it squandered eight weeks of hope and expectation.[101]

The October Days shook the confidence of deputies and became a major catalyst in curtailing much of the optimism in the new course of the National Assembly. In several instances the letters of deputies revealed how unnerved they were, and their constituents often became anxious in turn. Furthermore, a host of movements against the National Assembly undermined the fundamental hopefulness of the nation, although this loss of optimism did not translate into a lack of faith in the National Assembly itself; on the contrary, the nation offered encouragement to the deputies.[102]

One of the first such movements, and one that momentarily dispirited the Assembly, occurred in Dauphiné. Disconcerted by the October Days, the Intermediate Commission sought, on October 11, to convene the Estates of the province on November 2 to advise its deputies on the course of action they ought to follow in the circumstances. Initially this was an independent undertaking, viewed as a continuation of the tradition of the province and not directed against the National Assembly.[103] On October 10, however, the deputy Mounier, disillusioned by the fact that the Assembly had moved beyond the goals that he had originally envisioned, left Versailles – as did four other Dauphinois deputies around this time – in an effort to use the Estates, of which he had been secretary, to oppose the objectives of the National Assembly.[104]

For its part, the National Assembly remained determined to realize its new ideal of the polity and was unwilling to tolerate any interference from provinces, even Dauphiné, which had for so long been the symbol of the aspirations of the nation – a factor on which Mounier had counted.

---

(register), fols. 4v°, 5–5v°, 7; on the apparent impatience of society, AM Angoulême AA 19, no. 1.1; on the awareness of deputies of this impatience, AM Angoulême AA 19, no. 3.
100 Louis's equivocation on sanctioning the August decrees also provoked exasperation. See Harvard University Fr 1380.20*, fols. 387, 390–391.
101 For an example of the sense of relief that the National Assembly was finally beginning a program, see AM Douai AA 331, undated letter of Foucques. See also *Journal de la ville par Jean-Pierre-Louis de Luchet*, September 23, 1789.
102 On the letters of deputies, see AN AB^XIX 3562, dossier 1, document 4; AM Angoulême AA 19, no. 15; not all deputies were as discouraged, however; see AD Orne C 1227, document 205. On the encouragement and support expressed for the National Assembly, see AM Brest LL 47, p. 33; AM Lorient BB 13, letter from Lorient, October 23, 1789.
103 AD Isère C III 5*, fols. 390–393, 603–604. For more on the innocuous manner of the initial convening of the Estates, see AN B^a 75^A1, liasse 175, dossier 1, document 29.
104 Egret, *La Révolution des notables*, pp. 192–200.

On October 19, after learning of the intention of the Estates to convene, sixteen remaining deputies of the province gathered and charged Barnave and the comte de la Blache with writing a letter discouraging the Estates from convening. With liberal noble deputies now breaking with Mounier and committing themselves to the new ideal of the polity put forward by the Assembly, thirteen of the sixteen deputies signed the letter, which they sent on October 21. In it the deputies assured the commission of the safety of both the royal family and the National Assembly and asked the Estates not to convene. Since the Assembly had, in a reaffirmation of its new ideal, abolished orders for electoral and all other purposes on October 15, the convocation, due to its form, was illegal. Among other matters, the deputies pointed out that since Dauphiné had struck the first blow against the distinction of orders, it ought not now to be the only province to preserve them.[105]

The decision to convene the Estates gained little support outside of Grenoble and Valence; indeed, the deputies who returned did not receive the welcome they expected. One of them, the comte de Marsanne, was even arrested at Montélimar and held until the National Assembly ordered him released.[106]

The letter of the deputies decisively influenced the situation and forestalled the meeting of the Estates; on October 28, the Intermediate Commission deferred the opening of the Estates until December 14 and attempted to explain its decision to convene to the deputies of the National Assembly.[107] But on November 9 the Intermediate Commission received a packet from the minister La Tour du Pin containing the king's sanction of the decree of October 15 abolishing orders, a copy of the decree of the Assembly of October 26 prohibiting any convocation in assembly in the kingdom by order, and the king's acceptance of another decree of October 26 forbidding the convening of all provincial estates.[108] Since all of these criteria applied to the Estates of Dauphiné, the

105 *Lettre écrite à la commission intermédiare des Etats de Dauphiné par les députés de cette province à l'Assemblée nationale* (Paris, 1789). See also AN W 13, no. 227, no. 238; Egret, *La Révolution des notables*, pp. 205–208.

106 See *Chronique de Paris*, October 28, 1789; Egret, *La Révolution des notables*, pp. 201–203. For an indication of the support the National Assembly enjoyed in Dauphiné, see AN C 95, dossier 104, document 17, a decisive letter from Saint-Marcellin; see also AN C 95, dossier 107, documents 1, 14–15; dossier 108, documents 1–2; dossier 109, documents 10–11, 25–28. Valence also came to the support of the Assembly; see AN C 95, dossier 109, documents 8, 9[1].

107 AD Isère C III 5*, fols. 635–636; Egret, *La Révolution des notables*, p. 208. On the influence of the letter of the deputies at the local level, see *Délibération des citoyens de toutes les classes de la ville de Valence, du vingt-neuf octobre mil sept cent quatre-vingt-neuf, dans une des Salles de l'Hôtel de Ville* (N.p., n.d.), [Newberry Library, Case FRC 8906].

108 AD Isère C III 5*, fols. 696–697.

significance of the packet was unmistakable. Already lacking support in the province, and opposed by the National Assembly, the decision to convene the Estates did not have the support of the Crown either.

Indeed, it was becoming increasingly apparent that the convocation of the Estates was primarily a vehicle for one individual, Mounier, to express his personal opposition to the program of the National Assembly. Isolated and on the defensive, Mounier published a justification of his conduct on November 11 and resigned from the Assembly on November 15, and the effort to convene the Estates collapsed.[109] Mounier remained in Grenoble for several more months attempting to counteract the agenda of the National Assembly, but his efforts proved futile, and he left France in May, 1790. Perhaps the best contemporary insight into the entire episode was one that appeared in a Parisian newspaper after Mounier's departure from France, when it noted that "he had a constitution in his head: the National Assembly has made another one for us; he assures [us] that it is the National Assembly that is wrong."[110]

The convocation of the Estates of Dauphiné had not originally been directed against the National Assembly, and the attempt of Mounier to lead it in this direction had failed. But the defiance of Dauphiné and the estrangement of Mounier conferred greater legitimacy on contestation of the new ideal put forward by the National Assembly, and in other parts of France traditional bodies rose to take issue with it, although they almost invariably commanded little or no popular support.

An early declaration against the National Assembly by the vacation section of the *Parlement* of Toulouse in late September had gone largely unnoticed,[111] but in the aftermath of events in Dauphiné the number of challenges from traditional bodies increased. Indeed, one deputy, noting the unrest in Dauphiné as well as turmoil in Languedoc and Franche-Comté, wrote that he feared an insurrection of the provinces.[112] The *parlements* of Rouen and Metz issued defiant decrees in early November, which Louis, who had hastily agreed to the suspension of the *parlements*, condemned.[113] And in early November, in the most direct and explicit challenge to the authority of the National Assembly, the Intermediate Commission of the Estates of Cambrai and Cambrésis declared its

---

109 See Jean-Joseph Mounier, *Exposé de la conduite de M. Mounier dans l'Assemblée Nationale et les motifs de son retour en Dauphiné*, (Grenoble, 1789); Egret, *La Révolution des notables*, p. 211. On the unrest in Dauphiné in November, 1789, see AN AA 50, dossier 1416–1419, document 81. For an indication of Mounier's disillusionment with the course of the Revolution, and especially his estrangement from the consequences of August 4, see BM Grenoble Ms. R 6314 (14), III, fols. 57–79.
110 *L'Observateur*, July 15, 1790.        111 See AN AD$^{\text{XVIII}c}$ 10, no. 15 *bis*.
112 AN M 788, dossier 2$^{17}$, document 99.
113 AN C 33, dossier 279, documents 1–3, 9–14.

opposition to measures taken by the Assembly and sought to recall its deputies.[114] Even though the National Assembly continued to receive support and encouragement from the nation, it was clear by November, 1789, that a pervasive sense of discontent or unease had replaced the widespread hope and optimism of August and September.[115]

Although apprehension was obviously greatest in the areas of unrest, it was by no means limited to these regions. The provisioning crises and other difficulties that arose in the autumn of 1789 eroded the euphoria associated with the initial arrival and acceptance of the August decrees, and confidence in the National Assembly and its new ideal of the polity began to wane during the autumn of 1789 and into the winter of 1790.

The provisioning crises or other problems may have been the catalyst for diminished confidence, but it was compounded in many locales by a realization of the potential implications of the reorganization signalled by the report of the Committee of the Constitution on September 29. As the possible ramifications became clearer, the inhabitants of several regions became quite disconcerted. However attractive the destruction of privilege may have appeared in an abstract sense, its tangible local impact could be deeply unsettling, and this set off an intense competition between towns for the procurement of new institutions.[116] Beginning especially with the debate on the new administration in November, 1789, towns and cities began to attempt to gain some advantage in the new structure that was only beginning to take shape. Almost as soon as the municipality of Brest learned of the suspension of the *parlements*, for example, it importuned its deputies to secure the placing of a tribunal there when the judiciary was reorganized.[117] In addition, towns and cities began to position themselves favorably by writing to their deputies and pointing out the manifold advantages that would ensue by making their locale the site of a district or departmental *chef-lieu* or other governmental body.[118]

More typically, however, towns and cities, aware of the unrest convulsing France, would offer anew their submission to the National Assembly or renounce their privileges and take the occasion to point out the advantages of locating a *chef-lieu* or other administrative body in its locale. The town of Morlaàs in Béarn, for example, sent a message to the

---

114  See Ménard de la Groye, *Correspondance*, pp. 143–144, 146; BN Mss. Nouv. acq. fr. 4121, fols. 280, 284–285.
115  On the support received by the Assembly, see, for example, AM Lorient BB 13, letter from Lorient, October 26, 1789, no. 22, letter from Lorient November 4, 1789, no. 24, letter from Lorient, November 9, 1789; Ménard de la Groye, *Correspondance*, pp. 136, 146. See also *Chronique de Paris*, November 17, 1789.
116  See Margadant, *Urban Rivalries*.          117  AM Brest LL 47, fol. 39v°.
118  See, for example, AM Lorient BB 13, no. 30, letter from Lorient, November 23, 1789.

Assembly confirming its loyalty to the Assembly and offering decrees proclaiming its renunciation of its privileges, rights and franchises. It then indicated how painful the sacrifice of eight hundred years of its privileges was, and concluded by stating baldly that it hoped that its submission to the Assembly would lead the latter to make the town the site for a *chef-lieu* of a district and a tribunal in order to give the town "a new existence."[119]

Similarly, the deputies of the commune of Dijon also expressed concern for the fate of its citizens and wrote that they hoped that the Assembly would not abandon them "in their distress" and would locate in Dijon "some national establishments capable of offering it some resources that will protect it from Revolutionary politics."[120] Lodève, in a series of deliberations confirming the abandonment of its privileges and other declarations of loyalty, asked for the placement of administrative and judicial bodies.[121] The commune of Yvetot affirmed its adhesion to the night of August 4 and the abandonment of its privileges and then asked for a new tribunal to replace its seigneurial court, the largest in the region.[122]

Uncertainty over ramifications of the new configuration of the polity led scores of cities and towns – with some sensing opportunity, but more sensing loss – to seek to position themselves favorably, precipitating an intense competition between certain towns. In Laon, for example, where expectations had run high in August, a vigorous rivalry with Soissons began in December after the latter sent an address to the National Assembly seeking to obtain the *chef-lieu* for the department, leading Laon to do the same.[123] Furthermore, in addition to the flood of addresses or petitions, many towns sent delegations to Paris to meet with their deputies or the Committee of the Constitution to seek to become the *chef-lieu* for a department or a district, leading to even greater competition among towns.[124]

An examination of some cities, especially those that had been important administrative centers under the Old Regime, reveals the depth of

---

119 AN C 96, dossier 113², document 23.
120 AN C 97, dossier 117, document 11.
121 AN C 97, dossier 117, document 25.
122 AN C 97, dossier 118, documents 9–12. For other instances of this approach to the Assembly, see AN C 97, dossier 123, documents 17, 136; AN C 97, dossier 125², document 18; AN C 98, dossier 129, document 12.
123 AM Laon BB 46, fols. 31v°–33v°, 64v°–65; for the continuation of this rivalry, see AD Aisne L 628; Margadant, *Urban Rivalries*, pp. 263–264.
124 See Jean-Paul Rabaut de Saint-Etienne, *Nouvelles réflexions sur la nouvelle division du royaume, par M. Rabaut de Saint-Etienne, membre du comité de Constitution, adressées à ses commettans* (Paris, 1790), p. 8. See also AM Douai D³ 2, letter of Le Roux de Bretagne, February 2, 1790, for a good description of one such mission.

anxiety and concern that underlay this outpouring of addresses and sending of delegations. On November 26 in Toulouse a speaker addressed the municipal administration to warn of the deleterious effects that would result from the destruction of the *parlement*. As a result, the administrators decided to send an address to the National Assembly detailing the misfortunes threatening the city and, among other requests, to ask the favor of the Assembly in enabling Toulouse to reclaim the importance it had held up to that time. At the next meeting, on December 2, the address was read and approved, and it resembled many others that the Assembly received during this period. It began with a declaration of respect for the National Assembly, and then went on to express its unease at the implications for Toulouse of the recently enacted administrative reorganization and the impending judicial reform, which the municipality believed would entail even greater harm for the city. After a lengthy recitation of anticipated problems, the city asked the Assembly to recognize its plight when it made its decisions concerning the administrative and judicial reorganization of the kingdom.[125]

In late November, citizens of the town of La Rochelle, fearful that it would not be the *chef-lieu* of the department, gathered to make the "most lively representations" to the National Assembly, and all elements of the town were convoked to deliberate. Three days later, after a meeting on the "future of La Rochelle," the town sent a petition to the National Assembly.[126] Indeed, deputies clearly risked incurring the wrath of their constituents if the latter perceived that the deputies were not sufficiently representing their locale during the process of determining administrative sites.[127]

The town of Aix-en-Provence, however, offers perhaps the best illustration of the shift from optimism to apprehension that occurred during the autumn of 1789. In early September, Aix had enthusiastically welcomed the decrees of August 4 and had eagerly renounced its privileges. But by late autumn, many individuals within the town had become so disconcerted that a meeting of the municipal council in early January, 1790, witnessed the unleashing of recriminations at the haste with which the city had renounced its privileges and constitution. Reminding the council that he had warned at the time of the unfortunate consequences that could ensue, Dubreuil, a member of the council, recalled that the deputies had, in fact, solicited approval for their renunciation of the privileges of the province and that Aix, as well as most other municipalities, had complied. But, he argued, these abdications

---

125  AD Haute-Garonne C 303, fols. 183–190, 199–205.
126  AM La Rochelle BB 33, fols, 102v°–106.
127  See BM Lyon Ms. 2191, letters of December 9, 1789 and December 12, 1789.

had been made in isolation and the province itself had not gathered as a whole to offer them. He praised the one deputy from Provence in the Assembly, Bouche, who had resisted the division of the province into three departments. Arguing that ratification of the renunciation of privileges had not been unanimous, he implied that a retraction of some sort would be possible. Although the town did not attempt to renege on the renunciation of its privileges, Dubreuil's speech reflects the change of sentiment that took place in the last months of 1789.[128]

Whereas Aix-en-Provence had believed in the repudiation of privilege in favor of the new ideal of the polity that the night of August 4 had represented, the city of Strasbourg never had. As a result, in the uncertainty that beset France in the autumn of 1789, the debate on the fate of the privileges of the town – and the implications of its attempt to retain them – continued.

On December 7, the deputy Etienne-Joseph-François Schwendt, one of the representatives for Strasbourg in the National Assembly, wrote to explain that it was necessary for the town to renounce old ideas and old principles. Schwendt informed them that it was imperative for the inhabitants to submit themselves to the new constitution, to which the Assembly would make no exceptions.[129] The old ideas and old principles still had strong defenders, however, for a newly-founded newspaper had as its focus a debate over the new system represented by the Revolution versus the old system of privilege. Indeed, the series of articles opened with the observation that "the greater part of our fellow citizens seem to be in ignorance of whether or not we have already adopted the new body of laws begun by the National Assembly for the well-being of all the French."[130]

In fact, although the *Magistrat* registered and the aldermen of Strasbourg confirmed the decrees of August 4,[131] it is clear that the town remained wedded to its privileges rather than to the new ideal of the polity, for it continued to seek special treatment. Indeed, it wrote to Schwendt seeking a special exemption for the town from the newly-decreed system of municipal government, so that Strasbourg could have some permanent municipal administrators. Utterly exasperated, Schwendt wrote back that he was the only deputy to make such a request and that it was completely at variance with the principles established by

---

128 AM Aix BB 114, fols. 58–62v°; 142–145v°.
129 AM Strasbourg AA 2005ª, fol. 12.
130 See *Feuille Hébdomadaire Patriotique*, December 6, 1789, December 13, 1789, December 16, 1789 (supplement), December 20, 1789. See also *Réponse à Monsieur Hoffman par un bon citoyen de Strasbourg* (N.p., 1789) [Newberry Library, Case FRC 7831].          131 *Ibid.*, December 6, 1789.

the National Assembly, especially that of accountability to the citizenry. Clearly frustrated, he notified the municipality that there was nothing more that he could do, and pointedly noted that it was time for Strasbourg to decide if it was for or against the Revolution. In the event that the town refused to abide by the Revolution, he asked if they had the means to oppose themselves to and sustain themselves against the nation.[132]

With the erosion of the consensus in favor of the new ideal of the polity and a resurgence of adhesion to privilege, by the end of 1789, to a greater or lesser degree, unease was general throughout France. Virtually all of the former institutions of the kingdom – provincial estates, *parlements* and the like – had been suppressed, and new institutions, although legislated, had not yet been established. Furthermore, in many areas municipal government remained confused and irregular.[133] Even individuals favorably disposed toward the changes enacted by the National Assembly were disconcerted, as is best captured in an open letter to the Committee of the Constitution written and published by a Breton commentator, Jean-Baptiste-René Robinet, in early November, 1789. Brittany had been an exemplary model of a region accepting the changes enacted by the National Assembly, despite the loss of privileges and influence that this entailed. Robinet's pamphlet, however, illustrates that this did not occur without misgivings, amidst the uncertainty washing over France in the autumn of 1789 as the remaking of the polity by the National Assembly exceeded every expectation.[134] Robinet, in his letter, questioned the need for a territorial and physical division of the kingdom, when the Revolution was primarily a matter of politics, legislation and government. He regretted the overturning of all of the old administrative contours of the realm and deplored the consequences of administrative reorganization for the judiciary, and hoped that the parlements could continue, although staffed by all citizens. As a Breton, he said he welcomed the end of all exclusivity and the opportunity to blend with all other Frenchmen, but hoped to preserve the old provinces, believing that they would all be imbued with a spirit of the nation. Then, speaking to the Assembly, he stated:

There are no longer any provinces!... Instead, say that there are provinces, and that they are all national, all French, because there are no longer any distinctions, or privileges, or regimes, or interests or spirit of particularism. Patriotism is not in the names, but in the soul.

132 AM Strasbourg AA 2005ª, fols. 14–15.
133 See AD Seine-Maritime C 2, letter of comte de Saint-Priest to intendant of Rouen, November 13, 1789.
134 On the acceptance of the Revolution in Brittany, see AM Lorient BB 13, p. 111, letter from Lorient, November 23, 1789.

Let us conclude that new divisions are not necessary in order to abolish the spirit of particularism, that it is henceforth abolished, that everywhere it is replaced by national spirit...

You have made some indispensable destructions, some advantageous and infinitely useful destructions. It is necessary to take care not to push too far. It will no longer be regeneration: it will be abuse and excess.[135]

In a postscript to the letter, clearly alluding to the unease spreading throughout France, he added that the division of the kingdom was less pleasing than ever, at a time when Frenchmen should have been speaking only of reunion.[136] Indeed, doubtless aware of the unease in Brittany, the deputies from Nantes offered a detailed explanation to their constituents of the reasons that led them to accept the division of the province.[137] In addition, a large number of members of the Breton delegation wrote a letter that they had circulated throughout the province seeking to allay the concerns of their constituents.[138]

In other provinces as well individuals who were loyal to the Revolution were similarly disconcerted by the destruction of the provinces. In early November, 1789, an individual who had just travelled around France wrote to the president of the National Assembly to apprise him of his findings. He had, he indicated, been especially concerned with Brittany, Provence, and Dauphiné and all three were uneasy at the division of their province. In comments that echoed what Robinet had written, he reported that inhabitants were saying that they were French, that they had given the greatest example in this revolution, that they had abandoned their privileges so that nothing distinguished them any longer and they were asking what more one could want. The correspondent reported that inhabitants of these provinces asserted that the decrees of the National Assembly had enjoyed success because of the support of their provinces and that the Assembly now wanted to move against these same provinces.[139]

The ideal of the nation had come to fruition in 1789 within the traditional structure of the polity, and the destruction of provinces and *parlements*, whose existence stretched back centuries, was unnerving, even to those favorably inclined toward the Revolution. This suppression resulted directly from the course of events in the National Assembly –

---

135 AD Ille-et-Vilaine L 330, *Lettre XVIII. A Messieurs du comité de Constitution. Sur leur plan de division du royaume.*

136 *Ibid., Post-Scriptum à la lettre XVIII, relative au plan d'une nouvelle division du royaume.*

137 See *Etats-Généraux. Journal de la Correspondance de Nantes*, II: 553–557.

138 AD Loire-Atlantique L 176, documents 12, 15; BM Nantes Collection Dugast-Matifeux, t. 98, letter of December 18, 1789. On the unrest in Brittany, see also AD Ain 1 Mi 1, letter of December 8, 1789.     139 AN DIV 13, dossier 239, document 5.

especially the pact of association forged on the night of August 4 – with the Assembly absolutely determined to efface privilege and not to allow any entity that might later seek to reclaim its privileges to continue to exist.[140] However receptive many locales may have been in the summer of 1789 to the new ideal of the polity, it is indicative of the separate dynamic under which the Assembly operated for several months after August 4 that even those who subscribed to the new ideal and "national spirit" put forward by it were disquieted at the manner in which the National Assembly chose to realize these new values.

The pervasive unease at the monumental changes in the configuration of the polity was compounded by provisioning crises, not just in Paris, where the October Days were the best-known manifestation, but throughout much of the rest of France, and there were other difficulties as well. Indeed, there is evidence that the Crown sought to take advantage of the apprehension and uncertainty to attempt to turn public opinion against the National Assembly. In Amiens, for example, in December, 1789, the intendant became concerned about the potential for civil disorder in the city, but when he wrote to the comte de Saint-Priest to express his concern, the minister reacted almost casually to the intendant's alarm, noting that the matter, of which he had already been informed, had been referred to the National Assembly. The Assembly had issued a decree on the matter, he observed, and one could presume that this would restore calm. In fact, as the intendant later notified the ministers, there were no disturbances, but it was more the result of local efforts than anything else.[141] It is clear, however, that the Crown wished any onus for civil disorder to fall on the National Assembly, thereby discrediting it.

The incident also highlights another major factor contributing to the sense of unease late in 1789: growing doubt about the allegiance of the monarch to the new political order. This incertitude culminated with the arrest of the marquis de Favras on December 24, 1789, adding to the sense of anxiety that extended throughout France at the end of 1789.

Concurrent with this anxiety at the end of 1789, however, was a sense of both apprehension and wonder for all of the changes that the National Assembly had brought about and a recognition that it was the Assembly that was the political center of gravity in France, giving definition to the Revolution and realizing it by the sheer force of its will. When the

---

140 See AD Gironde C 4365, no. 44; AD Ille-et-Vilaine L 330, *Lettre XVIII. A Messieurs du comité de Constitution*. See also *Courier de Madon*, February 26, 1790.
141 AD Somme C 731, letter of intendant to comte de Saint-Priest, December 17, 1789, letter of comte de Saint-Priest to intendant of Amiens, December 20, 1789, letter of intendant of Amiens to various ministers, December 22, 1789.

electorate had assembled throughout France in early 1789, no one – including the men chosen as deputies – could have foreseen the magnitude of the changes that would issue from the National Assembly by the end of the year. In selecting deputies to the Estates-General there was a belief that that body would, to use the prevalent contemporary term, "regenerate" the kingdom, chiefly by addressing the financial crisis and producing a constitution, but it was believed that this regeneration would occur within the contours of existing institutions.

Although the night of August 4 evolved in part as a response to sentiments in the nation, out of it the National Assembly formulated a vision of the polity uniquely its own, inspiring both admiration and apprehension as the year 1789 ended. The reaction, as well as the realization that the Assembly was in control of the destinies of France, is reflected in a letter written in December, 1789, by two men sent by the Chamber of Commerce of Bordeaux to observe and report on the workings of the National Assembly. The focus of their letter was the fate of the slave trade and, after expressing their concern that slavery might, in fact, be abolished, they wrote:

The defect of all corporations up to this time has been wanting to defend the ideas that were special to them, without dreaming that principles have changed. They have believed that they can wrap themselves in the rules of the old regime and put them forward in a moment, where nothing relative is taken into consideration. Athens and Rome had slaves, one used to cite them in order to legitimize servitude, but it is no longer a question of taking as a model the ancients, one no longer speaks of them. They work for absolutely new laws. Commerce ought then to take its part in the regeneration and be proud of modifications based on reason and justice, in order to prevent a general overthrow. To wish to persist is to wish to destroy oneself, just as the nobility suddenly lost its privileges, the clergy its possessions and the *parlements* their existence.

... Rain spoils the best affairs and circumstances are the compass by which one always ought to lead. They have changed, one must not dissemble. Do not raise, then, too strong a resistance to the whirlwind of events, for fear of making the tree of commerce break suddenly.[142]

Circumstances had indeed changed, with the National Assembly in complete control of the nation and placing it on entirely new principles and foundations, with ramifications that affected the political, social, legal, commercial, administrative and religious spheres, as well as virtually every other facet of civic life. As 1789 ended, then, France waited expectantly, uneasy but fully aware that the course had been set by the National Assembly and was categorical and unalterable.

142  AD Gironde C 4365, no. 43. I would like to thank George Taylor and Elizabeth Fox-Genovese for calling my attention to the existence of this document. For a similar assessment, see AM Strasbourg AA 2005ᵃ fol. 14vᵒ.

# 6    The realization of the new ideal of the polity

> From Colloumiers-en-Brie – Every Sunday and holiday the mayor and
> municipal officers gather the people in a church, and read and explain to
> them all the decrees that the National Assembly has conveyed during
> the week, encouraging concord, peace and attachment to the con-
> stitution. All villages and hamlets ought to follow this example.
>
> *Journal des municipalités et assemblées administratives*, May 24, 1790

As the year 1790 began the nation existed in a void that was to be filled
by the National Assembly. Virtually all of its major institutions had
disappeared, and it was an indication of the omnipotence of the Assembly
that on a daily basis it reshaped the face of France, remaking provinces
into departments in a process that many deputies found stultifying even
as they recognized its overriding importance. But pockets of resistance to
the new ideals of the Assembly remained, and the anxiety created by the
air of uncertainty was palpable. This tension crystallized around two
incidents early in 1790: the summoning of a defiant Chamber of
Vacations of the *Parlement* of Rennes and the arrest and trial of the
marquis de Favras.

In January, 1790, the task of defining the boundaries of departments
was proceeding apace; by early January, in fact, approximately sixty
departments had been determined.[1] Although deputies recognized that
this was an undertaking of the highest magnitude, there were meetings
during this process when attendance was quite low, and most often the
Assembly simply adopted the advice of the Committee of the Constitution.[2] Apprehensive at the ramifications for their locales, countless
towns sent delegations that importuned the Committee of the Constitution, seeking to secure a *chef-lieu* of a department or district. But the
committee, confident of the moral grandeur of the new ideal of the polity,
and vested with the full confidence of the National Assembly, remained
unmoved. Impervious to the entreaties of delegations, it set the new

---

1 BN Mss. Nouv. acq. fr. 4121, fol. 374. Again, on the departments, see Ozouf-Marignier,
*La Formation des départements*; Margadant, *Urban Rivalries*, pp. 84–110, 220–321.
2 BN Mss. Nouv. acq. fr. 4121, fol. 384; Ménard de la Groye, *Correspondance*, p. 173.

contours of the polity, and took them before the Assembly, which almost invariably ratified its judgments.[3]

The progress made on realizing the new administration gave the Assembly increased confidence, as was evident in its handling of the recalcitrant Chamber of Vacations of the *Parlement* of Rennes. The Chamber had defied the National Assembly by not registering laws passed by the Assembly, which led the Assembly to summon the magistrates before it. In a dignified manner, the president of the Assembly questioned the president of the *Parlement* of Rennes and invited him to explain the conduct of the Chamber, observing that the National Assembly was a body in which justice did not destroy goodwill. The president of the *parlement*, de la Houssaye, behaved arrogantly, feigning at times, according to one deputy, to forget the existence of the National Assembly. In a declaration clearly at variance with opinion in the province, and which underscores the night of August 4 as the great watershed, de la Houssaye announced that the decree of the Assembly requiring the parlements to promulgate, in a timely fashion, laws passed by the Assembly contravened the privileges and franchises of the province, as well as the marriage contract of Anne of Brittany. He even implied that the imperative mandates of the deputies of the province remained valid because only the Estates of Brittany could retire them. The Assembly, however, with its view of the pact of association of August 4 as a binding covenant of the highest order, dismissed the explanation offered by de la Houssaye.[4]

The outcome of this episode revealed both the increased confidence of the National Assembly and the high-mindedness of its new ideal of the polity. The previous autumn, when it had been buffeted by the opposition of several traditional bodies, the Assembly had sought to work through the Crown in order to restore calm. By early 1790, however, with its confidence renewed by completion of the new administration,[5] a cornerstone of its new ideal, and unsure of the loyalty of the monarch, the Assembly met this new challenge independently and unaided, sum-

---

3 See Rabaut de Saint-Etienne, *Nouvelles réflexions sur la nouvelle division du royaume*, p. 8. One observer noted that there were approximately 3,000 delegates soliciting the Assembly for administrative sites, but he also stated that most would go away disappointed. See Lindet, *Correspondance*, p. 57. For an excellent description of one such delegation, see AM Douai D³ 2, letter of Le Roux de Bretagne, February 2, 1790. See also Margadant, *Urban Rivalries*, pp. 196–198.
4 BN Mss. Nouv. acq. fr. 4121, fols. 374–380; BN Mss. Nouv. acq. fr. 12938, fol. 309v°. On the satisfaction in Brittany with the suspension of the *parlements*, see AN C 100, dossier 160¹, documents 52, 53.
5 On the increased confidence of the National Assembly produced by the completion of the new administration, see AD Ain 1 Mi 1, letter of November 26, 1789.

moning the Chamber of Vacations before it rather than simply appealling for respect for its decrees or obedience to the law.

Furthermore, the resolution reached by the National Assembly emphasized its high-minded principles. Although the Chamber of Vacations clearly remained wedded to the repudiated standard of privileged corporatism and regarded the Assembly with disdain, the Assembly did not seek to make itself feared by jailing the magistrates or reacting in some other coercive fashion. Rather, citing the incompatibility between the beliefs of the magistrates and the new principles on which the polity was to be ordered, the Assembly proclaimed that the magistrates could not fulfill any public duties under a new constitution that they chose to ignore, and barred them from any public office until they took an oath of loyalty to the new constitution.[6] When the magistrates remained intransigent, the Assembly later dismissed the members of the Chamber of Vacations and appointed other men to replace them and, when these magistrates also refused to register the decrees of the Assembly, it created a provisional superior court in Rennes to replace the Chamber of Vacations.[7] Indeed, the National Assembly was habitually indulgent toward those who defied it or plotted against it, a stance that ultimately enhanced its moral stature and, in its lack of retribution or vengeance, served to distinguish it from the Old Regime. The comportment of the National Assembly was, in fact, in stark contrast to that of the Crown with the same body and province in 1765 and 1788, when in the course of disputes it had imprisoned magistrates or representatives of Brittany.

The other event contributing to the air of apprehension and un-certainty centered on the marquis de Favras, who had been arrested in late December, 1789; as details of his activities began to become known in early January a sense of alarm developed. Indeed, initial skepticism about a conspiracy yielded to belief in a large plot extending into various provinces and encompassing several important figures in the kingdom. The arrest of Favras, in fact, seemed an insufficient response to the conspiracy and Favras reinforced this notion at his arraignment when he demanded that the brother of the king appear and personally shift to Favras the plan to kidnap the king that was at the center of it. Furthermore, the notion of an intricate and extensive conspiracy gained additional credence with a deposition from the comte de Saint-Priest,

6 BN Mss. Nouv. acq. fr. 12938, fols. 309v°–310; Ménard de la Groye, *Correspondance*, p. 173.
7 See Ménard de la Groye, *Correspondance*, pp. 186–187; AD Ille-et-Vilaine 1 F 1648, letters-patent of the king establishing a provisional superior court at Rennes, February 4, 1790; AD Ille-et-Vilaine C 3843, fol. 894.

who indicated that he had been approached, during the previous August, about a plot to restore the lost privileges of the clergy and the nobility by raising 1,200 men to march against the municipality of Paris and the National Assembly, as well as other targets. When he asked who was directing this effort, he was told that it was Favras.[8]

The perceived scale of the alleged conspiracy raised great concern, especially since it also appeared to be directed against the National Guard, and agitation became so great that the Crown apparently believed it necessary to counter it in dramatic fashion. As early as January 21, a rumor – which proved untrue – arose that within twenty-four hours Louis would declare himself head of the Revolution, take the national uniform, regularly attend the meetings of the Assembly and make an extended tour of the kingdom to certify his acceptance of the Revolution and to enjoy the adulation due him as "restorer of French liberties."[9]

Some days later, as the trial was ready to begin, tensions were running high. Favras submitted a defense brief conceding the appearance of a plot in his conduct, but he denied any criminal intention. Another deposition disclosed that Favras had spoken of having at his disposal 20,000 Swiss, 12,000 German and 12,000 Sardinian troops.[10]

As additional details of Favras's activities accrued, it became evident that he had been assembling troops not only to assassinate Bailly and Lafayette, but also to "rescue" Louis from the Revolution. In itself the incident might have been of less importance, but coming as it did after the events of autumn – the dissembling of Louis, who was clearly following rather than leading the Revolution, the unrest and the provisioning crises – it appeared more menacing than it was. Observers saw the two events – the activities of Favras and the conduct of the Chamber of Vacations of Rennes – as last efforts by the formerly privileged clergy and nobility to forestall the Revolution.[11] Moreover, the continued passivity of Louis and his failure to respond to the disclosures heightened anxiety in late January and early February.

Political intrigues were not the only source of concern; unrest in various parts of France also heightened the sense of anxiety. Southwestern France, for example, experienced a wave of anti-seigneurial disturbances during the winter of 1789–1790 by peasants who were unhappy with the continuing collection of seigneurial dues and the tithe after what they thought had been the abolition of seigneurialism on

---

8 *Correspondance secrète*, de Lescure, ed., II: 414–416.    9 *Ibid.*, II: 417.
10 *Ibid.*, II: 418.    11 *Ibid.*, II: 414; Lindet, *Correspondance*, pp. 59–60.

August 4.[12] Although they were concentrated in the southwest, riots occurred elsewhere as well.[13] These outbursts, however, were less extensive than has generally been believed and were not directed against the National Assembly.[14] Nevertheless, the disturbances were an additional cause of tension in early 1790.

It was in this setting, then, that inhabitants of all locales outside of Paris – from the largest town to the smallest village – began to gather in January and February to elect new municipal governments, thereby beginning the realization of the new administration.[15] Because the procedure was new and unfamiliar, it often took weeks to complete; in La Rochelle, for example, the elections began on January 5 and concluded on January 23, although they were prolonged slightly by the fact that the first choice for mayor declined the post.[16] Similarly, in Toulouse the formation of the municipality began on January 25 and ended only on February 27.[17] In larger and medium-sized cities the tenor of the operation was quite businesslike, as was evident, for example, in Le Havre. The townsmen came together on January 23 and estimated that the population of active citizens was between 16,000 and 20,000 and that, according to the regulations put forward by the National Assembly, they would have to meet in five different assembly sites. In order to define who would qualify as an active citizen, they set the value of a day's labor at twenty *sous*, and the elections began on February 3.[18]

The spirit was quite different in the more sociable setting of smaller locales, such as the village of Vourez in Dauphiné. There the municipal officers gathered all of the inhabitants in the parish church on February 7 to explain the procedures; elections began on February 15 and concluded on February 18. The process began on February 15 with the *curé* of the parish, at the request of the municipal officers, explaining the reasons for the convocation according to article eight of the decree of the National Assembly of December 14, 1789. He delivered a speech to the villagers that indicates how deeply and how thoroughly the new ideal of the polity had already established itself.

He told the villagers that they were gathered in order to begin to enjoy the invaluable fruits of the enlightenment and wisdom of the august

12 See Steven G. Reinhardt, "The revolution in the countryside: peasant unrest in the Périgord, 1789–90," *Essays in the French Revolution: Paris and the Provinces,* ed. Steven G. Reinhardt and Elisabeth A. Cawthon, (College Station, 1992), pp. 12–37.
13 See the map in Tackett, *Religion, Revolution and Regional Culture,* p. 188.
14 *Ibid.,* pp. 187–189.
15 See Jean-Gabriel Gallot, *Adresse de M.Gallot, médécin, député du Poitou à l'Assemblée Nationale, aux habitans de la campagne de son canton* (Paris, n.d.).
16 AM La Rochelle BB 33, fols. 116v°–141v°.
17 AD Haute-Garonne C 303, fols. 287–298.
18 AM Le Havre BB 72, fols. 73v°–75v°, 76v°–86v°; K 1–5.

representatives of the nation and the benefits of their beloved monarch. Noting that they now knew no other master and no other empire than that of laws, nor any distinction among citizens, he reminded his listeners that all citizens now had the same right to the same laws and to prompt and enlightened justice. The villagers, he said, had been promised a constitution for their happiness, and the municipality they were about to create was its first proof. The *curé* enunciated the tasks that would be assigned to municipal officers, exhorted the inhabitants to make their choices honestly, and concluded by telling them that municipal affairs would contribute to the happiness of France. The elections then commenced.[19]

It was during the formation of municipalities throughout most of France that Louis visited the National Assembly on February 4. Just as his visit inspired a sense of common purpose with the Assembly, so, too, when news of it reached the provinces, it completely and instantly transformed the political atmosphere by dispelling underlying apprehension and affirming the basic unity between the nation and its monarch. In Nevers, for example, on February 6, as the balloting was about to begin, the voting was interrupted for the day and all sections rallied at the Hôtel de Ville, where a reading of the king's speech produced an emotional reaction among the inhabitants. The next day, Louis's speech was read again, along with a pronouncement from the bishop, and they resulted in resounding cries in favor of the king and the nation. A *Te Deum* was chanted "with emotion" and at the moment of prayer for the king, the acclamations resumed again. The *Te Deum* was followed by the firing of bursts of artillery, the playing of military and religious instruments in the public square and the church, and a general illumination of the town.[20]

The town of Bernay was also conducting elections for the formation of its new municipality when the news of Louis's visit to the Assembly arrived. It suspended the operations of its electoral assemblies in order to listen to a reading of Louis's speech, which produced a deep and respectful silence, and afterward the inhabitants pledged to use their lands and their life for the glory and happiness of the monarch. At the conclusion of a letter that they wrote to Louis, they reiterated the new sense of civic loyalty that the event had brought about.[21]

19 AN F$^1$c III Isère 1, document 196; see also documents 197–200. For more on municipal elections, see Jones, *The Peasantry in the French Revolution*, pp. 176–178.
20 AM Nevers BB 46, fols. 143–143v°, 144v°. A similar ceremony occurred in Toulon later in the month. See AM Toulon L 94, dossier D$^3$ 1, fols. 283–283v°.
21 AN F$^1$c III Eure 9, letter of citizens of Bernay to Louis, February 8, 1790. A similar reaction also occurred at Brest. See AM Brest LL 47, p. 58.

Similarly, in Rouen, the receipt of the news of Louis's visit to the Assembly led to an interruption of the municipal elections and the extraordinary convocation of a general assembly of the town at noon on February 6. The reading of Louis's "sublime" speech produced an emotional response in Rouen also and an outpouring of affection for the king. The gathering proclaimed that the monarch's visit to the National Assembly had "put the last seal on the glory of this beloved monarch, reconciled all spirits, joined all parties, blended all voices and dried up at their source the divisions which had afflicted all parts of the kingdom for several months."

The assembly at Rouen proclaimed that because Louis's action assured forever the prosperity of the nation, and rendered unshakeable the bases of the constitution and French freedom, it ought to be given some sign of thanks and public celebration. As a result, it ordered, by acclamation, that an address of thanks be sent to the king, that a *Te Deum* be solemnly chanted the next day, that a general illumination be held the following evening from 7.00 p.m. until 11.00 p.m. and that the king's speech, the letter of the comte de Saint-Priest that accompanied it and the present decree would be posted, read from the pulpit of parishes and given the greatest publicity possible.[22]

Indeed, the Crown made an exceptional effort to circulate the address of the king to the provinces, where it was in turn widely disseminated.[23] In Lyon the courier arrived at the Hôtel de Ville "in a moment of trouble," but again the reading of Louis's speech completely transformed the mood and produced a sense of common purpose. The deputies of the Intermediate Commission sought to reprint it and circulate it among the municipalities, as did the intendant.[24] The arrival of the text of the speech in Saint-Rambert-en-Forêts from the intendant at Lyon illustrates the effect that it had in smaller municipalities. When it initially arrived, the mayor read it to his colleagues, later read it from the pulpit of the parish and then had it posted throughout the town. The mayor noted that the event led to a general sense of joy, and a *Te Deum* was chanted and a

---

22 On the gathering, see AM Rouen Y 1, fols. 973–975; on the ceremony and the letter to the king, see *ibid.*, fols. 978–982; AD Seine-Maritime C 3, letter of intendant to comte de Saint-Priest, February 9, 1790.

23 See, for example, AD Herault C 5959, dossier 339, letter of intendant Ballainvilliers to subdelegate Favier, February 13, 1790, and circulars of February 13, 1790; AN F$^1$c III Marne 8, dossier 2, documents 229, 230; AN F$^1$c III Gers 11, letter of deputies of intermediate provincial commission of Gascony to comte de Saint-Priest, February 24, 1790.

24 AN F$^1$c III Rhône 8, letter of deputies of Intermediate Commission to comte de Saint-Priest, February 12, 1790; letter of intendant to comte de Saint-Priest, February 19, 1790.

general illumination held. In addition, the town decided that the event would also be commemorated each February 4 in the future.[25]

It would be difficult to overstate the change of spirit that occurred throughout France as a result of Louis's visit to the National Assembly. His action appeared to unify the Revolution once more, with the monarch and the nation again aligned in a common, harmonious outlook. In Paris, where the atmosphere had been so tense, and misgivings about Louis so pronounced, there were spontaneous assemblies held in various districts on February 4. The district of Saint-Jean-en-Grève urged members of the commune to take the same oath of loyalty to the nation, the law and the king and to the maintenance of the constitution that the deputies in the National Assembly had taken. The district of Minimes urged the commune to strike a medal to commemorate the event. In addition, the commune also offered a *Te Deum* on February 14 in thanks for "the intimate union of the king with the National Assembly" and, on February 15, the three districts of the faubourg Saint-Antoine voted in general assemblies to send a deputation of twenty-four members to carry to the king and queen in the name of the people of the *faubourg* a token of its affection, gratitude and respect.[26]

Although the immediacy of Paris to the event gave its response a special character, reaction was by no means limited to the capital; in the rest of France – from major cities to small villages – expressions of appreciation for Louis's visit to the Assembly were also extraordinary. In Bordeaux, the city recalled Louis's title of "restorer of French liberties" conferred on August 4, and his action produced a rapturous outpouring of affection and renewed solidarity as a result of his profession of loyalty to the constitution. Louis's speech was read throughout the city and elicited rousing cheers in favor of the monarch and his family. The municipal government of Le Havre characterized Louis's speech as "sublime" and circulated it to all of the sections of the city, where it was heartily applauded. The citizens of Charleville said that the event was unparalleled in history and wrote to Louis that his entry into the heart of the National Assembly would consolidate the foundations and hasten the work of the nation's happiness. The town of Châlons-sur-Marne also sent a message of thanks to the monarch and pledged homage and loyalty equal to that which their ancestors had earlier given to the greatest and

25 *Ibid.*, letter of mayor of Saint-Rambert-en-Forêts to unnamed addressee, February 17, 1790.
26 AN B I 5, extract from *procès-verbal* of district of Saint-Jean-en-Grève, February 4, 1790; address of district assembly of Minimes to commune of Paris, February 4, 1790; AN F$^1$c III Seine 27, letter of Bailly to comte de Saint-Priest, February 12, 1790; deliberation of three districts of Saint-Antoine, February 15, 1790.

best of Louis's ancestors. In Dijon a *Te Deum* was chanted in thanksgiving for Louis's action.[27]

If the reaction in larger towns was remarkable, it was equally extraordinary in the smaller setting of rural villages. Despite its hyperbole, the emotional impact of the news is evident in a letter from the village of Auronville in Normandy, which wrote that the more than 700 inhabitants had been on their knees in the church asking God for the safety of the king, and that it was at a loss to describe the tears of happiness, the love, gratitude and respect that Louis's speech to the National Assembly had inspired. During the *Te Deum*, the inhabitants wrote, fathers, children, the young and old all raised their hands and faces toward heaven to ask blessings for the king and his family, and they pledged to be forever faithful, grateful and submissive. In Aquitaine, the public reading of Louis's speech in a general assembly in the village of Begle produced an emotional outpouring of loyalty to the monarch. The village declared that henceforth February 4 would be a holiday and that the oath of loyalty to the king would be renewed every year, along with a reading of the king's speech. In conveying its gratitude to the king, the village of Airvant alluded to the unrest that had pervaded the realm, and said that it had transcribed the king's speech in its municipal register to preserve it forever. In the west, the village of Bouin claimed to have read Louis's "sublime" speech "with tears of joy and gratitude" and, characterizing his action as "a deed unique in the annals of the world," it went on to offer the warmest praise in appreciation for his visit to the National Assembly.[28]

A few days after Louis's visit, the National Assembly sought to reaffirm the sense of common purpose by putting forward its *Adresse aux François*, which it promulgated on February 11. Indeed, in a clear reflection of the new spirit of cooperation between the Crown and the Assembly, the Crown, in contrast to its conduct with the August decrees a few months previously, or with its attempts to discredit the Assembly

27  AN F¹c III Gironde 11, letter of inhabitants of Bordeaux to Louis, February 16, 1790; AN F¹c III Gironde 8, copy of letter written by citizens of Bordeaux meeting in twenty-eight districts to deputies of town, February 16, 1790; ordinance of mayor, lieutenant-mayor and others, February 11, 1790; AM Le Havre D² 1, fol. 161; AN F¹c III Ardennes 7, letter of inhabitants of Arches and Charleville to Louis, February 21, 1790; AN F¹c III Marne 8, dossier 2, documents 6–7; BM Dijon Ms. 1660, fol. 31. See also the remarkable sermon by the bishop of Mâcon. Gabriel-François Moreau, *Discours prononcé le dimanche 14 février 1790, par M. l'Evêque de Mâcon, dans l'Eglise Cathédrale, avant le TE DEUM par lui ordonné*. (Mâcon, n.d.).

28  AN F¹c III Seine-Inférieure 14, letter of inhabitants of Auronville to Louis, February 14, 1790; AN F¹c III Gironde 11, letter of municipal officers of Begle to Louis, February 28, 1790; AN F¹c III Deux-Sevrès 8, letter of inhabitants of Airvant to Louis, March 9, 1790; AN F¹c III Vendée 5, letter of municipal officers, notables and members of commune of Bouin, March 10, 1790.

only a few weeks earlier, assiduously circulated the Assembly's address, even sending out a correction of a minor typographical error that had occurred during the printing of it.[29] The new spirit was equally evident at the local level, for members of the Intermediate Commission of Brittany at Tréguier and Saint-Malo, despite their observation that their powers had been prorogued by the National Assembly, nevertheless circulated the address in the areas of their jurisdiction.[30]

The outpouring of affection for Louis had resulted from his resolution of growing doubts about his attachment to the emerging constitution, but the National Assembly also received high praise once again for its confidence, fortitude and perseverance in difficult circumstances. An address to the Assembly from the new municipality of Chalon-sur-Saône recalled that the members of the National Assembly had been called by the king to coordinate with him the regeneration of the empire and that they had been honored with the august title of representatives of the nation for this purpose. It commended the deputies for their reform of administration and their continuing attack on the hydra of privilege. For its actions, especially for reforming abuses which, by their long history, had nearly been transformed into legitimate rights, the Assembly had earned the gratitude of the French nation, as the adhesions and addresses it received daily indicated. But what was most flattering, according to the municipality, was the unpretentious request by the king to associate himself with the work of the Assembly.[31] It was apparent that the resurgent popularity of the monarch derived chiefly from his acceptance of the work of the Assembly.

Clearly, then, the elections for the new municipalities either concluded in or were followed shortly afterward by an atmosphere totally different from that in which they had begun. The strained political environment was completely transformed into a new spirit of common purpose and a belief in shared civic aspirations. Indeed, the municipal elections had a particularly significant impact in rural areas for, as one scholar has argued, for all of their magnitude, the Great Fear and the agrarian revolts

29 See AD Hérault C 5959, dossier 328, letter of intendant Ballainvilliers to subdelegate Favier, March 31, 1790, circular of intendant Ballainvilliers to *curés*; AD Côte d'Or C 1[bis], letter of intendant to comte de Saint-Priest, March 18, 1790; AD Côte d'Or C 3359, no. 128, letter of comte de Saint-Priest to Intermediate Commission of Burgundy, March 18, 1790; AD Ille-et-Vilaine C 3843, fols. 945–946; AD Ille-et-Vilaine C 3901, letter of Intermediate Commission of Brittany to commissioners of eight dioceses of Brittany, March 12, 1790; letter of comte de Saint-Priest to Intermediate Commission of Brittany, March 19, 1790; AD Ille-et-Vilaine C 6097.
30 AD Ille-et-Vilaine C 3901, letter of Intermediate Commission of Tréguier named by Estates of Brittany at Rennes, March 19, 1790; letter of Intermediate Commission at Saint-Malo to Intermediate Commission at Rennes, March 30, 1790.
31 AN C 111, dossier 246, document 10.

left many localities untouched, but the reorganization of municipal government "brought the revolution to every peasant's doorstep."[32]

In this setting the completion of municipal elections was a triumphant occasion representing an important event in the realization of the new ideal of the polity – the proverbial first step in a thousand mile journey. This new spirit is perhaps best captured in Auxerre, where the president of the Saint-Pierre-en-Vallée section, Guenot, who had recently been elected as a municipal officer, gave a speech at the conclusion of the elections pointing out the significance of what the electors had just accomplished. In an indication of the new aura of goodwill surrounding Louis, but also the primacy accorded to the work of the Assembly, he stated that a simple idea, the germ of which had existed in the heart of Louis XVI, but which had been developed in the heart of the National Assembly, was going to regenerate France, change principles and break all the shameful jurisdictions of the old regime. This idea was the bringing together of all administration, of all people and everything administered. Then, in a passage that reveals how the new ideal of the polity was felt to be realized through the nexus of the night of August 4, the new administration, and Louis's visit to the National Assembly on February 4, he said:

A sublime operation, I repeat, the only effective [means] to attain the happiness of a society as immense as that of twenty-four million individuals, that the new constitution invites to the public good and to their king, by the strongest bonds, those of unity of interest, of friendship, of brotherhood, of love of the fatherland, of reason and justice; but an operation that has had to defeat a formidable army of prejudice and privileges, from province to province, from town to town, from man to man and which demanded from all parts of this vast empire, from the king himself, the first of unexpected sacrifices.

For the happiness of France, they have made these sacrifices which astonish history and hold the attention of the world. It is on their base that the edifice begins to rise majestically. Do not doubt, gentlemen, it will succeed to its perfection; its foundations are cast; they are arranged with justice; they are sealed with the august oath of all French, with the oath of the supreme head of the nation who has solemnly promised to raise the heir to the throne... in the principles of the Revolution. It will assure for France the highest degree of internal prosperity and of respectable power externally.[33]

Elsewhere in Burgundy, the newly formed commune of Chalon-sur-Saône sent an address to the National Assembly praising it for its work

32 Jones, *The Peasantry in the French Revolution*, p. 169. For more on local government, see Alison Patrick, "French Revolutionary Local Government, 1789–1792," *The French Revolution and the Creation of Modern Political Culture : The Political Culture of the French Revolution*, ed. Lucus, pp. 399–420.
33 AD Yonne L 178, *Mot prononcé par M. Guenot, avocat, président de la Section de Saint-Pierre-en-Vallée, à la clôture de l'Assemblée.*

and swearing to maintain the "sublime" constitution that would make the French people "the first people of the universe," and the assembled citizenry of Dijon also lauded the National Assembly.[34]

Similar sentiments poured in from all over France. The commune of Aix-en-Provence wrote to the National Assembly that it considered it one of its first duties to express, in the name of the commune, its full adhesion to its decrees and its gratitude for the wisdom of its deliberations, and asserted that the organization of municipalities would be an epoch celebrated forever in the annals of the French people. The change in the political milieu was particularly evident in Aix-en-Provence for, in sharp contrast to the pessimism that had reigned in early January, the new municipality wrote of how auspicious it regarded the reception of the news of Louis's visit to the Assembly on the first day of elections and asserted that "a new political order succeeds the old as easily as if it was only the ordinary sequence and as if it had held to the same principles."[35] The cathedral chapter of Mende likewise observed that "a new constitution establishes itself in the kingdom: new ideas succeed those that we have respected until now, and this alteration is accomplished almost in an instant."[36]

Once formed, the municipalities did, in fact, become the base on which the new administration raised itself. Under the oversight of *commissaires du roi* appointed by the king to form the new departments, the municipalities were charged with drawing up lists of active citizens in order to convoke assemblies, a task made easier by the recent municipal elections. In several instances the *commissaires du roi* emphasized the importance of including all those who qualified as active citizens on the lists, for the number of electors allotted to a locale was determined by the number of active citizens.[37]

After the compilation of the lists the assemblies met, and it was in this setting that the new ideal of the polity came to be realized as citizens, grouped according to the guidelines of the National Assembly by neighborhood or arrondissement rather than by trade, profession or

34 AN C 111, dossier 246, document 10; AN C 112, dossier 268, document 23. Deputies in the Assembly were equally encouraged by the formation of new municipalities. See *Courier de Madon*, March 9, 1790.

35 AN C 111, dossier 249, document 8. For more on the reorganization of municipal government in Aix-en-Provence, see Christiane Derobert-Ratel, *Institutions et vie municipale à Aix-en-Provence sous la Révolution (1789–an VIII)* (N.p., 1981). For other similar examples, see AN F¹c III Ardeche 9, letter of mayor of Villeneuve-de-Berc to president of National Assembly, February 26, 1790; AN F¹c III Creuse 1, letter of *curé* of Saint-Domit, February 24, 1790. See also *Affiches d'Angers*, February 23, 1790.

36 AN T 643, memoir of cathedral chapter of Mende, May 10, 1790.

37 See, for example, AM Le Havre K 6, letter of *commissaires du roi* to inhabitants of Le Havre, April 7, 1790.

corporation, came together in the spring of 1790 to choose electors for the assemblies for the formation of departments.[38] As a result, in larger towns, especially those which had formerly been the site of a *parlement* or episcopal towns, the character of deliberations was totally transformed, as electoral assemblies acquired a complexion that would have been utterly inconceivable under the privileged corporate paradigm of the Old Regime. When, for example, in the city of Rennes, which had been so polarized in late 1788 and early 1789, François and Louis Biard, who were tanners, Laurent, a fishseller, Le Prieur, a carpenter and Sauvé, a baker, could work together with Defrieux, Fournel and Reslon, judges in the presidial court, and with Lesguern, formerly a judge at the *parlement*, to determine their common future, this was incalculably removed from the hierarchical political and social structure inherent in the Estates of Brittany of the Old Regime.[39] The same was true at Châteauneuf, where Pierre Olivier, a mason, Alain Olivier, a shoemaker, and Maurice Leunier, a carpenter, met in assembly with Etienne-Auguste Baude de la Vieuvile, the governor of the fort at Châteauneuf.[40] Similarly, in Grenoble, where it may have seemed slightly less extraordinary because of the spirit of cooperation between the orders in late 1788 and early 1789, it was nonetheless remarkable that de Barral, the president of the *parlement*, and Caze de la Bove and de Meyrieu, judges in the *parlement*, could meet together with Navizet, a baker, Chauvet, a carpenter, and Eymard, a locksmith, in a spirit of common purpose in the remaking of France.[41] Finally, in Toul, when the bishop of Toul, a captain in the royal artillery corps, the subdelegate, a captain of the infantry and a captain in the engineering corps participated in primary assemblies with coopers, wigmakers, vine-growers, hatmakers, booksellers, a cheese merchant, painters, wool-spinners and numerous day laborers, it was clear that the traditional contours of civic life had been totally redrawn.[42]

Nor should the metamorphosis of political life in rural areas be overlooked. That the village of Sel could convene 650 active citizens to choose five electors or the village of Saint-Servan could convoke 800 active citizens to choose eight electors to determine their own future was

---

38 See, for example, AD Meurthe-et-Moselle L 199, dossier Nancy.
39 AD Ille-et-Vilaine L 337, Extract from *procès-verbal* of nomination of electors, fourth district, Rennes, May 17, 1790.
40 *Ibid.*, List of citizens of Châteauneuf in primary assembly held in parish church of Saint-Nicolas, meeting of May 18, 1790.
41 *Rôle des citoyens de la ville de Grenoble, électeurs et éligibles qui doivent concourir à la formation de la nouvelle municipalité ordonné par les décrets de l'Assemblée Nationale, réédigé sur les rôles d'impositions directes et locales qu'ils payent dans la ville de Grenoble* (Grenoble, 1790), second district [Newberry Library, Case folio FRC 9843].
42 AD Meurthe-et-Moselle L 200, account of active citizens of municipality of Toul, April 21, 1790.

once again infinitely more equitable and immediate than the remote and inaccessible Estates of Brittany by which such villages had been ruled for centuries.[43]

Indeed, the magnitude of political change – in both spirit and substance – enacted by the National Assembly has, with the notable exception of R. R. Palmer and, more recently, Melvin Edelstein, Malcolm Crook and Patrice Gueniffey – generally been overlooked by historians.[44] There was nothing pernicious in the National Assembly's formulation of the electorate, for the intention of the chief architect of it, Sieyès, was to encompass as many individuals as possible, and to reduce the categories of exclusions to as few as possible.[45] Deputies, in fact, saw a large electorate as a safeguard against manipulation.[46] Consequently, to give but one example, the Assembly did not require active citizens to be literate, a requirement that could have significantly reduced their numbers had the Assembly been inclined to do so. In the town of Die, for instance, nearly one third of the active citizens were illiterate, and the percentage was higher in the surrounding countryside.[47] Literacy among active citizens was also an issue elsewhere.[48] In addition, the wage scale for a day's labor was almost invariably set low, a tendency encouraged by the National Assembly and, as Palmer noted, the National Assembly reformed taxation in such a way that liability to direct taxation extended

43 See AD Ille-et-Vilaine L 337, *Procès-verbal* of nomination of electors made in primary assembly held at Sel, May 17, 1790; *Procès-verbal* of nomination of electors made in primary assembly held at Saint-Servan, May 17, 1790. For a contemporary perspective, see especially BM Angers Ms. 1888, p. 162.
44 See R. R. Palmer, *The Age of the Democratic Revolution*, 2 vols. (Princeton, 1959–1964), I: 501, 522–528, especially the historical survey of the issue that comprises the latter section. More recently, historians have begun to recognize the significance of elections held during the period of the National Assembly. See Melvin Edelstein, "Vers une 'sociologie électorale' de la Révolution française: la participation des citadins et campagnards, 1789–1793," *Revue d'histoire moderne et contemporaine*, 22 (1975), 508–529; "L'apprentissage de la citoyenneté: participation électorale des campagnards et citadins (1789–1793)," *L'Image de la Révolution française. Communications présentées lors du Congrès Mondial pour le bicentenaire de la Révolution. Sorbonne, Paris, 6–12 juillet 1989*, 4 vols. (Paris, 1989–1991), I: 15–25; "Electoral participation and sociology of the Landes in 1790," (forthcoming); Malcolm Crook, "Les Français devant le vote: participation et pratique électorale à l'époque de la Révolution," *Les Pratiques politiques en Province à l'époque de la Révolution française. Actes du Colloque tenu à Montpellier les 18, 19 et 20 septembre 1987* (Montpellier, 1988), pp. 27–37; "Aux Urnes, Citoyens! Urban and Rural Electoral Behavior during the French Revolution," *Reshaping France*, ed. Forrest and Jones, pp. 152–167; Patrice Gueniffey, "Elections" and "Suffrage" *A Critical Dictionary of the French Revolution*, ed. Furet and Ozouf, pp. 33–44, especially pp. 33–38, and pp. 571–581, especially pp. 571–575.          45 AN 284 AP 4, dossier 3.
46 AM Bayonne AA 51, no. 37 (4), letter of October 31, 1789.
47 AN DIV 11, dossier 157, document 24; AN W 13, no. 145.
48 AN DIV 1*, entries 118, 119, 163.

far down the social scale.[49] Furthermore, as Norman Hampson pointed out, the pool of active citizens included many on the poverty line.[50] In fact, although it was a unique situation because of its local Old Regime tax structure, Toulon went from having over 90 percent of approximately 5,000 adult males disenfranchised to a *de facto* universal male suffrage in 1790.[51]

The Assembly was not, in fact, a disingenuous body – its high-mindedness was one of its most distinguishing characteristics – and, dedicated as it was to the primacy of a unitary and exalted ideal of the nation, it simply did not want that outlook undercut. As a result, it sought to preclude the participation in political life only of those whom it believed might be susceptible to the influence of others with ulterior motives.[52] It is clear that contemporaries understood the operations of the Assembly in such terms, as a newly founded journal intended for administrators makes clear.[53] The fatal incident in Rennes in January, 1789, in which lackeys of nobles had been involved, indicates that the concerns of the Assembly had merit, and this has been confirmed by modern scholarship.[54]

While the electoral system devised by the National Assembly may have

49 See, for example, AM Le Havre BB 72, fol. 75, where it was calculated at twenty *sous*. On the National Assembly, see *Procès-verbal de l'Assemblée nationale*, No. 175 (January 15, 1790), pp. 5–7; BM Lyon Ms. 2191, letter of January 16, 1790; *Journal des Décrets de l'Assemblée nationale, pour les habitans des campagnes*, January 9–15, 1790. For the observation of Palmer, *The Age of the Democratic Revolution*, I: 523. For the manner in which the National Assembly sought to make taxation as inclusive as possible, see *Journal de la municipalité, du département des districts & des sections de Paris, & correspondance des départements & des principales municipalités du royaume*, July 3, 1790.

50 Hampson, *Prelude to Terror*, p. 90.

51 Malcolm Crook, "The people at the polls: electoral behavior in revolutionary Toulon, 1789–1799," *French History*, 5 (1991), 164–179, especially 165–168. See also Malcolm Crook, *Toulon in War and Revolution: From the Ancien Régime to the Restoration, 1750–1820* (Manchester, 1991), pp. 89–90.

52 BM Nantes Collection Dugast-Matifeux, t. 98, letter of January 8, 1790. Indeed, as Norman Hampson noted, the *Comité de mendicité* of the National Assembly classified those paying only two or three days wages in taxation near the poverty level, and he pointed out that to enfranchise such people "was to invite them to sell their votes." Hampson, *Prelude to Terror*, pp. 88–89.

53 *Journal des municipalités et assemblées administratives*, May 3, 1790. Here I disagree somewhat with William H. Sewell, Jr., "Le citoyen/la citoyenne: activity, passivity and the revolutionary concept of citizenship," *The French Revolution and the Creation of Modern Political Culture: The Political Culture of the French Revolution*, ed. Lucas, pp. 105–123, in which Sewell argues that the National Assembly sought to limit active citizenship to an "educated, prosperous, propertied elite." The enfranchisement of illiterate men and the low threshold set for a day's labor undercut this contention.

54 See Sarah Maza, *Servants and Masters in Eighteenth-Century France* (Princeton, 1983), pp. 213–214, 218–219, 226–227, 306–307, although she also notes that servants took little part in the Revolution on either side. Paul Bois argued that the exclusion of domestics was a democratic measure to prevent masters from increasing their electoral power. See Paul Bois, *Paysans de l'Ouest* (Le Mans, 1960), pp. 227–228.

been flawed – and the imposition of a tax equivalent to ten days' wages of unskilled labor to qualify as an elector is usually cited, although Palmer argued that approximately half of the male population twenty-five or older qualified as electors, and this estimate has been generally corroborated by subsequent studies[55] – whatever flaws there may have been should not obscure the larger significance of the structure it established: the National Assembly, basing the electorate on taxes rather than property and freeing it of any religious affiliation, brought into being one of the most participatory and democratic national political structures in the world.[56] Furthermore, it extended complete legal equality and protection to every citizen. Indeed, aside from not being able to vote in primary assemblies, a restriction imposed only because of concern that they might not be independent participants, there were few limitations on passive citizens; a passive citizen could, for example, be elected to a judgeship.[57]

In his incisive study of French hatters in the eighteenth century, Michael Sonenscher, in discussing the narrow outlook of the *cahiers* of 1789, observed that "this concern with the parochial was also a claim upon the public sphere," and noted that the hatters demonstrated their awareness of their situation in their choice of deputies to the Estates-General.[58] One accomplishment of the institution of active citizen was that it inverted this equation by granting individuals a claim upon the public sphere through the universal medium of the nation rather than through the particularist mode afforded by the privileged corporate paradigm. In this way it completely transformed both quantitatively and qualitatively the character of the polity. Not only did the claim devised by the National Assembly encompass far more citizens, but it became habitual rather than episodic – as it had been under the Old Regime through the drafting of *cahiers* and the election of deputies to the Estates-General – and became a right, universally bestowed by the sovereign nation, rather than a favor granted to individuals or groups by the monarch. In the final analysis, it is ahistorical to criticize the National Assembly for not instituting universal manhood suffrage or a system closely approximating it. Just as the Old Regime must be understood on

---

55 Palmer, *The Age of the Democratic Revolution*, I: 501; Edelstein, "Electoral participation and sociology of the Landes in 1790." Again, although it must be pointed out that Toulon was not typical, Crook noted that the twelve month residency rule rather than poverty disenfranchised many Toulonnais. Crook, "The people at the polls," 168.

56 See Bois, *Paysans de l'Ouest*, p. 245. I would like to thank Melvin Edelstein and Elizabeth Dunn for helping me to clarify my arguments on this matter.

57 AN DIV 2*, p. 197.

58 Michael Sonenscher, *The Hatters of Eighteenth-Century France* (Berkeley, 1987), p. 161.

its own terms and not viewed merely as a prelude to the Revolution, so, too, the changes wrought by the National Assembly must be understood in terms relative to the Old Regime, and not measured against the aspirations of the post-Revolutionary era.

The compilation and verification of the lists of active citizens in the spring of 1790 inaugurated the formation of departments and districts,[59] a process that lasted well into the summer of 1790 due to differing commencement dates and varying rates of progress. The operation began, however, in a climate of wariness from within the National Assembly as well as in a few locales of France.

One element in the suspicion of the Assembly centered on the *commissaires du roi* appointed to oversee the formation of the departments. The commissioners had been approved in principle on January 8, 1790, and they had become an object of suspicion both in the Assembly and in some areas of the nation. Indeed, on March 29, the Assembly heard a letter from Troyes complaining that the executive power had named the *commissaires* and objecting to the wide range of their powers, leading the Assembly to act on the matter.[60] Speaking for the Committee of the Constitution, Le Chapelier observed that the nomination of the *commissaires du roi* had seemed necessary to the Assembly, but that the committee believed that their powers ought to be limited.

Robespierre spoke out against the powers of the commissioners, seeing in them a mechanism by which ministers could limit the powers of the electors and give them an inordinate influence over the assemblies. He asserted that the majority of commissioners were known enemies of the Revolution and that a host of individuals opposed to the Revolution were flattering themselves that they would be elected to departmental posts. He argued that the Assembly should negate this development by preventing those *commissaires du roi* already named from exercising their duties.

The deputy d'André responded to Robespierre, asserting that his concern and his proposal had little merit. He said that if there were individuals who were badly intentioned and who sought to threaten the constitution and public liberty, ninety-five percent of the French were ready to die in order to defend them. D'André did agree, however, that it was necessary to limit the power of the commissioners. Later in the debate, the deputy de Voidel proposed the publication of a list of all the commissioners so that the Assembly could know who they were and be apprised of their conduct.

59 See, for example, AD Charente-Maritime L 119, proclamation of *commissaires du roi*, April 29, 1790; AD Eure 8 L 1, dossier 1; AD Loire-Atlantique L 163, no. 51; AD Haute-Garonne 1 L 550, document 3.    60 See AN DIV 1, dossier 1, document 14.

The Assembly then decided, after hearing a reading of the commission and the instructions given by the king to the *commissaires du roi* for the formation of the assemblies that, among other measures, the powers of the commissioners would expire on the day on which the election of the administrators was completed, that the commissioners could provisionally decide any difficulties that might arise in the course of the elections, but that any major issues would have to be decided by the Assembly itself, and that the commissioners, before undertaking their duties, would have to take the civic oath before the municipality of the place in which the electoral assembly would be held.[61]

Mistrust of the commissioners, as the letter from Troyes suggests, was present in other parts of the nation as well.[62] Indeed, after March 29, deputies sought to assure their constituents that the commissioners would not be able to influence the forthcoming elections.[63]

The second element in the apprehension that was present as the formation of departments began was the larger backdrop to the mistrust of the *commissaires du roi*. It was the realization of the extraordinary importance of the elections to form the departments, for they represented the first *de facto* referendum on the work of the National Assembly. The formation of municipalities had proceeded smoothly, but they had been local elections in which local concerns had for the most part predominated. The formation of departments was entirely different, however, for not only was it the first time that the whole nation had mobilized since the elections to the Estates-General, it was also the first occasion on which the nation – through the men whom it elected to office – could indicate its endorsement or rejection of the ideals asserted by the National Assembly. The deputies in the Assembly were keenly aware of this, and did not want the elections subverted in any way.[64] Likewise, the nation

61 AN C 37, dossier 324, document 29; *Procès-verbal de l'Assemblée nationale*, No. 244 (March 29, 1790), pp. 6–8; AN KK 645, fols. 607–608; Poncet-Delpech, *Bulletins*, pp. 257–258. For the list of *commissaires du roi*, see AN BB³⁰ 157; on the instructions and commission given to the *commissaires du roi*. see AN BB³⁰ 157, dossier 1, documents 3–7, 9. See also *Journal des décrets de l'Assemblée nationale, pour les habitants des campagnes*, March 27–April 2, 1790.

62 See, for example, AM Douai K¹ 7, deliberation of municipal body of town of Vezelise, April 5, 1790; AM Bayonne BB 64, fols. 415–417. For more on the mistrust of the *commissaires du roi*, see *Journal des décrets de l'Assemblée nationale, pour les habitans des campagnes*, March 27–April 2, 1790.

63 See AM Lorient BB 13, letter of April 3, 1790; Queruau-Lamerie, "Lettres de Maupetit," XX: 369–370. See also *Journal des municipalités et assemblées administratives*, March 29, 1790.

64 See AN W 12, no. 203; Looten, "Lettres de François-Joseph Bouchette," 361; AD Bouches-du-Rhône C 1337, letter of Verdollin, February 10, 1790; AM Douai D³ 1, letter of Merlin, Aoust, Breuvard, April 29, 1790; Charles-Alexis Brulart de Sillery, *Adresse de M. Sillery, député de Reims à l'Assemblée nationale, aux assemblées primaires et de département du Département de la Marne* (Paris, n.d.). Robespierre had explicitly raised this concern in

recognized that this was its first opportunity to ratify or disclaim the new ideal of the polity put forward by the National Assembly[65] and, as the responses of deputies to their constituents reveal, it wanted to exercise its will in the most unfettered fashion possible.

As the formation of departments began there were inevitable disappointments among inhabitants over the placement of *chefs-lieux* and district seats – a process fraught with clear winners and losers[66] – but such disaffection did not translate itself into rejection of the new ideal of the polity put forward by the National Assembly. To the degree that there were resentments, they usually took the form of indignation against a competing town perceived to have gained an undue advantage through political influence or some other similar factor, but the new ideal of the polity was not challenged.[67] Its appeal rose above local disappointments or resentments, although this could not be known by the deputies, contributing to their apprehension about the formation of departments.

In addition, in some locales, especially formerly privileged areas, there was an acute sense of unease and anxiety. In Strasbourg, for example, where the loss of its ancient privileges had left the city aggrieved, the elections for the municipality, which further emphasized its homogeneity, had compounded the sense of loss.[68] As a result, as the elections for the departmental administration drew near, there was an air of tension surrounding them because of a fear that instead of strengthening the Revolution, the choice of men opposed to the Revolution as departmental administrators would weaken it.[69] Similarly, at Toulouse and at Châlons-sur-Marne, on the eve of the elections, an atmosphere of intrigue hung over them.[70] In some parts of France, there were even rumors that clerics and nobles would be massacred in the primary assemblies.[71]

In most regions of France, however, the elections began in a climate of hopeful expectation. The *commissaires du roi* appeared in the *chef-lieu* of the prospective department to take the civic oath and to inaugurate the proceedings.[72] Indeed, the mistrust of the *commissaires du roi* by deputies

---

the above-mentioned debate on the *commissaires du roi* when he asserted that many individuals opposed to the Revolution were anticipating that they would be elected to departmental posts.        65 AN H[1] 748 (244), no. 18.
66 See Margadant, *Urban Rivalries*, pp. 145–274, 287–321.
67 This is evident, for example, in the reaction of a fifteen year old girl cited in Margadant, *Ibid.*, p. 293.        68 AN F[1]c III Bas-Rhin 13, dossier 1, document 2.
69 BN Mss. Nouv. acq. fr. 4790, fols. 152–152v°.
70 AD Haute-Garonne 1 L 551, documents 3–9; Benjamin Bablot, *L'Observateur du Département de la Marne* (Châlons-sur-Marne, 1790), pp. 50–58.
71 AN 291 AP 1, dossier 2, liasse 13, letter of May 18, 1790.
72 See, for example, AD Meurthe-et-Moselle L 142, letter of *commissaires du roi* to president of National Assembly, April 8, 1790; AN H[1] 621, document 304.

in the National Assembly was misplaced, for they were sympathetic to the new ideal of the polity and took their position as intermediaries between the monarch, the National Assembly and the nation extremely seriously.[73] In Auxerre, for example, the chevalier Grand, the *commissaire* who opened the electoral assembly on April 12 did so with a bestowal of high praise on the work of the National Assembly. In the immensity of its works, he said, the division of the kingdom into eighty-three departments would be distinguished as a masterpiece of light, patriotism and wisdom, for it would form all of the empire into a single family.[74]

Similarly, in the Department of Calvados, the *commissaires du roi* made an invidious comparison between the old and the new administration, stating that the new one sought to attach citizens to the common good. They denounced the former administrative system as reflecting conquests and usurpations and for fostering a particularist spirit that opposed itself to the common good. Hailing its abolition, they praised the new division of the realm for being based on equality and asserted that it would produce a "great and sublime harmony." The *commissaires* then reminded the electors that "this precious institution, which should reconcile forever the rights of the prince with those of the people, is one of the first benefits from the National Assembly."[75] *Commissaires du roi* in other departments delivered similar addresses.[76]

After opening the assemblies, the *commissaires* determined who the oldest elector was and designated him dean in order to conduct an election for president of the assembly. They then retired, available only to resolve any uncertainties that might arise.[77] The operation of forming a department was virtually identical throughout France, so a brief examination of a single department will suffice to illustrate the process. In this regard, the Department of Loire-Inférieure is appropriate, not only because it was one of the earliest to be constituted, but also, because

---

73 Indeed, the selection process had, in fact, sought men who would be sympathetic to the ideals of the National Assembly. See AM Strasbourg AA 2005ᵃ, fols. 36, 48. Apparently aware of the mistrust of the Assembly, the *commissaires du roi* often sought to allay the concerns of the Assembly by working closely with it. See, for example, AN DIV 1, dossier 1, documents 21, 90; AD Meurthe-et-Moselle L 142, letter of *commissaires du roi* to president of National Assembly, April 8, 1790.
74 AD Yonne L 156, speech given by M. le Chevalier Grand, *commissaire du roi*, at opening of assembly of Department of Yonne, April 12, 1790.
75 AD Calvados L 10085, speech of *commissaires du roi* for the Department of Calvados at municipality of Caen.
76 See, for example, AD Puy-de-Dôme L 481, *Procès-verbal* of meetings of electoral assembly of Department of Puy-de-Dôme, June 4, 1790; AN C 121¹, dossier 368, document 2. And, although it was not a speech delivered at the electoral assembly, see AN H¹ 621, document 304.
77 For an example of how isolated the *commissaires du roi* were kept from the electors, see AN F¹c III Manche 1, *procès-verbal* of electoral assembly of Department of Manche, p. 5.

it evolved from the *pays d'états* of Brittany, it particularly exemplifies the transformation from the paradigm of privileged corporatism to the new ideal of the nation.

On April 3, 1790, after the prospective department had compiled its list of active citizens,[78] the *commissaires du roi* established themselves at Nantes and contacted one of the electors in order to explain the procedures that the electoral assembly would be following.[79] The elections began in Nantes on April 7 at 9.00 a.m., with the selection of the oldest elector as dean to preside over the meeting until the election of the president and the next oldest being made provisional secretary. The next three oldest men were designated as vote counters before the meeting adjourned at 1.00 p.m. The assembly reopened at 3.00 p.m. and devoted itself to the verification of powers, and the *commissaires du roi* were fully apprised of the proceedings.[80] On April 9, after attending Mass as a group, the assembly discovered some irregularities in the credentials of its members but, in the interest of completing the formation of the department expeditiously, decided to ignore them on this occasion only. On April 11, the assembly elected Costard de Massy as president and the next day elected Papin as secretary. The following day, April 13, three vote counters were elected. The actual election of administrators, in which a candidate had to receive a majority to be declared a victor, occasionally necessitating runoffs between the two leading candidates, began on April 15, with Costard de Massy being the first man selected. The elections continued until May 2, with the *commissaires du roi* making periodic reports to the Minister of the Interior on their progress.[81]

These were the mechanics of the formation of departments, but this description does not reveal the spirit that underlay the process. In many instances, the electoral assemblies, immediately after their formation, sent messages to the king or, more often, to the National Assembly, that indicated how enthusiastic the nation was for the new ideal of the polity and how deeply it felt a sense of gratitude to the National Assembly for conceiving it. When, on June 14, the eldest member of the electoral assembly of the Department of Bouches-du-Rhône was selected as dean, he opened the proceedings by paying homage to "the sublime deliberations of the National Assembly." On June 16, the assembly elected its

---

78  AD Loire-Atlantique L 164, dossier 1, document 1.
79  AD Loire-Atlantique L 163, document 52.
80  AD Loire-Atlantique L 167, document 1; AD Loire-Atlantique L 163, document 51.
81  AD Loire-Atlantique L 167, document 1. In a further reflection of the unitary ideal of the nation that came into being, avowed candidacy and open electioneering were not permitted due to the belief that they would be divisive. Electors were supposed to choose the most deserving individuals, but this could prolong the elections after refusals and the like. See Crook, "The people at the polls," pp. 171–172.

president, and the next day formed an editing committee, which defined its first task as making an address to the National Assembly in order to express its inviolable attachment to the immortal constitution that it had given them, and its profound respect for all of its decrees. One week later, on June 24, at the conclusion of the elections for departmental administrators, the editing committee presented its draft address in which it concluded by offering the National Assembly "the pure and sincere homage of our respectful attachment, of our unshakeable confidence and of our complete submission to the laws that your wisdom has already given us or for which it still prepares us" and assured it that its members "adhere heart and soul to all of your decrees."[82]

In Dijon, seat of another former *pays d'états*, and where the electoral assembly met in the *Salle des Etats*, the sense of enthusiasm for the ideals advanced by the National Assembly was evident in a speech given by M. de Brois after his selection as dean on May 10, 1790:

I forget at this moment the weight of my years, in order to feel the honor that they have gained for me of presiding over this respectable assembly. The time is not distant where I regretted having lived too long; my regrets have given way to the purest and most heartfelt joy. For too long I have seen my brothers submit to despotisms of all kinds ... The dawn of liberty brightens my last days. Ought I to regret finding myself the eldest of this family, when I see opening for my younger brothers a long course of prosperity?

And in what place could we feel more keenly the great benefits of an unhoped for regeneration? It is in this hall, which had been for so long the tomb of our liberty, where you were called only to cement ruin, that you are meeting in order to restore the edifice. What a great and happy metamorphosis! It is up to you, gentlemen, to assure your happiness and that of your posterity, in choosing administrators worthy of looking after the precious depository that you are going to confide to them. You will soon enjoy the fruits of their supervision. As for me, it will be enough to carry, to the end of my course, the assurance that my fellow citizens deserve the freedom which is offered to them.[83]

Likewise, at the end of the elections for administrators, the same electoral assembly sent a message to the National Assembly that included the following:

The assembly of electors of the Department of Côte d'Or hastens to offer the National Assembly the just tribute of admiration and gratitude, due to the immensity and to the wisdom of its works.

The most beautiful work that the human mind has been able to conceive is the regeneration of a vast empire, without internecine wars and by the sole force of public opinion and of reason: the most touching spectacle is the joy of a great people, treading underfoot its chains and blessing its liberators ...

82 AD Bouches-du-Rhône L 277, *Procès-verbal* of electoral assembly of Department of Bouches-du-Rhône..., pp. 2, 16, 28, 48–51.
83 AD Côte d'Or L 210, speech given by M. de Brois, dean of electors, May 10, 1790.

In vain partisans of the Old Regime accuse the National Assembly of having exceeded its mandates: each of its members had that of doing the greatest good possible. From all parts of the empire, a general cry asked for a constitution, and when our representatives have given us one that causes admiration and envy in all the peoples of Europe, if they have surpassed our expectations, they certainly have not overstepped their powers...

We declare then openly, sure of not being contradicted by those from whom we hold our powers: we regard the abolition of the so-called privileges of our province as a good deed, and the new division of the kingdom as the surest bulwark of freedom.[84]

This enthusiasm for the new ideal of the polity advanced by the National Assembly, and the sense of awe and respect for the constitution that would realize it, was equally evident in a speech given by the president of the electoral assembly of the Department of Charente-Maritime. After paying tribute to the courage of the deputies when the Crown had tried to employ armed force against them in July, 1789, he declared:

If I examine the constitution for which they have laid the foundations, the grandeur of the enterprise astonishes and overcomes me...What fecundity of ideas, what resources of the imagination, what sagacity, what foresight in the details, what humanity, what patriotism, finally [what] sublimity of genius! Oh my fatherland, be happy for having produced such great men. Neighboring nations ought to envy your lot, and perhaps one day, enlightened by the writings of wise legislators, they will owe them a new existence.[85]

Again, making every allowance for hyperbole, exaggeration and the sense of theater, as one must, it is nevertheless clear that participants regarded the moment as extraordinary.

Indeed, throughout France there were similar accolades bestowed on the National Assembly and its work.[86] In Béarn, for example, where the new ideal of the polity had briefly caused consternation, the electoral assembly for the new Department of Basses-Pyrénées hailed the work of the National Assembly and expressed its eagerness to see the constitution, which they claimed would assure the happiness of France, completed.[87]

84 *Ibid.*, address to National Assembly, May 25, 1790.
85 AD Charente-Maritime L 121, evening session of June 16, 1790.
86 See, for example, AN C 117, dossier 325, document 3; AN C 117¹, dossier 328, document 14; AN C 118, dossier 339^bis, document 4; AD Eure 3 L 1, session of July 26, 1790; AD Nord L 751, session of July 10, 1790; AD Puy-de-Dôme L 481, session of June 20, 1790; AN F¹c III Yonne 1, *Procès-verbal* of assembly of electors of Department of Yonne, session of April 17, 1790; AD Cantal L 149, *Procès-verbal* of electoral assembly of Department of Cantal, June 28, 1790 and following days, fol. 36; AD Sarthe L 199, *Procès-verbal* of electoral assembly of Department of Sarthe (1790), *cahier* 2, p. 3.
87 AN F¹c III Basses-Pyrénées 1, extract from register of deliberations of electoral assembly of Basses-Pyrénées, especially pp. 9–10. For more on the formation of this department, see Margadant, *Urban Rivalries*, pp. 265–267.

As concerned as they had been about the formation of departments as the first genuine referendum on their work, it is difficult to believe that the deputies of the National Assembly could have hoped for a more favorable outcome. In many instances, in fact, it was literally the case that the first and last actions of electoral assemblies were to salute the accomplishments and goals of the Assembly. Moreover, the electoral assemblies not only paid tribute to the Assembly for its past conduct and accomplishments, but they almost invariably swore an unconditional allegiance to all future legislation that it might enact, thereby immeasurably increasing the confidence of the National Assembly.

Although it was chiefly the National Assembly that received acclamation for the new administration, the nation also hailed Louis, largely as a result of his visit to the National Assembly on February 4, which had indicated his acceptance of its aspirations. Shortly after their election, for example, the new administrators of the Department of Creuse praised Louis for his support of the goals of the Assembly, saluting his "sublime patriotism" and alluding specifically to the visit of February 4.[88] Without question, the goodwill generated by the elections for the formation of departments seemed to unite the monarch, the National Assembly and the nation in an overwhelming sense of common purpose.[89]

Indeed, the complete absence of any perception of polarity or conflict between the nation and the monarch – and illustrative of the manner in which the *commissaires du roi* were also viewed as thoroughly imbued with the ideal of the nation – is perhaps best seen in the election of many *commissaires du roi* to one of the key administrative positions in the new departments, that of *procureur-général-syndic*, the executive figure in the departmental administration. In the Department of Marne, Jean Roze, one of the *commissaires du roi*, was elected by a wide margin as *procureur-général-syndic* on May 25, 1790; likewise, in Calvados, Côte d'Or, Côtes-du-Nord, Gard, Manche, Aude and Nord, *commissaires du roi* were elected as *procureur-général-syndic*.[90] As a result, these men, initially so

88 AN F¹c III Creuse 1, very respectful address of administrators of Department of Creuse to king, undated.

89 See, for example, AN F¹c III Hérault 10, address of electors of Department of Hérault to Louis, June 19, 1790.

90 AD Marne 1 L 256, *Procès-verbal* of meetings of assembly of electors of Department of Marne, p. 30; AD Calvados L 10084, *Procès-verbal* of meetings, session of June 25, 1790; AN F¹c III Calvados 1, letter of *commissaires du roi* to Necker, June 27, 1790; AD Côte d'Or L 210, dossier 1, *Procès-verbal* of election of administrators, session of May 28, 1790; AD Côtes-d'Armor 1 L 371, *Procès-verbal* of electoral assembly for formation of Department of Côtes-du-Nord, p. 28; AN B I 18, dossier Gard, *Procès-verbal* of operations of electoral assembly of Department of Gard, pp. 43, 45; AN F¹c III Manche 1, *Procès-verbal* of electoral assembly of Department of Manche, pp. 8–9; AN F¹c III Aude 1, *Procès-verbal*

distrusted by the National Assembly and the nation, were now key intermediaries between them as they became executors of the policies of the National Assembly. Such elections pleased, and apparently initially surprised, the Minister of the Interior, but the phenomenon obviously became more widespread.[91] Similarly, in several departments *commissaires du roi* were named to the directory of departments.[92]

Clearly the polity was almost universally regarded as a seamless web in which there were no longer any conflicting interests that could in any way supersede the grand and ultimate ideal of the nation. This attitude was evident in a speech by Le Veneur, the president of the electors of the Department of Orne, in early July, 1790, when he said "from this time, united by the bonds of confraternity, without any division of ranks, of dignities, or of any distinctions whatsoever, let us master our heart by this tender feeling. Let fraternal union maintain us all in a spirit of peace and general benevolence, which are the steady bases of public good."[93]

The departmental administration was of the greatest importance to the National Assembly,[94] but it was only the uppermost level of the new administrative structure. The districts, the entity between the municipality and the department that had been a major component of the project of the Committee of the Constitution that had won out over that of Mirabeau, remained to be formed, and to illustrate the continuing emergence of the new administration, the example of the Department of Loire-Inférieure is once again useful.

Following the completion of the elections for administrators of the

of electoral assembly of Department of Aude for nomination of administrators of the department, pp. 79–80; AD Nord L 751, *Procès-verbal* of electoral assembly, fols. 98–99.
91  On the surprise of the minister, see AD Marne 1 L 256, letter of comte de Saint-Priest to *commissaires du roi*, May 29, 1790.
92  See AN F[1b] II Isère 1, document 193; AN B I 18, dossier Bouches-du-Rhône, *Procès-verbal* of electoral assembly of Department of Bouches-du-Rhône, evening session, June 18; AN F[1c] III Nord 1, *Procès-verbal* of electoral assembly of department, July 13, 1790. In the Department of Nord, in fact, all three *commissaires* were elected to positions in the new departmental administration.
93  AD Côte d'Or L 151, dossier Orne, *Discours prononcé par M. Le Veneur ... le 7 juillet 1790*. The bishop of Angers ordered the chanting of a *Te Deum* to be sung in every church in his diocese in thanksgiving for the nomination of the administrators of the Department of Maine-et-Loire. *Affiches d'Angers*, June 12, 1790. For an earlier crystallization of this belief, which culminated with the formation of departmental administration, see AN C 114, dossier 298[4], document 7; AN C 114, dossier 300[3], document 4; *Affiches d'Angers*, February 23, 1790.
94  See AD Nord L 768, *mémoire* of Committee of the Constitution, July 16, 1790; AN F[1b] II Loire-Inférieure 1, opinion of Committee of the Constitution, September 21, 1790. AM Toulon L 106, dossier D[4] 12, letter of Noé to mayor and municipal officers of Toulon, August 15, 1790.

department, the *commissaires du roi* set a date for the convening of assemblies in the *chef-lieu* of each district in order to elect twelve district administrators. One *commissaire* was delegated to open each of these assemblies and to provide instructions to it.[95] The elections for departmental administrators in the Department of Loire-Inférieure concluded on May 2, and it is indicative of the significance attached to the completion of the new administrative structure that district elections began in Nantes and Savenay only a week later, on May 9, and on succeeding days in other districts, beginning on May 10, for example, at Paimbauf. The elections were conducted over three days at Nantes and in only two at Paimbauf and Savenay.[96]

Once again, however, the simple mechanics of the operation do not reveal the spirit that underlay them. As had been the case during the creation of departments, the process of forming districts was suffused with a deep respect and admiration for the work and goals of the National Assembly. The administrators of the district of Blain wrote to the National Assembly to render homage to it and to the wisdom of its decrees. They told the deputies that it was to them that the French nation owed its restoration and, among other tributes, wrote that their knowledge, courage, and activity had made the efforts of the enemies of the fatherland impotent. At Savenay, one of the electors told his colleagues that the formation of districts was one of the memorable epochs from which history would doubtless date the regeneration of France. He said the district was one of the principal bases on which the edifice of the constitution should rest, and he spoke of the constitution as "this superb monument raised by wisdom for the glory of the French empire and the example of the universe." The district of Nantes wrote to notify the National Assembly of the completion of elections, but indicated that their happiness would be complete only when the administrators could execute the decrees of the Assembly.[97]

By mid-summer of 1790, then, much, although not all, of the new administration had been formed, and almost everywhere the transition that the balloting represented went smoothly. In Strasbourg, where the atmosphere in the period preceding the elections for departmental

95 AD Loire-Atlantique L 163, document 52.
96 On Nantes, see AN F¹c III Loire-Inférieure 1, documents 147, 148; on Savenay, where only twenty-seven electors participated; AN F¹c III Loire-Inférieure 1, document 155; AN C 118, dossier 343, document 27; on Paimbauf; AN C 118, dossier 344, documents 2–4; for other examples, see AD Eure 11 L 9; AD Charente-Maritime L 133; AN C 119, dossier 352, document 10; AD Côte d'Or L 215, L 216, L 217, L 218, dossier 1.
97 On Blain, see AN C 118, dossier 339, document 6; on Savenay, AN C 118, dossier 343, document 27; on Nantes, AN C 118, dossier 343, document 24. For a similar tribute from another district in France, see AN C 118, dossier 342, document 20.

administration had been permeated by suspicion and tension, the elections proceeded without incident.[98] Likewise, at Toulouse, contrary to expectations, the elections were entirely uneventful and devoid of any counterrevolutionary activity.[99] There was a minor problem with respect to the boundary between the Department of Isère and that of Drôme before the elections began, but the Committee of the Constitution, eager to advance the formation of the administration, refused to reconsider its previous decrees.[100] There was also a slight problem in the Department of Isère concerning the site of the directory of the department that consumed four days of debate and occasionally led to a suspension of the assembly even before the choice of administrators.[101]

Only at Nîmes in the Department of Gard, in the great exception to the spirit of optimism that reigned in France at this time, was the process of the formation of a department seriously disturbed by the eruption of religious tensions in the *bagarre*, in which approximately 300 people were killed. Amidst alarming rumors and the sounds of gunshots and cannon fire, the electoral assembly – "in the example of the National Assembly," according to its *procès-verbal* – and the *commissaires du roi* persevered, leading to the successful conclusion of the elections and the formation of the department.[102] The violence in the Department of Gard, however, rooted as it was in old religious hatreds, shocked and horrified the nation, for it seemed to be the very type of phenomenon that the new ideal of the polity had consigned forever to the past.[103]

In all other areas of France, however, the installation of the new administrative officers was an occasion for exultation and excitement on the part of the populace – a new era in which dissension or discord seemed to have virtually disappeared. In the Department of Aisne, the Intermediary Bureau, which was being replaced, complimented the new departmental authorities, and the new *procureur-général-syndic*, Blin de la Chaussée, praised his predecessors in return. Furthermore, referring to Louis XVI as "the restorer of our liberty," the title conferred on him on August 4, Blin de la Chaussée stated that he had "surpassed the

98 AD Bas-Rhin 1 L 748, *Procès-verbal* of elections for deputies of administrative assemblies of Bas-Rhin.          99 AD Haute-Garonne 1 L 551, document 12.
100 AN DIV 1, dossier 1, document 34.
101 AN F¹c III Isère 1, documents 54, 71, 72, with the last, the *procès-verbal* of the electoral assembly, cleansed of all references to the major points of conflict that arose.
102 AN F¹c III Gard 1, *Procès-verbal* of operations of electoral assembly of Department of Gard, p. 37; AN F¹c III Gard 1, letter of president of electoral assembly of Department of Gard to president of the National Assembly, June 28, 1790. See also Gwynne Lewis, *The Second Vendée: The Continuity of Counterrevolution in the Department of the Gard, 1789–1815* (Oxford, 1978), pp. 16, 18–26, and Johnson, *The Midi in Revolution*, pp. 128–129.
103 See, for example, AN AB^XIX 3327, dossier 1, undated letter of Lindet to his brother.

wisdom and glory of Charlemagne."[104] At the same time, a group of *curés* from various villages of the new department, noting explicitly that they were not speaking as a corporation, paid their respects to the new departmental authorities, assuring them of their loyalty to the nation, to the law and to the king. They drew a parallel between the Christian message of brotherhood and the spirit of fraternity produced by the Revolution, telling the administrators "your religion is our religion" and asserting that "we have a common goal, however different our duties."[105]

In Aurillac, in the Department of Cantal, when the new departmental administration initially met, it read and approved a message to the National Assembly that clearly reveals the spirit of progress and triumph to which the inauguration of the new administration gave rise. The administration stated that it sought

to offer the homage of its respect for your persons and its attachment to all your decrees; proud to administer this ancient people who were the only ones whose liberty the Romans respected; with what ardor it is going to carry out the laws which assure that of the French.

And what laws!

Subservient to the will of a single individual, debased by the feudal regime, they groaned under arbitrary laws that favored the rich and powerful and weighed down only those whom they were supposed to protect. They were not free and [now] they are free under the single dominion of a common law founded on reason and equality.

You have made men.

The right of judging had become a property; their administrators, agents, plunderers for insatiable tax collectors, would invent every day some new means to consume their substance. Henceforth they will elect their judges and administrators: taxes will be proportional to the ability to pay and will be employed by them for the needs of the fatherland that you have given them.

You have made citizens.

Odious privileges, humiliating distinctions divided them into enemy groups; today everyone is equal in title and in rights, they comprise only a single family ...

---

104 AD Aisne L 566, compliment of Intermediate Bureau of Department of Laon; speech pronounced at opening of the first session of administrative body of the Department of Aisne. The ceremony here is of particulr significance because of the bitter rivalry between Laon and Soissons over which of them would be the *chef-lieu* of the new department. The tenor of the ceremony underscores the fact that whatever disappointments or resentments there may have been, they did not translate themselves into resistance to the new ideal of the polity. On the rivalry, see Margadant, *Urban Rivalries*, pp. 263–264.

105 *Ibid.*, undated address of *curés* of Chavignon, Chafueux, Ursel. For similar examples of the perceived affinity between religion and the ideals of the Revolution, see AD Charente-Maritime L 121, *Procès-verbal* of electoral assembly, evening session of June 19, 1790 and, although it was not connected to the formation of a new department, AN C 128, dossier 429, document 17.

Continue your glorious works, gentlemen; complete this immortal edifice in which each stone excites our admiration ... See only your fellow citizens armed in order to defend the constitution, your fellow citizens who so justly call you fathers of the fatherland and who long for the moment when they will see you in your homes to give an example of civic virtue and submission to laws.

We reiterate, gentlemen, in the name of all the inhabitants of the Department of Cantal, the inviolable oath that they carry in their heart to be forever faithful to the constitution, to the nation, to the law and to the king.[106]

In Nantes, the administration of the Department of Loire-Inférieure held an organizational meeting on June 14, 1790, and, declaring itself moved by sentiments of gratitude, devotion, love and fidelity, as its first act decided unanimously, by acclamation, to send an address to the National Assembly and to the king. It then decided to have a public installation ceremony, to be held two days later, and on June 17, the day after the ceremony, it sent its addresses to the National Assembly and the monarch. Some days later, in a further reflection of the excitement generated by the organization of the new administration, the first meeting of the departmental administration was heavily attended by the public.[107]

In a few locales the process of transferring power to the new administrative bodies encountered minor difficulties. In the Department of Saône-et-Loire, the new administration had to assert itself against the existing administration of the *comté* de Mâconnais over which body would draw up tax assessments for 1790.[108] Similarly, the new Departments of Côte d'Or and Saône-et-Loire encountered opposition from the *Elus Généraux* of Burgundy concerning the continuation of public works and other matters until the National Assembly intervened in favor of the departments.[109]

Unlike the late autumn of 1789, however, when the Crown had, as at Amiens, deliberately done little to discourage potential discord, in 1790 it complied fully in the transition from provinces to departments, encouraging provincial estates to cooperate with the departments, thereby reinforcing the sense of common purpose.[110] Difficulties were relatively rare, however; the experience of Ile-de-France was more typical. As had occurred in the Department of Aisne, the Intermediate Commission of Ile-de-France wrote a complimentary letter to its new

106 AD Cantal L 16, fols. 9–11.
107 AD Loire-Atlantique L 42, fols. 1–7v°; *Etats-Généraux. Journal de la Correspondance de Nantes*, V: 239.
108 AN H¹ 201¹, dossier 2, documents 50–75. In part this confusion resulted from an action of the Assembly itself, for on January 12 it had declared that the Intermediate Commissions of the *pays d'états* were authorized to draw up tax rolls.
109 AN H¹ 201², dossier 2, documents 27–67.
110 AN H¹ 748⁹⁹. See also AN 291 AP 1, dossier 2, liasse 40, letter of June 26, 1790, for another example of cooperation by the Crown, in this instance with respect to an intendant.

successors.[111] The transition was also smooth in Brittany.[112] Indeed, as one scholar noted in a study of the Midi, by the spring of 1790 most convinced counterrevolutionaries realized the strength of the Revolution and knew that they could not succeed in reversing it within a legal framework.[113]

After the installation of departmental administrators, a completely unanticipated development occurred, a development that displays another underlying attitude prevalent in 1790 – the belief that the population had formerly been divided against one another by privilege and was now joined in the solemn fraternity of the nation. Apparently at the suggestion of the administrators of the Department of Aisne, the new administrators not only tended to the regular, defined duties within their departments, but also established an active and continuing correspondence with each other that reveals how profound a transformation they believed had occurred in the change of administration from the paradigm of privileged corporatism to that of the new ideal of the polity.[114]

In June, 1790, for example, the administrators of the Department of Yonne wrote a letter to the administrators of the adjacent Department of Côte d'Or that indicates how divisive they believed the system of privileged corporatism had been and how the National Assembly had entirely transformed the polity. Noting the proximity of their departments, the common roads they shared and the opportunities that this offered to revive commerce and agriculture between them, the administrators of the Department of Yonne stated that "the prohibitions of tax officials, the difference in the type of taxes had in some ways made us strangers to each other; the National Assembly having by a sublime work reestablished men in their natural and primitive rights, the kingdom now presents only a single family, and its inhabitants have become brothers who throw out their arms to the most distant points. Animated by this spirit, we assure you of our sentiments of fraternity, and of the desire that we have of coordinating with you the operations relative to your administration."[115] Likewise, the Department of Ardèche wrote to other

111 AN H¹ 1448, report by the Intermediate Commission of former province of Ile-de-France to administrators of departments, September 1, 1790. By contrast, the new departmental administration of Isère rather curtly dismissed its predecessors, the intendant and the Intermediate Commission. See AD Isère L 105, fol. 1.
112 See AD Côtes-d'Armor 1 L 368, letter of Dufaure-Rochefort to members of directory of Department of Côtes-du-Nord, July 26, 1790.
113 Johnson, *The Midi in Revolution*, p. 126.
114 On the Department of Aisne as the originator of this correspondance, see AD Seine-Maritime L 215, letter of Department of Seine-et-Oise to administrators of all departments of the kingdom, July 28, 1790. See also AD Aisne L 567, undated address of administrators of Department of Aisne to administrators of other departments.
115 AD Côte d'Or L 151, dossier Yonne.

departments that "the privileges of provinces no longer exist, the general administration is subject to the same rules; it is necessary that the same directorships lead toward the general welfare. Only a steady correspondence between the administrative bodies can assure this."[116]

The most compelling illustration of the change of outlook that took root during the summer of 1790, however, is a similar declaration from the Department of Bas-Rhin in Strasbourg, the city which had aggressively defended its privileges so much longer and more vigorously than any other.

Until the moment of the most successful revolution, France could be regarded only as a vast body, in which no tie bound the parts. The provinces, isolated from each other, formed to some extent different nations: manners, customs, language, form of administration all tended to disunite them, and to make them indifferent to each other.

Today everything has changed. Our rights, our duties, our interests are the same; the privileges that divided us no longer exist; we are all brothers, all equal, all free: in a word, we are all French, and that is our most precious title. Reciprocally imbued with this public spirit, without which particular prosperity cannot exist, we have all sworn to uphold the revolution, to bring to the laws and decrees of the representatives of the nation the respect and obedience that is due them, of lending mutual help and assistance against the enemies of the public good. It is only by the most intimate union that we can fulfill all our duties, as citizens and as administrators; it is only in communicating among ourselves the results of our endeavors, of our diverse operations, in making our particular views that we conceive for the well-being of our fellow citizens known, that we will be able to succeed in establishing this unity of principles and execution, by means of which the administration of France will be only that of the very same family.[117]

The initiation of correspondence between departments, which became routine, brings to light another significant component of the political and emotional milieu of the summer of 1790 generated by the formation of the new administration.[118]

This overwhelming sense of cohesiveness and unity, and the various sentiments that underlay it – a deep feeling of gratitude toward the National Assembly and a continuing mandate, through the promise of total adhesion and complete obedience to all of its future laws and decrees, for the National Assembly to define the Revolution through its

116 AD Aisne L 567, undated letter of members of directory of administrative assembly of Department of Ardèche to Department of Aisne.
117 *Ibid.*, letter of president and members of administrative assembly of Department of Bas-Rhin to Department of Aisne, July 31, 1790. For an example of the manner in which the new ideal of the nation had manifested itself in Strasbourg, see *Le Modérateur*, April 14, 1790.
118 See, for example, AD Bouches-du-Rhône L 122, fols. 59, 60, 70, 73, 75, 122, 189; AD Côte d'Or L 151.

remaking of the polity, the belief that the new ideal of the nation constituted a virtual civic religion and the notion that France had been a nation of strangers under the system of privileged corporatism and that the inhabitants of the nation were now fraternally united under the new ethos framed by the National Assembly – are most visible in an address made by the administrators of the district of Aix-en-Provence to the National Assembly in early July, 1790.[119] (See Appendix) An awareness of this sense of exultation is necessary to comprehend fully the event that unquestionably marked the zenith, not only of the period 1789–1791, but of the Revolution as a whole, the *Fête de la Fédération* of 1790, a moment when the Revolution seemed to have reached its ultimate realization.[120]

Much like the night of August 4, of which it was in many respects the incarnation, it was an event that achieved its ultimate realization in Paris, but had, to some extent, been prefigured or anticipated earlier in the provinces. Early in 1790, in the climate of apprehension produced by uncertainty about Louis's allegiances and the arrest of Favras, young men from Brittany and Anjou had met at Pontivy to swear a "*pacte fédératif,*" declaring that they would "remain forever united by the tie of the most binding fraternity, to fight the enemies of the Revolution, to maintain the rights of man, to uphold the new constitution of the kingdom and to take, at the first sign of danger, as our rallying cry for our armed phalanxes, liberty or death!"[121] Approximately one month later, after Louis's visit to the National Assembly, they met again to declare that "no longer being Bretons nor Angevins, but French, we renounce all of our privileges and renounce them as unconstitutional; persuaded that the general combination of sentiments and strength should consolidate the revolution, we invite, we entreat, in the name of the fatherland, all French to adhere to the present coalition that will become the rampart of liberty and the strongest support of the throne."[122] In Dauphiné, in mid-February, 1790, the town of Romans held a remarkable federation, and in the following months there were similar celebrations in Troyes, in the university at Toulouse, in Laon and in Nantes.[123]

It was during the evening session of June 5 that a deputation from the commune of Paris appeared before the Assembly and, noting the various

119 AN C 120, dossier 359[1], document 16.
120 On the festivals, see Ozouf, *Festivals and the French Revolution*, especially pp. 1–60; Hunt, *Politics, Culture and Class in the French Revolution*, especially p. 35.
121 *Affiches d'Angers*, February 2, 1790.        122 *Ibid.*, March 2, 1790.
123 *Fédération de la ville de Romans, du 14 février 1790* (N.p., n.d.); *Procès-verbal des séances des députés des municipalités ... pour convenir d'un projet de confédération entre elles* (Troyes, n.d.); *Procès-verbal de prestation de serment de MM. les étudians des quatre facultés réunies de l'Université de Toulouse* (Toulouse, 1790); on Laon, AN C 117, dossier 326[bis], document 14; on Nantes, AN C 117, dossier 336[bis], document 5.

federations that had spontaneously formed in different parts of France, particularly that at Pontivy, proposed that each department send a delegation to Paris so that all of France could, in the presence of the National Assembly, swear to defend and maintain the new constitution. The delegation suggested July 14 as the date for the event. In what a preeminent historian of the Revolutionary festivals has oddly termed "a controversial, joyless birth," the National Assembly approved the suggestion, ultimately leading to what she called a "collective enthusiasm ... beyond their joyless projects."[124]

The festival was, in fact, to be a celebration of national unity and of the achievements of the Revolution; as one contemporary, a future deputy to the Legislative Assembly, noted, it was "the first time that French from all parts of this vast empire assembled together on a single point and seemed to form only a single family sharing the same sentiments on the great reforms that had just come into being."[125] The primary festival at Paris was replicated on a smaller scale in municipalities in the departments, and in a symbolic avowal of the unity of the nation, the ceremonies in the outlying municipalities were timed to coincide with the one in Paris so that the entire nation would take the civic oath at approximately the same time.[126]

As in Paris, local authorities made substantial preparations for the ceremony, almost invariably including the construction of an "altar of the fatherland," all of which imparted an extraordinary air of solemnity to the occasion. The extent of the arrangements can be seen in Aix-en-Provence, where a three-tiered altar of the nation was erected between the first two fountains of the promenade in the town. Across from the altar was an obelisk, at the top of which stood a globe which carried the inscription "Vive la Nation." The middle of the obelisk had an inscription that read "Vive la Loi" and below that "Vive le Roi." A set of columns formed a portico on each side of the obelisk and ended a short distance from the altar. Furthermore, the tone of the ceremonies – the idea of total unity between the monarch and the nation and the link with the night of August 4 – is also evident in Aix-en-Provence. Before the taking of the oath, a portrait of Louis XVI, with an inscription declaring him the "Restorer of French Liberties," was escorted around the city by both the National Guard and troops of the line, and was then placed in

124 *Procès-verbal de l'Assemblée nationale*, No. 310 (June 5, 1790), pp. 26–27; No. 312 (June 7, 1790), p. 10; No. 313 (June 8, 1790), pp. 5–7; *Journal des débats*, June 5–6, 1790; *Adresse des citoyens de Paris à tous les François* (Paris, 1790). For the characterizations, see Ozouf, *Festivals and the French Revolution*, pp. 43–44.
125 BM Angers Ms. 1888, p. 175.
126 As Mona Ozouf has noted, the only constraint placed on the provinces was simultaneity. As a result, there was a great deal of local variety to celebrations of the *Fête*.

the municipal building. After a speech by the *procureur* of the commune, the portrait of Louis was installed in the *Hôtel de Ville* as the mayor, to hearty applause, extolled his virtues, and the room in which the portrait had been placed was left open so that the public could view it.[127]

Indeed, a survey of speeches delivered in the departments on the occasion provides an insight into contemporary understanding of the Revolution, for the speakers, in commemorating, as it were, the first anniversary of the Revolution, sought to elucidate and affirm for the populace all that had occurred over the past year. Clearly, the essence of the event was to laud, even venerate, the accomplishments of the Revolution as defined by the National Assembly, and to celebrate the union and harmony that reigned as a result. A speaker in the Department of Nord offered the most succint evocation of the passage that had been effected between 1789 and 1790 when he said:

Citizens,
> When you assembled formerly, it was to notify you of the desire of a master. You no longer have any [master] other than the law.
> It is your own work since it is the work of the representatives that you freely elected.
> Friends of liberty, you have a constitution, you have sworn to defend it, and it is for your own interest.[128]

The overwhelming sense of union was captured by a speaker at Billons in the Department of Puy-de-Dôme, who told the assembly that this was the highly desired moment when the deputies of the nation, the true representatives of all the French, were assembled to join their minds, hearts and voices in order to join together and cry to the universe *Vive la nation, Vive la loi et le Roi*.[129]

Another theme that was present was the sense of overlap between the values of the Revolution and religion. In Nevers, for example, the celebration not only included a Mass, but the participation of clerics in the ceremony, both of whom praised the National Assembly effusively for its regeneration of the kingdom.[130] A rather unusual illustration of the solemnity of the observance – as well as the notion of the ideals of the Revolution as a virtual civic religion, not merely in a practical sense but even in a sacramental sense – can be seen in Laon in the Department of Aisne, where a wedding occurred during the *Fête de la Fédération*. A

---

127 AM Aix-en-Provence LL 248, federation of National Guard, and of troops of the line of town of Aix in presence of mayor and municipal officers.
128 AD Nord L 1244, document 52.
129 AD Puy-de-Dôme L 658, *Discours prononcé à Billons le 14 juillet 1790 à l'occasion du serment pour la fédération*.
130 AM Nevers BB 46, fol. 195. See also Ozouf, *Festivals and the French Revolution*, pp. 53–54.

"poor and virtuous girl" was endowed by different administrative bodies so that she could marry a soldier in the National Guard; as a result, the altar of the fatherland received "the double vow of conjugal union of these happy spouses, and the fraternal union of all citizens."[131]

Finally, the sense of the moment is seen in a speech by the *procureur* of the commune of Aix-en-Provence, who told the gathering:

> The vaunted halcyon days of Athens and Rome do not equal the famous day of July 14, the anniversary of which we celebrate; one saw marvels of valor and courage come about through the most ardent patriotism, the public cause triumphed over ministerial despotism, freedom conquered and the Fatherland was saved.
>
> ... We are all children of the Fatherland, we are all French, let us be joined by the most indissoluble bonds of fraternity.
>
> This sacred alliance will affirm our freedom, the rights of the nation and the legitimate authority of the King forever.[132]

Indeed, the moral cement provided by the *Fête de la Fédération* is particularly evident in Strasbourg – only a few months previously roiled by the loss of its privileges – where there was a major celebration.[133]

As in Paris, the solemnity of the daytime ceremony was followed by various celebrations that evening. In Aix-en-Provence there was an illumination and a ball was held in the promenade, as the people showed "their love for their king and their gratitude for the benefit of the constitution that becomes the precious promise of the happiness of the French people."[134] In Angers, the citizens met by neighborhood for communal family suppers and "the most innocent gaiety reigned."[135] At Questembert, in addition to the celebrations, the municipality provided a free meal to the poor, and later distributed money to those who had been too embarrassed to appear.[136]

As was the case with the night of August 4, there was something almost mystical about the *Fête de la Fédération*. One contemporary wrote that "it was necessary to have been a witness to the enthusiasm that manifested itself at this time in order to be convinced that July 14 was a truly national festival. The French were proceeding from the far corners

131 AD Aisne L 571, *Procès-verbal de ce qui s'est passé à Laon ... le 14 juillet 1790*.
132 AM Aix-en-Provence LL 248, *Féderation de la Garde Nationale*, pp. 11–13.
133 See François-Noël Le Roy de Sainte-Croix, "La Fédération de Strasbourg en 1790," *La Révolution française*, 1 (1881), 221–245, 248–302. As in other locales, the *Fête* had been anticipated in an earlier regional federation. See *Patriotisches Wochenblatt*, April 21, 1790. For the continuation of the ideal memorialized at the *Fête de la Fédération*, see *Journal de la municipalité, du département, des districts & des sections de Paris; & correspondance des départements & des principales municipalités du royaume*, August 28, 1790.
134 AM Aix-en-Provence LL 248, *Fédération de la Garde Nationale*, pp. 21–22.
135 *Affiches d'Angers*, July 17, 1790.
136 *Journal des départements, districts et municipalités de la ci-devant province de Bretagne. Par une société des patriotes*, July 28, 1790.

of France to embrace as brothers and to celebrate together the festival of the great family."[137] A modern scholar, observing that the *Fête* was seen as an "absorption of differences," has similarly noted, "it was not only a matter of aesthetic splendor. The mere fact of coming together seemed at the time to be a prodigious moral conquest: the festival celebrated the passage from the private to the public."[138]

It would be difficult to overstate the aura of unity and goodwill that the *Fête de la Fédération* generated throughout France, not only in the immediate aftermath, but for months afterward. If the *Fête de la Fédération* belonged chiefly to the National Assembly, the period afterward witnessed an accretion of gratitude toward Louis for his acceptance of the Revolution. As the mayor, municipal officers and notables of Toulon wrote to Louis:

The solemn oath that you have sworn before the altar of the fatherland, to maintain the constitution and to execute the laws, has finally reached us; our hearts are suffused with the deepest gratitude and it is with transport that we receive these words of comfort, of tenderness and of peace that you deign to make us hear.

Receive, Sire, receive the recompense of so many benefits, receive the offering of our hearts, they are unreservedly yours.

The oath of Your Majesty will be the pledge of our happiness, as it is that of our fidelity, of our respect and of our love.[139]

Similar messages arrived from all areas of France.[140]

In the final analysis, the *Fête de la Fédération* did for the formation of departments what Louis's visit to the National Assembly in February had done for the formation of municipalities – it instilled both a sense of unity of purpose and of progress.[141] As a future deputy to the Legislative Assembly stated, the multitude believed in the sincerity of these solemn promises.[142]

It was in the wake of the goodwill created by the *Fête de la Fédération*

---

137 BM Angers Ms. 1888, p. 175.
138 Ozouf, *Festivals and the French Revolution*, p. 54.
139 AN F¹c III Var 9, letter of mayor, municipal officers and notables of Toulon to Louis, July 30, 1790.
140 See, for example, AN F¹c III Charente 1, undated letter of administrators of Consolens to Louis; AN F¹c III Gers 9, undated letter of administrators of Department of Gers to Louis; AN F¹c III Vosges 8, letter of mayor, municipal officers and *procureur* of Saint-Die to Louis, July 20, 1790; AN F¹c III Ille-et-Vilaine 9, letter of administrators and *procureur-syndic* of district of Blain to Louis, August 12, 1790; AN F¹c III Hérault 10, letter of administrators of Department of Hérault to Louis, July 31, 1790; AN F¹c III Nord 11, undated letter of administrators of district of Lille to Louis.
141 See AN F¹c III Sarthe 7, undated letter of *commissaires* of Department of Sarthe to Louis, which emphasizes the centrality of the night of August 4; AN F¹c III Mayenne 7, letter of administrators of Department of Mayenne to Louis, July 9, 1790.
142 BM Angers Ms. 1888, p. 177 n.

that the National Assembly went on to complete work on the judiciary in August and September, 1790. In the autumn of 1790, then, after another frenetic round of competition between municipalities to gain district tribunals, electoral assemblies met throughout France in order to choose judges for them.[143] Although these elections, held under the auspices of local administrative authorities, were more businesslike[144] and less euphoric than those for the administrative posts – in the sense that they were not punctuated by addresses to the National Assembly – one should not underestimate the sense of progress and accomplishment that they produced. With the new administrative system everywhere established and in operation, the inauguration of the district tribunals appeared to conclude the grand design of the National Assembly for the French polity[145] – the rejection of privilege in favor of the rule of law.

Until the night of August 4, privilege and civil law had been synonymous, for civil rights were essentially authorizations granted to specified groups or individuals by the Crown. This was, in fact, the essence of the corporate paradigm of the Old Regime, in which natural rights were held custodially by the monarch, who in return accorded particular freedoms or prerogatives to those collectivities that had yielded their natural rights to his sovereign authority.[146]

It is precisely for this reason that law became so fundamental in the new ideal of the polity once the National Assembly repudiated privilege, not only in administration but also in the sphere of civil law. The protection of the law became an inalienable, universal and uniform entitlement bestowed on every individual and was regarded not only as the greatest benefit the nation provided, but as the fundamental bond among its citizens.[147] The centrality of law to the new ideal of the polity asserted by the National Assembly is seen most clearly in the Declaration of the Rights of Man. The first two articles restored the inalienable quality of natural rights, and several of the following ones outlined the new role of law – and thereby the new nature of civil rights – in the

---

143 Margadant, *Urban Rivalries*, pp. 287–321.
144 Indeed, the decreased level of apprehension by deputies, in comparison with the elections for the administration earlier in the year, is evident in AD Côtes-d'Armor 1 L 389, dossier Palasne de Champeaux 1790, letter of Palasne, October 11, 1790. Although it was not in conjunction with the judicial elections in Paris, for an insight into the spirit of electoral assemblies in the aftermath of the goodwill generated by the *Fête de la Fédération*, see Claude-Emmanuel-Joseph-Pierre Pastoret, *Discours prononcé après la prestation de serment des électeurs de la section des Champs-Elysées.* (October 17, 1790) (N.p., n.d.).
145 AN C 130, dossier 444, document 8.
146 Sonenscher, *The Hatters of Eighteenth-Century France*, pp. 6–7, and *Work and Wages: Natural Law, Politics and the Eighteenth-Century French Trades* (Cambridge, 1989), pp. 53–54.
147 See AN AD$^{XIXJ}$ 1, *Ministère public, devoirs et attributions*, October 1, 1790.

polity. The correlation between law and the nation had been apparent everywhere in the decoration for the *Fête de la Fédération*, where the inscription of *la nation, la loi, le roi* had been ubiquitous. Indeed, this formula had been elaborated in Paris on one of the four supports for the altar of the fatherland.[148]

It was not only those who favored the Revolution who regarded the formation of the new judiciary as concluding the establishment of the new fundamental framework of the polity; those in opposition to it viewed it in the same terms. In late September, 1790, for example, the vacation section of the *Parlement* of Toulouse issued two defiant statements, asserting that the French monarchy was touching on the moment of its dissolution and that "there will soon remain no trace of its oldest institutions and that the sovereign courts are going to be buried under its ruins." It went on to deny the validity of every major initiative undertaken by the National Assembly since it had come into being in 1789.[149] Indeed, in Aix, and doubtless elsewhere, the formal closure of the *parlement*, which necessarily preceded the installation of the new district tribunals, had been regarded by local officials with some trepidation, but the operation seems to have proceeded everywhere without incident.[150]

The election and installation of the new judicial officers led many contemporaries to believe that the passage to the new ideal of the polity advanced by the National Assembly was nearly complete. In Dijon, for example, the president of the electoral assembly, in opening the elections, spoke of the change that the election of judges represented from the past, noting that "men with a little money will no longer regard it as a business transaction," and warned that they would squander all of the great benefits extended by the National Assembly if they did not devote the utmost attention to their choice of judges.[151] The emotive power of the

---

148 See *Journal des Décrets de l'Assemblée Nationale, pour les habitans des campagnes*, July 10–16, 1790. The panel read *LA NATION, LA LOI, LE ROI* and below that:
   *LA NATION, c'est vous*
   *LA LOI, c'est encore vous, c'est votre volonté*
   *LE ROI, c'est le Gardien de la Loi.*
149 See AN AD$^{\text{XVIIIc}}$ 10, no. 15 *bis*.
150 On Aix, see AN DIV 20, dossier 393, document 6. For other locales, see AM Douai J³ 3, *Procès-verbal* of affixing of seals on *Parlement* of Flanders by mayor and municipal officers, September 30, 1790; AN C 129, dossier 440, document 38; on that of Pau, AN AB$^{\text{XIX}}$ 3327, dossier 1, undated letter of Lindet to his brother. Since 1789, in fact, the docility of the *Parlement* of Paris had been an object of surprise to many observers. See AD Gironde C 4365, no. 10; AN KK 645, fol. 371; BN Mss. Nouv. acq. fr. 12938, fols. 238–238v°. See also Henri Carré, *La Fin des parlements* (Paris, 1912).
151 AD Côte d'Or L 218, dossier 2, *Procès-verbaux* of elections of judges of district of Dijon, October 18, 19, 20, 1790. See also AN F¹c III Morbihan 11, address of *procureur-syndic* of district of Vannes to electoral assembly, October 4, 1790.

event was especially evident at Saint-Brieuc, where the election of judges became an occasion for spontaneous celebrations.[152]

It is particularly in the ceremony for the installation of judges that one can discern the belief that the formation of the new judiciary seemed to complete the realization of the new society envisioned by the National Assembly by concluding the transition from subject – ruled by the will of a monarch – to citizen – ruled by laws passed by elected representatives and administered or enforced by elected administrators or judges.[153] As a newspaper in Angers commented at the time of the installation of the district tribunal, "it is thus that the people, instructed by it, guided by it, will show itself the zealous observer of the laws that it has made."[154]

Indeed, the sense of completion, as well as the belief that the equity of the rule of law would produce harmony – in contrast to the inequity of privilege, which had produced divisiveness and conflict – are clearly evident in a speech by the mayor of Angers, who opened the installation by stating that "we have finally reached the happy moment when all the French, ruled by the same laws, are going to comprise only a society of brothers, having only one opinion, founded on justice and truth; free in following laws that we will have made, governed by virtuous magistrates that we have chosen, all promises us happiness under their administration because, subject to the laws themselves, they will use their power only for the maintenance of order and to contribute, in this manner, to the national success."[155]

Similarly, in the installation ceremony at Aix-en-Provence, the president of the city council, characterizing the day as "the triumph of laws" and of "the rights of the people," stated that the judicial order had been "reestablished on the sacred base of natural law." He extolled the benefits of the new judicial institutions in comparison with the old, and gave a description of the new system that would henceforth be in place. In an additional reflection of the sense of accomplishment, the event closed with a *Te Deum*.[156]

The format of the installation ceremonies also highlighted another difference between the new regime and the old. In contrast to the Old

152 *Journal des départements, districts et municipalités de la ci-devant province de Bretagne*, October 27, 1790.
153 See Sewell, "Le citoyen/la citoyenne," *The French Revolution and the Creation of Modern Political Culture: The Political Culture of the French Revolution*, ed. Lucas, pp. 105–106.    154 *Affiches d'Angers*, November 13, 1790.
155 *Ibid.* The mayor of Douai gave a very similar speech at the installation of the district tribunal of Douai. See AM Douai J⁵ 5, installation of district tribunal, December 17, 1790.
156 AM Aix-en-Provence LL 289, *Procès-verbal* of installation of judges of district of Aix, November 27, 1790. See also AM Grenoble LL 2, fols. 45–46; *Journal des municipalités, districts et départements de l'Ille-et-Vilaine, des Côtes-du-Nord, du Finistère, de la Loire-Inférieure et du Morbihan*, November 24, 1790.

Regime, when the intendant or subdelegate might often have been at odds with the *parlement* or local judicial body, the new administrators – mayors and municipal officers as well as other administrative officials – attended the ceremony, underscoring the manner in which the new administration and judiciary would reinforce and complement each other in the service of the new ideal of the nation. Moreover, the inclusion of both troops of the line and National Guard troops at some ceremonies further underscored the sense of common purpose.[157]

With the *parlements* formally closed, the transition to the new judiciary proceeded smoothly. A special tribunal occasionally sought to continue its existence, but such episodes were of little consequence.[158] There was also some confusion concerning the unprecedented procedures and duties to be followed in the new courts, but overall the new tribunals established themselves without major difficulty.[159] Indeed, from the outset the National Assembly demanded a total commitment from those serving the nation in the new judiciary.[160]

As the year 1790 drew to a close, then, the transformation that had occurred in the polity made it in many respects a year as remarkable as 1789 had been. The extirpation of privilege and the concomitant passage from absolute to constitutional monarchy seemed complete, even if it was not yet formally ratified by a fully promulgated constitution. Indeed, in both society and in the Assembly alike, there was a sense of impatience to complete the constitution by the end of the year.[161]

To be sure, the transition that occurred in 1790 had not been entirely peaceful – the bloodshed in Nîmes in June and in Nancy in August were the most notorious incidents – but this should not obscure the enormous changes that were accomplished peacefully.[162] Indeed, the moral authority of the National Assembly allowed it to implement perhaps the most thoroughgoing, virtually bloodless revolution in history.[163] Centuries-

---

157 See, for example, AD Indre-et-Loire L 74, fols. 70, 71v°; *Journal des municipalités, districts et départements de l'Ille-et-Vilaine, des Côtes-du-Nord, du Finistère, de la Loire-Inférieure et du Morbihan*, November 24, 1790.

158 See, for example, AN DIV 69, dossier 2088, document 1. For an earlier intance of an effort in 1790 to preserve a *marechaussée*, see AN C 113, dossier 276, documents 13–14.

159 On the uncertainty and confusion in the tribunals, see AN AA 49, dossier 1391, document 1; AN BB[29] 1; AN BB[29] 2. In addition, the Committee of the Constitution answered thousands of inquiries.     160 See AN DIV 6, dossier 86, document 34.

161 See *Journal des décrets de l'Assemblée nationale, pour les habitans des campagnes*, September 18–24, 1790.

162 See Samuel F. Scott, "Problems of law and order during 1790, the 'peaceful' year of the French Revolution," *The American Historical Review*, 80 (1975), 859–888.

163 Again, this is not to overlook the carnage at Nîmes or Nancy, but both seemed to represent reversions to the fanaticism or despotism of the Old Regime. At Nîmes, by far the bloodiest, the sectarian tensions were centuries old and the changes wrought by the Revolution were less a cause of the violence than a catalyst for it. See, for example, Johnson,

old institutions, from *parlements* to provinces, had yielded peacefully to newly created ones founded on totally antithetical principles. It is little wonder that contemporaries believed that it was indeed possible to establish a society that was harmonious and virtually conflict-free. Although a measure that would ultimately prove to be one of the greatest solvents to that unity and sense of harmony had recently been passed on November 27 – the requirement of an oath of loyalty to the Civil Constitution of the Clergy – its effects were not yet evident. As a result, the polity truly seemed to be a seamless web in which the law completely bonded the monarch and society,[164] and the completion of the constitution, which would formally ratify the changes in the contours of civic life seemed imminent.

*The Midi in Revolution*, p. 129. And, as Scott noted, many of the other incidents were the product of local conditions.

164 On the fundamental sense of harmony perceived at the end of 1790, see An F$^1$c III Nord 11, address of judges of district tribunal of Lille to Louis, December 1, 1790. For an underlying sense of unease, see AN F$^1$c III Creuse 9, decree of administrative assembly of Department of Creuse, November 27, 1790. Such unease, however, was much more the exception than the rule.

> At each proclamation, cries of "Long live the constitution, the nation and the king" made themselves heard everywhere. The purest satisfaction was expressed on the face of every individual who witnessed this majestic ceremony.
>
> *Affiches d'Angers*, September 27, 1791, describing the ceremony in that town celebrating Louis's acceptance of the Constitution

As the year 1791 began, the contrast with the beginning of the previous year could not have been greater. The year 1790 had begun in an atmosphere of deep unease, with most of the old institutions of the kingdom suppressed but the ones destined to supplant them not yet in place. At the beginning of 1791, however, the new departmental administrations were functioning smoothly, as were the district tribunals – except in Paris, where they would open in January, 1791 – and the establishment of the new institutions created a deep sense of pride and accomplishment.[1] Furthermore, at the beginning of 1790 there had been much uncertainty regarding Louis's attitude toward the Revolution, stemming especially from the arrest of the marquis de Favras. Louis's visit to the National Assembly on February 4 had dissipated these doubts, however, and the goodwill generated by that visit, as well as by the *Fête de la Fédération* of 1790, carried over well into 1791. Few in the nation doubted that Louis had completely aligned himself with the Revolution, and that the nation and the monarch were united in a sense of common purpose. It was, in fact, a reflection of the belief in the imminence of the completion of the constitution and the sense of common purpose and accomplishment that prevailed that the administrators of the Department of Creuse suggested to the other eighty-two departments that they form a delegation of two administrators from each department to express to the National Assembly and to the king the gratitude of the people for the benefaction of the constitution.[2] Indeed,

---

1 For an insight into the contrast, see AN C 125, dossier 406, document 6. See also AM Toulon L 616, dossier K 49, in which the deputy Ricard, during a visit to Toulon in early January, 1791, was honored with a ceremony by the municipal officials of the city.
2 AN F$^1$c III Seine-Inférieure 15, document 183.

many in France believed that the Revolution made them the envy of Europe. But the attitude of other monarchs toward the Revolution in the spring of 1791, and the passivity of Louis in the face of it, led to a revival of anxiety that culminated with the incident at the Tuileries in April, 1791, when a Parisian crowd refused to allow Louis's carriage to leave. Louis's subsequent declaration seemed to restore harmony between the monarch and the nation, which made his flight from Paris in June all the more shocking. But the nation rallied to defend the constitution and, after anger toward Louis had subsided, it, like the National Assembly, was ready to forgive him. As a result, the promulgation of the constitution in September was marked by a sense of happiness and accomplishment.

As 1791 opened, administrations were functioning smoothly at all levels – departmental, district and municipal. Although their election had unquestionably marked a change in spirit from administration under the Old Regime, the duties that the new administrators carried out were largely the same as those before 1789. Consequently, the new administrations, after the burst of enthusiasm at the time of their installation, attracted relatively little public attention before June because the transition was less dramatic.

Rather, what struck contemporaries much more was the new judiciary. One deputy to the National Assembly noted that the Assembly had sought to change altogether the nature of the judicial process – no longer was it to be "a question of combat; it was necessary to understand and to apply the law."[3] In the fraternal community of citizens envisioned by the National Assembly, in which rights were equal and universal rather than exclusive, justice would be administered in a rational and totally disinterested manner.[4] This is, in fact, the way in which the new judiciary began to be perceived, and initially the volume of litigation or potential litigation dropped sharply.

A key element in this development, as the National Assembly had intended, was the new office of the justice of the peace. Available to settle disputes anywhere, the justices of the peace became the vanguard of the beneficent new ideal of the nation,[5] and the capacity of the institution to promote social harmony in the name of the nation is evident in letters written by justices of the peace. The justice of the peace of Saint-Laurent (Haute-Vienne), for example, reported in mid-1791 that of the more than

---

3 Delandine, *De Quelques changemens politiques*, p. 166.
4 See Jean-Baptiste-Joseph-Innocent-Philadelphie Regnault-Warin, *Mémoires pour servir à la vie du général Lafayette et à l'histoire de l'Assemblée constituante*, 2 vols. (Paris, 1824), II: 145–146.
5 See, for example, *Journal de Département de l'Allier*, December 10, 1790; *Le Point du Jour*, January 25, 1791; AN DIV\* 2, fol. 163.

1,200 cases presented to him since he had taken office, more than 1,100 had been conciliated without any expense. Another 100 had been judged without a single appeal, with 70 of those closed with only the expense of a summons. Only five cases had advanced to the district tribunal of Saint-Junien, and this he attributed only to the stubborness of the parties. The justice praised the institution and his acclamation was echoed by the newspaper that published his letter.[6]

The situation was similar in other regions as well. In the canton of Triel, near Saint-Germain-en-Laye, between February 1, 1791, and June 1, 1791, only 18 out of 130 cases presented to the justice of the peace for conciliation proceeded to litigation, the majority of which, the justice of the peace claimed, stemmed from the Old Regime and therefore already entailed considerable expenses by each party. Furthermore, for audiences, the 155 cases that were judged produced only 300 *livres* of expenses, averaging about 40 *sous* per case. Moreover, it is illustrative of the character of the institution that many persons would spontaneously and voluntarily present themselves to the justice of the peace for resolution of disputes. With perhaps only a touch of hyperbole, the justice of the peace wrote of individuals who arrived from the countryside with submissiveness, entered the session with respect and left with tears in their eyes, raising their hands to the sky.[7]

Similarly, the justice of the peace of Ferté-Gaucherce wrote to the National Assembly to praise the institution, noting how many of the 150 cases that he had judged during the previous three months would have entailed great expense under the old regime. He even suggested that, if the settlements continued at such a rate, it might be possible to reduce the number of judges in the district tribunal.[8] Similarly, at Pont Saint-Esprit, during his first three months of activity, the justice of the peace settled the vast majority of disputes, preventing their advancement to litigation, and corresponding reports came from other areas of France as well.[9]

Paris, too, experienced similar results. The justice of the peace of the Ponceau section wrote to the National Assembly to observe that the benefits of what he called "this beautiful institution" were felt in the largest cities as well as in the countryside. He noted that during the previous six weeks he had terminated 187 cases, that only 72 had been

6 *Annales patriotiques et littéraires de la France, et affaires politiques de l'Europe*, July 3, 1791.      7 AN C 128, dossier 430, document 14.
8 AN DIV 62, dossier 1860, document 28.
9 AN C 133, dossier 473², document 112. For other areas, see AN C 127, dossier 428, document 55; *Le Point du Jour*, January 25, 1791, April 30, 1791; *Etats-Généraux. Journal de la Correspondance de Nantes*, VIII: 214.

judged in an audience and that the total expense of those cases had been only 100 *livres*, 12 *sous*. In a passage that illustrates how expeditiously the office operated, he reported that in only one case had he been obliged to call 10 witnesses, to visit the scene of the dispute twice, and to draw up a *procès-verbal*, and that this had only cost the parties 8 *livres*, including 6 *livres* of damages for wasting the justice's time! He closed by assuring the National Assembly that "all the citizens of our section bless your works, and notably the institutions of the tribunals of peace, whose sublime simplicity ceaselessly excites the gratitude of the friends of the constitution and forces admiration from its detractors."[10] Indeed, one contemporary referred to the justices of the peace as "angels of peace."[11]

Indeed, the moral authority of the justice of the peace derived from the nation itself, of which he was the representative in pursuit of the common good. For this very reason he did not need to overawe and therefore had no particular costume in the performance of his duties, but only a medallion symbolizing the authority of the nation.[12] He conveyed the ideals of equality and equity that the new ideal of the polity represented – in this instance that of the munificent nation conferring the benefits of accessible, fair and inexpensive justice to the citizenry.[13] In so doing, however, he could also undercut traditional mechanisms of social control in communities and confront citizens, often for the first time, with the direct authority of the nation in the most unimpeded and categorical way.[14]

The justices of the peace, however, although the most visible component of the new judiciary, were not the only element within it that served to embody the new ideal of the polity. There was also the bureau of peace and conciliation attached to each district tribunal, in which individuals were required to attempt to arbitrate their differences before a dispute could advance to actual litigation. Contemporaries regarded this institution with equal respect and approval.

The bureaus were, in fact, also quite efficacious in derailing litigation. In Beaune, for example, in its first few weeks of operation, from December 9, 1790, to January 31, 1791, the bureau received 240 cases and settled 135 of them so that they did not advance to litigation. The remainder were defaults, were insufficiently investigated or else the parties simply resisted all efforts at conciliation. Indeed, the demand for

10 *Le Point du Jour*, March 12, 1791.
11 *Annales patriotiques et littéraires de la France, et affaires politiques de l'Europe*, July 3, 1791.                    12 See especially AN DIV* 2, fol. 163.
13 See AN T 643, undated memoir on organization of new judiciary.
14 See T. J. A. Le Goff and D. M. G. Sutherland, "The Revolution and the Rural Community in Eighteenth-Century Brittany," *Past & Present*, 62 (1974), 96–119, especially 104–109.

the services of the bureau became so great that it had to expand its hours of operation from two days per week to three, and it remained open from 9.00 a.m. until 8.30 p.m.[15] By June 27, it had handled 720 cases of every variety, although the members noted that those least susceptible to conciliation were those inherited from the suppressed courts.[16] In Cahors, in its first few weeks of operation, the bureau settled many cases but informed the National Assembly that many legal representatives were undermining its work by telling their clients that appearance before the bureau was simply a formality that would not influence the judgment of the tribunal. As a result, it had been unable to settle these cases, and observed that "it is in this way that the badly-intentioned always place obstacles to the execution of laws that emanate from the august Assembly of our representatives."[17] Similarly, in Berniers, the bureau of peace and conciliation experienced a heavy demand for its services in the first few weeks of operation and was able to settle the vast majority of disputes before they advanced to litigation.[18]

Like the justices of the peace, then, the bureaus of peace and conciliation proved successful in resolving disputes and averting litigation. These two institutions, more than any others, seemed to represent the spirit of the new ideal of the polity. Whereas the paradigm of privileged corporatism had been relentlessly divisive, the new ideal of the polity was dedicated to harmony and equity. As the members of the bureau of peace and conciliation at Beaune stated, in contrasting the tribunals of the old regime with those of the new:

Envy, hatred and all the passions that degrade men manifested themselves in writings, by actions, and hearts embittered themselves to the point that a case was always the beginning of a constant enmity.

What a contrast! One comes to our bureau of peace with a satisfied look, the spirit already prepared for conciliation. A council opens in good time, a principle [is] summoned up: principles of a strict equity [are] presented by persons without interests in the cases, achieving reconciliation of citizens seeking only justice, certain of finding it in men animated only by public good, they give themselves up to their judgments, leave without acrimony, content and grateful for the benefit of the law, because the justice that they have obtained has been prompt, without expense, rendered solely on the basis of the facts and not drawn out by the tortuous expedients of chicanery.[19]

15 AN DIV 24, dossier 540, letter of *commissaires* of bureau of peace of Beaune to president of National Assembly, January 31, 1791.
16 AN DIV 24, dossier 530, document 8.
17 AN DIV 38, dossier 1028, document 23.
18 AN DIV 33, dossier 779, document 7.
19 AN DIV 24, dossier 540, letter of *commissaires* of bureau of peace of Beaune to president of National Assembly, January 31, 1791.

Similar opinions were advanced elsewhere in France as well. In Angers, one contemporary commentator noted the "double effect" that the justices of the peace and the bureaus of peace and conciliation would have and extolled the benefit that they would produce for the new civic framework, reconciling all those who "want to be brothers and friends, and who no longer want to be torn apart by disastrous lawsuits."[20]

The newly-defined role of law seemed to herald a new epoch in which litigation would no longer be a struggle for advantage but would represent the application of reason and wisdom, and could only be an action of last resort, when all other efforts to settle had failed.[21] Law would henceforth be the source of concord rather than a basis for division. It was in recognition of this new ideal that the departmental administration of Paris wrote to the Assembly that "we are children of the law," or that the directory of the administrative assembly of the Department of Somme, in a circular to its constituents, defined virtue, without which, it stated, freedom could not exist, as submission to the law.[22] Similarly, in more overarching views of the interconnection between the king, the law and the nation, the president of the Department of Loire-Inférieure saluted Louis for recognizing that the law was above him, while the administration of the Department of Vienne praised him as "the greatest and best of kings" because he had been so magnanimous to submit "to the law the most beautiful sceptre of the universe, because you wanted to make your people free."[23]

Traditional loyalty to the king had been strengthened by cognizance of the fact that, however inconsistent his course may have been between July, 1789, and February, 1790, Louis had forsworn the proprietary and corporate conceptions of kingship and submitted himself to the new principle of the primacy and rule of law, of which he was the executor.[24] Membership in the nation was now, in fact, predicated primarily on the equal protection accorded to all by the law and only secondarily on loyalty to the king. As a result, the nation realized that Louis himself had also made sacrifices in the reshaping of the polity, and it was his acquiescence to this new model of kingship that made him, by early 1791, not only admired but beloved, for he was an integral part of the nation.

20  *Affiches d'Angers*, May 17, 1791; June 7, 1791.
21  See, for example, AN DIV 6, dossier 98, document 2.
22  For Paris, AN C 58, dossier 582, document 30; AN F¹c III Somme 9, undated circular of directory of the administrative assembly of the Department of Somme to the French of the department.
23  AN F¹c III Loire-Inférieure 1, speech pronounced at reception for federal banner by Anne-Pierre Costard; AN F¹c III Vienne 8, document 69.
24  On the proprietary notion of kingship, see Herbert Rowen, *The King's State: Proprietary Dynasticism in Early Modern France* (New Brunswick, 1980); on corporate notions, see Sonenscher, *The Hatters of Eighteenth-Century France*, pp. 6–7.

Indeed, the degree of devotion and attachment to the king can be seen in the reaction to an apparently serious illness he experienced in early 1791. Expressions of joy and relief at Louis's recovery came from all over France, underscoring the sense of common purpose at this time between the monarch and the nation. The administrators of the directory of the Department of Seine-Inférieure expressed their concern about Louis's illness and conveyed their happiness at his recovery. The members of the directory cited Louis's identification of himself with the nation as one of the sources of the love of the nation for him, and assured him that the happiness of "the best of kings" would be the constant object of their prayers.[25] The commune of Compiègne wrote to Louis to observe that the most appropriate time to convince a king of the love of his subjects was unquestionably when they feared losing him. Noting the alarm that had been provoked by the news of his illness, they expressed the hope that this new assurance of constant and unlimited love would be of some value to him, and they assured him that sentiments of respect, affection and of devotion for his sacred person would be maintained forever.[26] The administrators comprising the directory of the Department of Hérault ordered a *Te Deum* sung throughout the department, and the one offered in Montpellier itself again highlighted the unity that the nation felt in early 1791. What the administrators called "this religious and civic" ceremony took place on March 27, and the administrative and judicial bodies attended, as did the National Guard and troops of the line, along with a large number of citizens. Furthermore, a general illumination of the city was held that evening.[27] The degree of affection for Louis XVI in early 1791 was extraordinary; it is doubtful that the French had felt so strongly attached to any monarch since Henri IV.[28]

Ironically, it was in the midst of this concern and outpouring of affection for Louis that uneasiness began to resurface in the nation. The emigration of two of Louis's aunts in February, 1791, aroused some resentment, but the catalyst for greater apprehensiveness derived from

25 AN F$^1$c III Seine-Inférieure 14, undated letter of administrators comprising directory of Department of Seine-Inférieure to Louis.
26 AN F$^1$c III Oise 7, undated letter of municipal officers and notables of commune of Compiègne to Louis.
27 AN F$^1$c III Hérault 10, letter of administrators comprising directory of Department of Hérault to Minister of Interior, March 28, 1791. Likewise, on an obviously smaller scale, the commune of Louvres (Seine-et-Oise) had a *Te Deum* sung in thanksgiving for Louis's recovery. AN F$^1$c III Seine-et-Oise 11, extract from deliberations of commune of Louvres, March 25, 1791.
28 See also AN F$^1$c III Côtes-du-Nord 1, letter of mayor and municipal officers of town of Saint-Brieuc to Louis, March 23, 1791; AD Nord L 1245, documents 5–6. On the scope of such ceremonies, see AM Toulon L 614, dossier K 47, list of attendees for *Te Deum*, March 25, 1791.

external events. The populace felt a deep sense of attachment to their king, which was reinforced by his acceptance of the changes wrought by the National Assembly, but they were far less sanguine about his fellow monarchs. As a result, in the spring of 1791, as the comte d'Artois circulated among foreign monarchs presenting what he saw as the plight of his brother, a profound concern about foreign intervention arose in France, although there was no explicit threat issued by any foreign ruler.[29]

It was this tension that underlay the incident at the Tuileries on April 18, when a Parisian crowd refused to allow Louis's carriage to leave for his trip to Saint-Cloud. The anxiety was not confined to Paris, however; it was present in outlying areas as well. The directory of the Department of Côte d'Or, for example, wrote to the president of the National Assembly to advise him that members of the National Guard of their department, alarmed by rumors of enemy armies threatening the fatherland, had rushed to the administration to offer their services and to renew their oath to defend the constitution to the last drop of their blood.[30] At the same time, however, it was illustrative of the sense of common purpose and trust that the nation felt in Louis that it looked to him to defuse or resolve the crisis. The directory and the *procureur-général-syndic* of the Department of Ille-et-Vilaine wrote Louis to remind him of his visit to the National Assembly on February 4, 1790, and his subsequent professions of support for the Revolution and asked him to break his silence and to reaffirm his commitment to it.[31]

Furthermore, the letter sent by the Department of Paris to the king after the April 18 incident received strong support and endorsement from other departments, again indicating that apprehension was not a phenomenon limited chiefly to Paris. The members of the directory of the Department of Aude, for example, wrote to Louis that the Department of Paris had spoken faithfully for all eighty-three departments. They alluded to August 4, to Louis's visit to the National Assembly and to the *Fête de la Fédération* and, echoing the Department of Paris, asked him to rid himself of those of his advisers who were opposed to the Revolution.[32] A similar endorsement of the message of the

---

29 See BM Lyon Ms. 2191, letter of April 2, 1791. On the general situation, see M. J. Sydenham, *The French Revolution* (New York, 1966), pp. 78–79; Lefebvre, *The French Revolution*, I: 193–195.
30 AN F$^1$c III Côte d'Or 8, dossier 3, letter of administrators of directory of Department of Côte d'Or to president of National Assembly, April 18, 1791.
31 AN F$^1$c III Ille-et-Vilaine 9, letter of administrators of directory and *procureur-général* of the Department of Ille-et-Vilaine to Louis, April 26, 1791.
32 AN F$^1$c III Aude 7, dossier 1, letter of directory of Department of Aude to Louis, April 30, 1791.

Department of Paris came from Quimper, where the directory of the Department of Finistère observed that it was the fate of kings to be deceived by the majority of those who drew near them and that it was the duty of true citizens to tell the truth. The directory then told Louis that this was precisely what the Department of Paris had done, for which the directory applauded its courage and judgment. After reiterating the faith of the people in him, the directory, among other requests, asked Louis to announce to foreign powers that the French had founded a constitution based on the rights of man and citizen and to inform them that they had a king resolved to maintain it with all of his power.[33] Similarly, the directory of the Department of Hérault wrote to Louis that its view was identical to that of the Department of Paris, and that it was also the view of all friends of the public good and of all Frenchmen concerned with the glory and happiness of his reign. The directory asked Louis to affirm to foreign powers his support of the Revolution, asserting that "it is time to announce to foreign nations that you have irrevocably accepted this constitution, and that you will be its strongest supporter. The revolution is complete; entire centuries would not suffice to reverse the work of some months, made ready by opinion and completed by wisdom."[34] The directory of the Department of Indre assembled in extraordinary session at 10.00 p.m. on April 22 to hear a reading of the address of the Department of Paris to the king. It unanimously endorsed the message and decided to write to the Department of Paris indicating its gratitude for its effort and to encourage it to continue to engage Louis to maintain the constitution with all of his power and to turn away all enemies of the public good. The directory decided to send a copy of its deliberation to the National Assembly as well.[35]

With apprehension running so high, Louis's unequivocal declaration to foreign powers produced another remarkable outpouring of emotion in the nation. The directory of the Department of Ille-et-Vilaine immediately followed up its earlier message to Louis, in which it had asked him to break his silence, and indicated its pleasure that he had fulfilled their wish, telling him that all hearts had been penetrated with the deepest gratitude and that a universal joy had erupted at the report of this new evidence of his love. The administrators stated that the only dissatisfaction among the public resulted from the fact that he was unable

33 AN F$^1$c III Finistère 1, letter of directory of Department of Finistère to Louis, April 25, 1791.
34 AN F$^1$c III Hérault 10, letter of directory of Department of Hérault to Louis, April 27, 1791.
35 AN F$^1$c III Indre 7, extract from deliberations of directory of Department of Indre, April 22, 1791. See also *Journal des décrets de l'Assemblée nationale, pour les habitans des campagnes*, April 23, 1791.

to witness personally the joy and happiness that reverberated throughout Rennes at the news.[36] Likewise, the Jacobin Club at Saintes in the Department of Finistère wrote a lengthy letter to Louis, observing that the happiness present in the National Assembly was equally present in the nation. In a passage that revealed the primacy of law, they told Louis that in acceding to the wish of an anxious people on a freedom so dear to them, "the French and the Law saw in him more and more a defender and a father." They informed him of their profound gratitude for "the sublime writing" that traced so well the sentiments of his heart. It concluded by telling Louis that if the letter he had dictated had delivered the last blow to the enemies of freedom and of laws, it had also reassured good citizens forever, and banished the alarms that an instant of mistrust had formed in them.[37] The directory of the Department of Côte d'Or, which also had earlier sent a message to Louis informing him of concern within the department about the situation, posted the news of Louis's announcement in the city of Dijon and sent him an expression of appreciation for his action.[38] In Bordeaux as well the reading of Louis's letter produced a strong reaction of gratitude.[39]

Louis's declaration restored confidence in the monarchy to the levels it had been in August, 1789, February, 1790, or July, 1790. As a result, when he fled Paris only a few weeks later, the sense of betrayal was all that much the greater. It seemed incomprehensible that he would have fled after such an unequivocal declaration and when completion of the constitution seemed so close at hand. Two newspapers, both of which had a primarily rural readership, perhaps best captured the welter of emotions that the news of Louis's flight produced. The *Journal des Décrets* proclaimed:

This king, who had secured the admiration of the universe, the love and gratitude of the French, who seemed to pride himself on reigning over a free people, who had declared himself the head of the revolution; this king who had renewed, so many times and freely, the solemn and sacred oath to maintain the new laws, who had notified foreign powers of this resolution, who even said in one of his last speeches to the National Assembly, *have confidence in me*; this king has just

36 AN F¹c III Ille-et-Vilaine 9, letter of directory of Department of Ille-et-Vilaine to Louis, April 28, 1791.
37 AN F¹c III Finistère 1, letter of members of Society of Friends of the Constitution at Saintes to Louis, May 9, 1791.
38 AD Côte d'Or L 368, address of directory of Department of Côte d'Or to citizens of the city of Dijon, April 27, 1791; address of the directory of Department of Côte d'Or to the king, April 28, 1791.
39 AN F¹c III Gironde 11, letter of administrators of Department of Gironde to Louis, April 30, 1791. For other examples, see AN C 125, dossier 407, documents 23–24; AN F¹c III Aisne 12, undated address of directory of Department of Aisne to Louis (cover letter dated April 24, 1791).

forgotten his duty and his oaths, he has disappeared with his spouse, his brother and his sister.[40]

Similarly, the *Feuille Villageoise* doubtless captured the feelings of many when, speaking of the king and the enemies of the Revolution, it stated:

What a moment they have chosen in order to betray us! Calm was reestablished everywhere; the National Assembly hastened its progress. The court seemed to content itself with being able to do only good. The administrations and justice resumed their beneficial activity. The people were prepared to pay their new taxes and to name the new representatives. Men allowed us to hope for peace; nature promised us abundance.[41]

Despite such dismay, the populace remained calm and official opinion at every level expressed unlimited faith in the National Assembly.[42] Indeed, unlike July, 1789, the Assembly did not stand alone nor have to rely on spontaneous action, but had a complete supporting apparatus in the administrative structure it had established, which rallied quickly and unreservedly to the National Assembly and the constitution. In fact, the assurance and poise of administrators at all levels in the departments mirrored the calmness and confidence of the National Assembly; at every leve of jurisdiction – municipal, district and department – the administration immediately moved to galvanize the citizenry.

The first instinct of these administrators was to place complete faith in the National Assembly and to encourage the citizenry to do the same. The administrators of the Department of Gers, for example, exhorted the populace to rely on the National Assembly and on their administrators, promising that whatever happened they would never abandon the position confided to them by the populace and would, if necessary, die defending their constituents.[43] The directory of the Department of Deux-Sèvres, in extraordinary session, also urged inhabitants of the department to rely on their representatives and, recalling the bravery of the deputies in the past, urged the citizenry to follow exactly the decrees put forward by the National Assembly. They also ordered that, at 8.00 a.m. the next morning, all citizens, National Guardsmen and troops of the line assemble to swear publicly and individually the oath to maintain the constitution.[44] On learning of the news of Louis's departure, the

40 *Journal des décrets de l'Assemblée Nationale, pour les habitans des campagnes*, June 21, 1791.
41 *Année de la Feuille villageoise*, June 30, 1791. See also AN F[1]c III Orne 12, dossier 1, address to citizens of Department of Orne, undated.
42 See, for example, AN F[1]c III Finistère 9, document 35; AN D XXIX[bis] 36, dossier 374, document 13.
43 AN F[1]c III Gers 11, proclamation and decree of the Department of Gers, June 25, 1791.
44 AN F[1]c III Deux-Sèvres 8, extraordinary session of directory of Department of Deux-Sèvres, June 23, 1791.

administrators of the Department of Nord decided to convene the general council of the department. After ordering a number of actions, and after receiving a letter from their deputies to the National Assembly, the administrators wrote a reply. Referring to the deputies of the National Assembly as "fathers of the Fatherland," the departmental authorities reaffirmed the common outlook they shared with the Assembly and assured them of the complete submission of the department.[45] Similar appeals for reliance and belief in the National Assembly were issued by departmental authorities in every area of France.[46]

Likewise, district and municipal authorities issued similar declarations. The directory of the district of Issoire in the Department of Puy-de-Dôme, also referring to the deputies as "the fathers of the fatherland," expressed gratitude for the decrees of the National Assembly concerning the measures it should take with respect to the flight of the king.[47] At Thiers the district administrators expressed full confidence in the National Assembly and wrote that although the event was distressing, they regarded it as a new occasion to show, with more energy than ever, their zeal and devotion to the constitution.[48] The directory of the district of Château-du-Loir in the Department of Sarthe proclaimed that they sought to direct hearts and minds and to regulate the actions of political bodies on a uniform plan that could be dictated only by the representatives of the nation.[49] Similarly, in an address to the inhabitants of Bordeaux, the general council of the commune urged all citizens to surrender their individual wills to constituted authority which, in turn, would yield to the will of the National Assembly. It asserted that the constitution was complete, that it was known, that the French loved it and had sworn to maintain it. The general council noted that the French had a rallying point in the National Assembly, that they also had their

---

45  See AD Nord L 110*, fol. 165v°; AD Nord L 106*, fols. 121v°–123v°, 128–128v°; for the address, see AD Nord L 8119, dossier 1, address of general council of Department of Nord to National Assembly. Another copy may be found in AN M 664, dossier 21, document 18. For more on activity in Lille, see also AN AA 1, plaquette 2, document 13.
46  See, for example, AD Loir-et-Cher L 116, fol. 24; AN F$^1$c III Creuse 9, extract from registers of deliberations of the directory of Department of Creuse, June 23, 1791; An F$^1$c III Orne 12, dossier 1, address to citizens of Department of Orne, undated; AN F$^1$c III Vendée 7, document 15; AN F$^1$c III Finistère 9, document 35; AD Bouches-du-Rhône L 54, fol. 153v°.
47  AD Puy-de-Dôme L 543, extract from minutes of the directory of district of Issoire, June 24, 1791.
48  Ibid., letter of administrators and procureur-général-syndic of Thiers to administrators of Department of Puy-de-Dôme, June 23, 1791.
49  AD Sarthe L 259, dossier Château-du-Loir, extract from register of deliberations of directory of the district of Château-du-Loir, June 24, 1791.

administrators and judges, as well as the National Guard, which they termed "this invincible rampart of liberty."[50]

In many *chefs-lieux* of departments, the three administrations – departmental, district and municipal – came together to strengthen the response of the locale to Louis's flight.[51] The directory of the Department of Loir-et-Cher stated that the present circumstances led it to believe that it was its duty to coordinate its actions with all centers of authority in the *chef-lieu* of the department in order to assure calm, and together they enacted a series of measures.[52] In Nantes, the municipal, district and departmental authorities, which had often quarrelled over various minor matters in the past, came together in a sense of common purpose to address the situation and to issue a joint statement to the citizenry.[53] Indeed, they claimed that there had been 2,000 new enrollments in the National Guard, as citizens understood the dangers of apathy.[54] In Paris as well, the municipal government sought to work with the National Assembly.[55] Furthermore, in several places the authorities not only sought to harmonize their actions within their own department but, building on the correspondence they had opened with each other shortly after their formation in 1790, several departments began to communicate with each other to better organize their activity.[56] Nowhere was there a movement in favor of the king; indeed, the reaction of the nation was perhaps best captured in the characterization of the administrators of the Department of Isère, who wrote to the National Assembly that the citizens of their department had "rallied heart and soul to their august representatives, they have shown themselves more than ever worthy of the freedom that they have conquered through the efforts of the Constituent Assembly."[57]

50 AD Haute-Garonne 1 L 324, document 38. In Lyon, the authorities simply asserted that at that moment the National Assembly was "the only point where the plentitude of national authority resides." See AD Rhône 1 L 259, no. 259.
51 See, for example, AD Orne L 140, fols. 78–78v°; AD Charente-Maritime L 98, fols. 90–93v°; AD Bas-Rhin 1 L 760, document 27; AD Rhône 1 L 259, no. 259; AN F$^1$c III Marne 8, dossier 2, document 251; AN D XXIX$^{bis}$ 36, dossier 374, document 13; AN D XXIX$^{bis}$ 36, dossier 369, document 16.      52 AD Loir-et-Cher L 116, fol. 24.
53 AD Loire-Atlantique L 45, fols. 160–161. On some of the disputes, see AN F$^1$a 418, Department of Loire-Inférieure, extract from registers of administration, meeting of June 22, 1790, evening session; AN F$^1$b II Loire-Inférieure 1, letter of mayor and municipal officers of Nantes to Guignard, July 12, 1790; letter of members of directory of Department of Loire-Inférieure to Guignard, July 29, 1790; advice of Committee of Constitution, September 21, 1790.      54 AN D XXIX$^{bis}$ 36, dossier 369, document 30.
55 See BHVP Ms. 805, fols. 201–221.
56 See, for example, AD Sarthe L 153, fols. 260–261; AD Haute-Garonne 1 L 324, document 44.
57 AD Isère L 103, fols. 133–134. See also AN C 129, dossier 437, document 52. For a rare exception – that of an individual who did speak against the National Assembly at this time – see AD Nord L 12570 (9).

Louis's flight occurred as electoral assemblies in many departments had convened to elect deputies to the Legislative Assembly, the successor body to the National Assembly. As a result, although confidence in the National Assembly was extremely strong in the polity, there was also a realization that ultimately citizens had to direct their loyalties toward more enduring foundations. In the absence of the king, the most immediate and apparent focus of allegiance was the constitution, the permanent legacy of the National Assembly. Indeed, the crisis revealed the importance of the new constitution for contemporaries, from urban centers to small towns. The administrators of the Department of Bouches-du-Rhône, for example, proclaimed that "the kingdom of the French, created by the constitution, from this time provides for itself."[58] In Strasbourg, the directory of the Department of Bas-Rhin, the directory of the district of Strasbourg and the general council of the commune of Strasbourg, in a joint statement, invited their fellow citizens "to share our confidence in the efficacy of the measures that have been taken, to concur in the principles of our sublime constitution, which no enemy power can impair."[59] In Blois, the three administrative bodies declared that "the kidnapping of the king and of the royal family no longer permits any doubt that a constitution ought to form the well-being (bonheur) of France."[60] The ideal of the constitution had also penetrated smaller towns; even allowing for exaggeration or a desire to please by administrators, the reaction of small towns and rural areas was nevertheless remarkable. In the Department of Maine-et-Loire, for example, the municipal government of Chemillé convened the populace, which declared that it would "sacrifice its lands and a thousand lives if it could for the defense of the fatherland and the constitution," and similar sentiments came from citizens of the town of Vihiers.[61] Similarly, in the rural Department of Landes, the departmental administrators reported simply that despite the unhappiness produced by the desertion of the king and his family, virtually every individual of the department had shown the greatest desire to maintain the constitution and freedom.[62]

If the constitution was the tangible symbol on which the polity focused, the ethos of that document was the rule of law, and the implications of this for Louis in 1791 were portentous. The predicament

58 AD Bouches-du-Rhône L 54, fol. 153v°. See also AD Côtes-d'Armor 1 L 576, letter of administrators of Department of Côtes-du-Nord, June 26, 1791.
59 AD Bas-Rhin 1 L 760, document 27.    60 AD Loir-et-Cher L 116, fol. 24.
61 AD Maine-et-Loire 1 L 351, letter of citizens of Chemillé to directory of Department of Maine-et-Loire, June 24, 1791; letter of administrators of directory of district of Vihiers to directory of Department of Maine-et-Loire, June 30, 1791.
62 AN F¹c III Landes 9, letter of administrators of Department of Landes to Minister of the Interior, July 1, 1791.

for Louis was not simply the fact that the nation had rallied to the National Assembly in a crisis; this had also occurred in July, 1789, when Louis had sought to dissolve the Assembly, but his lack of success had not entailed any direct or immediate diminution of his position. By June, 1791, however, the tenets and principles of the National Assembly had so thoroughly permeated the polity that, unlike July, 1789, an alternative notion of sovereignty, based on the ideal of the rule of law and rooted in the constitution, had fully crystallized. The new conception of sovereignty was in no way synonymous with republicanism, which was but one element, and an extremely small one at that, of this new precept. Rather, the new standard was essentially the supplanting of divine-right monarchy and proprietary dynasticism by a belief in the rule of law and the ideal of the nation. In the final analysis, the central element of the nation was no longer the monarch but the law. As a result, in the crisis precipitated by Louis's flight, when the nation was, for the first time, forced to make a choice between sources of authority, law gained a genuine autonomy that had hitherto been largely implicit and theoretical because it had been interwoven with the role of the king as its chief executor. Furthermore, although it was articulated chiefly by administrators, it is nevertheless clear that this belief in the primacy of law, rather than the person of the king, as the quintessence of the nation was deeply embedded in society at large and is one reason that Louis garnered no support when he fled.[63]

The principle was abundantly clear, for example, in the statement that the administrators of the Department of Orne had disseminated and posted throughout the department when they learned of the flight of the king, which opened in the following terms:

Citizens!... If you do not enjoy the presence of your king, your laws exist and laws are the sovereigns of free men.

Citizens! Without a religious respect for the law true liberty cannot exist. If you have sworn to live free or die, then make this religious respect for the law a condition of your existence.

Citizens! Do you want to know liberty? It is the equal submission of all before law, assented to by the people or its representatives.[64]

Similarly, the administrators of the Department of Gers issued a proclamation to their constituents urging them to rally around the law

---

63 Reflecting this development, the deputy Ricard, after Louis's return to Paris, wrote to his constituents at Toulon that Louis's flight, which at first glance had seemed to throw the polity into confusion, had, in fact, strengthened its real foundations. AM Toulon L 338, dossier H³ 13, letter of Ricard, June 27, 1791.
64 AD Orne L 140, fol. 78. Another example may be found in AN F¹c III Orne 12, dossier 1, address to the citizens of Department of Orne, undated.

and to let it be the aegis and safeguard for everyone.[65] The administrators of the Department of Vendée told the inhabitants that they were invincibly attached to the law, which was their common aegis, while those of the Department of Nord declared to their constituents that friends of the Fatherland and of the constitution could not better manifest their sentiments at this difficult moment than by the strictest obedience to the law.[66]

The degree to which Louis's position had been diminished by the new principles that had taken root in the polity is particularly apparent in the declaration issued in Nantes by the three administrative bodies to the residents of the Department of Loire-Inférieure. The administrators began by stating that

the king has left, but the true sovereign, the nation, remains, and the French, worthy of liberty, are more than ever masters of their fate. The constitution is done, the destiny of the empire is fixed and its duration has taken on the eternal bases of reason and justice, never being allowed to depend on the will and presence of a man.

The power that he exercised and that he has abolished by his flight, was it not ours? Was it not the nation that delegated it to him? It remains then still entirely at its source.

They went on to state that the National Assembly was the repository of the national will and that it could now retrieve that power in the name of the nation, and keep it or delegate it for the interest and health of the fatherland. They professed total confidence in whatever course the Assembly chose to follow, exhorted citizens to rally to the constitution and closed their address with the words "fidelity to the nation and to the law." This declaration was posted throughout the department.[67]

The populace had extraordinary confidence in the ability of the National Assembly to maintain the rule of law and for this reason rallied to it completely. Indeed, members of the National Assembly sent out from Paris during the crisis uniformly encountered overwhelming sentiment in favor of the Assembly.[68]

As a result, when the National Assembly confirmed Louis's suspension after his return to Paris, it was conforming to public opinion as much as it was leading it; belief in the primacy of law was virtually universal. The acquiescence of the nation to the measure was, in fact, a striking illustration of how far the National Assembly had brought the polity during the preceding two years. Later reflecting on the series of decrees

65 AN F$^1$c III Gers 11, proclamation and decree of Department of Gers, undated.
66 AN F$^1$c III Vendée 7, document 15; AN F$^1$c III Nord 13, decree of directory of Department of Nord, June 22, 1791.     67 AD Loire-Atlantique L 45, fol. 161v°.
68 AN C 71, dossier 702, document 23; AN W 13, no. 312; AN F$^7$ 4385$^1$, dossier 5.

that confirmed the suspension of the king, one contemporary observed that, at the beginning of the Estates-General, the *bailliages* would certainly have had difficulty believing that their deputies would name the tutor of the heir to the throne to the exclusion of the monarch and his family.[69]

It would be difficult to exaggerate the degree of isolation of Louis or to overestimate the overwhelming respect enjoyed by the National Assembly in the aftermath of the Varennes episode.[70] Confronted with an event that was not merely unanticipated, but virtually inconceivable, the Assembly had remained master of the situation and guided the polity through the crisis. Indeed, meeting continuously for more than five days, the Assembly had demonstrated its utter and selfless devotion to the cause of the nation and the constitution.[71] The populace had already held the National Assembly in high regard, but admiration for it reached new heights after Varennes. An address sent to the National Assembly by the directory of the Department of Cantal on June 29, after Louis's return to Paris, reflects the attitude of much of the nation at this time.

What a great spectacle France gives at this moment to the earth! The foremost civil servant of the state, abandoning the post assigned to him by the law, doubtless believing that all authority would be dissolved, that the constitution would self-destruct and that despotism would soar over its ruins, but you instantly became the center of all authority just as you had never ceased to be that of confidence; the French rallied themselves around you; they deposited in your hands the oath that they had taken up; to live free or of not outliving freedom; ... they quickly moved against the enemy with this calm firmness that inspired them. The sense of their strength and of their worthiness; and we, too, gentlemen, wish to serve the fatherland and support your bountiful works; we swear to be faithful to the nation and to the law, to watch over vigilantly public peace and the circulation of grains, the collection of taxes and to die, if necessary, victims of an unbridled zeal for the upholding of the constitution that you have decreed.[72]

The isolation of Louis is equally apparent in a letter written to him by the administrators of the directory of the Department of Deux-Sèvres after his return, which chided him, firmly but politely.

Sire,
    The news of your departure has dismayed France; the news of your arrest ought to be and becomes the prize of its legitimate uneasiness. You abandoned,

69 Bibliothèque Méjanes (Aix) Ms. 535, p. 307.
70 See AM Douai D³ 8, letter of municipal commissioners of Douai to National Assembly, July 13, 1791; AN C 124, dossier 404¹, document 2.
71 See, for example, AM Le Havre D² 2, fols. 165v°–166.
72 AD Cantal L 76, entry 2234. The municipality of Aurillac also offered the highest praise to the National Assembly. See AN F¹c III Cantal 2, decree of municipality of Aurillac, June 29, 1791. See also AN F¹c III Ardennes 9, document 481.

Sire, your friends and your children; this powerful reproach that our heart dictates, is the only one which ought to be made to the king of the French... Loved, adored by a people who put this love in the foremost of its duties, what more was necessary to the ambition of a sensitive king? You saved France by breaking its chains; you gave an example to an astonished Europe of the powerful truth, that of ruling over hearts by reason and equity. Did Your Majesty suddenly change? And the soul of Louis XVI, in the middle of the happiness that he brought about, was it sorry for its work and conceived the scheme of destroying it?

Remember your oaths, remember your promises; the Constitution is our happiness, the Constitution comprises our renown, you swore to uphold it, you promised to defend it, and the French and their king are not made for perjury.

But forget the storm, when calm reappears over our heads. Show us that we were worthy of possessing the monarch who fled us; the habits of love and respect are the only bonds with which we want to shackle ourselves.[73]

If Louis needed any additional reminder of his isolated position in the nation, it came during the *Fête de la Fédération*, at the very time that the National Assembly debated his fate. The tenor of the ceremonies in 1791 was, in fact, markedly different from the ceremonies of 1790. The triad of *la nation, la loi et le roi*, so ubiquitous in 1790, was absent in 1791, in favor of almost exclusive praise for the National Assembly or of the autonomy of the law.

In the Department of Nord, for example, the vice-president of the directory of the department, speaking from the altar of the Fatherland, noted that the National Assembly had fulfilled the desires of all Frenchmen and that the purpose of the day was for all citizens to come together to take an oath binding all the individuals of the great family that comprised the state. He underscored that the purpose of the *Fête* was to recognize and support the National Assembly, and at no point did he mention Louis. He told his audience that they were there to swear to live only for the defense of the Fatherland and of liberty. A municipal official followed the vice-president and reminded the assemblage that the day was the great festival of the Fatherland and that they were gathered in order to swear eternal loyalty to the Fatherland. He then pronounced the oath that the citizens were to take, which was "I swear to use the arms placed in my hands for the defense of the fatherland, and to uphold against all internal and external enemies the constitution decreed by the National Assembly, to die rather than suffer the invasion of French territory by foreign troops, and to obey only orders given as a result of

73 AN F¹c III Deux-Sèvres 8, letter of administrators of directory of Department of Deux-Sèvres to Louis, June 28, 1791. In a reflection of the fact that these addresses were not merely pro forma, the Minister of the Interior answered this letter for Louis. See *Ibid.*, letter of Minister of the Interior to administrators of the directory of Department of Deux-Sèvres.

decrees of the National Assembly." After the oath had been taken there was enthusiastic applause and resounding cries of "*Vive la nation!*"[74]

The same oath was sworn by troops of the line and National Guard members in the Department of Marne, after which the vice-president of the directory of the department addressed the *fédérés*, reminding them that they had just renewed the sacred obligation of defending the law and liberty at the risk of their lives. He then said that, having received their oaths, the administrative and judicial bodies were going to renew, in the name of all citizens, the pledge that united them to the constitution and made of them a people of brothers. Each member of those institutions then took the oath, which produced enthusiastic applause that culminated with a second salvo of artillery.[75]

In Le Havre, where the municipal officers had been informed that the oath had been changed only to the extent of rallying the populace to the principal object of repelling a foreign invasion and would otherwise be the same as the preceding year,[76] the municipality still amended it, slightly but significantly, in a manner that showed how deeply the constitution had established itself. After giving his speech from the altar of the Fatherland, the mayor pronounced the oath to be taken as "We swear to remain faithful to the nation, to the law and to the constitutional king, to maintain with all our power the constitution decreed by the National Assembly and accepted by the constitutional king." The oath was then repeated by the bishop and clergy, the administrative bodies and all citizens present.[77]

As the rephrasing of the oath demonstrated, or especially as the communication to Louis from the Department of Deux-Sèvres indicated, despite Louis's extraordinary isolation, there was still a relatively large reservoir of goodwill on which he could draw as long as he was willing to abide by the constitution. Although admiration for the National Assembly had been and was paramount, sympathy and a willingness to forgive Louis had been present since his arrest. The directory of the Department of Var, for example, had written to the Minister of the Interior that it had received news of the arrest of Louis from the Department of Bouches-du-Rhône and had immediately announced it to the public, which had greeted it with great satisfaction and joy. It went on, however, to observe that everywhere they had "received evidence of

---

74 AD Nord L 1244, document 62.
75 AD Marne 1 L 378, fol. 70. For another similar example, see AN F¹c III Dordogne 1, extract from register of town and commune of Mareil, July 14, 1791.
76 AM Le Havre K 39, letter of directory of Department of Seine-Inférieure to mayor and municipal officers of Le Havre, July 13, 1791, letter of municipal bureau of Rouen to municipal officers of Le Havre, July 13, 1791.
77 AM Le Havre D¹ 1, fols. 105v°–106.

the most burning love for the Constitution and Liberty, of the deepest gratitude toward the National Assembly, of the most tender concern for a king who is still loved, of the deepest esteem for his excellent ministers."[78]

The constitution clearly had primacy, and the National Assembly remained the guardian of and focal point for the aspirations of the nation, but there was, at the same time, in addition to a reservoir of traditional loyalty to the monarch, understanding and sympathy for Louis, and it seems to have grown as the debate on his fate approached. On the very eve of that debate, for example, on July 12, the directory of the Department of Rhône, in a message to the department, appropriated the ubiquitous metaphor of the family and used it in Louis's favor, asking "if monarchical government was always considered as the image of paternal government, from this time should not the children hasten to forget the vexation that a father gives them?"[79]

By the time discussion of the report on Louis began on July 13, then, there was a favorable reserve of understanding for him in the nation which, if it did not excuse in any way what he had done, was willing to forgive him for his mistake and even for his betrayal. As a result, when the National Assembly decided at the end of the debate to maintain the king if he agreed to accept the constitution, it was once again, as with the maintenance of Louis's suspension in June, fulfilling public opinion as much as it was shaping it.

This conjunction was evident in a letter sent by the administrators of the directory of the Department of Aube to the National Assembly, which opened by stating that, at the time of the flight of the king, the directory had taken the solemn engagement to await and to receive with submission the decree that the National Assembly would convey on what they termed "this memorable event." It then stated that "we have been rewarded for our confidence by a decision that fulfills our wishes and those of all true citizens."[80]

Similarly, the administrators of the district of Saint-Jean d'Angély notified their representatives in the National Assembly that their constituents had learned "with total satisfaction" the news of the decree of July.[81] They followed this communication with a succinct letter to the entire National Assembly that revealed their understanding of the issue

78 AN F[1]c III Var 11, document 23.        79 AD Rhône 1 L 259, no. 269.
80 AN C 124, dossier 404[2], document 38. The directory also circulated an address to the inhabitants of their department. See *Ibid.*, document 39.
81 AD Charente-Maritime 4 J 1574 (28), letter of administrators of the directory of the district of Saint-Jean d'Angély to deputies of Saint-Jean d'Angély at National Assembly, July 25, 1791.

that the Assembly had to reconcile, as well as its willingness to forgive Louis. The letter, in its entirety, read:

Gentlemen:

Louis XVI, protesting against the constitution and quitting his post, has doubtless exposed the state to an imminent danger; but King Louis XVI was inviolable; you have strengthened this great principle by your decree of the 15th of this month.

We have sworn to defend the Constitution and to die for it; we swear to live and to die under monarchical government. May this sentiment be etched forever in the hearts of all French.[82]

Endorsements of the action of the Assembly arrived from all over France. The administrators comprising the directory of the Department of Seine-Inférieure commended the National Assembly for the course it had followed. A contrary decree, they noted, would have represented the triumph of the enemies of the Fatherland because, among other things, it would have disturbed the bases of the constitution and put the National Assembly in contradiction with itself. They reminded the Assembly that it was the nation that it represented, and stated that it was only in the heart of the National Assembly that the French would find their true friends.[83]

Similarly, the administrators of the directory and the *procureur-général-syndic* of the Department of Haute-Saône wrote to the Assembly in the most approving terms, telling the deputies that their works had just received a new luster and that they had gained for the deputies an eternal right to national gratitude. The administrators went on to assure them that by their decision they had given the constitution a "grandeur and stability above all praise."[84]

In Grenoble, the directory of the Department of Isère wrote to the National Assembly that this great event demonstrated that the Assembly had more than ever shown itself worthy of the confidence of the nation. Reflecting the belief that foreign powers sought to intervene in France, the directory praised the Assembly for the decrees, asserting that it had struck the ultimate blow against the enemies of France. Indeed, it used a colorful maritime analogy to convey its admiration for the steadfastness of the Assembly throughout the events of June and July:

Immobile, like rocks in the depths of the sea, you have just seen break at your feet the fleets stirred up by the mistake of deluded people. Proud henceforth of your courage, surrounded by our respect, strong in the confidence and the energy of a free people, you can brave all the tempests that one would dare to raise still, and

---

82 AN C 129, dossier 441², document 87.
83 AN C 130, dossier 443, document 6.    84 AN C 130, dossier 442, document 20.

to show to the tyrants of the earth that their attempts against our liberty will serve only to hasten their fall.[85]

The decrees of July represented the culmination of an extraordinary period during which the National Assembly had resolutely guided the nation through one of the most severe and unique political crises in the history of France. The decision of the National Assembly, while it fulfilled the wishes of the nation, also appeared magnanimous and served to enhance its stature even further. Indeed, the moral position of the Assembly with respect to the king was absolutely unassailable. Whereas Louis had been secretive and duplicitous in determining his course of action, the Assembly had arrived at its decision through an open debate waged on principles rather than passions. Whereas Louis had broken his solemn oath to uphold the constitution, the Assembly had faithfully affirmed it by preserving the principle of the inviolability of the monarch. Furthermore, the manner in which the Assembly had done so had magnified the cardinal precept of the rule of law, and the nation recognized and appreciated virtually all of the elements that ultimately figured in the decision. A representative example is the tribute that the directory and the *procureur-général-syndic* of the Department of Haute-Saône offered in a letter to the National Assembly, which stated that "the general assent of the French to the imperturbable wisdom that guides you is the only worthy homage to the depth of purpose, the delicacy of tact, and the political adroitness that brings back the head and members of the State. The supreme Law will be your work; it is to us to strengthen it, and to you to discern the triumph that is owed to you."[86]

It is, in fact, an indication of this "general assent" and the widespread support enjoyed by the National Assembly that the killings at the *Champ de Mars* of those protesting the decision of the Assembly evoked little sympathy. On the contrary, there was anger against those involved in the demonstration, both because they seemed to represent a threat to both the National Assembly and to the constitution and because, in a society predicated on the rule of law, republicanism seemed to be the negation of that ideal as much as the absolute will of a monarch, for in the view of most contemporaries the demonstrators had clearly violated the law.

A characteristic judgment is that of the administrators of the Department of Indre-et-Loire, who wrote to the National Assembly that

85 AD Isère L 103, fols. 143–144.
86 AN C 130, dossier 442, document 20. See also AD Seine-Maritime L 2347, letter of administrators of directory of Department of Seine-Inférieure to administrators of district of Rouen, July 20, 1791. For other representative messages from administrators, see AN C 124, dossier 404[2], document 17; AN C 125, dossier 408, document 112; AN C 126, dossier 413, document 26; AN C 126, dossier 423, document 28; AM Toulon L 80, dossier D 37, undated address of directory of district of Toulon to National Assembly.

enemies of the Revolution, factions and "mad journalists" were combining their "sacriligious efforts" to lead the people astray and to make the representatives of the nation suspect. Their efforts were futile, however, because of confidence in the National Assembly and the devotion of the populace to the constitution. The administrators then exhorted the deputies to maintain "across the storms and the factions, this majestic, imposing immobility that has already saved the fatherland; hasten especially to conclude the Constitution, since it is the only means to assure the happiness of France."[87] Likewise, the administrators of the Department of Aube praised the decision of the National Assembly and then stated that they knew that criminals were daring to criticize the most magnificent act of wisdom of the assembly and were seeking to lead people astray. Pledging to resist their efforts, the administrators urged the Assembly to "continue its memorable works; surrounded by respect, by confidence and the gratitude of the true friends of liberty, it will no longer lack in its renown to struggle with the slanders of factions."[88]

The threat that contemporaries saw in republicanism is evident in a passage from a letter to the National Assembly from the administration of the Department of Haute-Saône, in which it told the deputies that they had "fixed an honorable end to the Revolution, that happiness and liberty equally approve, and the monarchy, tempered by the prudence of your decrees, secures us from the chains of despotism and from the convulsions of republicanism."[89]

Virtually as one, the nation had spoken and given primacy to the constitution and the rule of law, and had indicated to Louis that he could reassume his throne if he merely agreed to abide by the constitution that he had already solemnly sworn to uphold. The only dissonant note came from some Jacobin clubs, but even within the Jacobin club network those who disagreed were in a distinct minority.[90] Furthermore, it was done in a respectful manner that indicated that they were a loyal opposition, committed to the rule of law. A letter from the Jacobin club at Alais is representative:

The friends of the constitution were able to profess an opinion contrary to yours as long as this matter could appear to them undecided or uncertain; but from the

87 AN C 126, dossier 422, document 7.
88 AN C 124, dossier 404², document 38. For other examples, see AN C 130, dossier 443, document 6; AD Charente-Maritime 4 J 1574 (28), letter of administrators of directory of district of Saint-Jean d'Angély to deputies of Saint-Jean d'Angély at National Assembly, July 25, 1791; AM Toulon L 80, dossier D 37, address of municipal body of Toulon to National Assembly, July 24, 1791.
89 AN C 130, dossier 442, document 20. See also AD Loir-et-Cher L 176, fol. 164; AN C 129, dossier 440, document 44.
90 Again, see Kennedy, The Jacobin Clubs in the French Revolution: The Early Years, pp. 269–278, but he overemphasizes this opposition.

moment that the Law has spoken, that the general will has made itself heard, this opinion, earlier an error, would become a crime.[91]

Similarly, the club at Bédarieux wrote to the National Assembly:

Although our opinion was not exactly in conformity to that which you have sanctified by your decrees of the 15th and 16th of this month, we hasten to inform you that we will comply no less. We respect your motives and we do justice to your views: when the law has spoken we know only to obey and to be faithful to it.[92]

Other messages of disagreement were similar in tone,[93] but comprised only a small proportion of the messages received; most clubs professed support for the decisions of the Assembly.[94] Furthermore, committed, as they were, to the ideal of the rule of law, the Jacobins also had little sympathy for the protestors who had been killed at the *Champ de Mars*.[95]

A concurrent object of outrage in the polity was the group of 290 deputies who refused to participate in the deliberations of the Assembly. The spectacle of these deputies placing their will above that of the Assembly as a whole, and that of the law – and the perception that they sought to revive the concept of orders – upset many. Not surprisingly, since some of them had just abided by a decision with which they had not agreed, it was the Jacobins who were most dismayed.[96] Such anger was not confined to the Jacobins, however, and contributed further to division in the polity.[97]

In July, the electorate resumed its selection of deputies for the Legislative Assembly – and it is significant that even at this stage the

91 AN C 124, dossier 404$^1$, document 58.
92 AN C 124, dossier 405, document 67.
93 See, for example, AN C 124, dossier 404$^1$, document 20; AN C 124, dossier 405, documents 56, 101; AN C 127, dossier 426, document 61.
94 See, for example, AN C 124, dossier 404$^1$, documents 84, 116; AN C 124, dossier 404$^2$, documents 22, 60–61, 78; AN C 125, dossier 408, document 23; AN C 125, dossier 409, document 20; AN C 126, dossier 413, document 36; AN C 125, dossier 407, document 11; AN C 125, dossier 408, documents 44, 49; AN C 126, dossier 419, document 22; AN C 129, dossier 437, document 17; AN C 129, dossier 439, document 21; AN C 129, dossier 440, documents 42–43; AN C 129, dossier 441$^1$, document 20; AN C 130, dossier 449, document 44; AN C 130, dossier 453, document 21; AM Toulon L 80, dossier D 37, letter of extraordinary convocation of citizens at Jacobin Club of Toulon to National Assembly, July 25, 1791.
95 AN C 124, dossier 404$^1$, document 4; AN C 128, dossier 433, document 44; AN C 129, dossier 438, document 9; AN C 129, dossier 439, document 21.
96 See AN C 127, dossier 425, document 39; AN C 129, dossier 438, document 4; AN C 129, dossier 440, document 4; AN C 129, dossier 441$^1$, document 68.
97 AN C 129, dossier 440, document 11; *Adresse envoyé à l'Assemblée nationale, au nom de 1,670 citoyens de la ville de Montauban; sur la protestation faite par 290 députés, membres de la ditte Assemblée. Avec leur adhésion formelle aux décrets de l'Assemblée nationale.* (Paris, n.d.).

electorate chose men who believed in the king[98] – while the National Assembly, beginning in August, set about revising the constitution to take into account the unprecedented events of June. During this period, the political situation was obviously irregular but, because of the confidence the nation had in the National Assembly, there was no overriding sense of crisis. Rather, there was a sense of hopeful expectation as the nation awaited the definitive resolution of the predicament, which only Louis could determine.

Approximately seven weeks after the Assembly's decision of July, the National Assembly presented the constitution to the monarch. When Louis informed the Assembly of his acceptance of it, the Assembly dispatched special couriers to the departments, who in turn announced it to district and municipal authorities within their jurisdiction.[99]

The news of Louis's acceptance of the constitution precipitated several spontaneous celebrations and often produced letters to Louis by administrators of the departments. In Le Havre, when the municipal authorities learned of Louis's acceptance they convened and, surrounded by a detachment of troops of the line and the National Guard, went to various *places* in the town to announce it. This was followed by the firing of artillery blasts, the ringing of church bells and the offering of a *Te Deum* in thanksgiving. In Vesoul, *chef-lieu* of the Department of Haute-Saône, the arrival of the news caused "an inexpressible joy" in the administrators and happiness in the populace; a *Te Deum* was offered and the town held a general illumination that evening. Likewise, the city of Grenoble also ordered a general illumination to mark the occasion.[100]

Several departmental administrations also immediately sent letters to the king, which provide a useful insight into contemporary official thinking because of their spontaneity. The directory and the *procureur-général-syndic* of the Department of Ille-et-Vilaine wrote to Louis to praise his acceptance, by which he had shown himself to be "the father of the French" and had earned new claims to their loyalty. The address, however, also pointedly underscored for Louis the new governing ideals

98 C. J. Mitchell, *The French Legislative Assembly of 1791* (Leiden, 1988), pp. 214–215.
99 See, for example, AD Seine-Maritime L 14, fol. 204; L 225, document 128; AM Aix-en-Provence LL 314, letter of president of administrative assembly of Department of Bouches-du-Rhône to mayor and municipal officers of Aix, September 18, 1791; AN F$^1$c III Cher 8, letter of administrators of directory of Department of Cher to Minister of the Interior, September 22, 1791.
100 AD Seine-Maritime L 225, document 128; AN F$^1$c III Haute-Saône 11, document 23; AM Grenoble LL 13. For other examples of such spontaneous celebrations, see AD Nord L 5874, dossier 2, letter of administrators of directory of district of Bergues to directory of Department of Nord, September 17, 1791; AD Nord L 1245, document 3; AN F$^1$c III Oise 10, letter of administrators of directory of Department of Oise to Minister of the Interior, September 15, 1791; AM Aix-en-Provence LL 75, fols. 152v°–153.

of the nation, for the administrators concluded by stating "resolved to live and die free, all the citizens of the Department of Ille-et-Vilaine swear, and we swear with them, to spill the last drop of our blood for the maintenance of laws, of the constitutional throne and of liberty."[101] The mayor and municipal officers of the town of Gisors praised Louis's acceptance fulsomely, but also noted that "the throne of Your Majesty, as much as the smallest property of the lowest citizen, rests on the sacred edifice of the laws."[102] The administrators of the Department of Bouches-du-Rhône convened extraordinarily and sent Louis a letter hailing his acceptance of the constitution and informing him that the news had been greeted happily by the citizenry, but reminding him also that henceforth the French would live "under the empire of the Law."[103]

Other administrators referred to the constitution as "sublime" or evoked the night of August 4 by recalling Louis's title of "Restorer of French Liberty."[104] The evocation of August 4 or the characterization of the constitution as sublime was appropriate to the moment for, in several parts of France administrators marked the occasion of Louis's acceptance to advance such ideals as forgiveness and reconciliation.

A circular put forward by the administrators of the Department of Aude to inhabitants of the department best reflected the higher ideals associated with the constitution when they urged their constituents to use Louis's acceptance to forget, forever, the divisions that had convulsed them. They expressed the hope that all hatreds would be extinguished and encouraged the populace to be forgiving toward those who had emigrated, in the hope that Louis's action would induce them to return.[105]

101 AD Ille-et-Vilaine L 193, letter of administrators of directory and *procureur-général-syndic* of Department of Ille-et-Vilaine to Louis, September 16, 1791; another example may be found in AN F$^1$c III Ille-et-Vilaine 9, undated letter of directory and *procureur-général-syndic* of Department of Ille-et-Vilaine to Louis.
102 AN F$^1$c III Eure 9, letter of mayor and municipal officers of town of Gisors to Louis, September 16, 1791.
103 AD Bouches-du-Rhône L 123, fol. 299. For other invocations of the ideal of the rule of law, see AN F$^1$c III Eure 9, letter of administrators of directory of Department of Eure to Louis, September 19, 1791; AN F$^1$c III Aveyron 8, letter of administrations of directory of Department of Aveyron to Louis, September 26, 1791; AM Le Havre D$^1$ 1, fols. 111–111v°.
104 See AN F$^1$c III Maine-et-Loire 9, letter of administrators of directory of Department of Maine-et-Loire to Louis, September 21, 1791; AN F$^1$c III Pas-de-Calais 10, letter of administrators of directory of Department of Pas-de-Calais to Louis, September 16, 1791; AN F$^1$c III Deux-Sèvres 8, letter of administrators of directory of Department of Deux-Sèvres to Louis, September 17, 1791; AN F$^1$c III Somme 9, letter of members of National Guard, general council of commune of Amiens and others to Louis, September 18, 1791; AN F$^1$c III Vosges 8, letter from administrators of district, municipality, National Guard and others of Bruyères, September 25, 1791; AN C 126, dossier 412, document 31; AN C 127, dossier 428, document 67; AN C 129, dossier 441$^2$, document 89.
105 AN F$^1$c III Aude 8, document 147. See also AN F$^1$c III Meurthe 9, address of directory of Department of Meurthe to citizens of department, September 16, 1791.

Likewise, the electors of Boulogne, responding to Louis's exhortation in his letter of acceptance for the nation to forget the divisions of the past, wrote him to state that "yes, Sire, it will forget everything, this generous nation, and you will find in the sentiments that you demand the proof of its respect for its king, and of its love for his brothers; may the moderation to which it has recourse bring home those who have gone astray acting in good faith."[106]

Similarly, the municipal officers of Nevers wrote to Louis to express the happiness of the town at his acceptance of the constitution, and told him:

They are indeed precious to us, Sire, these words of peace that concluded your letter to the National Assembly. We would be unworthy of the name of French, if we did not know how to follow so noble and so generous an example. Far from us, then, any idea of hate and vengeance: peace and harmony, submission to laws, inviolable attachment to the King of the French; such are our wishes, Sire, such are our sentiments: may they be the presage of your happiness, and of the prosperity of the most beautiful of empires.[107]

There was a clear readiness on the part of the nation to forgive Louis and to consider his acceptance of the constitution as a new beginning. After a *Te Deum* and other spontaneous celebrations of Louis's acceptance, the vice-president of the directory of the Department of Nord told the assembled citizenry that "this happy day extinguishes forever all germs of division among the French, it is truly today that they are going to form only one family, one people of brothers who are going to enjoy liberty and happiness."[108]

Beyond a willingness to forgive the king, however, what the nation felt above all was a sense of relief; a phrase that recurred in several different letters was that of Louis's acceptance marked "the return of order and peace."[109] The return of order signified the end of uncertainty over the political structure in France that had been present since late June – the mayor and municipal officers of Gisors captured this concern best when they praised Louis for accepting "the constitution that gives a form, a

106 AN F¹c III Pas-de-Calais 10, letter of electors of Boulogne to Louis, September 16, 1791.
107 AN F¹c III Nièvre 6, undated letter of municipal officers of Nevers to Louis.
108 AN F¹c III Nord 13, copy of *procès-verbaux* of meetings of directory of Department of Nord, September 15, 1791. See also AN F¹c III Haute-Garonne 10, address of municipal body of town of Bagnerres to citizens, September 21, 1791.
109 See AD Seine-Maritime L 225, document 128; AN F¹c III Haute-Saône 11, document 23; AN F¹c III Charente 12, extract from registers of deliberation of directory of Department of Charente, September 16, 1791; AN F¹c III Vosges 10, document 10. Similarly, the administrators of the Department of Nièvre welcomed the return of "peace and tranquility." AN F¹c III Nièvre 6, letter of administrators of directory of Department of Nièvre to Louis, September 16, 1791.

character to the government."[110] The return of peace resided in the expectation that, with its acceptance by the king, the constitution would henceforth be an object of near universal consensus. Indeed, some locales, with more hope than acumen, wondered whether the constitution could any longer have enemies after Louis's acceptance.[111]

The official commemoration of the event took place in the departments on September 25, and in several locales its scope and intensity rivalled the *Fête de la Fédération* of 1790. Indeed, at Dijon, the components from the *Fête* of 1791 were used to erect a large structure to celebrate Louis's acceptance of the constitution. It served as a podium from which the mayor read Louis's letter to the National Assembly, producing cries of *Vive la Constitution* and *Vive le Roi*, and it was followed by a fireworks display and salvos of artillery. That evening there was an illuminaton of the city. The acceptance, however, was not confined to public commemoration; on the rue des Forges a grocer set up a small altar, on which there was an inscription and a vase with a flame, to mark the event.[112]

In Orléans also the ceremony reminded observers of the *Fête de la Fédération*, but the altar used for the commemoration of the constitution was embellished even more than it had been for the *Fête*, with the planting of greenery before each of the four faces of the altar. The celebration in Orléans lasted all day and culminated that evening with a special illumination.[113]

In Tours, the National Guard, carrying the banner of the department, and the thirty-ninth regiment of the troops of the line, carrying its regimental flags, marching in two columns accompanied by music, escorted the judicial and administrative bodies of Tours to several places in the town to read the official proclamation of the constitution. After the readings a bonfire was lit, several salvos of artillery were fired and the ceremony culminated that evening with a general illumination.[114] A similar celebration occurred in Nantes, during which the mayor gave a speech to the citizenry urging harmony, tolerance, respect and submission to the law. The bishop also spoke for the occasion.[115]

110 AN F¹c III Eure 9, letter of mayor and municipal officers of town of Gisors to Louis, September 16, 1791.
111 See AN F¹c III Pas-de-Calais 10, letter of electors of Boulogne to Louis, September 16, 1791. See also AN F¹c III Gironde 11, address of the directory of Department of Gironde to citizens of department, September 18, 1791.
112 BM Dijon Ms. 1660, fol. 90; AD Côte d'Or L 36, fol. 123v°.
113 AD Loiret 2 Mi 3114, entry for constitutional festival of 1791; AD Loiret 2 Mi 3115, p. 65.                          114 AD Indre-et-Loire L 82, fol. 23–23v°.
115 AD Loire-Atlantique L 46, fols 102v°–103. See also *Journal de correspondance de Paris à Nantes et du département de la Loire-Inférieure*, September 30, 1791 (supplement). For other similar ceremonies elsewhere and the emotion they generated, see AM Douai D⁵ 1, proclamation of the Constitution, October 2, 1791; *Affiches d'Angers*, September 27, 1791.

The celebration of the achievement of the constitution was in no way an emotionally hollow or thoughtless ritual. To be sure, divisions were present in the polity, particularly as a result of the Civil Constitution of the Clergy. Although a slight majority of parish priests took the oath of allegiance in 1791, this left a substantial minority who did not,[116] but its divisiveness should not be overstated, at least not for 1791. As John McManners has noted, the oath was almost identical to the civic oath of February 4, 1790, which most of the clergy in France had taken, and it was therefore possible to view the oath as little more than a general assent to the new order in France.[117] This was, of course, precisely what was being celebrated on this day, and virtually all but the most reactionary viewed the new system as preferable to the old. It was, as a result, a deeply-felt commemoration of the realization of the new ideal of the polity, embodied in the constitution.

A letter to Louis from the town of Saint-Chamas in the Department of Bouches-du-Rhône illustrates how thoroughly the new values, originally articulated by the National Assembly and carried out by the nation, had permeated France. After expressing their happiness at the "so desired news" of Louis's acceptance of the constitution, the populace praised him in effusive terms. Then, modestly but doubtless correctly referring to themselves as "secluded inhabitants of an extremity of the empire," they told Louis that "we worship liberty, we cherish the constitution that secures it, and our king who will uphold it." They admonished those opposed to the Revolution, stating that the King of the French had retaken the avenging sword of the law, and observing that "we want to enjoy finally the advantages of a revolution as illustrious as [it is] fortunate in the calm shadow of our olive tree." They averred that the foremost sentiment of their heart would be for two henceforth reunited objects: the Fatherland and the king.[118]

Unlike the spring of 1789, when inhabitants of various locales had sometimes drafted *cahiers* with only a vague understanding of their meaning or import, in the autumn of 1791 the significance of the constitution was almost universally known: the monarch ruled in accordance with the constitution through the medium of laws common to all. It was for this reason that there was such rejoicing, for Louis's acceptance ended doubt and ambiguity and marked the return of accord and consensus. It was, the inhabitants of Saint-Chamas acknowledged in their letter, perhaps the first time that Louis had ever heard Saint-Chamas mentioned. It is noteworthy, however, that it was to affirm the

116 Tackett, *Religion, Revolution and Regional Culture*, especially pp. 40–41.
117 McManners, *The French Revolution and the Church*, p. 50.
118 AN F$^1$c III Bouches-du-Rhône 8, undated letter of citizens of Saint-Chamas to Louis.

work of the National Assembly that "the citizens of the small town of Saint-Chamas" had self-consciously sought to express themselves to their monarch for the first time. It was, in a sense, the ultimate tribute to the work of the National Assembly that they had had the confidence to do so.

# Conclusion

> Our free and peaceable constitution is, then, the work of God for the happiness of man.
>
> Speech of the priest Charles Hervier during a celebration of Louis's acceptance of the constitution, September 25, 1791

Various generations of historians have tended to view the Constitution of 1791 unfavorably, albeit for different reasons. Mathiez, for example, asserted that privilege of wealth replaced that of birth, and Soboul echoed this judgment when he wrote of the French throwing off the yoke of privilege based on birth but replacing it with privilege based on money. Similar judgments have continued to the present era.[1] Such criticisms, however, concentrate on only one aspect of the constitution and are overstated in any case.[2]

Indeed, the degree of political involvement – in political clubs, popular societies or elections, especially the elections of 1790 – belies any notion of a plutocracy. Contemporaries clearly regarded the constitution with respect and were strongly attached to it. To most, it represented the replacement of a corporative, hierarchical society of orders and privilege by one based entirely on new principles of equity, equality and the rule of law.[3] It is not surprising, then, that most Frenchmen viewed the work

1 Albert Mathiez, *The French Revolution* (New York, 1928), p. 132; Soboul, *The French Revolution*, p. 227. For current recapitulations, see Joan B. Landes *Women and the Public Sphere in the Age of the French Revolution* (Ithaca, 1988), p. 122; Barbara Luttrell, *Mirabeau* (Carbondale, 1990), p. 170.

2 In his study of Pont-de-Montvert, for example, Patrice Higonnet found that of approximately 310 potential voters there, 225 were active citizens, and comparable ratios are found elsewhere. Patrice L.-R. Higonnet, *Pont-de-Montvert: Social Structure and Politics in a French Village, 1700–1914* (Cambridge, Mass., 1971), p. 84. See also Sheppard, *Lourmarin in the Eighteenth Century*, p. 183; Bois, *Paysans de l'Ouest*, pp. 230–241. Indeed, Bois noted that in the commune of Thoigné, seven active citizens had their occupation listed as "indigent" (*pauvre*).

3 See, for example, AN F$^1$c III Nièvre 7, dossier 2, document 5; AM Arles AA 23, fol. 634; *Feuille hebdomadaire patriotique*, December 13, 1789, December 20, 1789. Once again, Pont-de-Montvert provides a useful example of the manner in which the constitution seemed to symbolize the triumph of equity: as a predominantly Protestant village, most of its inhabitants would have enjoyed few rights before 1787, and even then the Crown had

of the National Assembly so favorably. The Jacobin club of Loches, for example, wrote the following to the National Assembly in late September, 1791, after Louis's acceptance of the constitution:

Two and one-half years of work have redressed the unhappiness of fourteen centuries; in fourteen centuries the gratitude that we express to you today for the completion of so sublime a work will not yet have weakened in the hearts of the French.[4]

The extraordinary homages rendered to the National Assembly and to Louis after his acceptance of the constitution testify to its merit and importance in the eyes of so many contemporaries. Had it been broadly viewed as instituting an "aristocracy of wealth", or implementing a system of "privilege based on money", it is highly unlikely that so many tributes would have been offered.

It was not that social tensions had disappeared, that competition or resentments between towns had ceased, that the poor were being succored or that religious misgivings associated with the Civil Constitution of the Clergy had vanished. Tensions obviously existed but, except among extreme conservatives, there was a recognition that whatever flaws there may have been in the new constitution, the principles on which it rested were infinitely superior to those of the Old Regime. It was this recognition that formed the basis for widespread acceptance of the Constitution of 1791.

More recently, historians have criticized the National Assembly for the primacy placed on unity and on ferreting out plots, which they associate with the beginning of an intolerance that would reach full fruition in the Terror.[5] Criticism of the National Assembly for its obsession with conspiracies is justified, as long as one realizes that its efforts were occasionally the object of attempted subversion. In addition, one must recognize how remarkably tolerant it was of the defiance and opposition that came from traditional, constituted bodies. Finally, one must also realize how free, serious, principled and wide-ranging the debates in the National Assembly were. Issues were thoroughly discussed, without imputations of disloyalty or treason, before being enacted into law.[6] Although ill-will and bitterness might linger beyond the

granted only toleration and not equality. See Clarke Garrett, "Religion and revolution in the Midi-Toulousain, 1789–1790," *Essays on the French Revolution*, ed. Reinhardt and Cawthon, p. 44.

4 AN C 127, dossier 427, document 3. See also AN C 127, dossier 428, documents 67, 91.

5 See, for example, Furet, *Interpreting the French Revolution*, pp. 52–54; Hunt, *Politics, Culture and Class in the French Revolution*, pp. 38–42; Hampson, *Prelude to Terror*, pp. 106–110, 190.

6 Margadant, *Urban Rivalries*, pp. 452–453, makes a similar argument with respect to the National Assembly and the formation of departments and districts.

resolution of a debate, their scope was personal – as in the duel between Barnave and Cazalès[7] – and they had nothing in common with the murderous, collective proscriptions that emerged during the Terror.

Another reproach levelled against the National Assembly stems from its failure to extend political rights to women. The disparity between the apparent universality of the Declaration of the Rights of Man and the treatment accorded to women by the Assembly is obvious, but the failure of the Assembly to act must be examined in its contemporary context. In its destruction of the corporate structure of the Old Regime, the National Assembly had recast the French polity into what one scholar has called a new "individual-state relationship."[8] Members of the Assembly believed that extending political rights to women had the potential to splinter the family – broadly accepted as the bedrock of society – at the same time that it was atomizing society through its remaking of the polity.[9] Indeed, the National Assembly considered the most glaring disparities of power within the institution of the family and enacted measures that raised the standing of women from the position they had occupied before the Revolution.[10]

Furthermore, although there were certainly individuals such as Condorcet, Olympe de Gouges or Etta Palm d'Aelders who argued for the rights of women, most scholars of women in the early years of the Revolution agree that the great majority of women were not seeking the right to vote nor formal participation in the political process – most, in fact, seem to have favored a system whereby the household was represented in politics by the male.[11] Indeed, one scholar has argued that even such activist women as Olympe de Gouges or Etta Palm d'Aelders saw themselves more as Revolutionaries who believed in equality between the sexes than as advocates of women's rights, and the circumstances under which several women's political clubs were founded

7 On this duel, see *Journal National*, August, 1790.
8 Lynn Hunt, *The Family Romance of the French Revolution* (Berkeley, 1992), p. 46.
9 *Ibid.*; Madelyn Gutwirth, *The Twilight of the Goddesses: Women and Representation in the French Revolutionary Era* (New Brunswick, 1992), pp. 225–226.
10 Hunt, *Family Romance*, pp. 40–41. In addition, even as passive citizens married women in particular enjoyed far more rights than they had under the old Regime, when the authority of the husband over the wife was virtually absolute.
11 See Olwen Hufton, *Women and the Limits of Citizenship in the French Revolution* (Toronto, 1992), p. 22. Nor was this unique to France. In the United States, for example, in July, 1848, at the Seneca Falls convention, female reformers passed a series of controversial resolutions insisting on sexual equality and other measures. The only one not to pass unanimously was one by Elizabeth Cady Stanton advocating that women fight to gain "their sacred right to the elective franchise." See Ronald G. Walters, *American Reformers 1815–1860* (New York, 1978), p. 108. I am grateful to Elizabeth Dunn for calling this to my attention.

in 1790 and 1791 does seem to indicate that enthusiasm for the Revolution was the primary consideration.[12]

With the prevailing cultural view of women held by both men and women, it is unlikely that any appeal for the rights of women could have succeeded.[13] The failure to extend political rights to women is undeniably another example of the failure of the National Assembly to realize ideals it had so boldly proclaimed, as Olympe de Gouges highlighted when she published her Declaration of the Rights of Woman and Citizen in 1791. In the final analysis, however, it seems to be more of an opportunity missed than an opportunity denied, and should not obscure other achievements of the National Assembly – achievements underscored by the enthusiasm with which women founded Revolutionary political clubs in 1791.

From an entirely different vantage point, François Furet has criticized the radicalism of the Assembly, decrying its propensity "to explore every aspect of a given decision and yet choose the most adventurous course out of their passionate desire to burn all bridges with the past."[14] Yet these were men who, in the years preceding the convening of the Estates-General, had seen clearly the failure of traditional policies, vacillation and half-measures. The Estates-General itself had come about through political decline and bankruptcy, and the National Assembly evolved out of continuing political paralysis. It seems inappropriate, then, to criticize the deputies of the National Assembly for seeking to break with a system that they correctly believed to be a complete failure. Furthermore, such criticism overlooks the fundamental respect with which the National Assembly treated other traditional institutions, especially the monarchy.

To see antecedents of the Terror in the politics of 1789 is misguided, for it fails to allow for critical historical disjunctures. The central element to any debate on the Terror, particularly that of the thesis of circumstances, is the war. Furet has challenged the thesis of circumstances – the notion that the Terror was a reaction to the war as an external event – by pointing out that it was the deputies of the Legislative Assembly

---

12 On Olympe de Gouges and Etta Palm d'Aelders, see Candice E. Proctor, *Women, Equality and the French Revolution* (Greenwood, Ct., 1990), p. 48. On the founding of women's political clubs, see Suzanne Desan, "Constitutional Amazons: Jacobin Women's Clubs in the French Revolution," *Re-creating Authority in Revolutionary France*, ed. Bryant T. Ragan, Jr. and Elizabeth A. Williams (New Brunswick, 1992), pp. 14–15.
13 Gutwirth, *Twilight of the Goddesses*, p. 225; Proctor, *Women, Equality and the French Revolution*, p. 116; Landes, *Women and the Public Sphere*, pp. 116–117; Nina Rattner Gelbart, *Feminine and Opposition Journalism in Old Regime France : Le Journal des Dames* (Berkeley, 1987), p. 301. In this respect, most scholars view the betrayal of the rights of women as occurring particularly with the later republican regime.
14 Furet, "A Commentary," *French Historical Studies*, 16 (1990), 795.

who wanted and brought about the war.[15] His arguments have merit, but there had been a clean break between the National Assembly and the Legislative Assembly because of the self-denying ordinance, rendering notions of continuity inapposite. Indeed, for all of its historical significance, the transition from the Estates-General to the National Assembly ultimately represented less of a rupture than that from the National Assembly to the Legislative Assembly. Discontinuity is clearest, in fact, on the issue of war. During the crisis between England and Spain over the Nootka Sound, the National Assembly had renounced all wars of conquest and pledged never to use its forces against the freedom of any people;[16] the Legislative Assembly, in contrast, would prove bellicose and antagonistic.

The rupture entails larger principles as well. Until 1789 the governing ideals of the polity had been historical tradition and privilege, but these had been repudiated on June 17 and August 4. The National Assembly, initially through the Declaration of the Rights of Man and then, more definitively, through the constitution, replaced tradition and privilege with the rule of law. The overthrow of the king in August, 1792, annulled the rule of law, but no new governing precept emerged to replace it. In this vacuum – and the termination of the rule of law was definitively confirmed by Louis's execution – the operative tenet became expediency, particularly after the outbreak of war. Whatever its origins – and there is no doubt that the Legislative Assembly played the pivotal role – the war became an absolute struggle for survival, and the imperative of survival of the Revolution, rather than the politics of 1789–1791, became the engine of the Terror.

Furet has also argued that the National Assembly, while not necessarily laying the foundations for the Terror, "failed to perceive that its conceptions might some day be used as means to establish a democratic despotism."[17] Once again, however, such criticism seems misdirected. The deputies of the National Assembly debated issues and resolved them with the passage of laws. Once laws were passed, particularly con-stitutional ones, they expected that all parties would abide by them; anything less would show contempt for the law. The crucial belief governing the National Assembly was that, through the Constitution of 1791, law – as the expression of the general will – would be the over-arching principle to which all subscribed.

15 Furet, "A Commentary," 796.
16 Because of the Family Compact, it appeared that France might have to provide support to the Spanish. The National Assembly instead asserted that the right to declare war belonged to the nation rather than to the monarch, and issued its declaration.
17 Furet, "A Commentary," 795.

In August, 1792, and beyond, the general will continued to be invoked, but it was a much more malleable concept because it was not moored to any overarching instrument. As a result, contending factions could invoke general will with equal legitimacy, and in pursuit of general will various factions resorted to violence. The crucial difference between 1789–1791 and the Terror is precisely the absence of any larger structure, notably the rule of law. This is not to posit a "good" 1789 versus a "bad" 1793, as Furet imputes to a critique by David Bien,[18] but parallels between the National Assembly and the National Convention are inappropriate, in large measure because of this critical difference.

Indeed, one cannot understand the development of the French Revolution without taking into account the ruptures that occurred. From the outset, in fact, these disjunctions were critical, for although it may seem paradoxical, the French Revolution was not, strictly speaking, the product of the crisis that preceded it. For all of the considerable merits of the book from which the term is drawn, this is the major flaw of Jean Egret's concept of the "pre-Revolution." The term assumes a teleology and linear progression that was absent. The various problems that arose between 1787 and 1789 led to the convening of the Estates-General, but the program devised by French society to address them – defined chiefly in the *cahiers* and the mandates given to deputies – was that of an Estates-General. To be sure, the agenda had a sense of urgency due to the seriousness of the crisis, but the defining precepts of the French Revolution arose from an altogether separate dynamic, rooted in the stalemate that developed immediately after the opening of the Estates-General.

Indeed, the deadlock at the Estates-General refracted the historical process, rendering the *cahiers*, instructions and mandates given to the deputies useless; it was, in part, their conflicting dictates that had produced the impasse. Caught in a historical vacuum in which past precedents were meaningless, the deputies at Versailles suddenly had to develop a new method of deliberation. After several weeks without progress, the National Assembly emerged as a solution to the stalemate. Its members pursued an agenda rooted in an emerging unitary ideal of the nation rather than one predicated on the diversity of interests of social groups and geographical regions of the kingdom.

Even at this stage, however, the National Assembly limited its goals and remained within the confines of existing institutions, as the report of

18  See Furet, "A Commentary," 794. For the critique of Bien, see David Bien, "François Furet, the Terror, and 1789," *French Historical Studies*, 16 (1990), 777–783. See also the contribution of Donald Sutherland, "An Assessment of the Writings of François Furet," *Ibid.*, 784–791.

the Committee of the Constitution to the National Assembly on July 27 made clear.[19] But the night of August 4, with its incalculable emotional intensity, transformed the perspective of the National Assembly, elevating its concept of the nation to an altogether different level. Whereas the initial concept of the nation had emerged from a theory of common rather than competing interests, understanding of it trans-cended this assumption after August 4. After August 4 the National Assembly viewed the nation as a source of equity, rectitude and high-mindedness, and it proceeded to remake the polity in accordance with its new ideals.

The power of the new ideal of the polity proved compelling, and most locales and social groups throughout France willingly relinquished control of their destiny to the National Assembly. The National Assembly remade France, creating institutions to realize the new principles it had conceived. The spirited debate that often characterized the undertaking resulted not from disagreement about whether there should be change but on the degree of change desirable.[20] It was on this issue that differences arose, but change was the overarching object of consensus.

The propelling force of the Revolution, in its critical formative stage from 1789 to 1791, was the National Assembly. It gave the Revolution definition as it imparted new ideals through the creation of institutions that completely reshaped the nation. Indeed, Mme. de Staël – hardly a conservative or a counterrevolutionary – observed that the National Assembly treated France like a colony with no past.[21]

At the same time, Frenchmen reinforced the new ideals of the National Assembly by electing men to serve in the newly-established institutions. The program of the National Assembly was realized without imposition or coercion and completely without violence. The major recourses to violence were, on the contrary, perpetrated by forces clinging to the values of the Old Regime – most notably, the attempt to dissolve the National Assembly, the actions of Catholics in the Department of Gard or of the marquis de Bouillé at Nancy. The first of these is, of course, the most critical, and the violent action spontaneously produced a violent reaction, but it was a reaction unsolicited and unanticipated by the National Assembly. While it can only remain a hypothesis, one cannot help but believe that the escape of the National Assembly from

---

19 It will also be recalled, for example, that the deputies from Provence were working for a separate constitution for their province until the night of August 4.

20 As Furet has noted, even the leader of the *monarchiens*, Mounier, accepted the principle of sovereignty of the nation. See Furet, ed., *Terminer la Révolution*, p. 8.

21 Anne-Louise-Germaine Staël-Holstein, *Considérations sur les principaux événemens de la Révolution française*, 3 vols. (London, 1818), I : 368.

overwhelming military force in July, 1789, when its only asset was the moral authority of its aspirations for reforming the polity, accounts, in large measure, for the subsequent confidence of the Assembly that its new ethos would be accepted by the nation as a whole, and that coercion and violence were not only unnecessary, but futile.[22] In the end, the overwhelming majority of Frenchmen freely accepted the new ideals advanced by the National Assembly and energetically participated in the new institutions formed to realize those ideals.

Ultimately, then, the French Revolution, in the decisive period from 1789 to 1791, is best understood as a collaboration between the National Assembly and the French nation, in which the National Assembly served as the architect and the nation as the builder. To be sure, the process was not untroubled. Many regions that had initially greeted the new ideal of the polity enthusiastically began to have misgivings in the autumn of 1789 as Louis's vacillation and the potentially inimical implications of the new ideal for their own locale became clearer. Louis's visit to the National Assembly in February, 1790, however, dissipated most of the uneasiness and restored a sense of optimism that culminated with the *Fête de la Fédération* of 1790. Thereafter, although there was a period of doubt during the spring of 1791, a generally cooperative and optimistic mood prevailed until Louis's flight from Paris in June, 1791.

The crisis of Louis's departure marked a watershed in the history of the National Assembly and revealed how indissoluble the partnership between the National Assembly and the French nation had become. Forced to make an absolutely unprecedented choice between the monarch and the National Assembly, the nation decisively embraced the latter. Under the aegis of the National Assembly, which had formulated and systematized it, the new ideal of the polity had completely superseded the paradigms of proprietary dynasticism and privileged corporatism. The resolution of the crisis heightened recognition of the high-mindedness and magnanimity of the National Assembly, further enhancing its eminence and moral stature.

The settlement of 1791 was not the panicky and hastily-arranged program that is often supposed, but an orderly process that sought to accommodate matters of concern from all sectors of the political spectrum, except for the far right. As a result, within the National Assembly, the constitution became an object of common assent – only 190 of between 1,100 and 1,200 deputies, many of whom would not have

22 See AD Ain 1 Mi 1, letter of August 18, 1789; AM Bordeaux D 227, no. 1, copy of letter of Nairac, July 15, 1789. The popular insurrection in Paris was what saved the Assembly, of course, but the rising, as Godechot argued, was an endorsement of the idea of the nation, which the National Assembly embodied. Godechot, *The Taking of the Bastille*, p. 270.

recognized any constitution, refused to accept it. Not only was the constitution a matter of consensus within the National Assembly, but the resolution of Louis's flight and the constitution met with the overwhelming approval of the nation.

Above all, the men of the National Assembly sought to preserve the rule of law by making the constitution independent of the person of Louis XVI. Louis could either accept the constitution or reject it, but if he opted for the latter he would revert to the status of ordinary citizen. This was not coercive or unjust, for Louis could not logically perform public duties or functions in opposition to the will and governing ideal of the nation; as a private citizen he could freely dissent. In the final analysis, the National Assembly invited Louis, despite his disloyalty, to become once again an integral part of the nation. All that was asked of him was to subscribe to its principles, as embodied in the constitution.

It is little wonder, then, that the deputies took pride in their accomplishment. They had recast the state along the most high-minded principles, seeking to subordinate private interests to the well-being of the nation itself.[23] The deputies commemorated their accomplishment with a medal given to each member, and that common endeavor forged a solidarity among them that transcended much of the bitterness of the period after the Terror. The bond of a common and unprecedented achievement made subsequent political differences appear trivial by comparison.[24]

If the situation was so apparently stable in September, 1791, why did radicalization and deterioration occur so quickly afterward, leading to the demise of the constitution within a year? Two factors are of paramount importance.

The first was a product of the rupture of continuity entailed in the self-denying ordinance. The men of the National Assembly, for most of their duration as deputies, had worked with the deep conviction that Louis accepted the Revolution and was a willing, fully cooperative participant in the transformation of the polity. The shock of Varennes came at the end of their tenure, during which time they had seen the monarch at his best – at the presentation of the August decrees, for example, or in the meeting of February 4, 1790, or at the *Fête de la Fédération* of 1790. Even

---

23 Among other results, France became the first nation in the Western world not to allow any religious limitations on participation in political life.

24 Based on his acquaintance with him in the National Assembly, for example, under the Directory Reubell saved the life of the abbé de Pradt, an erstwhile adversary in the Assembly. Similarly, under the Restoration, d'André, then head of the police, saved his former National Assembly colleague, Larevellière-Lepeaux, from deportation. See Henry Bergasse, *Histoire de l'Assemblée des élections de 1789 aux élections de 1967* (Paris, 1967), p. 28. See also AN AA 50, dossier 1439–1441, document 50.

if they found his flight incomprehensible, most were still willing to trust him afterward, sincerely believing that Louis had realized his error of judgment.

The Legislative Assembly never had any such perspective. Although its members believed in Louis,[25] the shadow of Varennes hung heavily over the Legislative Assembly and significantly narrowed the margin of trust in the monarch. Without the perspective or counsel of members of the National Assembly – who had not only greater experience in dealing with the monarch but also a deeper understanding of, and attachment to, the constitution – relations deteriorated, especially when Louis exercised his veto power with a frequency many regarded as excessive.[26]

Ultimately, the edifice constructed by the National Assembly failed less from internal contradictions than from the refusal of the monarch to abide by it unconditionally and in good faith. This is not to posit a "good Revolution, bad king" argument, for Louis was, in fact, more weak than malevolent, but indecision punctuated by frequent use of the veto could plausibly appear to others – including men of integrity, not merely demagogues – as bad faith.[27]

As trust withered and political life stagnated, different constituencies – legislators, ministers and the Crown – began to view war as a desirable policy, but obviously for different reasons. For Louis, the advantage of war was that a French defeat would enable him to throw off the constitution. Although the motives of many deputies – self-promotion and advancement – were hardly admirable, they were not, unlike those of the king, treacherous. The declaration of war, then, was the second factor in the collapse of the constitution.

In the feverish atmosphere produced by war, what had been construed as bad faith now appeared treasonous, and as that impression of treason grew, the urge to act became irresistible. With the inviolability of the monarch guaranteed by the constitution, such action could only be extra-

25  See Clapham, *The Origins of the War of 1792*, p. 103; Mitchell, *The French Legislative Assembly of 1791*, pp. 214–215.

26  The single greatest deficiency of the constitution, a deficiency that arose again from a deep and fundamental sense of respect for the king, was the suspensive veto. Its problem was not that it gave Louis too little power, but that it gave him too much, so that he should have used it sparingly. The theoretical sovereignty of the nation seemed to matter little when the monarch could forestall legislation for years. The powers of the monarch seemed more tangible – even preponderant – and heavy use of that power led to a perception of bad faith.

27  On the belief of one deputy that the constitution would have succeeded if the monarch had abided by it, see Dubois-Crancé, *Analyse de la Révolution française*, p. 71. R. R. Palmer observed that the Revolution was over "if the constitution was firmly established, if all concerned would live under it peaceably, if it had no dangerous enemies either inside France or beyond its borders." As Palmer also noted, "these conditions did not obtain." Palmer, *The Age of the Democratic Revolution*, I: 502.

constitutional. The National Assembly, with its respect for the institution of monarchy, had defined treason narrowly;[28] it was that narrow definition that led to the demise of the Constitution of 1791, rather than internal contradictions or shortcomings. The Constitution of 1791 was much more an object of consensus – both within the Assembly itself and in France at large – than has generally been recognized, and the achievements of the Assembly deserve greater acknowledgement than they have heretofore received.

Indeed, it is indicative of the sense of achievement that the creators of the constitution felt that, even on the verge of its demise, they continued to feel a deep sense of pride in it.[29] Although the physical component of the remaking of France was a success – indeed, its core endures to this day – the effort to instill the new ideal of the polity was not. The vision of the polity to which the National Assembly aspired was destroyed by the overthrow of Louis XVI, which produced divisions in France that have never truly healed.

"The Revolution is a block," Georges Clemenceau's famous judgment, has often been cited with approval by historians. This is ironic, for it was not the conclusion of a serious, detached scholar, but the presumably offhand remark of a fiercely partisan politician who wished to rehabilitate the portion of the Revolution from which his party claimed its heritage. In his effort to graft the coercive and militant phase of the Revolution onto its consensual period, Clemenceau implicitly conceded that there were disjunctions in the Revolution. Indeed, it is precisely for this reason that historians differ so markedly on even the chronology of the Revolution, especially its terminating date.

One should, in fact, recast Clemenceau's statement into a fuller and more accurate metaphor: the form of the Revolution as it unfolded resembled a section of a tree trunk, with the period 1789–1791 akin to the core, providing the basic structure and properties for subsequent rings. In significant later accretions, the National Convention forcefully

28 With the precedent of Varennes in mind, the National Assembly limited action against the king only in the event that he placed himself at the head of a foreign army or if he ordered his generals to use the army against the nation. Neither of these conditions applied to the situation of 1792.

29 In May, 1792, a former member of the National Assembly living in Chatillon-les-Dombes in the Department of Ain, sought his medal, unclaimed due to an illness at the time that the National Assembly disbanded. His intermediary, Robin, obtained the medal on June 9, 1792, and must have brought it back to his friend, the former deputy. Ironically, however, only weeks after the deputy received the medal that he had so cherished, the achievement memorialized in that medal was eradicated when the constitution was overturned. See AN C 133, dossier 480, documents 5–6. See also *Correspondance patriotique, entre les citoyens qui ont été membres de l'Assemblée nationale constituante* (Paris, 1791–1792).

persevered to defend the core values of 1789–1791 when they were threatened with extinction, and the Directory self-consciously sought to return as much as possible to the Constitution of 1791.[30]

Such a metaphor would also emphasize the unparalleled position of the National Assembly. The men of the National Assembly have been criticized for intolerance for not allowing a plurality of views to develop, but such criticism is misplaced because it misunderstands the context and unique situation of the National Assembly. Its foremost mission, after being summoned as the Estates-General following the political breakdown of 1787–1789, was to draft a constitution and ultimately – after August 4 – to forge an entirely new political and social order for the French polity. Debates produced competing ideas for reshaping the polity, and decisions reached usually reflected a compromise view, but the consensus reached was frequently not honored by all. Indeed, as the Assembly remade France, its efforts were often challenged by individuals and institutions who wished to restore the system of privilege. In this regard, the accusation of intolerance is unjustified, for the Assembly was often dealing not with a loyal opposition but with men who wished to subvert its work altogether. Furthermore, the usual response of the Assembly – to deny such individuals access to public life and public office until they were prepared to abide by the constitution governing these activities – was eminently fair and reasonable. In the final analysis, there could be only one point of reference for public life, requiring the adhesion of all and, to the degree it can be adduced at all, the charge of intolerance should more properly be levelled against those opposed to the National Assembly rather than against the Assembly itself.

The men from diverse *bailliages* and *sénéchaussées* in France, who came together in the National Assembly between 1789 and 1791, reinvented their world, with principles which they believed had universal value. They further believed – as did much of the French nation – that the attraction of these ideals was so powerful, and their utility so self-evident, that they would spread peacefully to the rest of Europe. Unfortunately, they were only half right, but the quarter-century of conflict that began under their immediate successors should not overshadow the enormity of their accomplishments or diminish the loftiness of their ideals.

---

30 Palmer, *The Age of the Democratic Revolution*, II: 214; Lucas, "The First Directory and the rule of law." Indeed, in this instance the lines of continuity are much greater from the Convention to the Directory, for whereas the self-denying ordinance severed all continuity between the National Assembly and the Legislative Assembly, the Two-Thirds Decree assured a great deal of continuity between the Convention and the Directory.

# Appendix

---

July 9, 1790

August representatives of the nation,

All peoples have received from you a great example, and France the most precious of benefits. Twenty-five million men, for so long strangers to one another in the midst of their Fatherland, divided by prejudices of vanity, superstition and ignorance have suddenly become friends and brothers. You have achieved this political wonder in proclaiming the natural and imprescriptible rights of man. The book of nature [and] that of religion are the sources from which you have drawn your precepts: all of your decrees emanate from these unadulterated and divine sources.

A universal cry of admiration, of love and of gratitude suddenly raises itself in the kingdom: it resounds energetically to the most distant ends. This free homage given to the sublimity of your works merely precedes the happiness that they will prepare for the French people.

The most noble means for us of strongly expressing our respect, our submission and our enthusiasm, is to walk with zeal and courage in the route that you have traced for us. It is in understanding the extent and the limits of the powers that you have confided to us; it is in unreservedly sacrificing oneself to the performance of our duties; it is in striving to follow the most enlightened, the most economical, the most just principles of administration that we will render to the constitution, of which you are the fathers, the most deserving homage, of it and of you.

A national confederation, forever memorable in the annals of Europe, is going to cement the union of all wills, of all French hearts. We will not have the pleasure of being witnesses to it; but our vows will accompany our legislators and our brothers. We will repeat with them, [on] the same day and at the same hour, the same oath. While our brothers in arms and we swear on the altar of the Fatherland to maintain, at the risk of our lives, the Constitution, we will add to this oath that of working for them, for their happiness, in the heart of the administration entrusted to us.

The administrators of the district of Aix,
Department of Bouches-du-Rhône

Source: AN C 120¹, dossier 359, document 16.

# Research note and list of manuscript sources

Research on the National Assembly is complicated somewhat both by the circumstances of its evolution and by its own internal rules. Although there are published records or accounts of the proceedings of the clergy and nobility, the nature of the impasse that developed at the Estates-General determined that there would be few official records for the Third Estate, so one must rely primarily on journals or letters of deputies to gain knowledge of events. When the commons assumed the title of National Assembly on June 17, 1789, it began a *procès-verbal* numbered sequentially from that day.

The *procès-verbal* is a necessary source, but not a sufficient one. Its advantage is that the previous day's *procès-verbal* was read each day and corrections were made immediately, so its accuracy is its greatest strength. Its major weakness is that it is not comprehensive, but only an outline, and must therefore be supplemented by other sources.

The one most often utilized is the *Archives parlementaires*, but the criticisms of Alphonse Aulard, Armand Brette and Philippe Sagnac have made clear its limitations, so it should be used with caution. Despite its defects, however, it conveys an accurate sense of what occurred in the National Assembly and, after cross-checking with the *procès-verbal*, I have used it for quotations or greater detail on debates.

There are several contemporary sources that may be usefully consulted. The best starting point is Series C of the *Archives nationales*, which provides great insight into the interconnection between the National Assembly and France. This series is also significant because on February 15, 1790, the National Assembly decided that protests of individual towns or provinces would not be included in the *procès-verbal*, so it should be checked to gain a fuller understanding of events. These documents should be complemented by the Series DIV, the records of the Committee of the Constitution, which acted as a virtual steering committee for the National Assembly.

Two newspapers, *Le Point du Jour* and *Journal des Etats-Généraux*, had recorders or transcribers in the National Assembly and were highly regarded by deputies, who often recommended them to their constituents. Other newspapers began originally as letters sent by deputies to constituents, and these can also be quite valuable. The most useful published set of letters is the ten volume collection written by Urbain René Pilastre de la Brardière and J. B. Leclerc, *Correspondance de MM. les députés des communes de la province d'Anjou avec leur commettants relativement aux Etats-Généraux ... en* 1789.

There are two caches of letters that are particularly useful because they extend over much of the time of the National Assembly's duration. In the municipal archives at Brest, LL 46, is a large set of letters that encompasses the entire period of the Estates-General/National Assembly. Although they are of shorter duration than those found in Brest – they virtually end with Louis's flight – the single most useful collection of letters is that written by the deputy François Ménard de la Groye, which have recently been published in their entirety. Unlike most letters, which were meant to be public and might seek to influence opinion or to convey a point of view, these were private letters to his wife. Never intended for public dissemination, they are the innermost thoughts of a back-bencher and provide great insight into the intent of the National Assembly.

A listing of secondary sources is impractical because of the abundance of literature, especially local studies. Readers are asked to refer to the notes for the most pertinent works.

ARCHIVES NATIONALES

Series B Elections et votes
Bª – Elections aux Etats-Généraux
    9, 10, 11, 13, 14, 16, 17, 20, 22, 24, 25, 26, 27, 29, 31, 33, 35, 37, 38, 41, 43,
    47, 48, 49, 50, 57, 60, 74, 75, 76, 80
B I – Elections diverses
    5, 18, 19, 20
Series C – Assemblées nationales
    12–134
Series D – Missions des représentants du peuple et comités des Assemblées
DIV – Comité de constitution
    1–67
Series F¹ – Ministère de l'Intérieur: Administration générale
    F¹b II – Série département
    Aisne 1
    Cantal 1
    Gironde 1
    Ille-et-Vilaine 1
    Isère 1
    Loire-Inférieure 1

    F¹c III – Esprit public et elections
    Ain 7, 8
    Aisne 1, 12
    Allier 9
    Ardèche 9
    Ardennes 1, 7, 9
    Aube 1
    Aude 1, 7, 8
    Aveyron 8, 10
    Bouches-du-Rhône 1, 8
    Calvados 1, 10
    Cantal 1, 2, 8

Charente 1, 12
Charente-Inférieure 2
Cher 1, 8
Corse 1
Côte d'Or 8
Côtes-du-Nord 1, 12
Creuse 1, 12
Deux-Sèvres 9
Dordogne 1
Doubs 1, 11
Drome 11
Eure 9
Eure-et-Loire 8, 9
Finistère 1, 9
Gard 1, 10, 11
Haute-Garonne 1, 10, 13
Gers 9, 11
Gironde 8, 11
Hérault 10
Ille-et-Vilaine 1, 6, 9, 11
Indre 7
Indre-et-Loire 9, 10
Isère 1
Jura 9, 10, 13
Landes 9
Loir-et-Cher 8
Loire 7
Haute-Loire 7, 8
Loire-Inférieure 1, 10
Lot-et-Garonne 12
Maine-et-Loire 9, 10
Manche 1, 7, 12
Marne 8
Mayenne 1, 7, 8
Meurthe 9, 15
Meuse 10
Morbihan 8, 11
Moselle 1, 10
Nièvre 6, 7
Nord 11, 13
Oise 7, 10
Orne 12, 13
Pas-de-Calais 14
Puy-de-Dôme 9
Basses-Pyrénées 1
Bas-Rhin 1, 13
Haut-Rhin 10, 11
Rhône 6, 8

Haute-Saône 11
Sarthe 7, 10
Seine 25, 26, 27
Seine-Inférieure 14, 15
Seine-et-Marne 10
Seine-et-Oise 11
Somme 9
Tarn 11
Var 1, 11
Vendée 5, 7
Vienne 8
Haute-Vienne 9, 10
Vosges 8, 10
Yonne 1, 9

Series $F^7$
$3688^1$
$4385^1$
4767
Series H – Administrations locales et comptabilités diverses
Series $H^1$
148, 149, 201, 203, 207, 409, 419, 554, 555, 556, 563, 564, 620, 621, 670, 702, 704, $748^{99}$, $748^{244}$, 942, 997, 1139, 1238, 1240, 1361, 1447, 1448, 1455, 1681
Series K – Monuments historiques
163, 164, 684
Series KK
641, 642, 643, 644, 645, 646, 647, 679, 1105
Series M – Ordres militaires et hospitaliers, universités et collèges, titres nobiliaires. Mélanges
663, 788, 856, 890
Series T – Papiers privés tombés dans le domaine public
$397^1$, 643, 1108/3
Series W – Jurisdictions extraordinaires
12, 13, 14, 15, 294, 306, 342
Series AA – Collection de lettres et pièces diverses
1, 48, 49, 50
Series $AB^{XIX}$ – Documents isolés et papiers d'erudits
189, 600, 3198, 3258, 3259, 3319, 3359, 3449, 3492, 3494, 3562, 3886, 3887, 3888, 3889
Series AP – Archives personnelles et familiales
150 AP 1
284 AP 2
284 AP 3
284 AP 4
349 AP 1
Series $BB^{30}$ – Ministère de la Justice. Versements de 1904, 1905, 1908, 1929, 1933, 1936, 1941, 1943–1944, 1956, 1959, 1961
16, 21, 82, 85, 95, 157

ARCHIVES DE GUERRE (VINCENNES)

A4 56

ARCHIVES DEPARTEMENTALES

Ain
  1 Mi 1
Aisne
  L 566, 567, 571, 628, 1598, 2704, 2755, 2779
Bouches-du-Rhône
  C 101, 102, 103, 255, 999, 1046, 1241, 1337, 1380, 1381, 1383
  L 54, 56, 122, 123, 277, 567, 568, 577
Calvados
  C 6345, 6346, 6347, 6348, 6349, 6350, 6351, 6352, 6353, 6354, 6355, 6356,
    6357, 6358, 6359, 7629, 7630
  F 780
  L 10024, 10025, 10065, 10084, 10085, 10090, 10099
Cantal
  L 16, 76, 112, 149, 150
  Collection Jean Delmas
  106, 154, 155, 156, 160, 176, 177, 189, 190, 193, 205
Charente-Maritime
  4 J 1523, 4 J 1574 (28)
  L 98, 119, 120, 121, 133, 754*
Côte d'Or
  C 1$^{\text{bis}}$, 2975, 2976, 2977, 2987$^{6*}$, 3359, 3367, 3465, 3475, 3475$^{\text{bis*}}$, 3476, 3843
  E 642
  L 36, 176, 198, 210
Côtes-d'Armor
  1 L 368, 371, 389, 399, 576
Eure
  5 F 63
  3 L 1
  4 L 1, 3
  8 L 1
  11 L 8, 9, 11
Haute-Garonne
  C 42, 62, 303
  1 L 324, 533, 550, 551, 552
Gironde
  C 4363, 4364, 4365, 4366
  3 L 82
Hérault
  C 878, 5958, 5959
Ille-et-Vilaine
  C 1799, 1803, 1804, 1805, 1806, 1808, 1809, 1810, 1812, 3129, 3130, 3131,

3843, 3898, 3899, 3900, 3901, 3903, 6095, 6096, 6097, 6134, 6135, 6136, 6137, 6138, 6139, 6203, 6204, 6205

1 F 1648, 1738, 1739, 1740, 1741, 1742, 1743, 1744, 1745, 1746, 1747, 1748, 1841, 1842, 1843, 1844, 1845, 1846

5 FF 33

L 193, 281, 282, 330, 337, 376

Indre-et-Loire
  C 739
  L 74, 82
  L$^m$ 221
  L$^z$ 692

Isère
  III C 3, 4★, 5★
  L 103, 105

Loir-et-Cher
  1 C 258
  L 116, 117, 176, 239, 256, 300, 840, 841, 842

Loire-Atlantique
  C 626, 627, 628, 648
  L 42, 45, 46, 154, 163, 164, 167, 176

Loiret
  2 J 1983, 1984

Maine-et-Loire
  1 L 351, 410

Marne
  1 L 138, 146, 256, 271, 272, 291, 369
  4 L 104
  10 L 189

Meurthe-et-Moselle
  L 142, 143, 199, 200, 201, 212, 1832

Morbihan
  1 Mi 240

Nièvre
  1 L 165

Nord
  L 101, 106★, 109★, 110★, 111★, 768, 787, 789, 791, 792, 793, 1244, 1245, 4899, 5874, 8119, 12570 (9)

Orne
  C 1183, 1185, 1225, 1226, 1227, 1228
  L 73, 79, 80, 81, 137, 140, 1295, 1296, 1297, 1298, 1299, 1300, 1869, 2213

Puy-de-Dôme
  F 140, 141
  4 J 2, 3, 4, 6, 9
  L 481, 543, 658

Pyrénées-Atlantiques
  C 1377, 1601

Pyrénées-Orientales
  C 2119

Bas-Rhin
  1 J 116
  19 J 452
  1 L 748, 760
Rhône
  9 C 58, 59, 60, 61, 62, 63
  1 L 259*, 260*, 369, 370, 371
  35 L 1, 2, 3, 4, 5
Sarthe
  C 90, 91, 92
  10 J 122
  L 34, 153, 185, 199, 259
Seine-Maritime
  C 2, 3, 2113, 2152, 2185, 2186
  L 12, 13, 14, 200, 215, 225, 2309, 2347
  LP 6974*[2], 8363, 8454
Somme
  C 731
Yonne
  L 156, 169, 178, 191, 194


ARCHIVES MUNICIPALES

Aix-en-Provence
  AA 5
  BB 5, 113, 114, 115
  LL 65, 75, 248, 289, 314
Angoulême
  AA 17, 19, 20
  BB 20
Arles
  AA 21, 22, 23
  BB 56
  D 1, 2
Aurillac
  II 7
Bayonne
  AA 50, 51
  BB 64
Bergerac
  Fonds Faugère, I
Bordeaux
  D 220, 227
Brest
  LL 44–48, 281
Châlons-sur-Marne
  E supp. 4812*
Douai

AA 330, 331
$D^3$ 1–10
$J^3$ 3, 5
$J^5$ 4, 5
$K^1$ 7
Grenoble
  AA 41
  BB 128, 146
  LL 2, 13
Laon
  BB 46
La Rochelle
  BB 33
Le Havre
  AA 44–50, 52
  BB 72
  $D^1$ 1
  $D^2$ 1, 2
  $D^3$ 27, 38, 39
  $H^2$ 165
  $I^3$ 5
  K 1–7, 41–42
Lorient
  BB 12, 13
Nantes
  AA 82
  BB 112
  II 151
Nevers
  BB 46
Perigueux
  AA 26, 41 (now O E DEP 5004, 5005)
Rouen
  $D^3$ $1^c$
  $I^5$ 1
  Y 1
Strasbourg
  AA 2002–2005, $2005^a$, $2005^b$
Toulon
  L 80, 104, 107, 338, 614, 616

BIBLIOTHEQUE NATIONALE

Manuscrits Fonds Français 6687, 10883, 13713, 20703, 20706
Manuscrits Nouvelles acquisitions françaises 307, 308, 312, 1777, 2633, 2671, 4121, 4790, 4816, 4789, 12938, 17275, 21565, 21566

BIBLIOTHEQUE HISTORIQUE DE LA VILLE DE PARIS

Ms. 736, 737, 787, 793, 805

BIBLIOTHEQUES MUNICIPALES

Bibliothèque Méjanes (Aix)
    Ms. 534, 535, 536
Bibliothèque municipale – Angers
    Ms. 1888, 1889, 1890
Bibliothèque municipale – Dijon
    Ms. 1660, 2074, 2522
Bibliothèque municipale – Grenoble
    Ms. R 5949, 6202, 6203, 6204, 6205, 6314, 7082, 7109, 7906 (225, 226)
Bibliothèque municipale – La Rochelle
    Ms. 21, 22
Bibliothèque municipale – Lyon
    Ms. 2191, 2193, 5430
Bibliothèque municipale – Nantes
    Collection Dugast-Matifeux
    12, 44, 98
Bibliothèque municipale – Versailles
    Ms. F 823

# Index